The Evolution of Intelligence

The Evolution of Intelligence

Edited by

Robert J. Sternberg
Yale University

James C. Kaufman
*Center for New Constructs
at Educational Testing Service*

LAWRENCE ERLBAUM ASSOCIATES, PUBLISHERS

2002   Mahwah, New Jersey   London

Lawrence Erlbaum Associates, Inc., Publishers
10 Industrial Avenue
Mahwah, NJ 07430

Cover design by Kathryn Houghtaling Lacey

Library of Congress Cataloging-in-Publication Data

The evolution of intelligence / Robert J. Sternberg and
James C. Kaufman, editors.
        p. cm.
    Includes bibliographical references and index.
ISBN 0-8058-3267-X (alk. paper)
1. Intellect. 2. Genetic psychology. 3. Psychology, Comparative.
    I. Sternberg, Robert J.   II. Kaufman, James C.
BF431 .E89 2001
155.7—dc21   00-061737
                                                       CIP

Books published by Lawrence Erlbaum Associates are printed on acid-free paper, and their bindings are chosen for strength and durability.

Printed in the United States of America
10 9 8 7 6 5 4 3 2 1

For my children, Seth and Sara.
                                —RJS

For my grandparents,
Hannah and Seymour Bengels,
and (the late) Blanche and Max Kaufman with love.

                                —JCK

Contents

Preface

We know that intelligence is important in our everyday lives, but we do not know very well what it is, as shown by the fact that hot debate rages in the field of intelligence—today as at the turn of the last century—regarding the nature of intelligence. Although psychologists of diverse backgrounds have tried to answer the question of what intelligence is, too often they have fallen back on conventional psychometric intelligence tests that, for the most part, were constructed in the absence of an empirically demonstrated theory of intelligence—as the criterion against which to assess their theories.

Some psychologists have sought approaches other than intelligence testing to understand the nature of intelligence. For example, some psychologists have studied response times, error rates, or biological correlates derived from performance on cognitive tasks as bases for understanding the nature of human intelligence. But they have then turned around and validated their measures by correlating estimated parameters with conventional psychometric measures of intelligence. The result is that, even with some of these new approaches, the psychometric tests still rule as the ultimate arbiters of what is intelligence and what is not.

An alternative approach is to seek criteria other than psychometric-test performance as the standard for deciding what intelligence is. One such criterion is a distinct evolutionary history. This criterion has been suggested by a number of individuals over the past, from Charles Darwin in the more distant past to Howard Gardner, Stephen Gould, Steven Pinker, Carl Sagan, David Stenhouse, and many others in the more recent past. Perhaps we can understand what intelligence is by elucidating how and why it has evolved. Or perhaps not: The coformulator of the theory of evolution, Alfred Russell Wallace, believed that evolution could account only for life-sustaining traits, not for higher order skills that went beyond such traits. So we find ourselves with three major questions in this book:

1. Does evolutionary theory help us understand the nature of human intelligence?
2. If so, what does it tell us about the nature of human intelligence?
3. And if so, how has intelligence evolved?

These three questions are addressed in many of the chapters in the book, and form the basis for the final integrative chapter.

The goal of this book is to present diverse points of view on the evolution of intelligence as offered by leading experts in the field. In particular, it may be possible better to understand the nature and societal implications of intelligence by understanding how and why it has evolved as it has. This book is unique, to our knowledge, in its offering of a diversity of points of view on the topic of the evolution of human intelligence.

The book perhaps can be brought into the current surge of interest in evolutionary psychology, a field that has been pioneered by David Buss, Richard Byrne, Leda Cosmides, Gerd Gigerenzer, John Tooby, and more recently, by Steven Pinker, among others. Evolutionary models are now being used widely, to account for phenomena as diverse as morality and ethical behavior, interpersonal attraction, creativity, reasoning, perception, and intelligence. The focus of the current book is exclusively on human intelligence and its evolution.

A book such as this one does not develop in isolation. We are grateful to the U.S. Office of Educational Research and Improvement (Grant R206R000001), which has supported some of our research in the area of intelligence. Of course, the findings and opinions expressed in the book do not reflect the positions or policies of this agency. We also are grateful to Sai Durvasula for help in preparing the manuscript and to Judi Amsel for contracting the book. Finally, we thank the authors who have contributed to the book for their help in putting together what we hope will be an influential collection of viewpoints regarding the interface between evolution and human intelligence.

1

The Search for Criteria: Why Study the Evolution of Intelligence?

Robert J. Sternberg
Yale University

Perhaps the most difficult challenge in the study of intelligence is figuring out the criteria for labeling a thought process or a behavior "intelligent." How does one decide?

A number of different approaches have been tried to figure out what criteria one can use to decide what constitutes "intelligence." The thesis of this chapter is that evolutionary arguments constitute one of three such criteria that can be readily incorporated, given a conventional definition of intelligence in terms of adaptation to the environment.

DEFINITIONS OF INTELLIGENCE

Conceptual Definitions

Conceptual definitions are opinions of experts or laypersons about what constitutes intelligence, or intelligent thought and behavior. Two major symposia have directly addressed this issue.

One symposium ("Intelligence and its Measurement," 1921) involved 14 experts giving their views on the nature of intelligence. This symposium produced definitions such as "having learned or ability to learn to adjust oneself to the environment" (Colvin, 1921), "ability to adapt oneself adequately to relatively new situations in life" (Pintner, 1921), and "the capacity to inhibit an instinctive adjustment" (Thurstone, 1921). Note that a major theme in these definitions was the role of adaptation to the environment.

The second symposium (Sternberg & Detterman, 1986) involved opinions of 24 experts in the field of intelligence and produced answers that overlapped with those in the earlier symposium. There was perhaps greater emphasis in these later definitions on metacognition. But the main theme once again was adaptation to the environment.

Definitions also may be extracted from experts or from laypersons by studying these individuals' implicit theories of intelligence. This route was followed in two separate investigations (Sternberg, 1985; Sternberg, Conway, Ketron, & Bernstein, 1981) and produced a variety of responses, depending in part on whether the individuals were professionals or laypersons, and, if professionals, on their field of study. For example, laypersons suggested practical problem-solving ability, verbal ability, and social-competence abilities, whereas experts placed more emphasis on academic skills. However, the skills they emphasized depended on the skills they needed to succeed in their own fields. Implicit-theory studies also have been done cross-culturally, with extremely diverse results (see review in Sternberg & Kaufman, 1998).

Operational Definition

Definitions can also be sought that skirt the issue altogether. For example, Boring (1923) achieved what little fame he has in the field of intelligence for his famous remark that intelligence can and should be defined operationally as that which the intelligence tests test. The circularity of this definition—the tests are designed to measure intelligence, which then is defined in terms of whatever they measure—has made the definition unappealing to many theorists in the field.

THEORIES OF INTELLIGENCE

A second approach is to propose a theory of intelligence, from which some kind of definition is supposed to follow somehow. These theories can be classified in a number of different ways. One scheme is in terms of the metaphor of mind they presuppose. These metaphors characterize the grounds through which intelligence needs to be understood.

Sternberg (1990) suggested that many theories can be viewed as falling under one of seven metaphors. What are these seven metaphors?

First, the geographic metaphor is based on the notion that a theory of intelligence should provide a map of the mind (see Brody, 2000; Carroll, 1993; Horn, 1994; Spearman, 1927; Thurstone, 1938;). Intelligence then comes to be defined in terms of underlying factors of the mind, which Vernon (1971) likened to lines of longitude and latitude for understanding how the mind works.

Second, the computational metaphor envisions the mind as a computing device and analogizes the processes of the mind to the operations (software) of a computer (see Deary, 2000; Hunt, 1980; Lohman, 2000; Sternberg, 1983). The operations of the mind are then characterized in terms of processes, strategies, and mental representations used in processing information.

Third, the biological metaphor (which includes evolutionary notions) seeks to understand intelligence in terms of the workings of the brain (Ertl & Schafer, 1969; Haier et al., 1988; Haier, Siegel, Tang, Abel, & Buchsbaum, 1992; see Jerison, 2000; Vernon, Wickett, Bazana, & Stelmack, 2000). Biological theorists often attempt to map cognitive activity onto various portions of the brain, or to show that certain kinds of responses emitted by the brain (e.g., evoked potentials) relate to psychometrically measured intellectual performance. Or they may try to understand the evolutionary origins of intelligence.

Fourth, the epistemological metaphor, due primarily to Jean Piaget (e.g., Piaget, 1972), seeks to understand intelligence as an equilibration between assimilation and accommodation. Individuals assimilate new objects into existing mental schemas, or change existing schemas to accommodate objects that do not well fit into old schemas.

Fifth, the anthropological metaphor views intelligence as a cultural invention (e.g., Berry, 1974; Greenfield, 1997). On this view, the mental processes underlying intelligence may or may not change as a function of culture, but the behaviors considered to be intelligent certainly do. What is considered intelligent behavior in one culture may be considered to be unintelligent in another (Serpell, 2000).

Sixth, the sociological metaphor considers how socialization affects intellectual development (e.g., Feuerstein, 1980; Vygotksy, 1978). One might examine, for example, how children internalize experiences they first encounter in an interpersonal context (see Chen & Siegler, 2000).

Seventh, the systems metaphor tries to understand the various aspects of intelligence and how they work together as a system (e.g., Gardner, 1983, 1999; Sternberg, 1985, 1997, 1999). According to this metaphor, the various approaches to intelligence need to be systemically integrated.

The different metaphors vary in a tremendous number of respects. But interestingly, they have one thing in common with the diverse definitions. It typically is assumed that the core concept underlying intelligence is adaptation to the environment, broadly conceived.

THREE ADAPTATIONIST CRITERIA

If intelligence is to be understood as adapation to the environment, broadly conceived, then how might we go about discovering the mental processes and behaviors that can be labeled as intelligent? Three criteria suggest themselves. These criteria differ from largely arbitrary listings of criteria (e.g., Gardner, 1983) in that they all derive from the virtually universally accepted notion of intelligence as adaptation to the environment.

Criterion 1: Correlations with Success

Success is often defined in terms of *cultural adaptation*. When it is so defined, it makes sense to correlate performance on measures of intelligence with multiple measures of success; however, they may be culturally defined. These measures will differ from one culture to another. But the variation in what constitutes success is not limited to cultural adaptation. Adaptive success also varies with biological niche. Success for a bird is certainly different from success for a human. And even humans need different skills to succeed in different environments, such as in cold mountainous regions versus hot tropical rain forests.

Criterion 2: Mental Skill Development

All organisms are designed to become increasingly independent and better able to adapt to the environment with increasing age, up to a certain point. Then, in the later portion of their lives, their adaptive skills may decrease with age. Binet and Simon (1905/1916) were among the first to recognize that a scale for measuring intelligence could be constructed on the basis of items on which performance differed as a function of age. The whole notion of mental age, although no longer in general use, derived from the view that mental growth during childhood was such as to render an individual more adaptive to the environment. Increases in age can result in increases both in cultural adaptation, considered in the first criterion, and biological adaptation, considered in the third criterion.

Criterion 3: Evolutionary Origins and Development

If we start with biological adaptation as the core of intelligence, then a primary means for understanding what intelligence is would have to be in terms of the evolutionary antecedents of thought and behavior. This approach has not been widely used, although its origins are not particularly recent (Darwin, 1859, 1872/1965; see also Stenhouse, 1973).

This volume is an attempt to remedy the relative dearth of literature on the evolution of intelligence in comparison with, for example, the psychometric correlates of intelligence or the development of intelligence. From an adaptationist standpoint, evolutionary considerations probably deserve special status in understanding intelligence. Yet theorists of intelligence probably have devoted the least attention to them.

CONCLUSION

In sum, the proposal here is that three criteria for understanding the nature of intelligence are nonarbitrary, given a definition of intelligence as broad adaptation to the environment. The first is correlation of a target thought or behavior with cultural success (cultural adaptation). The second is mental skills development (cultural and biological adaptation). The third is evolutionary origins and development (biological adaptation). This book examines the third and, arguably, most important of these three criteria, the evolutionary one.

ACKNOWLEDGMENTS

Preparation of this chapter was supported by Grant REC-9979843 from the National Science Foundation and by a grant under the Javits Act Program (Grant No. R206R000001) as administered by the Office of Educational Research and Improvement, U.S. Department of Education. Grantees undertaking such projects are encouraged to express freely their professional judgment. This chapter, therefore, does not necessarily represent the position or policies of the National Science Foundation, Office of Educational Research and Improvement or the U.S. Department of Education, and no official endorsement should be inferred.

REFERENCES

Berry, J. W. (1974). Radical cultural relativism and the concept of intelligence. In J. W. Berry & P. R. Dasen (Eds.), *Culture and cognition: Readings in cross-cultural psychology* (pp. 225–229). London: Methuen.

Binet, A., & Simon, T. (1916). *The development of intelligence in children*. Baltimore: Williams & Wilkins. (Original work published 1905)

Boring, E. G. (1923, June 6). Intelligence as the tests test it. *New Republic*, 35–37.

Brody, N. (2000). History of theories and measurements of intelligence. In R. J. Sternberg (Ed.), *Handbook of intelligence* (pp.16–33). New York: Cambridge University Press.

Carroll, J. B. (1993). *Human cognitive abilities: A survey of factor-analytic studies*. New York: Cambridge University Press.

Chen, Z., & Siegler, R. S. (2000). Intellectual development in childhood. In R. J. Sternberg (Ed.), *Handbook of intelligence* (pp. 92–116). New York: Cambridge University Press.

Colvin, S. (1921). What I conceive intelligence to be. *Journal of Educational Psychology, 12*, 136–139.

Darwin, C. (1859). *The origin of species*. London: Murray.

Darwin, C. (1965). *The expression of the emotions in man and animals*. Chicago: University of Chicago Press. (Original work published 1872)

Deary, I. J. (2000). Simple information processing. In R. J. Sternberg (Ed.), *Handbook of intelligence* (pp. 267–284). New York: Cambridge University Press.

Ertl, J., & Schafer, E. (1969). Brain response correlates of psychometric intelligence. *Nature, 233,* 421–422.

Feuerstein, R. (1980). *Instrumental enrichment: An intervention program for cognitive modifiability.* Baltimore, MD: University Park Press

Gardner, H. (1983). *Frames of mind: The theory of multiple intelligences.* New York: Basic.

Gardner, H. (1999). Are there additional intelligences? The case for naturalist, spiritual, and existential intelligences. In J. Kane (Ed.), *Education, information, and transformation* (pp. 111–131). Upper Saddle River, NJ: Prentice-Hall.

Greenfield, P. M. (1997). You can't take it with you: Why abilities assessments don't cross cultures. *American Psychologist, 52*(10), 1115–1124.

Haier, R. J., Nuechterlein, K. H., Hazlett, E., Wu, J. C., Pack, J., Browning, H. L., & Buchsbaum, M. S. (1988). Cortical glucose metabolic rate correlates of abstract reasoning and attention studied with positron emission tomography. *Intelligence, 12,* 199–217.

Haier, R. J., Siegel, B., Tang, C., Abel, L., & Buchsbaum, M. S. (1992). Intelligence and changes in regional cerebral glucose metabolic rate following learning. *Intelligence, 16,* 415–426.

Horn, J. L. (1994). Theory of fluid and crystallized intelligence. In R. J. Sternberg (Ed.), *The encyclopedia of human intelligence* (Vol. 1, pp. 443–451). New York: Macmillan.

Hunt, E. B. (1980). Intelligence as an information-processing concept. *British Journal of Psychology, 71,* 449–474.

Intelligence and its measurement: A symposium. (1921). *Journal of Educational Psychology, 12,* 123–147, 195–216, 271–275.

Jerison, H. J. (2000). The evolution of intelligence. In R. J. Sternberg (Ed.), *Handbook of intelligence* (pp. 216–244). New York: Cambridge University Press.

Lohman, D. F. (2000). Complex information processing and intelligence. In R. J. Sternberg (Ed.), *Handbook of intelligence* (pp. 285–340). New York: Cambridge University Press.

Piaget, J. (1972). *The psychology of intelligence.* Totowa, NJ: Littlefield Adams.

Pintner, R. (1921). What I conceive intelligence to be. *Journal of Educational Psychology, 12,* 139–143.

Serpell, R. (2000). Intelligence and culture. In R. J. Sternberg (Ed.), *Handbook of intelligence* (pp. 549–580). New York: Cambridge University Press.

Spearman, C. (1927). *The abilities of man.* London: Macmillan.

Stenhouse, D. (1973). *The evolution of intelligence: A general theory and some of its implications.* New York: Harper & Row.

Sternberg, R. J. (1983). Components of human intelligence. *Cognition, 15,* 148.

Sternberg, R. J. (1985). *Beyond IQ: A triarchic theory of human intelligence.* New York: Cambridge University Press.

Sternberg, R. J. (1990). *Metaphors of mind: Conceptions of the nature of intelligence.* New York: Cambridge University Press.

Sternberg, R. J. (1997). *Successful intelligence.* New York: Plume.

Sternberg, R. J. (1999). The theory of successful intelligence. *Review of General Psychology, 3,* 292–316.

Sternberg, R. J., Conway, B. E., Ketron, J. L., & Bernstein, M. (1981). People's conceptions of intelligence. *Journal of Personality and Social Psychology, 41,* 37–55.

Sternberg, R. J., & Detterman, D. K. (1986). *What is intelligence?* Norwood, NJ: Ablex.

Sternberg, R. J., & Kaufman J. C. (1998). Human abilities. *Annual Review of Psychology, 49,* 479–502.

Thurstone, L. L. (1921). What I conceive intelligence to be. *Journal of Educational Psychology, 12,* 201–207.

Thurstone, L. L. (1938). *Primary mental abilities*. Chicago: University of Chicago Press.

Vernon, P. A., Wickett, J. C., Bazana, P.G., & Stelmack, R. M. (2000). The neuropsychology and psychophysiology of human intelligence. In R. J. Sternberg (Ed.), *Handbook of intelligence* (pp. 245–264). New York: Cambridge University Press.

Vernon, P. E. (1971). *The structure of human abilities*. London: Methuen.

Vygotsky, L. S. (1978). *Mind in society: The development of higher psychological processes*. Cambridge, MA: Harvard University Press.

2

Evolutionary Psychology: Promise and Perils

James B. Grossman
Yale University

James C. Kaufman
*Center for New Constructs
at Educational Testing Service*

Over the past few years, a discipline known as *evolutionary psychology* (EP) has become increasingly prominent in the public imagination. Promoted by such popular and semipopular texts as Steven Pinker's *How the Mind Works* (1997), Daniel Dennett's *Darwin's Dangerous Idea* (1995), Robert Wright's *The Moral Animal* (1994), and David Buss' *The Evolution of Desire* (1994), EP is the latest model in a venerable tradition of attempts to explain human behavior and cognition as mechanisms shaped by the forces of natural selection. According to EP, our evolutionary heritage is apparent in modern humans through the organ of our "adapted mind" (in the phrase of Barkow, Cosmides, & Tooby, 1992); that is, our inherited mental architecture evolved to solve particular adaptive problems of survival and reproduction faced by our ancestors. We utilize these same mental adaptations or *modules* in our modern existence, although while often navigating a very different physical and cultural landscape. Thus, cognition and intelligence have a history; to fully understand them, we must look back to the evolutionary past that formed them. But before we can truly examine the evolution of intelligence, we need to examine the evolutionary framework itself.

The vocabulary and ideas of EP have infiltrated the different branches of psychology to varying degrees. A significant evolutionary component has been present within developmental psychology for some time, ever since Bowlby (1969) synthesized ideas from ethology and infant research into modern attachment theory. Within social psychology, excitement as well as controversy have surrounded research concerning the evolutionary aspects of human mate selection (see Buss, 1994; Singh, 1995). Many cognitive psychologists have largely accepted the tenets of EP, for example that complex phenomena such as perception and memory can be understood by reverse-engineering their structures from the perspective of evolutionary "design." (A kind of natural affinity also appears to be in operation here, with cognitive scientists concerned with artificial intelligence [e.g., Dennett, Pinker] often being particularly enthusiastic about evolutionary concepts.) Evolutionary psychology may thus be seen to address an array of issues related to human cognition and behavior. Perhaps most important, EP may be seen as a novel organizing framework for psychology, a form of *metatheory* for conceptualization and research across various domains of the field.

EVOLUTION AND HUMAN INTELLIGENCE

The use of evolutionary theory as a basis for explaining human intelligence can be traced back to Charles Darwin, whose revolutionary work *On the Origin of Species* (1859/1989) presented the first complete account of the mechanism of evolutionary change. Darwin established that the process of natural selection—the differential reproductive success associated with heritable variation—is the primary organizing force in the evolution of living beings. Despite the storm of reaction that accompanied Darwin's seminal work, the *Origin* was concerned primarily with the source of the earth's biological diversity as a whole and said little about the evolution of humankind per se. Indeed, Darwin went only so far as to say that "light will be thrown on the origin of man and his history," (p. 311) but his message was clear that humanity was by no means exempt from the scope of natural selection. Darwin did not elaborate on his views until his 1871 work *The Descent of Man* (1871/1989), where he argued that the properties of the human mind displayed essential continuities with characteristics of other species: "The difference in mind between man and the higher animals," he wrote, "great as it is, certainly is one of degree and not of kind" (p. 126). Although his specific arguments in support of this position were necessarily hypothetical and sometimes contrived (as in his supposition that an analog for human religion could be seen in a dog's love for its master), Darwin's ideas in *Descent* were more important for their overall implications rather than for their strict scientific validity. Darwin (in contrast with his "codiscoverer" of natural selection, Alfred Russell Wallace) specifically included humanity's lofty mental capacities within his evolutionary model; his theory affirmed that human intelligence was, like the features of any other living being, a biological phenomenon ultimately explicable by evolutionary theory.

EVOLUTION AND INTELLIGENCE AFTER DARWIN

In the period between Darwin's writings and the advent of World War II, many researchers carried the banner of evolutionary theory while attempting to illuminate the inner workings of the human mind. Sadly, the majority of these figures used supposed science and empiricism to justify views and policies that, by today's standards, would be considered racist and sexist (Gould, 1981). Furthermore, included among those who preached this brand of evolutionary theory were the "founding fathers" of the field of intelligence.

Darwin's cousin, Sir Francis Galton, was a multitalented scientist who pioneered numerous advances in statistics, testing, and measurement in the latter half of the nineteenth century. He had a firm belief in the inherent quantifiability of all natural phenomena, including intelligence. He based his landmark mental tests on perceptual and motor skills, and tried to trace out the heredity of "greatness" by looking at the family trees of known geniuses. Galton coined the term *eugenics* to refer to the societal goal of encouraging the smartest individuals to have the most children, while discouraging those of the least intelligence. His contemporary, Paul Broca, best known for localizing cerebral functions such as language, was a vociferous defender of the relationship between intelligence and racial characteristics such as brain size, skull shape, and skin pigmentation. Broca also compared male and female brains and skulls, concluding that from anatomical evidence alone, men had greater intellectual capacities. Both Galton and Broca, while indisputably important figures in the history of science, also used the new evolutionary "science" to perpetuate and validate a then socially prevalent racist and sexist ideology (Gould, 1981).

Working in Galton's wake, and incorporating Mendel's revolutionary discoveries concerning the basic mechanisms of genetics, were a whole new wave of eugenicists, who assumed all undesirable traits could be linked to genes and could be eliminated with proper strictures on breeding. H. H. Goddard, the man who brought IQ tests to America, was the first to give labels to different levels of mental deficiency (popularizing such terms as *idiot* and *moron*). He placed every subgroup of society on a scale according to their innate intellectual and moral potential, with criminals, alcoholics, and prostitutes as the inherently "feeble-minded" bottom; the typical, mentally "dull" individuals comprising the working class in the middle; and an elite intelligentsia at the top. Thus, he advocated a "benevolent aristocracy" in which the smartest men ruled "in comfort and by right" (Goddard, 1919). The policy implications of Goddard's vision are disturbing (to say the least), including the sterilization of "morons" and exclusion of immigration by most foreign ethnic groups, who were considered mentally defective. Lewis M. Terman, one of the founders of the modern IQ test, agreed with Goddard, arguing that those whose low intelligence precludes their making a moral contribution to society must be prevented from reproducing. This American evolutionary "science" was later to be an important influence upon German Nazi ideology (Chorover, 1979). By placing racial and intellectual prejudices in an empirical context, these scientists provided an academic justification for social policies that might otherwise have appeared immoral.

(While these biological-based theories of intelligence are ideologically and empirically bankrupt by today's standards, some aspects of these ideas have been revived in modern scientific research. For example, Willerman, Schultz, Rutledge, and Bigler, 1991, 1992 have found significant correlations between IQ scores and, controlling for body size, brain size.)

Sociobiology

In the post-World War II era, a reaction to the horrors of Nazism and the predominance within psychology of behaviorism created a lull in the evolution-based study of humanity. Not until the 1960s did a new generation of researchers begin to attempt a rigorous, scientific application of evolution to human behavior and cognition. By then, the well-established field of evolutionary biology had introduced ideas that would serve as the basic building blocks of a new human evolutionary science (see Hamilton, 1964; Trivers, 1971; Williams, 1966). In his controversial 1975 opus, *Sociobiology*, E. O. Wilson synthesized the disparate elements of this emerging paradigm into a book-length argument that both nonhuman and human social behavior could be explained by the use of evolutionary concepts. Wilson discussed the possible evolutionary origins of varied aspects of human social organization, communication, and culture; his book, as well as Richard Dawkins' *The Selfish Gene* (1976/1989) and Wilson's later *On Human Nature* (1978), were manifestos for the ultimate application of the Darwinian program to humanity's higher faculties.

The sociobiologists of the 1970s created a stir by suggesting that human beings, as much as the rest of the animal kingdom, are shaped and constrained by their Darwinian ancestry. To a certain degree, of course, this is hardly controversial. Today, only religious creationists would still try to argue that humanity as a biological species is not a product of evolution, or that natural selection has not played an important role in making us what we are. Sociobiology raised the ire of many scientists and educated laypeople, however, because it was seen as reducing the complexity of human experience to a simple genetic determinism. E. O. Wilson's primary subject of expertise was the social behavior of insects, and sociobiology seemed to argue that Homo sapiens were blindly acting out the dictates of their "selfish genes" as slavishly and unfreely as ants and termites.

TENETS OF EVOLUTIONARY PSYCHOLOGY

People are not ants, the new breed of evolutionary psychologists wish to reassure us. An important advance of today's EP over earlier attempts to incorporate evolutionary theory into the understanding of human behavior is its recognition that humans are not mindless "fitness maximizers." The canonical texts of sociobiology seemed to paint a picture of humans as robots to their instincts, motivated only to survive and reproduce. EP, however, takes pains to stress that humans are not slaves to their genes: for example, people choose to use birth control, regardless of the grievous limitations that may impose on their Darwinian reproductive success. An EP perspective would argue that human beings are designed to find sex pleasurable and desirable because in our ancestors' time such feelings were adaptive to leaving behind more offspring. For modern humans, however, such inherited instincts are mediated by our advanced cognitive abilities and technological adaptations, and the outcome will not necessarily fall in our genes' favor.

In humans' "maladaptive" use of birth control, evolution is thwarted because it could not have anticipated modern technological advances. This highlights an important aspect of contemporary evolutionary theory, a concept that Bowlby (1969) first labeled the *environment of evolutionary adaptedness* (EEA). The EEA refers to the environment whose selective pressures formed the physical and behavioral adaptations we possess today—certainly a vastly different environment from that of any modern, industrialized human society. Because evolution proceeds almost inconceivably slowly by human time-scales, little in our biology is likely to be an adaptation to modern human history (*modern* here defined as the past 10,000 years or so since the advent of agriculture). The period that shaped our genotypes may be seen as the roughly 2 million years in which Homo sapiens and their protohuman ancestors spent living as nomadic hunter–gatherers. Thus, in using evolution to understand the mind, it is important to remember that the traits we now possess evolved not because they are necessarily adaptive *today*, but because they conferred a selective advantage during the crucible of humanity's evolution, many thousands of years ago.

Evolutionary psychology does not attempt to reduce all the complexities of human behavior to some rigid form of genetic determinism, however. EP makes a distinction between *ultimate* causes of human behavior and cognition (a history of differential transmission of inherited structures from one generation to the next) and *proximal* causes (the particular combination of genetic, environmental, and psychosocial factors that shape the life experience of a given individual). These are not alternative but rather complementary explanations, with human behavior determined ultimately by the legacy of inherited mechanisms that motivate and constrain the entire species and proximally by the specific manner in which those mechanisms interact with other forces across an individual's life span (McGuire & Troisi, 1998). Complex human attributes such as intelligence cannot be understood only from the perspective of evolved mechanisms; rather, an evolutionary perspective may complement other approaches. Thus, a coherent evolutionary perspective should not be understood as implying that, for example, observed group differences in intelligence must be essentially genetic in origin. In recent years, much notoriety has attended the work of certain researchers offering genetics-based explanations of racial IQ disparities. Canadian researcher J. Phillipe Rushton (1988) espouses a highly controversial and disputed (see Cain & Vanderwolf, 1990) "evolutionary" model that rank orders the overall intelligence of Asians, Caucasians, and people of African ancestry. Herrnstein and Murray (1994) argued in their much debated best seller *The Bell Curve* that racial differences in intelligence are substantially determined by genetic factors. However, the mainstream of contemporary EP is concerned primarily with universal features of the mind, rather than with the traits that set apart certain individuals or groups. As Pinker argued (1997), EP mainly studies the "signal" (the universal mental architecture shared by all members of the human race), with individual differences being just "noise."

Reverse-Engineering

According to the contemporary evolutionary perspective, we can best understand various features of the mind through a process of what Pinker (1997) called "reverse-engineering the psyche," that is, interpreting aspects of our mental architecture in terms of the purposes for which selective forces might have shaped such adaptations. Of course, evolution has no actual purpose—rather, the evolution of replicating organisms over vast spans of time has slowly and gradually created complex structures that give the *appearance* of having been engineered to allow their owners to survive and reproduce. The reverse engineering of anatomical structures is a common practice in biology, where the theory of natural selection provides the only successful account of the origin of what Darwin called "organs of extreme perfection and complication" (Dawkins, 1986). To understand, for example, the mechanisms of echolocation in bats, biologists must recognize they constitute a system "designed" by natural selection for the purpose of allowing navigation in the dark. According to evolutionary psychology, then, the human mind is a similar complex organ (or system of organs) designed by natural selection to solve the particular kinds of problems our ancestors faced.

Thus, from the standpoint of EP, to understand human intelligence we must reverse engineer the different specialized mental faculties or modules that constitute cognition, recognizing them as features that evolved in order to boost fitness and perpetuate genes. As Pinker and Bloom (1990) argued, human language ability is such an adaptation. Children in every culture of the world, unless they are severely brain damaged or deprived of verbal stimuli, become fluent speakers of complex grammatical sentences by the age of 3, without benefit of formal instruction. As Chomsky (1965) demonstrated, all languages are complex computational systems sharing common structural features or "deep grammar." For these and other reasons, Pinker and Bloom argued that the human "language instinct" is the product of Darwinian natural selection, a species-specific, task-specific biological ability, like echolocation in bats, that helped our proto-human ancestors to survive and reproduce.

Logical Reasoning and Evolutionary Psychology

At its best, the evolutionary perspective provides a novel and intellectually generative framework for understanding psychological phenomena. One interesting phenomenon observed by Cosmides (1989) is that people perform significantly better at certain forms of logical reasoning when problems are posed in the context of social interactions. This is especially true when the situations concern the likelihood of being cheated by another person.

Cosmides conducted research using the Wason selection task (Wason & Johnson-Laird, 1972). This task involves participants being presented with four two-sided cards. Each card has either a numeral, which can be odd or even, or a letter, which can be a vowel or a consonant. The participants are then given conditional statements such as, "If a card has a vowel on one side, then it has an odd number on the other side." The participants must then decide whether the statement is true or false by turning over the minimum number of cards necessary. So, for example, if they are presented with four cards that read A, 6, H, 9, then they must turn over both the A and the 9 to ascertain the statement's truth. Most participants will recognize that they must turn over the A to confirm that there is an odd number on the other side, but they will not recognize that they must also turn over the 9 as well (to disconfirm that there will be a consonant on the other side).

Griggs and Cox (1982) demonstrated that participants can solve the Wason task more accurately when the problem is posed in the context of a social interaction. For example, participants might be given the scenario that they are police officers at a bar, and they must ensure that no underage drinking is taking place. With this context, participants would be presented with four cards representing individuals with the following four characteristics: 22 years old; drinking beer; 17 years old; drinking soda. Participants would then be asked to select the card or cards that would definitely need to be turned over to determine whether or not the bar patrons are violating the law. Under these new conditions, a significantly higher percentage of people correctly solve what is virtually the same problem (the correct answer is to check the individual drinking beer to make sure he or she is over 21 and to check the 17-year-old to make sure he or she is not drinking beer).

Why would people reason more effectively on a task that usually proves diffi-cult when the domain of the task concerns a social domain, especially cheating behavior? Cosmides' (1989) explanation is that although humans have not evolved much of a natural capacity for logical reasoning, the demands of our so-cial environment necessitated that we evolve a module for detecting cheaters; that is, it was important in the past to guard against those who might deprive us by deceit of valuable material or reproductive resources. To Cosmides, our sen-sitivity to potential cheaters, in contrast with our generally poor facility with formal logic, is too robust to be the product of learning alone. (Gigerenzer, 1998, has demonstrated a similar disparity between humans' ability to engage in probabilistic reasoning versus reasoning in natural frequencies.) Thus, when applied effectively, EP may provide us with a basis for understanding facts about our mental makeup that are otherwise truly puzzling.

Evolution and Cognitive Disorders

One seeming contradiction given such an evolutionary perspective is the exis-tence of apparently genetically based mental disorders such as schizophrenia and autism. If there is a genetic component to these disorders, which involve major deficiencies in cognition and information processing, why should the rel-evant genes have evolved and been maintained in the human gene pool? Indi-viduals with schizophrenia, for example, have compromised fitness in evolutionary terms—they have shorter life expectancies and lower reproduc-tive rates than healthy individuals (Gottesman, 1991), and, consequently, they pass on fewer copies of their genes to the next generation. How, then, has such a devastating, and comparatively common, disorder been maintained in the world population?

Numerous studies have established that there *is* a genetic component to schizophrenia (Gottesman & Shields, 1982; Meehl, 1989). Although there is not *a* gene that inevitably *causes* schizophrenia, the converging evidence of nu-merous twin, adoption, family, and linkage studies indicates that there is a ge-netic factor, most likely made up of multiple genes, that contributes to vulnerability to the disease. This presents evolution-minded researchers with something of a puzzle.

EP has looked for an answer to this conundrum by analogy with certain ge-netically transmitted medical diseases that are maintained by forces of selection whose effect is to favor genetic variability in the population. For example, in the phenomenon referred to as *balanced polymorphism*, genetic traits can be expressed differently or at different degrees of severity depending on whether an individual carries both or only one allele; though the full-blown, homozygous version of such a trait may be disadvantageous, the lesser, heterozygous version that occurs in a relative may carry a selective advantage. If the selective advantage of the mixed form is high, both that trait and the deleterious trait will be maintained in the population.

The classic example of this genetic phenomenon is sickle-cell anemia, which afflicts many individuals of African descent. Although few individuals who carry both copies of the gene (recessive homozygotes) survive to reproduce, the allele is nevertheless maintained in relatively high frequency in certain African populations because individuals who are heterozygous for the trait (carriers) gain enhanced protection from malaria. Because malaria is a strong enough selective force to winnow out dominant homozygotes who carry no sickle-cell gene, sickle-cell anemia persists even though the trait is usually lethal for those with the dual genetic loading (Childs, Moxon, & Winkelstein, 1992).

Sickle-cell anemia is not a direct analog for schizophrenia. It is highly unlikely that a single gene or major locus is responsible for the disorder; some form of multifactorial, polygenic threshold model will ultimately be needed to explain schizophrenia, with different combinations of multiple genes and environmental stressors resulting in liability (Gottesman, 1991). However, if the predisposition that may result in schizophrenia is inherited in graduated form, then schizophrenia itself may exist today as the price paid by some individuals for the existence of a related trait that is adaptive—or was adaptive in our evolutionary history.

There is some evidence that a milder, more common variant of schizophrenia may exist. According to Meehl (1989), schizophrenia has its roots in the inheritance of a predispositional substrate that in most individuals leads to the development of a *schizotypal* personality rather than schizophrenia proper. Labeled schizotypal personality disorder in the *DSM–IV* (APA, 1994), it is characterized by a pervasive pattern of peculiarities in behavior and ideation, but not to the florid degree observable in full-blown schizophrenia. Thus, the large majority of schizotypic individuals (Meehl estimates 90%) never experience a schizophrenic breakdown, but rather exhibit a less severe pattern of eccentricity, odd beliefs, or "magical" thinking. Although there is some dispute concerning schizotypal personality disorder as a discrete diagnostic entity, there does appear to be a higher prevalence of schizotypy among first- and second-degree relatives of schizophrenics as compared with individuals who do not have schizophrenia in their families (Kendler, 1985).

Although schizotypal personality disorder may represent a milder variant of schizophrenia, it still far from adaptive in our contemporary society. Evolution-minded researchers, however, have speculated whether the schizotypal trait might have conferred selective benefits at some point in the past. Earlier in the century, the anthropologist Alfred Kroeber advanced the idea that many tribal shamen and medicine men may be mildly schizophrenic by the standards of Western society (Silverman, 1967). Although the bizarre cognitions and behavior of schizotypal individuals may be socially isolating today, in the more tribal social organizations of ancestral humans schizotypal individuals may have made charismatic leaders. Sapolsky (1997) and others argued that the founders of many religious forms and rituals may have had schizotypal personalities; in a prescientific era, their eccentric behavior and metamagical thought may have shaped the beliefs of their societies (and such individuals may have been rewarded with greater reproductive success, hence perpetuating their characteristics).

A similar evolutionary perspective has also been applied to autism, another profoundly impairing, although much rarer, cognitive and affective disorder that appears to have a significant genetic component (Bailey et al., 1995; Bolton & Rutter, 1990). A current influential theory (Baron-Cohen, Leslie, & Frith, 1985) about autism posits that the fundamental deficit of the disorder is the absence of a *theory of mind*, that is, a mental mechanism for understanding others' mental states. Evolution-minded researchers have used this paradigm to argue that natural selection has produced specific and discrete modules of the mind responsible for various aspects of social cognition in humans; they cite the apparent absence of "mindreading" abilities both in individuals with autism and, to varying degrees, in nonhuman primates as evidence that in autism, the theory of mind module is absent or damaged (Baron-Cohen, 1995; Leslie, 1991). This has spawned a related theory as to why the trait of autism should persist in the gene pool despite its deleterious effects. Lesser variants of autism, involving milder but still disadvantageous cognitive and social deficits, appear to be reflected in some first-degree relatives of individuals with autism (Bolton & Rutter, 1990). A speculation is that, in a milder form where full-blown autism is not expressed, the genes responsible for the social, mindreading deficit may provide a cognitive advantage—the ability to rapidly analyze information into its constituent parts (Baron-Cohen & Hammer, 1997).

Thus, a seeming loophole in the evolutionary paradigm—the existence of genetically driven disorders such as autism and schizophrenia entailing inarguably maladaptive cognitive traits—may in fact be explicable under an evolutionary model. The current evolutionary perspective recognizes that there are multiple genotypes within a population at any given time, and the differential selection of alternate combinations of genes and their associated phenotypes may result in the continued survival in the species of apparently dysgenic phenomena. An emerging subdiscipline of evolutionary psychopathology may help to illuminate the evolutionary nature of genetically based cognitive disorders and may thus supplement our understanding of adaptive intelligence's evolution.

CRITIQUES OF EVOLUTIONARY PSYCHOLOGY

Although evolutionary psychology has taken hold in the popular press—indeed, for many of the educated lay-public, it is now assumed to be an established subfield of mainstream science—within the sciences itself it is not fully accepted, either as a branch of psychology proper or as a general theoretical or methodological orientation. Why this schism between the public acceptance of EP and practicing scientists' acceptance of the discipline? Multiple objections have been voiced concerning the emerging field.

First, some argue that EP is just the latest incarnation of a racist, sexist tradition utilizing the veneer of science to justify various social inequities (e.g., Horgan, 1993, 1995). EP is thus sometimes invoked in the same breath as political conservatism, Social Darwinism, and even Nazism. Although today's evolutionary psychologists have largely tried to distance themselves from the sweeping social implications of some practitioners of sociobiology, nevertheless their claims cannot help but fall on ofttimes unsympathetic ears. The previously mentioned controversial research by Rushton (1988) and Herrnstein and Murray (1994) has been widely criticized as reactionary. Research by Buss and others (e.g., Buss, 1994; Singh, 1995) on divergent male and female sexual strategies does convey at least an implicit message that the persistence of gender stereotypes may reflect real personality differences between women and men. Evolutionary psychologists may rightly claim that there is a fundamental difference between the way nature *is* and the way we *ought* to treat one another and organize our society. Because something is natural (i.e., has some evolutionary basis) means neither that it is immutable (e.g., IQ) nor that it is morally right (e.g., warfare, infanticide). To some, however, this articulation of EP's moral neutrality in relation to its subject matter will always appear slightly evasive.

As a second obstacle to EP's acceptance into mainstream psychology, EP is widely seen as representing a form of genetic reductionism, advocating that all that is worth studying is "what's in the genes." This stands in sharp opposition to the field of psychology's emphasis on the importance of environmental and social factors influencing individual development and behavior. Although most evolutionary psychologists would deny they are concerned only with nature to the exclusion of nurture, EP does deemphasize individual and cultural differences (Pinker's "noise"), arguing instead that some basic human nature is the most essential unit of analysis. This so-called noise is of vital importance to most psychologists, however, who are concerned with differences among individual humans as well as with general laws of human behavior. Moreover, in their efforts to present the strongest case for the evolutionary paradigm, evolutionary psychologists sometimes omit or gloss over crucial issues concerning the relative influence of culture versus inherited characteristics. Cultural context is enormously important to the existence and expression of many aspects of cognition, making it difficult to speak of universal human abilities (Sternberg & Kaufman, 1998). The very notion of intelligence, for example, is highly culturally bound. Western conceptions of intelligence typically emphasize verbal ability and processing speed, whereas the Chinese culture, for example, has two central perspectives: the Confucian perspective, which values benevolence, and the Taoist perspective, which places a greater emphasis on such traits as humility and self-knowledge (Sternberg, Conway, Ketron, & Bernstein, 1981; Yang & Sternberg, 1997). (In addition, ubiquity alone does not prove that a trait is the product of natural selection. As Dennett (1995) observed, different human cultures will tend to rediscover "obvious good moves" over time; for example, humans need not have an evolved mental mechanism concerning house-building in order to figure out that it is helpful to have some kind of shelter from the elements.)

Adaptationism Versus Spandrels

EP also faces other, internal obstacles to integration with mainstream science. A debate within the field of evolutionary biology has opened up the question of how central adaptational processes truly are to the evolution of complex structures, physical or mental. In a highly influential 1979 paper, Gould and Lewontin criticized what they called the "Panglossian paradigm" in evolutionary science (referring to the character in Voltaire's *Candide* who believes that everything, no matter how absurd or unjust, occurs so as to bring about the best of all possible worlds). This paradigm is premised on explaining every evolved trait in terms of how it had been designed by natural selection for optimum utility and thereby maximized the success of the organism who possessed it. In contrast with this prevailing "adaptationist program," however, Gould and Lewontin argued that the major category of important evolutionary features does not arise as actual adaptations but rather as nonadaptive side effects, or *spandrels*, of much rarer, truly adaptive changes. "Since organisms are complex and highly integrated entities," wrote Gould (1997), "any adaptive change must automatically 'throw off' a series of structural byproducts—like the mold marks on an old bottle" (p. 47). Such byproducts might later be co-opted for useful purposes, but they did not arise in the first place as adaptations, and thus their existence cannot be explained through the kind of adaptationist reverse engineering Pinker and others espouse.

Thus, Gould argued that most higher cognitive faculties in humans, such as reading and writing or mathematical ability, must have originated as side effects of a general evolutionary trend toward primate brain growth: "Natural selection made the human brain big, but most of our mental properties and potentials may be spandrels—that is, nonadaptive side consequences of building a device with such structural complexity ... and therefore outside the compass of evolutionary psychology." (Gould, 1997). Lewontin (1990) argued that all of language, and perhaps even consciousness, are mere spandrels, beyond the realm of evolutionary explanation. Even Chomsky (1991), despite the immense contribution his linguistic theories have made to our understanding of the biological basis of language, doubted that natural selection can account for the existence of "the language organ," appealing instead to some as yet undetermined basic physical law.

Despite the influence of Gould and Lewontin's claims, the adaptationist program they ridicule is far from discredited. Many other biologists challenge the thesis that nonadaptational mechanisms play a central or even significant role in evolution (see Dawkins, 1986; Maynard Smith, 1988). Pinker, Bloom (1990), Dennett (1995), and others also strongly contest their critics' claim that EP is a misapplication of Darwinian theory to explain essentially nonadaptive mental structures. They grant that certain human abilities must be side effects in some sense—the ability to play chess or perform calculus obviously did not evolve to abet survival during the Pleistocene, but must instead represent modern sequelae of other evolutionary gains. Nevertheless, as Pinker noted (1997), natural selection is still the only mechanism we currently have to explain the evolution of complex biological structures such as eyes, hands, or indeed, the human brain. How else, then, can we explain the existence of something as marvelous and intricate as language?

Minds Leave No Fossils

Lewontin (1990) went even further in denying the utility of Darwinian theory, arguing that the evolutionary paradigm is essentially useless for understanding human cognition. He claimed we will never be able to reconstruct the evolutionary history of the mind—that is, how intelligent processes have developed across nonhuman ancestral species up to our present forms—because minds leave behind no fossil evidence for us to examine; thus, any such enterprise is hopelessly speculative.

Given this relative paucity of physical evidence and the emphasis on what he sees as misguided adaptationist reasoning, Gould recently (1997) pronounced the nascent discipline of evolutionary psychology to be stillborn. Appealing to some selective advantage in a distant and perhaps unknowable past as a means of explaining features of the mind may result too often in what he derides as "just-so stories"—unfalsifiable, and therefore essentially unscientific, post hoc accounts of how things came to be.

Lewontin's warnings are well taken, but he is most likely wrong to gainsay the entire enterprise of trying to reconstruct the evolution of human cognition. Although the constraints on our knowledge are daunting, there are still valid conclusions to be drawn from archaeological and anatomical evidence (e.g., comparing cranial and vocal structures of ancestral protohuman species) and comparative studies of living nonhuman primates (Jerison, 1991; Mithen, 1996; Povinelli & Eddy, 1996)

Regarding Gould's charge of just-so stories, it is admittedly a slippery slope from semiplausible evolutionary explanations to ridiculous, posthoc storytelling with no scientific basis. Even some of the more compelling evolutionary accounts may ultimately be unfalsifiable. Can this storytelling mode of science be reconciled with modern psychology as a discipline guided by empirical research?

The leaders of evolutionary psychology would answer yes. Pinker (1997) made the case that there is a difference between good and bad adaptationist explanations. Evolutionary explanations should offer a rigorous engineering analysis of the phenomenon of interest (answering the question, why would natural selection design this behavior?) and yield testable predictions that can be evaluated empirically, in the lab or in the world at large. Pinker's model of research is the more clear-cut example of visual perception, where a reverse-engineering approach is obviously appropriate (we know the eye was designed for the purpose of sight). If EP is to be accepted into the mainstream of psychological research, it must offer testable theories that can be verified or disproven. EP's storytelling must be joined with a commitment to empiricism.

CONCLUSION

A survey of EP's contribution to our understanding of the mind lays to rest, or at least assuages, several common fears expressed about the evolutionary approach. First, evolutionary psychology as commonly practiced is not Social Darwinism in a new guise; it does not seek to prove a genetic basis for inequalities among different human subgroups, nor does it seek to justify the existence of injustice or any form of human suffering by declaring it to be "natural" and therefore good. Certain evolutionary theories may still elicit a hostile reaction, such as those concerning relative differences in cognitive abilities between males and females, but such theories are normally advanced only to explain generally observed disparities between the sexes, such as differences in spatial abilities (e.g., Silverman & Eals, 1992) and arise from a framework that views men and women, and all humans in general, as essentially alike in most respects. Second, evolutionary psychology does not equal biological determinism; it does not seek to argue that everything important about the mind or intelligence is in essence genetic. Rather, it adopts the uncontroversial view that all complex human traits are determined by the interaction between innate, inherited characteristics and environmental experience. Of course, EP emphasizes the role of evolved behaviors, but only in the context that, for human beings, such behaviors are modifiable by culture and learning and are mediated by our advanced cognitive faculties.

Last, the new evolutionary psychology is capable of making real contributions to the enterprise of empirical cognitive science. Darwinian theory as applied to the human mind can be more than "pure guesswork in the cocktail party mode," as some have denigrated it (Gould, 1997).

Although the models and methods of evolutionary psychology may themselves need some time to evolve, the potential contributions of the evolutionary approach should not be overlooked. As the biologist Theodosius Dobzhansky noted (1951), "Nothing in biology makes sense except in the light of evolution." Evolutionary theory can anchor our understanding of the full complexity of human psychology in the basic processes known to govern all life. Clearly, while the framework of EP is a controversial one, it is nonetheless a viable one for the study of intelligence.

As Buss (1991) observed, "the crucial question is not *whether* evolution is relevant to the understanding of human behavior but *how* it is relevant" (p. 461). Evolution is a fundamental facet of our existence; it must ultimately be incorporated into any true model of human cognition. Rather than waiting for the ramparts to fall, psychology should open its doors now.

REFERENCES

American Psychiatric Association. (1994). *Diagnostic and statistical manual of mental disorders* (4th ed.). Washington, DC: Author.
Bailey, A., LeCouteur, A., Gottesman, I., Bolton, P., Simonoff, E., Yuzda, E., & Rutter, M. (1995). Autism as a strongly genetic disorder: Evidence from a British twin study. *Psychological Medicine, 25,* 63–77.
Barkow, J., Cosmides, L., & Tooby, J. (Eds.). (1992). *The adapted mind: Evolutionary psychology and the generation of culture.* Oxford: Oxford University Press.
Baron-Cohen, S. (1995). *Mindblindness: An essay on autism and theory of mind.* Cambridge, MA: MIT Press.
Baron-Cohen, S., & Hammer, J. (1997). Parents of children with Asperger syndrome: What is the cognitive phenotype? *Journal of Cognitive Neuroscience, 9*(4), 548–554.
Baron-Cohen, S., Leslie, A., & Frith, U. (1985). Does the autistic child have a "theory of mind"? *Cognition, 21,* 37–46.
Bolton, P., & Rutter, M. (1990). Genetic influences in autism. *International Review of Psychiatry, 2,* 67–80.
Bowlby, J. (1969). *Attachment* (Vol. 1). New York: Basic Books.

Buss, D. M. (1991). Evolutionary personality psychology. *Annual Review of Psychology, 42,* 459–491.

Buss, D. M. (1994). *The evolution of desire.* New York: Basic Books.

Cain, D. P., & Vanderwolf, C. H. (1990). A critique of Rushton on race, brain size, and intelligence. *Personality and Individual Differences, 11,* 777–784.

Childs, B., Moxon, E. R., & Winkelstein, J. A. (1992). Genetics and infectious diseases. In R. King, J. Rotter, & A. Motulsky (Eds.), *The genetic basis of common diseases* (pp. 71–91). New York: Oxford University Press.

Chomsky, N. (1965). *Aspects of the theory of syntax.* Cambridge, MA: MIT Press.

Chomsky, N. (1991). Linguistics and cognitive science: Problems and mysteries. In A. Kasher (Ed.), *The Chomskyan turn* (pp. 26–53). Cambridge, MA: Blackwell.

Chorover, S. (1979). *From genesis to genocide.* Cambridge, MA: MIT Press.

Cosmides, L. (1989). The logic of social exchange: Has natural selection shaped how humans reason? Studies with the selection task. *Cognition, 31,* 187–276.

Darwin, C. (1859/1989). *On the origin of species.* New York: New York University Press.

Darwin, C. (1871/1989). *The descent of man.* New York: New York University Press.

Dawkins, R. (1976/1989). *The selfish gene.* Oxford: Oxford University Press.

Dawkins, R. (1986). *The blind watchmaker.* New York: Norton.

Dennett, D. C. (1995). *Darwin's dangerous idea.* New York: Simon & Schuster.

Dobzhansky, T. (1951). *Genetics and the origin of species.* New York: Columbia University Press.

Gigerenzer, G. (1998). Ecological intelligence: An adaptation for frequencies. In D. D. Cummins & C. Allen (Eds.), *The evolution of mind* (pp. 9–29). Oxford: Oxford University Press.

Goddard, H. H. (1919). *Psychology of the normal and subnormal.* New York: Dodd, Mead, & Co.

Gottesman, I. I. (1991). *Schizophrenia genesis.* New York: W.H. Freeman.

Gottesman, I. I., & Shields, J. (1982). *Schizophrenia: The epigenetic puzzle.* Cambridge: Cambridge University Press.

Gould, S. J. (1981). *The mismeasure of man.* New York: Norton.

Gould, S. J. (1997, June 26). Evolution: The pleasures of pluralism. *New York Review of Books,* 47–52.

Gould, S. J., & Lewontin, R. C. (1979). The spandrels of San Marco and the Panglossian paradigm: A critique of the adaptationist programme. *Proceedings of the Royal Society of London, 205,* 581–598.

Griggs, R. A., & Cox, J. R. (1982). The elusive thematic-materials effect in Wason's selection task. *British Journal of Psychology, 73,* 407–420.

Hamilton, W. D. (1964). The genetical evolution of social behavior, Parts 1 & 2. *Journal of Theoretical Biology, 7,* 1–52.

Herrnstein, R. J., & Murray, C. (1994). *The bell curve.* New York: Free Press.

Horgan, J. (1993, June). Eugenics revisited. *Scientific American,* 5–12.

Horgan, J. (1995, October). The new Social Darwinists. *Scientific American,* 46–51.

Jerison, H. J. (1991). *Brain size and the evolution of mind.* New York: American Museum of Natural History.

Kendler, K. S. (1985). Diagnostic approaches to schizotypal personality disorder: An historical perspective. *Schizophrenia Bulletin, 11,* 538–553.

Leslie, A. (1991). The theory of mind impairment in autism: Evidence for a modular mechanism of development? In A. Whiten (Ed.), *Natural theories of mind.* Oxford: Blackwell.

Lewontin, R. C. (1990). The evolution of cognition: Questions we will never answer. In D. Osherson & E. E. Smith (Eds.), *Thinking: An invitation to cognitive science,* (Vol. 3). Cambridge, MA: MIT Press.

Maynard Smith, J. (1988). *Did Darwin get it right? Essays on games, sex and evolution.* New York: Harvester Wheatsheaf.

McGuire, M., & Troisi, A. (1998). *Darwinian psychiatry.* Cambridge, MA: Harvard University Press.

Meehl, P. E. (1989). Schizotaxia revisited. *Archives of General Psychiatry, 46,* 935–944.

Mithen, S. (1996). *The prehistory of mind.* London: Thames & Hudson.

Pinker, S. (1997). *How the mind works.* New York: W.W. Norton.

Pinker, S., & Bloom, P. (1990). Natural language and natural selection. *Brain and Behavioral Sciences, 13,* 707–727.

Povinelli, D. J., & Eddy, T. J. (1996). *What young chimpanzees know about seeing.* Monographs of the Society for Research in Child Development, (Serial No. 247).

Rushton, J. P. (1988). Race differences in behavior: A review and evolutionary analysis. *Personality and Individual Differences, 9,* 1009–1024.

Sapolsky, R. M. (1997). *The trouble with testosterone.* New York: Scribner.

Silverman, J. (1967). Shamans and acute schizophrenia. *American Anthropologist, 69*(1), 39–47.

Silverman, I., & Eals, M. (1992). Sex differences in spatial abilities: Evolutionary theory and data. In J. H. Barkow, L. Cosmides, & J. Tooby (Eds.), *The adapted mind: Evolutionary psychology and the generation of culture* (pp. 533–549). Oxford: Oxford University Press.

Singh, D. (1995). Female judgments of male attractiveness and desirability for relationships: Role of waist-to-hip ratio and financial status. *Journal of Personality and Social Psychology, 69,* 1089–1101.

Sternberg, R. J., Conway, B. E., Ketron, J. L., & Bernstein, M. (1981). People's conceptions of intelligence. *Journal of Personality and Social Psychology, 41,* 37–55.

Sternberg, R. J., & Kaufman, J. C. (1998). Human abilities. *Annual Review of Psychology, 49,* 479–502.

Trivers, R. L. (1971). The evolution of reciprocal altruism. *Quarterly Review of Biology, 46,* 35–57.

Wason, P. C., & Johnson-Laird, P. N. (1972). *Psychology of reasoning: Structure and content.* London: B.T. Batsford.

Willerman, L., Schultz, R., Rutledge, J. N., & Bigler, E. D. (1991). In vivo brain size and intelligence. *Intelligence, 15,* 223–228.

Willerman, L., Schultz, R., Rutledge, J. N., & Bigler, E. D. (1992). Hemisphere size asymmetry predicts relative verbal and nonverbal intelligence differently in the sexes: An MRI study of structure-function relations. *Intelligence, 16,* 315–328.

Williams, G. C. (1966). *Adaptation and natural selection.* Princeton, NJ: Princeton University Press.

Wilson, E. O. (1975). *Sociobiology: The new synthesis.* Cambridge, MA: Harvard University Press.

Wilson, E. O. (1978). *On human nature.* Cambridge, MA: Harvard University Press.

Wright, R. (1994). *The moral animal.* New York: Pantheon.

Yang, S.-Y., & Sternberg, R. J. (1997). Conceptions of intelligence in ancient Chinese philosophy. *Journal of Theoretical Philosophy and Psychology, 17,* 101–119.

3

Social Cognition, Inhibition, and Theory of Mind: The Evolution of Human Intelligence

David F. Bjorklund
Florida Atlantic University

Katherine Kipp
University of Georgia

Intelligence, or more generally, cognition, is usually thought of as an active process. We search, classify, evaluate, reason, and so on, in order to solve some problem. In general, when thinking, we activate knowledge or mental strategies, and those of us who do a better job of such activation are usually considered to be more intelligent that those of us who are cognitively less active. But there's more to intelligence than the activation of knowledge from our long-term memories or the implementation of plans or strategies. Sometimes intelligence requires not activating some mental routine or actually inhibiting some mental action from taking place. What we don't think or do is sometimes as important as what we do think or do.

The major theme of this chapter is that cognitive inhibition—the ability to inhibit certain thoughts and behaviors at certain times—plays an important role in intelligence and played an important role in the evolution of intelligence in our species. More specifically, we propose that pressures for greater cooperation and competition in our ancestors led to increased brain size, specifically of the neocortex. This resulted in greater voluntary inhibitory control of sexual and aggressive behaviors, which contributed to increased social harmony. Over time, inhibitory mechanisms became increasingly under cortical (and thus intentional) control. Brain circuits that were initially involved in the control of emotional behavior could then be used for inhibiting other social behaviors and cognitions and played a critical role in the evolution of the cognitive architecture of modern humans (Bjorklund & Harnishfeger, 1995). Moreover, we propose that, in some contexts, there was greater pressure on ancient human females than males to develop good inhibitory abilities and that remnants of this ancient heritage can be observed in contemporary men and women (Bjorklund & Kipp, 1996).

In the following sections we first provide a definition of what we mean by intelligence and how we believe that social pressures to cooperate and compete were the driving force behind human intellectual evolution. We then examine the role of inhibition in contemporary modern thinking, followed by a brief look at the neural basis of such inhibition. We then provide some evidence for our hypothesis that it was inhibitory mechanisms, evolved initially to deal with control of emotional responding, that were subsequently co-opted for more general use in intellectual functioning.

THE SOCIAL NATURE OF INTELLIGENCE

What is unique about human beings is our intelligence. Not that we are the only thinking animal to inhabit the earth, but that our intelligence, more than any other attribute, is responsible for our place in the world. We have survived as a species and have come to dominate the world, for better or worse, but not because we are stronger or faster than other animals, or because we have superior camouflage, armor, or sensory skills. Rather, our flexible intelligence has permitted *Homo sapiens* to live in the widest range of environments of any mammal and to invent culture, which has changed the way humans live at a rate much greater than could have been accomplished strictly by biology. Through our intelligence we make technological changes that, in the course of years and decades—not millennia and eons—result in whole-scale changes in how we live as a species. Cultural change has sometimes been slow, as reflected by the seeming stability of human existence and tools over the course of more than 1 million years (see Binford, 1983; Mithen, 1996). But since the advent of agriculture, about 12,000 years ago, the rate of change has been increasing, and there is no sign of it slowing down. Yet even today, there remain tribes of hunter–gatherers and agriculturists, who possess the same brain and intellect as Internet-using moderns. Thus, rapid cultural change cannot be the definition of human intelligence. How can we describe the intelligence of contemporary humans across the globe, and what forces might have caused human intelligence to take the course that it did?

We believe that Sternberg (1997) captured the essence of *intelligence* when he defined it as "the mental activities necessary for adaptation to, as well as shaping and selection of, any environmental context. According to this definition, intelligence is not just reactive to the environment but also active in forming it. It offers people an opportunity to respond flexibly to challenging situations" (p. 1030). When talking about the evolution of intelligence, one must pay close attention to the context in which it developed. So, when Sternberg stated that intelligence offers people "an opportunity to respond flexibly to challenging situations," we must ask what type of situations did ancient men and women face that demanded intelligence, and are any of these situations relevant for people today? As all other species, our hominid ancestors faced situations in which they needed to make a living—find food and shelter, and avoid becoming food for other animals. (Hominids refers to the class of bipedal animals that includes humans and our ancient ancestors. *Homo sapien* is the only surviving member of this class.) In many respects, the demands of the physical environment must have been similar for our ancestors as they were for other large mammals living in Africa over the past 5 million years or so. If that's so, why are we so intellectually different from our closest cousins, the chimpanzees and bonobos (pigmy chimpanzees)? The primary reason, we believe, is not because we became better hunters or gathers but because, due to a host of interacting factors, the social complexity of hominid groups increased, and we became more intelligent in order to deal with each other.

Of course, looking for any simple cause–effect explanation for the evolution of human intelligence would be just that—simplistic. A multitude of pressures, interacting over hundreds of thousands of years' time, are responsible for the amazing brain contained in our heads today. But one set of factors that we believe cannot be overlooked, when studying intelligence in either contemporary people or in the evolution of the species, is the social nature of our kind. We are a social species, and many theorists have proposed that our intelligence evolved primarily to deal with fellow human beings (Alexander, 1989; Bjorklund & Harnishfeger, 1995; Byrne & Whiten, 1988; Crook, 1980; Dunbar, 1993; Humphrey, 1976). As the social complexity of hominid groups increased, individuals who could better understand their social world gained more of the benefits in terms of available resources and mates and passed those characteristics along to their offspring. An important function of the brain in "higher" animals is to create a form of reality that permits it to function in its world. The greater social complexity of hominid groups required a greater awareness of ourselves and the needs and motivations of others so that we could better understand, and perhaps manipulate, others.

One function of language, for example, is social, and language may have served a similar role for early humans that social grooming does for chimpanzees. Dunbar (1993) proposed that language evolved so that individuals could learn about other group members faster than would be possible by direct observation alone. Dunbar noted that about 60% of conversation among modern humans deals with gossip about human relations and personal experiences. In other words, language evolved because of social pressures to handle unique social problems.

As social complexity increased, the need to cooperate among members of the group increased. Success in hunting and food gathering is more likely among people who are cooperating with one another. To cooperate, it helps to have ideas of what the group goals are and how others will behave in certain situations. (If I circle around this side, will he circle around the other?) Groups of hominids who failed to cooperate could find themselves victims of other, better organized (i.e., more cooperative) groups.

What type of intelligence must develop in order to deal with these new social pressures? Humphrey (1976) was one of the first to suggest the significance of self-consciousness—the ability to experience one's own feelings and behavior—as an important factor in human intellectual evolution. Being self-conscious puts us in a better position to interpret and predict the feelings and behaviors of others, a valuable tool for a social animal. This latter set of abilities has been studied lately under the term *theory of mind*. Children develop what has been termed *belief-desire reasoning* (Wellman, 1990) around 4 years of age. They recognize that people's behavior is based on what they believe (know, suppose, expect, doubt) and what they desire (want, wish, hope), and that other people's beliefs and desires can be different from their own. This type of reasoning is critical for life in any human social setting. And although some researchers believe that chimpanzees demonstrate some evidence of theory of mind (see, e.g., articles in Byrne & Whiten, 1988), others doubt it (Povinelli & Eddy, 1996; Povinelli, Bering, & Giambrone, in press), and few would credit even the brainiest chimpanzee with a theory of mind as sophisticated as that of an average 4-year-old human child. (We have more to say about theory of mind in both children and apes later in this chapter.)

A related intellectual skill is deception. Although deception has been observed in baboons and chimpanzees (Whiten & Byrne, 1988), those animals are novices compared to humans. Deception is perhaps the ultimate political skill. Concealing one's true feelings and motives is important in many social exchanges, as in cases of social tact ("Oh, you colored your hair. How lovely."), love ("Of course I'll respect you in the morning."), war ("Leave me alone or I'll get my big brother after you."), and games ("The pair of threes sees your $5, and raises you $10.").

We believe, as others, that the social pressures to cooperate and compete with other members of the group was the driving force of human intelligence. Human beings are more intelligent than necessary to eke out an existence on the savannas of Africa. In fact, so also are chimpanzees. According to Humphrey (1976), most of the technological genius of humankind is not used in our daily lives. If alien anthropologists had observed Albert Einstein during a typical day, they would likely infer that he had a hum-drum mind. If our genius is used only rarely, what are our big brains for most of the time? The answer is that we do use our keen intelligence everyday but not for inventing tools or solving abstract problems of mathematics or physics: we use our intelligence in dealing with other members of our species. We became smart not so much to cope with the demands of a hostile physical world but to meet the demands of hostile members of our own species. According to Richard Alexander (1989), hominids essentially evolved a new hostile force of nature—themselves.

Social intelligence is often viewed as "soft" or "warm" or "fuzzy" in comparison with the "hard" or "cold" intelligence reflected by mathematics, formal reasoning, or the many other topics that cognitive psychologists have spent a century studying. We argue that social intelligence is actually the more primitive, or core, human intellectual ability, and that analytical reasoning, spatial thinking, and other forms of hard cognition evolved on the abilities developed to deal with social problems. And central to our claims, we believe that one critical ability in the evolution of social intelligence and in the subsequent development of other forms of cognition is the ability to inhibit thoughts and behaviors in certain contexts.

Inhibition, as we think of it, is a *domain-general* ability. That is, the ability to inhibit thoughts or behaviors is believed to cut across domains, or types of cognitive tasks, and thus is not limited to any one particular domain or task (such as social cognition). But contemporary evolutionary psychological theory proposes that most important aspects of cognition are *domain-specific* in nature. That is, most adaptive cognitive mechanisms evolved to solve specific problems of our ancestors (such as mating, hunting, and dealing with other members of our species). These skills are said to be *modular*, in that they are self-contained and are not influenced by other cognitive abilities (Buss, 1995; Tooby & Cosmides, 1992). Theory of mind, for example, is proposed to be such a modular ability (Baron-Cohen, 1995). This is illustrated in cases of autism, in which children may have relatively normal language and general intellectual abilities, but they treat other people in the same way they treat objects, being seemingly unaware that other people have minds and that their actions are based on their desires and beliefs. Baron-Cohen (1995) referred to such people as having mindblindness.

If theory of mind, and other important aspects of social cognition, are domain specific in nature, how can changes in a domain-general ability play an important role in their evolution and development? We do not argue against the position that most aspects of adaptive cognitive abilities, including important aspects of social cognition, are domain-specific in nature. However, we (Bjorklund & Kipp, 1996) and others (e.g., Mithen, 1996) have argued that domain-specific cognitive abilities coexist in contemporary people with domain-general ones and that this has been the case through human evolution. More to the point, we argue that enhanced domain-general skills, such as inhibition or speed of mental processing, may have been required before more domain-specific abilities could be developed. For example, early hominids' increased brain size may have resulted in greater overall inhibition abilities; these abilities could then be used for more specific tasks, such as to inhibit a desired response when one knows that it will produce a benefit in a social situation. More specific cognitive abilities could then be evolved once the requisite general abilities were in place. From this perspective, inhibition and other domain-general abilities, played a *permissive* role on human cognitive evolution. More advanced cognitive abilities, of both the domain-general and domain-specific kind, could not have evolved until a certain level of inhibition was achieved.

THE ROLE OF INHIBITION IN COGNITION

Inhibition is the component of intelligence that allows us to withhold immediate responding long enough to execute the more sophisticated and complex cognitive analyses that are necessary for intelligent or thoughtful responses. The suspension of action or decision is essential in our adaptation to a changing environment. We become a force in environmental change when we are able to withhold immediate reaction to the environment.

Although inhibition may be an ubiquitous process in human behavior, our primary interest here is on the role of inhibition in human cognition and intelligence. Inhibition contributes to a variety of cognitive functions, including basic cognitive processes (such as attention), developmental differences in cognition, and individual differences in cognition and behavior.

At a general level, inhibitory processes control the contents of consciousness and the operation of processing activities (Harnishfeger, 1995). With cognitive inhibition, we suppress previously activated cognitive contents or processes; clear irrelevant actions or attention from consciousness; and resist interference from potentially attention-capturing processes or contents. That is, cognitive inhibition allows us to restrict our attention and thereby execute cognitive processing more efficiently.

Failure to maintain control through inhibitory efficiency may be detrimental to performance in some contexts, such as during tasks requiring speedy responses and frequent changes in response. One of the clearest forms of cognitive inhibition is the suppression of attention to external stimuli that are irrelevant to current concerns (Bjorklund & Harnishfeger, 1995). Selective attention to relevant stimuli requires efficient inhibition of wandering or captured attention. Inhibitory processes permit the control of internal distractors (e.g., task-irrelevant activations in working memory or spontaneous task-irrelevant cognitive processes, such as daydreaming) as well as the control of external distractors (e.g., task-irrelevant features in the environment or cognitive processing that become tangential during problem solving).

Inhibition may be controlled at a conscious or a preconscious level (Harnishfeger, 1995). Inhibition on a conscious level occurs as in the monitoring of task performance and the deliberate control of consciousness. For example, a person might recognize that his or her thoughts have wandered from the topic of the book he or she is reading (to an enticing daydream, perhaps), and the person makes a conscious effort to refocus attention from that daydream to the task at hand. Inhibition on a preconscious level occurs when our cognitive system suppresses activation or processing before it reaches conscious awareness. For example, the fact that one does not think about night-flying mammals while reading about bats in a baseball story is due to preconscious inhibition, not to selective activation of the supposedly correct meaning of the word (e.g., Lorsbach, Katz, & Cupak, 1998; Swinney & Prather, 1989).

Inhibitory processing changes contribute to changes in intellectual functioning across the lifespan. The efficiency of cognitive inhibition increases with age in childhood and decreases with age in later adulthood. In infancy, inhibitory processes contribute to developmental improvements in the ability to withhold prepotent responses (e.g., Diamond, 1985). In childhood, increasingly efficient inhibitory processes contribute to developmental improvements in children's abilities to selectively attend to relevant information in perceptual and cognitive tasks and to keep task-irrelevant information from interfering with task processing (e.g., Bjorklund & Harnishfeger, 1990; Lehman, McKinley-Pace, Wilson, Savsky, & Woodson, 1997). In later adulthood, decreasing inhibitory efficiency contributes to older adults' failure to moderate the contents of working memory during memory tasks and discourse processing (Hamm & Hasher, 1992).

Inhibition and Theory of Mind

Consistent with our hypotheses concerning the evolution of social cognition, inhibitory abilities have also been linked empirically to the acquisition of theory of mind (e.g., Perner & Lang, in press; Perner, Stummer, & Lang, 1999). A variety of tasks containing inhibitory components have been examined in this literature, including Stroop-type tasks and variants of the Wisconsin Card Sorting

Test (WCST) that are modified for young children. For example, Frye, Zelazo, and Palfai(1995) modified the WCST for young children by including just two dimensions (color and form, with green cars, green flowers, yellow cars, and yellow flowers) for matching. Children first sorted according one dimension (e.g., form) and then the rules were changed so that sorting was done by the other dimension (e.g., color). Children between the ages of 3 and 5 years typically had a great deal of trouble with the task after the change in instructions, presumably in part because of the requirement to inhibit the previously correct responses.

Performance on similar tasks that include an inhibitory component has been compared to performance on variants of the false-belief test of theory of mind. For example, in the deceptive container task children are asked to guess the contents of a distinctive Smarties candy box (Perner, Leekam, & Wimmer, 1987). Most children respond that there are Smarties in the box. Next, the children are shown that the Smarties box holds pencils, not Smarties. When the box is closed again and children are asked what another person (one who hadn't looked in the box) would think was in the box, the 3-year-olds are unable to respond correctly, stating what they know to be true. Similar to the problems they have in sorting tasks used by Frye, Zelazo, and their colleagues, young children have difficulty resolving the conflicting information that another person may have knowledge different than their own, and one source of their difficulty appears to be related to a failure to inhibit an established response. For example, when 3-year-old children are shown a series of windows, some of which have candy treats in them, they never receive the treats when they select the "treat" window. They only get the treat when they select a nontreat window. Despite the negative outcome associated with choosing the treat windows, young children have a difficult time inhibiting the obvious responses and repeatedly select the treat window and get nothing for their efforts (Russell, Mauthner, Sharpe, & Tidswell, 1991).

This literature suggests that the inhibition tasks and the theory of mind tasks are mastered at about the same developmental time (e.g., Russell et al., 1991). Perner et al. (1999) report an average correlation between performance in the two types of tasks between $r = .30$ and .60, with a significant correlation remaining even after age is partialled out. Although the exact nature of the relationship between theory of mind and inhibition in development is not clear, it does appear that there is some common functional relationship between the two (cf. Perner & Lang, in press; Perner et al., 1999).

Thus, cognitive inhibition changes with development, and this change affects such other cognitive processes as memory, reasoning, problem solving and discourse processing, and possibly theory of mind. Inhibitory processes have been proposed as explanatory mechanisms of developmental change by numerous researchers. These approaches link changes in behavior and cognition. For example, the inhibition of prepotent responding, which improves over infancy and early childhood, is thought to contribute to the development of self-regulation and a sense of personal control, fostering cognitive and social-emotional development and a positive sense of agency and self-concept (Bjorklund & Harnishfeger, 1995).

Differences in the efficiency of inhibition may also contribute to individual differences in cognitive processing (Harnishfeger & Bjorklund, 1994). As some age groups have more difficulty than others inhibiting off-task activations and processing, some individuals have more difficulty with inhibition than others. For example, inhibitory deficits have been found in the cognitive performance of children with attention deficit hyperactivity disorder and in individuals suffering from various psychiatric dysfunctions, such as conduct disorder, psychopathology, schizophrenia, and obsessive-compulsive disorder (e.g., Flor-Henry, 1983; Malloy, 1987). Inhibitory deficits have also been found in the cognitive performance of children with mental retardation and reading and learning disabilities, providing further evidence of the link between inhibition and cognition (e.g., Ellis & Dulaney, 1991). Inhibition is likely a cognitive function that is normally distributed in the population, and individuals have been found to differ in the sensitivity they show to interference in their everyday lives (e.g., Tipper & Baylis, 1987).

INHIBITION AND THE BRAIN

The Neural Basis of Inhibition

There is substantial evidence that the control of behavior through inhibitory mechanisms can be localized in functional areas of the neocortex. Neuropsychological research has identified the primary locus of behavioral inhibition to be the associative cortex of the frontal lobes, or the prefrontal cortex (Fuster, 1984; Luria, 1973). This area is structurally defined as the part of the cerebral cortex that receives projections from the mediodorsal nucleus of the thalamus. It is a functionally heterogeneous area, with various functions falling together in a pattern related to the temporal organization of behavior, including the suppression of interference, or inhibition (Fuster, 1984; Goldman-Rakic, 1987).

The prefrontal cortex is one of the last areas of the brain to reach full maturity in development. Development of the frontal lobes in humans is rapid between birth and approximately 2 years of age. There is another, less pronounced growth spurt between approximately 4 and 7 years of age, with subsequent growth being slow and gradual into young adulthood (Luria, 1973).

Development of the frontal lobes takes several forms, including increases in the size and complexity of neurons, increased myelination, and changes in the density of synapses in the area. The density of synapses—the connections between neurons—reaches its peak in the frontal areas between 1 and 2 years of age (Huttenlocher, 1979). The number of connections per neuron is higher in the first few years of life than at any other age, with subsequent development involving the pruning of neurons via a process known as selective cell death (Goldman-Rakic, 1987). Experiences during this time may determine which neurons will live, their functionality, and their dedication to various brain operations (e.g., Edelman, 1987; Greenough, Black, & Wallace, 1987). The process of myelination of the frontal areas begins relatively late in development (compared to myelination of the sensory and motor cortices) and is not complete until adulthood (e.g., Yakovlev & Lecours, 1967). Myelin is the fatty tissue that surrounds neurons, producing fast transmission of nerve signals and less electrical interference from surrounding neurons. The emotional and cognitive inhibitory processes of the brain appear to depend on the full development of the prefrontal cortex, including proliferation of the neurons and synapses, myelination, and selective cell death (e.g., Goldman-Rakic, 1987).

Several research programs have linked the inhibitory control of behavior to the prefrontal cortex. The research suggests that variations in prefrontal function may account for developmental differences and individual differences in patterns of inhibitory control. For example, evidence from comparative research, in which animals with extensive ablation of the prefrontal cortex are compared with intact control animals, suggests that the prefrontal cortex controls the inhibition of behavior, including motor, appetitive, aggressive, and sexual response (e.g., Fuster, 1984; Goldman-Rakic, 1987). Evidence from comparative developmental research suggest that the protracted developmental course of the prefrontal cortex, compared with other areas of the neocortex, plays a role in young animals' difficulties in completing tasks that require the inhibition of prepotent responses (e.g., Goldman-Rakic, 1987). Evidence from human neuropsychological research suggests that humans with prefrontal damage present a host of behavioral deficits that include inhibitory deficits, such as the inability to regulate conscious attentional processes, to control behavior verbally, and to inhibit prepotent responses (e.g., Luria, 1973; Schacter, Moscovitch, Tulving, McLachlan, & Frendman, 1986). Evidence from clinical research links some clinical psychiatric syndromes that are characterized by inhibitory deficits, such as obsessive-compulsive disorder, to dysfunctions of the frontal lobes (e.g., Flor-Henry, 1983; Malloy, 1987). Finally, human developmental research suggests that the protracted development of the frontal lobes in humans is related to young children's deficits in inhibitory control of their motor and perceptual behavior (e.g., Diamond, 1991; Diamond & Taylor 1996).

Evolution of the Human Brain

Perhaps it is obvious, but increased human intelligence over evolutionary time is directly linked to increased brain size and organization. This is perhaps the most obvious physical difference between humans and both our australopithecine ancestors and our modern genetic cousins, the great apes (chimpanzees, bonobos, gorillas, and orangutans). Looking at the fossil record, changes in skull size are the most notable differences between modern people and our ancestors. One of the earliest members of the hominid family line (*Australopithecus afarensis*) walked erect as we do but had a skull capacity not much different from that of a modern chimpanzee (about 420 cc). Skull capacity gradually increased over the next several million years, from *Homo habilis* (about 650 cc) to *Homo erectus* (about 950 cc) to modern humans (about 1350 cc) (Eccles, 1989; Tobias, 1987). It is not just size of the skull, and thus presumably the size of the brain, that is important, however. If that were the case, blue whales would be the most intelligent animals alive today, and elephants would rule the land. What is critical is brain size relative to body size, which has been termed the *encephalization quotient* (Jerison, 1973). Compared with most other mammals primates generally have larger brain to body ratios, but this trend is exaggerated in humans.

Although one can get a good idea of how large the brains of early hominids were by looking at their skulls, one cannot know much about the organization of the brain. Brains do not fossilize, and although skulls sometime show the impression of the brains they once held, such impressions provide little information about the structure of the brains themselves. We are able to get a better (or at least different) idea of how brains have changed over the past 4 million years by comparing the brains of modern people with those of our closest living relatives, the chimpanzees. Paleontologists have suggested that common chimpanzees (and their close relative, the bonobos) are a conservative species, having changed relatively little, particularly in comparison with humans since they and *Homo sapiens* last shared a common ancestor, approximately 5 to 6 million years ago. (Recall that the skull size of the earliest hominids was approximately the same as that of modern chimpanzees.) When we compare the brains of modern humans and chimpanzees, we essentially see no new brain structures in humans. What differs between the species is the size of the brains, although some areas of the brain have increased more than others over evolutionary time (see Eccles, 1989). Most notable is the difference in the neocortex, the part of the human brain most associated with complex human thought. Included in this expansion of the neocortex are the prefrontal lobes, which have been implicated in cognitive inhibition. As we noted earlier, the prefrontal cortex has many connections with the limbic system, or the "emotional" brain. One pur-

ported role of the prefrontal cortex important for our hypothesis is the inhibition of inappropriate emotional responses. It is worth noting that the human
limbic system also shows a substantial increase in size relative to chimpanzees.
Thus, any evidence of greater humans' abilities to control their emotions (relative to chimpanzees) cannot be attributed to a reduction in emotionality; humans remain highly emotional creatures. Rather, any such enhanced ability to
inhibit impulses arising from the limbic system can be better attributed to
greater prefrontal control.

THE EVOLUTION OF INHIBITION MECHANISMS

As should be quite obvious, inhibition is not a new neural mechanism in evolution but presumably one that is possessed by all animals that have a nervous system. But, we argue, ancient *Homo sapiens* raised the use of inhibition of social
responses to a new level. Such control of behavior may have been particularly
important in keeping sexual and aggressive behaviors in check (likely their initial purpose), which fostered the cohesion and cooperation of the social group.
With these abilities in place, inhibition skills could be used for other purposes,
chief among them the withholding of information (a form of deception) and
eventually better control of one's own thoughts, which may have lead to the development of a theory of mind—perhaps the most critical component in modern humans' social intelligence. From this point, we propose, inhibition abilities
were co-opted for other basic cognitive abilities and may have made possible
(although, did not "cause") many forms of higher cognition, such as reasoning
and language.

Although we believe that improved inhibition abilities are species-typical
characteristics that evolved over hundreds of thousands of years, we also propose that there were greater pressures in ancient human females than in males
for the use of certain classes of inhibition abilities and that remnants of these
pressures and inhibition abilities can be found in modern men and women
(Bjorklund & Kipp, 1996). In the following sections, we look at the pressures
under which our hominid ancestors lived and how those pressures may have led
to increased inhibition abilities and, in turn, increased intelligence.

Not Responding in Social Contexts

We, as others, have suggested that it was pressures of having to deal with other
members of one's immediate group that played a major role in the evolution of
the modern human mind (Alexander, 1989; Bjorklund & Harnishfeger, 1995;
Byrne & Whiten, 1988; Humphrey, 1976). Primates generally are social creatures. Chimpanzees, for example, not only compete with other members of the

group for access to resources (food, mates), but they also form coalitions and co-operate with one another in order to achieve specific goals (e.g., hunting, raid-ing other groups, settling within-group conflicts). Dealing with other members of a group requires social intelligence, or what has sometimes been referred to as Machiavellian intelligence (Byrne & Whiten, 1988), reflecting the political goals of almost all social interactions.

What type of cognitive functioning is necessary for good social intelligence? Among the many skills that might be involved are the recognition of kin, distin-guishing and remembering friends and foes, remembering who has done favors for whom and when those favors have been repaid, detecting cheaters, forming coalitions, planning one's "moves" and anticipating the "moves" of others, and sometimes withholding information in order to protect or garner important re-sources. Social cognition is as complex, or perhaps more complex than the cold cognition used to read a book or solve math problems, and no simple listing of specific skills will do the topic justice. However, we contend that at the root of adept social cognition is the basic ability to inhibit—to withhold responses and information under certain circumstances. At its most sophisticated level, this may involve conveying misinformation with a straight face (inhibiting the facial signals associated with lying) or not divulging some pertinent information to a competitor while making a deal. At a more basic level, this may involve not looking in the direction of a desired resource while in the presence of a rival or the withholding of sexual and aggressive responses.

The wisdom of controlling one's aggressive and sexual urges in public places seems quite obvious to us today but may not have been obvious to our ancestors. However, as the social fabric of hominid society became more complex, the need to inhibit these "animal" urges became increasingly important. Once the neural architecture underlying such inhibition abilities had evolved to deal with the control of sexual and aggressive behaviors, it could be used for other pur-poses, some social (deception, theory of mind), and some nonsocial (tool use, reasoning).

Control of Sexual and Aggressive Responses

It is not just humans or our immediate ancestors who need to control sexual and aggressive urges. In many species of primates, there is substantial conflict among males for access to females, particularly when females are in estrus. Higher ranking males often prevent lower ranking males access to estrus fe-males and often threaten (or partake in) violence to achieve this goal. In some species, lower ranking males are permitted to copulate with females when they are not in estrus. Conflict occurs when the possibility of reproduction (as evi-denced by external signs of fertility in the female) is real (see Geary, 1998).

It is interesting that copulation sometimes occurs with nonestrus female chimpanzees, despite the fact that conception is not possible at these times. This reflects in primates a shift of sexual behavior from hormonal and limbic-system control to neocortical control (Beach, 1947), which is most fully developed in humans. The greater neocortical control of sexual behavior means that sex can now be increasingly under the influence of social factors rather than simply the product of chemistry (i.e., hormones). This is coupled in humans with changes in females that mask the time of ovulation. Unlike most other primates, human females do not go through a period of estrus. Other than during menstruation, there are no clear signs of whether or not a woman is ovulating. Women show few if any outward signs of sexual receptivity when they are ovulating, making it difficult for a man to know when she is most likely to become pregnant. Women also have permanently swollen mammaries, which have become a sexual signal for males, despite the fact that they are unreliable indicators of ovulation or sexual interest and, in comparison to males, show little outward signs of sexual arousal. In addition, like her male counterparts, a woman is also potentially sexually receptive continuously throughout her cycle. However, human females could just as likely be said to be continuously *nonreceptive* (Alexander & Noonan, 1979) because few women are indiscriminate in their choice of a sexual partner.

This pattern causes some problems. For males, there are few reliable signs of female interest that do not take some time to evaluate. This requires an inhibition of males' sexual advances toward females until additional information can be gained. Also, if females didn't inhibit their sexual receptivity, it could easily result in constant conflict among males for access to females and "guarding" of females by possessive males to prevent access by other males. The result would be social chaos. The unique combination of greater neocortical control of sexual behavior, concealed ovulation, and continuous (but ambiguous) female sexual receptivity necessitated increased inhibitory control, in both males and females, of sexual behavior.

Human females need male support. Human infants have a prolonged period of immaturity, and support from males (i.e., the fathers) increases the likelihood that children will survive and thrive (see Geary, 1998; 2000). If mating were promiscuous, with neither males nor females inhibiting their sexual behaviors, paternity would be uncertain (due to concealed ovulation) and male support for a female's offspring would not likely be forthcoming. In this way, as well as in its interaction with other physical changes that occurred over the course of human evolution, inhibition played an important role in developing the sexual strategies of both sexes. Not only was the control of sexual and aggressive impulses implicated in pair-bonding—an important social characteristic of our species—but it also provided an atmosphere that permitted other complex social interactions to develop.

It is also worth noting that inhibiting sexual responses and associated behaviors may have been (and might continue to be) of greater consequence for prehistoric females than for males (Bjorklund & Kipp, 1996). This is because of the greater potential investment women have in any act of mating, relative to men. A man's investment in reproduction may be as little as a few minutes, and the number of offspring he can sire is restricted only by the number of fertile women with whom he has sex. A woman's investment in any sexual encounter, in contrast, is potentially much greater. Should conception occur, the woman must carry the child for 9 months and then is (traditionally) the principal source of food for the child for the next 3 or 4 years. Even in modern society, and in cultures that provide paternal leave as well as maternal leave, women provide a disproportionate amount of the child care (see Geary, 1998; Lamb, Frodi, Hwang, & Frodi, 1982; Whiting & Whiting, 1975, for a review). The differential consequences of sex for males and females is described by *parental investment theory* (for applications to humans see Bjorklund & Shackelford, 1999; Buss & Schmidt, 1993; Geary, 1998; Trivers, 1972). Because women would like to mate with men who not only will provide good genes but who will also provide resources for them and their offspring, they must be more cautious than men when committing to a sexual encounter.

In support of this hypothesis of greater inhibitory abilities in females than in males, proposed by Bjorklund and Kipp (1996), there is some evidence that women are better than men in inhibiting sexual arousal (Cerny, 1978; Rosen, 1973). Women have also been found to be better than men in concealing emotions, despite the fact that females are more emotionally expressive than males. For example, in research in which people are to display a positive emotion after a negative experience (e.g., pretending that a foul-tasting drink tastes good) or vice versa, females from the age of 4 years are better than males in controlling their emotional expressions (i.e., fooling a judge who is watching their reactions) (e.g., Cole, 1986, Feldman & White, 1980; Saarni, 1984).

Successful Parenting

Another domain that seems to require substantial inhibition skills, and which females seem to better master, is the parenting of young children. Humans have a longer period of immaturity than any other primate. We are born helpless and remain dependent on our parents for 4 or 5 years, and we then spend another decade or more as pre-reproductives. Effective parenting involves the inhibition of many responses. Parents (again, mostly mothers) must often put the needs of their infants first, delaying their own gratification and resisting distractions that would take them away from their infants. They must also be able to inhibit many aggressive reflex responses to an often difficult and aversive infant. One reads all too often of an adult (usually a male) losing his temper and injuring or killing an infant or young child who would not stop its persistent crying, who soiled his or her pants, or who otherwise misbehaved. A parent must also deal with toddlers and young children who engage in activities that are dangerous, both to themselves and to others in their surroundings. Young children believe that they are more capable than they actually are (Bjorklund, Gaultney, & Green, 1993; Plumert, 1995), and the result often is a child who attempts tasks that can produce injury to themselves or others or damage to personal property. To be an effective parent under these circumstances requires patience and the ability to withhold unreasonable aggressive responses to minor childhood transgressions.

In contemporary societies, mothers who raise securely attached children tend to be emotionally warm and sensitive to their children's signals of physical and emotional need (Ainsworth, Blehar, Waters, & Wall, 1978). Securely attached infants tend to become curious, socially competent, and self-assured children (Cassidy, 1988; Cohn, 1990; Erickson, Sroufe, & Egeland, 1985). Although parenting styles do vary across cultures, and we can never know how our ancient ancestors dealt with their young children, it would seem that these same characteristics—inhibition of aggressive responses and delay of gratification while attending to infants' needs—would have characterized effective hominid mothers. Similar to the findings of gender differences in social situations (e.g., control of facial expressions), there is evidence that females are somewhat better than males on tasks that involve resisting temptation (e.g., Kochanska, Murray, Jacques, Koenig, & Vandegeest, 1996; Slaby & Park, 1971) and delaying gratification (e.g., Kochanska et al., 1996; Logue & Chavarro, 1992), exactly the pattern that one would predict if pressures associated with taking care of young children were greater on hominid females than males (see Bjorklund & Kipp, 1996).

Deception

We have emphasized the social roots of human intelligence and the role that inhibition plays in such cognition. Although restraining sexual urges and aggressive behavior (toward other adult members of the group or toward one's young children) are obviously social in nature, human social intelligence, and likely the social intelligence of our primate relatives, is much more complex. Cooperation requires not just inhibiting aggressive responses or sexual overtures toward an ally's mate, but also planning, identifying shared goals, and working together to meet those goals. Competition with conspecifics (other members of one's species) likely involves even greater social intelligence. It requires realizing that one's goals might often conflict with those of others and developing ways in which one can "defeat" competitors, or perhaps arrive at mutually satisfying goals. One skill that is critically involved in such social intelligence is *deception*.

Deception can involve as little as withholding a response (e.g., not looking at a desired object when in the presence of a more dominant peer), concealing an emotion (e.g., acting unhappy when, in fact, the outcome is quite acceptable to you), or exhibiting such complicated maneuvers as implanting false beliefs in other people, lying, and getting others to go along with "the plan." Each type of deception, from the simplest not looking at a desired object to the intricately de-signed ruse, involves inhibition. To deceive, one must realize that doing or say-ing something in a particular context is not in one's best interest, even if one is prone to normally do or say these things. But once this realization is attained, one must inhibit (not respond) in order to *not* share information with another individual.

Of course, inhibiting a response is only one of several factors that is impor-tant in deception. One must have a specific goal in mind and keep it in mind, re-alize that a competitor has a different goal in mind (and one that is not to your advantage), and that not responding (that is, deceiving) can help you achieve your goal at the expense of your competitor. Thus, inhibition plays only a per-missive role in deception. However, without the ability to inhibit natural ten-dencies, none of the other complicated mental operations involved in deception, or other forms of higher cognition, could function properly.

We do not think it is necessary to expand on the role that deception (broadly defined) plays in social intelligence and everyday human functioning. From the simple "white" lies we tell one another to grease the wheels of social functioning to the operations of the legal system and military tactics, deception, in one form or another, is found. And we argue that, at all levels, deception involves inhibition.

Although human beings have raised the art of deception to a level unsur-passed in the known universe, we are not the only social species to deceive. Some animal deception has a strong genetic basis to it and, because of this, is quite dissimilar from what humans do. For example, some insects look like sticks or leaves, nonpoisonous butterflies mimic a toxic species, and some birds will lure predators away from an egg-filled nest. These are examples of deception, but they cannot be used flexibly. Rather, they are part of the basic bodily struc-ture of an animal (such as walking sticks and mimicking butterflies) or are elic-ited "instinctively" and without choice whenever a particular situation arises (as in the case of some birds). But the type of flexible, inhibition-based decep-tion that we see in humans has also been found in lesser degrees in monkeys and apes. Most primates are social creatures, and it should not be surprising that, at times, deceiving a conspecific would be in an animal's best interest. A number of researchers have observed cases of deception in wild or captive primates. For example, Whiten and Byrne (1988) sent questionnaires to 115 primatologists asking for any evidence of deception in their subjects. The primatologists responded with 79 examples, most involving concealment or distraction. Next, we provide a few examples from this literature (from Bjorklund and Harnishfeger, 1995):

> Goodall (1986) reports that male chimpanzees would sometimes inhibit their distinctive cry during orgasm when copulating with a favorite female. In this way, they avoid having to share the female with other males.
>
> Premack (1988) and Savage-Rumbaugh and McDonald (1988) each report evidence of deception in language-trained chimpanzees. For example, Austin and Sherman of the Yerkes laboratory have perfected ways of escaping from their cages, but have never allowed humans to knowingly watch them while doing it (Savage-Rumbaugh & McDonald, 1988). Premack (1988) reports that chimps quickly learned to distinguish between a trainer who provided them with food rewards and one who did not, and suppressed responding in the presence of the hostile trainer (or, in one case, actively misled the trainer), but not in the presence of the benign one.
>
> In research by Menzel (1974), one chimp, Belle, was shown the location of hidden food and would then lead the small group of chimps to it. She ceased leading the group directly to the food, however, when Rock (the dominant male) was present, because Rock would kick or bite her and take the food. When Rock was present Belle would wait until Rock left before uncovering food. On a few occasions, Belle actually led the troop in the opposite direction from food, then, while Rock was searching, she doubled back to get the food. On other trials, the experimenter hid extra pieces of food in second place. On those trials, Belle would lead Rock to this second, smaller source, and then go to the main cache. A similar observation of not retrieving or looking at a banana until after a more dominant chimp had left the area, was reported for the juvenile chimp Figan by Goodall (1971).
>
> A female baboon approached a male baboon who had some meat, which he showed no willingness to share. The female edged up to the male and began grooming him until he lolled back, at which time she grabbed the meat and ran (Jolly, 1985). (pp. 165–166)

In general, deception was more sophisticated in apes (gorillas, chimpanzees) than in monkeys (including baboons), which is consistent with the idea that inhibition abilities, particularly when involved in social contexts, are greater in humans' nearest relatives (apes) than in our more distant relatives (monkeys). We do not mean to imply that a chimpanzee, for example, has the deceptive ability to become a skilled poker player or a major mover and shaker in the political machinations of a small government. As we've mentioned before, skilled deception requires not only inhibition but also planning and a knowledge of other people's desires and goals (and that they may be different from one's own). But, we argue, inhibition is the necessary first operation in these political skills. The apparent presence of these abilities in our close relatives suggests that the rudiments of deception, and thus complex social intelligence, has deep evolutionary roots, likely extending to the common ancestors of modern apes and humans, and perhaps beyond (i.e., the ancestors of apes and monkeys). We believe that tactical deception, of the types shown by apes, was built on the inhibition skills used to control sexual and aggressive responses. That is, Machiavellian intelligence had its beginnings in the control of sexual and aggressive urges.

THEORY OF MIND

Perhaps the single most critical ability (or, more realistically, set of abilities) to successful social intelligence is possessing a theory of mind. As we discussed earlier, we say that a person possesses a theory of mind when he or she understands that other people's behavior is based on beliefs and desires and that such beliefs and desires may be different from one's own. Theory of mind has been one of the most researched topics in the field of cognitive development over the past decade, and for a good reason. Not only does it reflect an important aspect of cognitive change over early childhood, but it serves as the basis for all subsequent understanding that is characteristic of everyday human social intercourse. Understanding that belief-desire reasoning typifies not only one's own thinking but also the thinking of others is the basis of all folk psychology (i.e., the theory that all normal humans apply when trying to predict or to understand another person's behavior). Theory of mind is the basis of social intelligence. Although there are substantial individual differences in social intelligence based on a host of information-processing mechanisms (Crick & Dodge, 1994; Dodge, 1986), there would be little of what we consider normal social cognition if we did not possess a theory of mind.

Children are said to acquire an adultlike theory of mind by approximately 4 years of age, with younger children behaving on many tasks as if they did not realize that the desires of other people often conflict with their own and thus with the attainment of their goals. We also noted that children's performance on theory of mind tasks is related to performance on tasks of executive function, particularly tasks that involve inhibition of previous responses (see Perner & Lang, in press; Perner et al., 1999). We propose that the inhibition skills used to solve more basic social problems, such as the control of sexual responses, and simple not responding in some contexts, were recruited for understanding that one's own thoughts and desires are not always shared by others.

It might seem that the deception shown by monkeys and apes discussed in the previous section would indicate that these animals also possess at least a rudimentary theory of mind. Although this is possible, it is not necessarily so. The deception of monkeys and apes described earlier certainly requires inhibition of responses only in certain situations (i.e., it is used flexibly). But it does not necessarily require that one animal understands the mind of another. For example, an animal could have learned a particular response in a specific situation (e.g., when Belle goes directly to the cache of food when Rock is around, Belle loses it). In these situations, it may be not be the case that an animal is reading the mind of another, but only that a particular behavior has been unsuccessful in a particular situation and inhibiting that behavior is in the animal's best interest.

Support for the interpretation that the social behavior of chimpanzees does not reflect a theory of mind comes from research by Povinelli and Eddy (1996). In a series of experiments, they demonstrated that chimpanzees did not understand that a person with prior or current knowledge of the location of a desired food in fact possessed that knowledge. They were just as likely to approach a naive observer or one who could not see the desired object (e.g., who wore a blindfold) as they were an observer who possessed the requisite knowledge that would help them achieve their goal of getting a treat. Thus, although deception is an important social skill and implies an ability to inhibit responses, it does not necessarily imply a theory of mind.

Why should theory of mind require the ability to inhibit responses? As we noted earlier, what is required in most theory-of-mind tasks is the resolution of conflicting information. People must deal with the fact that the knowledge and beliefs they posses are sometimes at odds with those of another. In order to behave in their own best interests, they must sometimes inhibit a desired response (pick the window with the candy treat) when, by doing so, the outcome is undesirable (they never get the treat when they choose it, only when they choose the nontreat window, Russell et al., 1991).

We propose that a theory of mind evolved in our ancestors as the social complexity of groups grew and the pressures for a greater understanding of the motives, knowledge, and desires of other group members increased. We also propose that a prerequisite for developing a theory of mind was the attainment of executive function so that people could have some insight into their own thoughts and the thoughts of others. Such executive function involves inhibition of thoughts as well as action—of keeping irrelevant information out of working memory at times (such as what you believe to be true) so that it doesn't compete with other activated information (such as what someone else believes to be true). Again, inhibition would have served a permissive role in the acquisition of a theory of mind. The abilities to withhold certain behaviors, such as looking at a desired object or suppressing sexual cries in some situations, would have served as the basis for developing greater executive control and the inhibition of interfering response tendencies.

Did the degree of inhibition necessary for theory of mind develop before the symbolic abilities necessary to represent and contrast one's own beliefs and desires with those presumed to be possessed by others? For example, might chimpanzees, and our common ancestor, have the necessary inhibitory skills to perform theory of mind tasks but lack the mental-representational abilities necessary to understand concepts such as beliefs and desires, both in themselves and others? That is, perhaps, even if chimpanzees possess the requisite inhibitory skills, they have nothing pertinent (with respect to theory of mind) to inhibit. Although we feel certain that the advanced representational skills necessary for developing an understanding of theory of mind evolved in hominids since chimpanzees and humans last shared a common ancestor, it is equally clear that inhibition abilities have also evolved. Although inhibition of responses in chimpanzees for the purpose of deception has been observed a number of times by primatologists, such behavior is noteworthy because it is the exception to the rule. Chimpanzees typically find it difficult to withhold prepotent, or well-established, responses, even when it is in their best interest to do so. We are not in a position to state the order skills evolved in the hominid line, and we will likely never be in the position to do so. Rather, we argue that both representational skills (i.e., representing one's own thoughts and the thoughts of others) and inhibition skills likely evolved side-by-side and that those individuals possessing greater abilities in these areas developed a better understanding of themselves and their group members; they thus were better able to compete and reproduce than those less competent in these skills.

It has long been suggested that chimpanzees posses some rudiments of symbolic representation, as reflected in their limited ability to learn language (Gardner & Gardner, 1978; Savage-Rumbaugh et al., 1993) and their ability to show deferred imitation (i.e., imitate a behavior after some significant delay (Bering, Bjorklund, & Ragan, 2000; Bjorklund, Bering, & Ragau, 2000; Tomasello, Savage-Rumbaugh, & Kruger, 1993). However, these symbolic abilities have been observed only when the animals are reared in a humanlike environment, as human children are reared, and have been seriously questioned by other researchers (Terrace, 1979). It seems, then, that changes in mental representational abilities, observed infrequently in apes (and presumably in apes' and humans' common ancestor) and not unambiguously, would have to undergo substantial changes before they reached the level required for complex social understanding (Bering, 2001). Inhibition abilities, in contrast, are possessed by the great apes but simply to a lesser degree than they are possessed by humans. We propose that the gradual improvement in inhibitory skills over the course of hominid evolution permitted the evolution of other important cognitive skills, possibly symbolic representation. Not until individuals possessed sufficient executive control to keep some thoughts out of mind while considering others could the embryonic mental-representational abilities of our ancestors flourish. Our model, although necessarily speculative, suggests that changes in cognitive inhibition evolved gradually over generations, much as Darwin (1859) proposed that evolution occurs. However, once inhibition abilities reached a particular level, they permitted the relatively rapid development of symbolic abilities, characteristic of the punctuated equilibration model proposed by Eldredge and Gould (1972) (i.e., relatively abrupt change over a brief period of geological time).

Co-Opting Inhibition Abilities for More "Cognitive" Tasks

To this point, we have focused on the role of inhibition in social cognition. This is appropriate, because we believe that our species' advanced inhibition abilities evolved first to deal with social problems and that contemporary humans display their substantial intellectual abilities most frequently in the social realm. However, despite the importance of social intelligence in our everyday functioning, modern society owes its existence to the intellectual feats in nonsocial realms. Writing has changed the nature of human culture and the transmission of knowledge, and the advent of agriculture, cities, weapons, mass transportation, medicine, art, and electronic communication, among other things, is due to intellectual accomplishments in the areas of biology, mathematics, chemistry, and physics, among others. How has inhibition played a role in the evolution of these uniquely human skills?

Science, and perhaps religion, can be thought of as exploration of one's environment—looking for not just what's around the next bend but for the reason why the world is structured as it is. Stenhouse (1974), in a theory of human intellectual evolution that gave inhibition a central role, proposed that exploration required withholding nearly all alternative behaviors, except those in response to danger. An important characteristic of human intelligence is the ability to deal with novelty (Sternberg, 1985), which has reached its zenith in humans. One can only approach the novel when one inhibits more established responses to one's environment.

Earlier in this century, the influential philosopher Thomas Dewey (1933/1964) proposed that reflective thought played a central role in human intelligence and that the alternative to reflective thought is "inconsiderate impulse, unbalanced appetite, caprice, or [responding to] the circumstance of the moment" (p. 258). The role of inhibition in reflective thought, as viewed by Dewey, is obvious.

Several scientists have proposed that the evolution of language required first the development of a certain level of inhibition. For example, Bickerton (1990) noted that apes have great difficulty inhibiting alarm calls associated with the presence of predators or food. Yet, as we saw in the section on deception, suppressing such calls (and vocalizations involved in copulation) can sometimes be to an animal's advantage. Bickerton believes that suppressing vocalizations would have been particularly beneficial to *Australopithecus afarensis*. Because of the their small size (about 25–35 kg) and presumed lifestyle of spending much time on the ground, when this species made a noise at the wrong time disastrous consequences might have occurred. Forest-dwelling animals of comparable size and abilities would have suffered less disaster. Bickerton proposed that the voluntary suppression of vocalization would have had strong selection value, and the neural circuits underlying such an ability may have been an important step in the evolution of language.

We noted in an earlier section how contemporary cognitive psychologists have implicated inhibition mechanisms in many, if not most, cognitive tasks. For example, being able to selectively attend to a task (i.e., concentrate) requires the inhibition of competing thoughts, and several researchers have suggested the importance of inhibition in keeping irrelevant information out of working memory, and thus influencing performance on memory and problem-solving tasks (e.g., Harnishfeger, 1995; Hasher & Zacks, 1988). Our contention is that the inhibition necessary to solve both mundane and more esoteric cognitive tasks arose from the abilities that evolved to deal with social problems. Also, few gender differences are found on cognitive tasks (Bjorklund & Kipp, 1996). This is consistent with the idea that such inhibition is derived from the more domain-specific mechanisms used for social cognition, for which there is a female advantage.

CONCLUSION

Humans are not special in their possession of inhibition abilities. Cognitive inhibition, similar in nature to that observed in *Homo sapiens*, is found in our primate relatives, although not to the same degree. Also, most complex social and cognitive tasks are characterized by complicated reasoning, strategic, and symbolic (mental-representational) abilities, with inhibition playing only a background role. However, we propose that few advanced social or cognitive tasks could be accomplished without the requisite level of cognitive inhibition that modern humans possess. We propose that, both in evolutionary time and for contemporary people, the ability to inhibit responses (overt or covert) played, and continues to play a permissive role, setting the stage so that more complex cognition could develop. Moreover, we propose that the roots of such inhibition abilities can be found in the pressures ancient humans and their ancestors faced in dealing with one another and that the neural circuits we use today to solve complex problems in a multitude of areas are evolved from the neural circuits used initially to withhold sexual and aggressive behaviors, to not make an overt response in some contexts, and, eventually, to understand the beliefs of desires of oneself and others.

REFERENCES

Ainsworth, M. D. S., Blehar, M. C., Waters, E., & Wall, S. (1978). *Patterns of attachment: A psychological study of the strange situation.* Hillsdale, NJ: Lawrence Erlbaum Associates.

Alexander, R. D. (1989). Evolution of the human psyche. In P. Mellers & C. Stringer (Eds.), *The human revolution: Behavioural and biological perspectives on the origins of modern humans* (pp. 445–513). Princeton, NJ: Princeton University Press.

Alexander, R. D., & Noonan, K. M. (1979). Concealment of ovulation, parental care, and human social evolution. In N. A. Chagnon & W. Irons (Eds.), *Evolutionary biology and human social behavior* (pp. 436–453). North Situate, MA: Duxbury Press.

Baron-Cohen, S. (1995). *Mindblindness: An essay on autism and theory of mind.* Cambridge, MA: MIT Press.

Beach, F. A. (1947). Evolutionary changes in the physiological control of mating behavior in mammals. *Psychological Review, 54,* 297–315.

Bering, J. M. (2001). Theistic percepts in other species: Can chimpanzees represent the minds of non-natural agents? *Journal of Cognition and Culture.*

Bering, J. M., Bjorklund, D. F., & Ragan, P. (2000). Deferred imitation of object-related actions in human-reared juvenile chimpanzees and orangutans. *Developmental Psychobiology, 36,* 218–232.

Bickerton, D. (1990). *Language & species.* Chicago: University of Chicago Press.

Binford, L. R. (1983). *In pursuit of the past: Decoding the archaeological record.* New York: Thames & Hudson.

Bjorklund, D. F., Bering, J., Ragan, P. (2000). A two-year longitudinal study of deferred imitation of object manipulation in an enculturated chimpanzee (*Pan troglodytes*) and orangutan (*Pongo pygmaeus*). *Developmental Psychobiology, 37,* 229–237.

Bjorklund, D. F., Gaultney, J. F., & Green, B. L. (1993). "I Watch, therefore I can do": The development of meta-imitation during the preschool years and the advantage of optimism about one's imitative skills. In M. L. Howe & R. Pasnak (Eds.), *Emerging themes in cognitive development: Competencies* (Vol. 2, pp. 79–102). New York: Springer-Verlag.

Bjorklund, D. F., & Harnishfeger, K. K. (1990). The resources construct in cognitive development: Diverse sources of evidence and a theory of inefficient inhibition. *Developmental Review, 10,* 48–71.

Bjorklund, D. F., & Harnishfeger, K. K. (1995). The role of inhibition mechanisms in the evolution of human cognition. In F. N. Dempster & C. J. Brainerd (Eds.), *New perspectives on interference and inhibition in cognition* (pp. 141–173). New York: Academic Press.

Bjorklund, D. F., & Kipp, K. (1996). Parental investment theory and gender differences in the evolution of inhibition mechanisms. *Psychological Bulletin, 120,* 163–188.

Bjorklund, D. F., & Shackelford, T. K. (1999). Differences in parental investment contribute to important differences between men and women. *Current Directions in Psychological Science, 8,* 86–89.

Buss, D. M. (1995). Evolutionary psychology. *Psychological Inquiry, 6,* 1–30.

Buss, D. M., & Schmidt, D. P. (1993). Sexual strategies theory: An evolutionary perspective on human mating. *Psychological Review, 100,* 204–232.

Byrne, R., & Whiten, A. (Eds.) (1988). *Machiavellian intelligence: Social expertise and the evolution of intellect in monkeys, apes, and humans.* Oxford: Clarendon.

Cassidy, J. (1988). Child–mother attachment and the self in six-year-olds. *Child Development, 59,* 121–134.

Cerny, J. A. (1978). Biofeedback and the voluntary control of sexual arousal in women. *Behavior Therapy, 9,* 847–855.

Cohn, D. A. (1990). Child–mother attachment of six-year-olds and social competence at school. *Child Development, 61,* 152–162.

Cole, P. M. (1986). Children's spontaneous control of facial expression. *Child Development, 57,* 1309–1321.

Crick, N. R., & Dodge, K. A. (1994). A review and reformulation of social information-processing mechanisms in children's social adjustment. *Psychological Bulletin, 115,* 74–101.

Crook, J. H. (1980). *The evolution of human consciousness.* Oxford: Clarendon Press.

Darwin, C. (1859). *The origin of species.* New York: Modern Library.

Dewey, J. (1964). *How we think: A restatement of the relation of reflective thinking to the education process.* In R. D. Archambault (Ed.), *John Dewey on education.* New York: Modern Library. (Original work published 1933)

Diamond, A. (1985). Development of the ability to use recall to guide action as indicated by infants' performance on AB. *Child Development, 56,* 868–883.

Diamond, A. (1991). Frontal lobe involvement in cognitive changes during the first year of life. In K. R. Gibson & A. C. Petersen (Eds.), *Brain maturation and cognitive development* (pp. 127–180). New York: Aldine de Gruyter.

Diamond, A., & Taylor, C. (1996). Development of an aspect of executive control: Development of the abilities to remember what I said and to "Do as I say, not as I do." *Developmental Psychobiology, 29,* 315–324.

Dodge, K. A. (1986). A social information processing model of social competence in children. In M. Perlmutter (Ed.), *Minnesota symposium on child psychology* (Vol. 18, pp. 77–125). Hillsdale, NJ: Lawrence Erlbaum Associates.

Dunbar, R. I, M. (1993). Co-evolution of neocortex size, group size, and language in humans. *Behavioral and Brain Science, 16,* 681–735.

Eccles, J. C. (1989). *Evolution of the brain: Creation of the self.* Routledge: London.

Edelman, G. M. (1987). *Neural Darwinism: The theory of neuronal group selection.* New York: Basic Books.

Eldredge, N., & Gould, S. J. (1972). Punctuated equilibria: An alternative to phyletic gradualism. In T. J. M. Schopf (Ed.), *Models in paleobiology* (pp. 83–115). San Francisco: Freeman.

Ellis, N. R., & Dulaney, C. L. (1991). Further evidence for cognitive inertia of persons with mental retardation. *American Journal of Mental Retardation, 95,* 613–621.

Erickson, M. F., Sroufe, L. A., & Egeland, B. (1985). The relationship between quality of attachment and behavior problems in preschool in a high-risk sample. In I. Bretherton & E. Waters (Eds.), Growing points of attachment theory and research. *Monographs of the Society for Research in Child Development, 50* (Serial No. 209).

Feldman, R. S., & White, J. B. (1980). Detecting deception in children. *Journal of Communication, 30,* 121–128.

Flor-Henry, P. (1983). *Cerebral basis of psychopathology.* Boston: John Wright.

Fry, D., Zelazo, P. D., & Palfai, T. (1995). Theory of mind and rule-based reasoning. *Cognitive Development, 10,* 483–527.

Fuster, J. M. (1984). The prefrontal cortex and temporal integration. In A. Peters & E. G. Jones (Eds.), *Cerebral cortex: Association and auditory cortices* (Vol. 4, pp. 151–177). New York: Plenum.

Gardner, R. A., & Gardner, B. T. (1978). Comparative psychology and language acquisition. *Annals of the New York Academy of Sciences, 309,* 37–76.

Geary, D. C. (1998). *Male, female: The evolution of human sex differences.* Washington, DC: American Psychological Association.

Geary, D. C. (2000). Evolution and proximate expression of human paternal investment. *Psychological Bulletin, 126,* 55–77.

Goldman-Rakic, P. S. (1987). Development of cortical circuitry and cognitive function. *Child Development, 58,* 601–622.

Goodall, J. (1986). *The chimpanzees of Gombe.* Cambridge, MA: Belknap.

Greenough, W. T., Black, J. E., & Wallace, C. S. (1987). Experience and brain development. *Child Development, 58,* 539–559.

Hamm, V. P., & Hasher, L. (1992). Age and the availability of inferences. *Psychology and Aging, 7*, 56–64.

Harnishfeger, K. K. (1995). The development of cognitive inhibition: Theories, definitions, and research evidence. In F. N. Dempster & C. J. Brainerd (Eds.), *New perspectives on interference and inhibition in cognition* (pp. 175–294). New York: Academic Press.

Harnishfeger, K. K., & Bjorklund, D. F. (1994). Individual differences in inhibition: Implications for children's cognitive development. *Learning and Individual Differences, 6*, 331–355.

Hasher, L., & Zacks, R. T. (1988). Working memory, comprehension, and aging: A review and a new view. In G. H. Bower (Ed.), *The psychology of learning and motivation: Advances in research and theory* (Vol. 22, pp. 193–224). San Diego, CA: Academic Press.

Humphrey, N. K. (1976). The social function of intellect. In P. P. G. Bateson & R. A. Hinde (Eds.), *Growing points in ethology* (pp. 303–317). Cambridge: Cambridge University Press.

Huttenlocher, P. R. (1979). Synaptic density in human frontal cortex—developmental changes and effects of aging. *Brain Research, 163*, 195–205.

Jerison, H. J. (1973). *Evolution of the brain and intelligence.* Academic Press. New York.

Jolly, A. (1985). *The evolution of primate behavior* (2nd ed.). New York: Macmillian.

Kochanska, G., Murray, K., Jacques, T. Y., Koenig, A. L., & Vandegeest, K. A. (1996). Inhibitory control in young children and its role in emerging internalization. *Child Development, 67*, 490–507.

Lamb, M. E., Frodi, A. M., Hwang, C.-P., & Frodi, M. (1982). Characteristics of maternal and paternal behavior in traditional and nontraditional Swedish families. *International Journal of Behavioral Development, 5*, 131–141.

Lehman, E. B., McKinley-Pace, M. J., Wilson, J. A., Savsky, M. D., & Woodson, M. E. (1997). Direct and indirect measures of intentional forgetting in children and adults: Evidence for retrieval inhibition and reinstatement. *Journal of Experimental Child Psychology, 64*, 295–316.

Logue, A. W., & Chavarro, A. (1992). Self-control and impulsiveness in preschool children. *Psychological Record, 42*, 189–204.

Lorsbach, T. C., Katz, G. A., & Cupak, A. J. (1998). Developmental differences in the ability to inhibit the initial misinterpretation of garden path passages. *Journal of Experimental Child Psychology, 71*, 275–296.

Luria, A. R. (1973). *The working brain: An introduction to neuropsychology.* Basic Books.

Malloy, P. (1987). Frontal lobe dysfunction in obsessive-compulsive disorder. In E. Perecman (Ed.), *The frontal lobes revisited* (pp. 207–223). New York: IRBN Press.

Menzel, E. W. (1974). A group of young chimpanzees in a 1-acre field: Leadership and communication. In A. M. Schrier & F. Stollnitz (Eds.), *Behavior of nonhuman primates* (Vol. 5, pp. 83–153). New York: Academic Press.

Mithen, S. (1996). *The prehistory of the mind: The cognitive origins of art, religion and science.* London: Thames & Hudson.

Perner, J., & Lang, B. (in press). Theory of mind and executive function: Is there a developmental relationship? In S. Baron-Cohen, H. Tager-Flusberg, & D. Cohen (Eds.), *Understanding other minds: Perspectives from autism and developmental cognitive neuroscience* (2nd edition). Oxford: Oxford University Press.

Perner, J., Leekham, S. R., & Wimmer, H. (1987). Three-year-olds' difficulty with false belief: The case of conceptual deficit. *British Journal of Developmental Psychology, 5*, 125–137.

Perner, J., Stummer, S., & Lang, B. (1999). Executive functions and theory of mind: Cognitive complexity or functional dependence? In P. D. Zelazo, J. W. Astington, & D. R. Olson (Eds.), *Developing theories of intention: Social understanding and self control* (pp. 133–152). Mahwah, NJ: Lawrence Erlbaum Associates.

Plumert, J. M. (1995). Relation between children's overestimation of their physical abilities and accident proneness. *Developmental Psychology, 31*, 866–876.

Povinelli, D. J., Bering, J., & Giambrone, S. (in press). Toward a science of other minds: Escaping the argument by analogy. *Cognitive Science*.

Povinelli, D. J., & Eddy, T. J. (1996). What young chimpanzees know about seeing. *Monographs of the Society for Research in Child Development, 61*, (3, Serial No. 247).

Premack, D. (1988). 'Does the chimpanzee have a theory of mind?' revisited. In R. W. Byrne & A. Whiten (Eds.), *Machiavellian intelligence: Social expertise and the evolution of intellect in monkeys, apes, and humans* (pp. 224–237). Oxford: Clarendon Press.

Rosen, R. C. (1973). Suppression of penile tumescence by instrumental conditioning. *Psychometric Medicine, 35*, 509–514.

Russell, J., Mauthner, N., Sharpe, S., & Tidswell, T. (1991). The 'windows tasks' as a measure of strategic deception in preschoolers and autistic subjects. *British Journal of Developmental Psychology, 9*, 331–349.

Saarni, C. (1979). Children's understanding of display rules for expressive behavior. *Developmental Psychology, 15*, 424–429.

Saarni, C. (1984). An observational study of children's attempts to monitor their expressive behavior. *Child Development, 55*, 1504–1513.

Savage-Rumbaugh, E. S., & McDonald, K. (1988). Deception and social manipulation in symbol-using apes. In R. W. Byrne & Whiten (Eds.), *Machiavellian intelligence: Social expertise and the evolution of intellect in monkeys, apes, and humans* (pp. 16015179). Oxford: Clarendon Press.

Savage-Rumbaugh, E. S., Murphy, J., Sevcik, R. A., Brakke, K. E., Williams, S. L., & Rumbaugh, D. M. (1993). Language comprehension in ape and child. *Monographs of the Society for Research in Child Development, 58* (Serial No. 233).

Schacter, D. L., Moscovitch, M., Tulving, E., McLachlan, D. R., & Frendman, M. (1986). Mnemonic precedence in amnesiac patients: An analog of the AB error in infants. *Child Development, 57*, 816–823.

Slaby, R. G., & Parke, R. D. (1971). Effects of resistance to deviation of observing a model's affective reaction to response consequence. *Developmental Psychology, 5*, 40–47.

Stenhouse, D. (1974). *The evolution of intelligence: A general theory and some of its implications*. London: George Allen & Unwin.

Sternberg, R. J. (1985). *Beyond IQ: A triarchic theory of human intelligence*. Cambridge: Cambridge University Press.

Sternberg, R. J. (1997). The concept of intelligence and its role in lifelong learning and success. *American Psychologist, 52*, 1030–1037.

Swinney, D. A., & Prather, P. (1989). On the comprehension of lexical ambiguity by young children: Investigations into the development of mental modularity. In D. S. Gorfein (Ed.), *Resolving semantic ambiguity* (pp. 225–238). New York: Springer-Verlag.

Terrace, H. (1979, November). How Nim Chimpsky changed my mind. *Psychology Today*, 65–76.

Tipper, S. P., & Baylis, G. C. (1987). Individual differences in selective attention: The relation of priming and interference to cognitive failure. *Personality and Individual Differences, 8*, 667–675.

Tobias, P. V. (1987). The brain of *Homo habilis*: A new level of organization in cerebral evolution. *Journal of Human Evolution, 16*, 741–761.

Tomasello, M., Savage-Rumbaugh, S., & Kruger, A. C. (1993). Imitative learning of actions on objects by children, chimpanzees, and enculturated chimpanzees. *Child Development, 64*, 1688–1705.

Tooby, J., & Cosmides, L. (1992). The psychological foundations of culture. In J. H. Barkow, L. Cosmides, & J. Tooby (Eds.), *The adapted mind: Evolutionary psychology and the generation of culture* (pp. 19–136). New York: Oxford University Press.

Trivers, R. L. (1972). Parental investment and sexual selection. In B. Campbell (Ed.), *Sexual selection and the descent of man* (pp. 136–179). Chicago: Aldine.

Wellman, H. M. (1990). *The child's theory of mind*. Cambridge, MA: MIT Press.

Whiten, A., & Byrne, R. W. (1988). The manipulation of attention in primate tactical deception. In R. W. Byrne & A. Whiten (Eds.), *Machiavellian intelligence: Social expertise and the evolution of intellect in monkeys, apes, and humans* (pp. 211–223). Oxford: Clarendon Press.

Whiting, B. B., & Whiting, J. W. (1975). *Children of six cultures: A psycho-cultural analysis*. Cambridge, MA: Harvard University Press.

Yakovlev, P. I., & Lecours, A. R. (1967). The myelogenetic cycles of regional maturation of the brain. In A. Minkowski (Ed.), *Regional development of the brain in early life* (pp. 3–70). Philadelphia: F. A. Davis.

4

The Evolution of Intellect: Cognitive, Neurological, and Primatological Aspects and Hominid Culture

John L. Bradshaw
Monash University

INTRODUCTORY ISSUES

Although we all may think we know the meaning of the word *intelligence*, there is little agreement on what to measure, how to measure it, and how to compare the result across individuals, cultures or species (see e.g., Sternberg & Kaufman, 1998). Are there multiple intelligences, corresponding to various discrete abilities, and how might they correlate? Is there a general (*g*) underlying or unifying factor? In this chapter, I ask how intelligence might relate to problem-solving ability (speed, accuracy, efficiency), where in the brain might it be mediated, how it might correlate with measurable brain processes (electrophysiological, metabolic, or conductive), and what selective processes might have operated in hominid evolution. I then ask how it might be reflected in such behaviors as tool use, language and art on the one side, and social or Machiavellian intelligence on the other. What might a comparative study of our closest relatives, the African apes, tell us about our common ancestors' intellectual capacities, and what is there to be seen in the fossil or archaeological record? This chapter surveys developments relevant to the evolution of intellect from the basic elements of response processes, via mediating brain structures and mechanisms, upward to gross aspects of behavior and culture, in the contexts of neuropsychology, primatology, and paleoanthropology.

A view of intelligence as the ability to solve novel problems that are ecologically relevant to an individual's or species' niche will resonate with a primatologist's report (Hauser, 1988) of a wild vervet monkey discovering how to extract nutritive sap with dry pods. A psychometrician may agree with Calvin (1994) that intelligence is the ability to juggle, wield, or manipulate several ideas simultaneously. A student of evolutionary theory and a neuropsychologist would find common ground in a view of intelligence as an ability to deal adaptively with the ever-changing demands of the environment, to proceed efficiently to appropriately set goals, and to identify commonalities across varying situations or experiences—aspects, perhaps of prefrontal executive function.

This last view of intelligence, a fluid problem-solving ability in dealing with novel situations, contrasts with the application of "crystallized" intelligence employing existing skills and knowledge, as in language and tool behavior (Cattell, 1963; Horn & Cattell, 1967). Its possible locus, in the dorsolateral prefrontal cortex places it close to orbitofrontal regions probably involved in social or Machiavellian intelligence; conversely, clinical neurology has long demonstrated the discrete effects of often posterior lesions in generating such specific deficits as aphasia (acquired language loss), apraxia (loss of ability to use objects meaningfully), and agnosia (loss of ability to recognize objects). Such clinical observations, according to the localizationist Geschwind's (1965) model and in line with thinking in cognitive science (Fodor, 1983), have seen the brain as locally specialized and the architecture of the mind as consisting of discrete independent and encapsulated modules; nevertheless, we nowadays increasingly view the brain in terms of highly interconnected circuits and the mind in terms of distributed processing and massively parallel interactive networks. That, however, does not stop the search for those regions or circuits, which by lesion, or latterly by imaging studies, are apparently most involved in particular cognitive processes. Such an approach is consonant with Gardner's (1983) view of intelligence as comprising a number of loosely related functions such as language, musical ability, logical and mathematical reasoning, spatial reasoning, body movement skills, and social sensitivity. Such a view also chimes with evolutionary concepts of our intellect as being honed in the practice of navigation, digging, peeling, cutting, tracking, hunting, wielding tools and missiles, constructing, communicating, dissembling and deceiving. The question of course is the extent to which the practice of such activities, and the brain regions mediating them, interact or remain relatively independent. There is also the issue, addressed next, of how a range of behavioral and electrophysiological techniques may index individual differences in cognitive ability.

COGNITIVE PROCESSES, NEUROSCIENCE, AND INTELLIGENCE

Whether or not there is a general (g) underlying or unifying factor, it still makes operational sense to talk about someone's general intellectual ability, while accepting different performance levels, and intercorrelations, with specific tests. Deary and Caryl (1997) reviewed correlations that have been reported between IQ-type scores and such behavioral measures as reaction time (RT) and inspection time (IT). Reaction time, the interval between the appearance of a stimulus event and an associated response, measures speed of preparatory and initiation processes. Significant correlations have been shown between various RT procedures and mental test scores (Jensen, 1987). Inspection time is a less direct but equally important measure of the speed of processing stimulus events, but without an immediate or speeded response component; it is a psychophysical measure of the ability to make accurate (according to a preset criterion) judgments with very brief exposure durations. Thus someone able to resolve, to a 75% accuracy criterion, the temporal noncoincidence of two events with very brief asynchronies is thought to be able to process such events faster than someone who requires longer asynchronies to achieve the same criterion (Kranzler & Jensen, 1989). A related approach, the attentional blink (Shapiro, Arnell, & Raymond, 1997), involves the rapid, serial presentation, at fixation, of a series of letters wherein two targets are embedded. The first, physically defined by reverse contrast, focuses attention; the second, identified by name, follows after a variable number of intervening nontargets. It assesses temporal changes in processing availability, while probe identification accuracy, as a function of intertarget interval, assesses attentional capacity. Durations can thus be quantified for which, in an individual, attentional processes, which are thought to reflect dorsolateral prefrontal operation, are occupied and cleared.

Evoked response potentials (ERPs), quantified in terms of latency, magnitude, and shape, may reflect attentional processes, reliability, or speed of processing (Deary & Caryl, 1997), which again raises the question of whether smarter brains run faster, or whether low intelligence is correlated with unreliable (i.e., highly variable), rather than slow transmission, as reflected in ERP variability. Conversely, do highly intelligent individuals make fewer information-processing errors, such that interitem correlations between ERPs are higher?

Nerve-conduction velocities, measured in the arm, were reported by Vernon and Mori (1992) to correlate fairly well with IQ indices, though Wickett and Vernon (1994) were unable to replicate the earlier finding; the latter authors note that sex differences may be an important variable. Reed and Jensen (1991), using somewhat different techniques, also failed to obtain a significant effect, but did find a similar relationship to that reported by Vernon and Mori (1992) when instead ERP techniques were used to measure nerve-conduction velocities in the brain. Any underlying mechanism may be one of neural efficiency rather than transmission speed. Indeed, intelligent performers may be able to use shorter and more efficient cortical pathways and may require less processing power. This would account for the observation that metabolic imaging techniques may only indicate operating brain regions in those individuals who are less able and more extended (i.e., having to work harder) (Kutas & Federmeier, 1998); in normal or high-functioning individuals, imaging may not always reveal functionally relevant regions.

How do these intervening variables, mental speed, neural efficiency, and, especially, spare capacity, relate to quantity of available neural tissue? Because of variability in scalp and skull thickness, head size correlates poorly with IQ, though moderate correlations between brain volume and IQ (especially verbal) appear with magnetic resonance imaging (MRI; see Wickett, Vernon, & Lee, 1994); indeed, good correlations appear between the degrees of decrease in brain volume and performance IQ as a function of aging (Bigler, Johnson, Jackson, & Blatter, 1995). Therefore, with high intelligence, is there more complex circuitry available; more efficient neurotransmitter production, release, and uptake; greater metabolic efficiency; thicker myelination; more synaptic or dendritic expansion? Are any specific regions, particularly perhaps the prefrontal grey matter, especially important? This is the issue addressed in the following section.

LOCALIZATION OF STRUCTURES MEDIATING COGNITIVE BEHAVIOR

Cabeza and Nyberg (1997) reported a meta-analysis of 101 subtractive task comparisons in 73 imaging studies of sustained and selective attention; the perception of objects, faces, and locations; language (listening to and producing words, reading); and memory (phonological, visuospatial, episodic, semantic, procedural, and priming). For each process they identified activation patterns, including the most consistently involved areas, which constitute important components of the putative network of brain regions that seem to underlie that process. One may conclude from their analysis that the cerebellum is involved in episodic memory retrieval, procedural memory, and a variety of cognitive (as well as motor) activities (and see also Leiner, Leiner, & Dow, 1995; Schmahmann, 1997). The basal ganglia and thalamus are involved in procedural memory and motor learning, while the hippocampus and parahippocampal gyrus are involved in episodic memory and retrieval. The occipital cortex is involved in perception and perceptual priming and memory, the parietal lobe in attention, spatial perception, working memory, episodic retrieval and skill learning—all spatial and attentional processes—while the temporal lobe, ventrally, is concerned with face and object perception, and on the left with language comprehension and semantic processing. The anterior cingulate is active during selective attention, top-down processing, working memory, and memory retrieval, (i.e., response selection and action initiation generally). It has major links to other frontal lobe regions involved in higher cognitive processes, especially those of a top-down nature and those involving executive functions (Shallice, 1988)—monitoring, organizing, planning, and working memory (see e.g., Stuss, Eskes, & Foster, 1994). However, the frontal lobes, which are of major evolutionary significance, partition into important subregions, each of which control discrete aspects of behavior and engage with particular striato-pallido-thalamic feedback loops. I address these fronto-striatal pathways in the next section, but should first note, with Mesulam (1998), that although upstream unimodal association areas encode basic sensory features (e.g., color, motion, form, and pitch), and more complex aspects (e.g., objects, faces, words, spatial locations, and sound sequences) become encoded in more downstream unimodal areas, heteromodal and transmodal networks operate at the highest cognitive level. A network for spatial awareness is based on epicenters in the posterior parietal cortex and frontal eyefields; the language network on Wernicke's and Broca's areas; the explicit memory/emotion network on the hippocampal-entorhinal complex and amygdala; the face–object recognition network on the midtemporal and temporopolar cortices; and the working memory/executive function network on the posterior parietal and, especially, the lateral prefrontal cortex. It is to the prefrontal cortex and associated pathways that I next turn.

FRONTO-STRIATAL PATHWAYS

Five major, parallel circuits have been identified linking the frontal lobes with subcortical (basal ganglia) structures: motor, oculomotor, dorsolateral prefrontal (DLPF), orbitofrontal (OF), and anterior cingulate (AC; e.g., see Foti & Cummings, 1997). The first two circuits, mediating the initiation, execution, and maintenance of limb and eye movement, do not concern cognitive or intellectual functioning. All share common structures and organization, originating in the frontal lobes, with sequential projections via the striatum (input circuit) and globus pallidus (output circuit) of the basal ganglia (which may play a major filtering, selecting, and sequencing role, see Brooks, 1995) and thalamus, back to the frontal cortex. They are all mutually adjacent but remain anatomically segregated. Generally, their inputs are broad and may include functionally related structures outside the circuit, while their outputs are more specific to localized cortical areas. In the context of problem solving and social intelligence,

- the DLPF circuit originates and ends in the frontal convexity. Disruption leads to deficits in executive functioning (Shallice, 1988; i.e., in maintaining or shifting set, generating organizational strategies, retrieving memories, and maintaining fluent cognitive processes).
- the OF circuit originates and ends in the inferolateral prefrontal cortex; it is important in inhibiting interference from external cues and in self-monitoring. Disturbance affects fundamental personality aspects and leads to disinhibition, irritability, impulsivity, aggression, and antisocial or poor social functioning.
- the AC circuit, with associated limbic pathways, is critical for drive and motivation. Damage leads to apathy and reduced initiative, and in extreme cases akinetic mutism (i.e., effectively a motionless, mute state, even though underlying cognitive functions may not be so severely affected).

Differential breakdown of these three circuits contributes to the essentially human neuropsychiatric disorders of attention deficit disorder with hyperactivity, obsessive compulsive disorder, Tourette's syndrome, and probably autism and schizophrenia (Pantelis & Brewer, 1996), although fragments of such pathological behaviors may appear in appropriately treated primates.

Reason, logic, cost–benefit analysis, working memory calculations, and conscious unemotional weighing-up of the pros and cons of a situation are clearly one way, via the DLPF cortex, of intelligent problem solving in real-life situations. Damasio (1994), however, noted that we also operate using gut feelings, or emotions; he invokes the role of the limbic structure, the amygdala, whose activity can automatically draw our attention, emotionally, to the positive or negative valency associated with a situation's various outcomes. This rapid pathway may allow us unconsciously to avoid or dismiss various alternatives immediately, without further analysis, thereafter allowing the rational DLPF to perform a final analysis or choice. He sees it as a biasing device that derives from ancestral limbic mechanisms, and which explains intuition, in comparison with the potentially fallible reason; it cannot be excluded from any analysis of apparently intelligent behavior. Patients with damage here seem unable to make good decisions, in life or in experimental situations, even though able otherwise to describe what should be done, and these patients typically show little emotion when choosing bad strategies (Bechara, Damasio, Tranel, & Damasio, 1997;

Vogel, 1997). Prefrontal cortex, with associated limbic and basal ganglia modulation, clearly plays a major role in human problem solving in both the physical and social worlds. How have these structures evolved in concert with the rest of the brain?

ENCEPHALIZATION AND THE GROWTH OF THE BRAIN

In accordance with allometric principles (Harvey, 1986), where across-species brain size is plotted as a function of body mass, the former generally increases more slowly than the latter and follows a power function with an exponent of around 0.75 (Aboitiz, 1996). Encephalization, the additional processing capacity beyond that required for routine control of body functions (Jerison, 1986), accelerated with primate evolution. The quantitative aspects of brain growth seem to be achieved by increasing the number of cortical columns rather than by changing neuronal density (Karten, 1991); qualitative evolutionary changes in brain function may be achievable by altered patterns of area connectivity and function.

Target adult brain (and body) size is largely determined during embryogenesis, with, in humans, the brain growing for up to a year after birth, much like that of a giant ape's body, whose development is slower than that of the brain (Deacon, 1990). Large infant brains pose obstetric problems, and, as an investment, may only pay off in a lifelong time scale via a quantum increase in behavioral complexity. The latter, in our case, may be the combined product of a large brain, slow development, extended parental care, and enhanced learning. At a cultural level, these evolutionary developments are associated with the appearance of a home base, food sharing, a division of labor by sex, the development of the family, and the evolution of language and culture.

Our increased encephalization is clearly linked to our species' intellectual capacity, although a major internal reorganization probably occurred during hominid evolution consequent upon selection for perhaps a few key functions, such as speech, social, and manipulative skills; this process would have resulted in increased overall intellectual capacity, rather than, for example, speech and praxis being a consequence of otherwise-selected increases in cognitive capacity (Deacon, 1986a, 1986b). Such changes may in turn have increased the potential for the emergence of new abilities, which themselves would now have selected for further reorganization or encephalization or both (Kien, 1991). Increases in encephalization could thus occur via a series of plateaux, rather than exhibiting a steady state growth, as indeed would seem to be the case with respect to the changing cranial capacities in hominid evolution (Holloway, 1995). However, as Hauser (1997a) observed, we have the paradox of hominid brains increasing greatly in size over a long period, with little apparent consequence in the stone tool record, and then staying the same or even decreasing during a more recent period of major behavioral change or evolution.

Creative thinking, planning for future actions, decision making, artistic expression, aspects of emotional and social behavior, working memory, "theory of mind" tasks, and control of language and motor functions are, as we saw, all attributed to the frontal lobes and thought of as prototypically human intellectual functions. The frontal lobes comprise the largest sector of the hemispheres and are often said to be relatively larger and more developed in humans than in any other primate (Blinkov & Glezer, 1968). However, Semendeferi, Damasio, Frank, and Van Hoesen (1997) found that although the absolute volume of both the brain and all sectors (dorsal, medial, and orbital) of the frontal lobes are indeed largest in humans, in absolute terms, the relative proportions are constant across primate species. Although their findings are preliminary, they conclude that aspects other than relative volume of those structures must underlie our cognitive specialization. Maybe, however, their absolute size is all that really matters; perhaps once they have exceeded a certain critical mass, they may be able to take on new, emergent functions. What then might have been the limits of our primate ancestors' cognitive capacities?

COGNITIVE CAPACITIES IN NONHUMAN PRIMATES

Some inkling of the cognitive capacities of our primate ancestors common with the African apes can be gained from studying the latters' abilities, although these species must also have undergone further evolution. At a gross, observational level we are always intrigued by our superficial social and behavioral similarities. Thus, for example, both native peoples and wild chimpanzee troops may ingest certain nonnutritional plant species to control parasites and relieve gastro-intestinal upsets (Huffman, 1997). At a more cognitive level, Boysen, Berntson, Shreyer, and Hannan (1995) reported that a chimpanzee, experienced in counting arrays of zero to seven items and trained to comprehend number symbols, spontaneously displayed such indicating acts as pointing, touching, and rearranging items during counting. Significant correlations occurred between the number of items, the cardinal number the animal selected, and the number and type of indicating acts. Thus, the animal's indicating acts may have had a functional significance, serving as an organizing schema comparable to similar behaviors in children learning to count.

Counting transcends mere rehearsal in the ascending sequence of the codes or symbols for number. To count, you must individuate individual objects, group them, and tag them with some sort of value that allows you to keep track of the count. If nonhuman primates can demonstrate such abilities, even if only after extensive training, then not only would the roots of mathematical capability be shown to extend into infrahuman species, but it would appear that mathematical talent does not necessarily depend on language. Hauser and Carey (1998) noted that measurements of how long rhesus monkeys watch the appearance and disappearance of eggplants behind a screen suggest that the animals comprehend that "1 plus 1 equals 2, and not 3." That they were not merely attending to the total mass of material was indicated by their responses (apparent surprise) when one large eggplant was substituted for the two smaller, expected ones. Moreover, they could apparently grasp the concept that 1 squash plus 1 carrot equals 2 things, and that, for example, 3 is greater than and not merely different from 2. Similarly, Brannon and Terrace (1998) found that monkeys, first trained to respond to exemplars of the numerosities 1 to 4 in an ascending numerical order, could represent the ordinal relations that exist from 1 through 9; thus they generalized the rule of touching the lower number of items before the higher one when shown stimuli containing set sizes that they had not previously been taught (e.g., 5 vs. 7).

Dehaene, Dehaene-Lambertz, and Cohen (1998) reviewed the extents to which human infants, chimpanzees, monkeys, dolphins, rats, pigeons, and parrots possess a concept of abstract numerosity (a tacit awareness of number, independent of the nature of the individual items involved), as tested by such techniques as habituation and dishabituation of looking times with confirmation or violation of expectancies respectively, when for example objects are surreptitiously added or removed behind a screen, and with control of spacing, location, size, density, identity, and so on. They noted that a knowledge of numerosity and elementary arithmetic is present in many species in simple form, even though extended training may be required to demonstrate it. Numerosity may be apprehended intermodally (i.e., with simultaneous or successive visual and auditory presentations), and numerical distance and number size effects demonstrated. (With the numerical distance effect, discrimination between two numbers, represented as dots or even as Arabic numerals, is better the bigger the separating distance between them; with the number size effect, for an equal numerical distance, the discrimination of two numbers worsens, according to Weber's law, as the numerical size increases.) They concluded that although a domain-specific cognitive concept of numerosity spontaneously emerges in human development, it is present in simpler form in other species; in humans, lesion studies (Gerstmann's syndrome), imaging, and electrophysiological evidence implicate inferior intraparietal regions, especially on the left, in the processing of number, though with more right-sided representation than occurs with language. Wynn (1998) likewise reviewed recent work with infants in the first few months of life and similarly concludes that they can enumerate sets of entities (objects, sounds, and even physical actions and action sequences, heterogeneous as well as homogeneous, with control for duration and tempo) and perform numerical calculations (addition and subtraction). She rejected the argument that these abilities arise from general cognitive capacities not specific to number, instead claiming, with Dehaene et al. (1998), that we possess a specialized mental mechanism for number, which we share with other species and that has evolved (in some unspecified way) through natural selection. However, while it is clearly adaptive for individuals (human, or of other species) to thus be able to operate in a world of discrete, numerical entities (e.g., to know that if three predators had been in the vicinity and two had left, you were still at risk from one remaining predator), it is not clear that numerical competence, any more than language, should be treated as a discrete Fodorian (Fodor, 1983) module, encapsulated and distinct from other abilities, specific or general. (According to Fodor, 1983, the mind consists of a number of discrete, independent, encapsulated modules, all operating in a semiautonomous fashion and separately evolved.) Clearly, a concept of numerosity is not restricted to adult humans, and the capacity to acquire it may be present in many species. What is the evidence for other cognitive capacities previously thought to be exclusively human, such as tool use, in other species?

TOOL BEHAVIOR IN OTHER SPECIES

In a troupe, apparently intelligent behavior may not reflect individual problem-solving behavior as much as proficient imitation or social learning (Visalberghi & Fragaszy, 1990), although even the latter behaviors require considerable cognitive capacity. Nor is it always clear whether an individual is imitating another animal or has independently rediscovered the process, perhaps from attending to the relevant context. Successful monkeys seem not to copy potential models exactly, doing better with contextually directed trial-and-error learning. We should therefore distinguish between copying a motor act by rote and finding a guiding rule—the difference between bottom-up and top-down processing. Tool use is uncommon among monkeys (but not apes) in the wild (Bradshaw, 1997) and involves learning rules relating to action, object, and outcome from the behavior of an effective model. Learning rules by trial and error may be easier than straight imitative copying, whereas monkeys may not be particularly good at either (Visalberghi & Fragaszy, 1990). Thus capuchin monkeys, though very successful tool users in captivity, rarely modify tools before using them. However, even when not natural tool users, and otherwise rarely encountering artifacts, captive cotton-top tamarins can distinguish between the relevant and irrelevant properties of a potential tool (Hauser, 1997b). They choose tools that already have, or can be easily converted to having, adaptations most suitable for certain purposes (e.g., reaching). They seem to possess an intuitive understanding of the relevant laws of physics.

In the wild, chimpanzees prepare a range of suitable probes for termite "fishing," chew leaves to make sponges to transport water, crack nuts with a hammer and pestle, and the mother may even apparently coach her young in the use of such techniques (Caro & Hauser, 1992). Although, again, we must distinguish between teaching and social learning. Indeed, it seems that the mother understands what her pupil does not know and recognizes how performance can be improved; she seems to have a theory of mind, an important aspect of Machiavellian or social intelligence.

Many species successfully employ tools in a more or less stereotyped fashion. Perhaps only the higher primates can use the same tool for more than one end (e.g., a stick as a probe or a rake). Perhaps only apes and humans can readily use different tools for the same end or combine more than one tool (e.g., hammer and anvil). Perhaps only humans systematically put tools aside for future use, thereby evidencing forward planning and advanced, typically prefrontal behaviors, or use tools to make other tools. Otherwise there is a progression, rather than a sharp transition, between the repertoire of apes and the cognitive behavior, as inferred from the fossil record of our hominid ancestors (Bradshaw, 1997).

HOMINID TOOL USE

Homo habilis, appearing around 2.2 million years ago, is conventionally regarded as the first true human and toolmaker. However, the oldest Oldowan (and therefore hominid) tools are now known to date to 2.5 to 2.6 million years ago in Ethiopia (Semaw et al., 1997), contemporary with australopithecines and earlier than the most ancient members of the genus *Homo* reported by Kimbel et al. (1996). Several attempts have been made to infer, from fossils, the toolmaking capabilities of hominid hands from such preserved features as areas of muscle attachment, bone and joint surface configurations, relative metacarpal robusticity, and other hand and arm data. Moreover, Marzke et al. (1998) used electromyography to monitor the activity of hand muscles in experienced modern manufacturers during the production of Oldowan-type tools and to identify the muscles that were most likely to be involved.

Whether or not *H. habilis* was indeed the first user of Oldowan-style tools, it had an allometrically larger brain than its australopithecine ancestors or chimpanzees. The Oldowan stone tool assembly associated with it is surprisingly sophisticated in its control of fracture mechanics, although for another 1 million years there was comparatively little advance. Evidence suggests such tools were used to fashion other, wooden implements, now vanished, and contributed to food sharing, division of labor (male to hunt, female to gather), reciprocity, and cooperation (Bradshaw, 1997), all of which would have contributed to our cognitive evolution. However, there is debate as to whether Oldowan tools exhibit evidence of shared knowledge. Although apes can be taught to make and use tools almost of an Oldowan level, and captive bonobos (pygmy chimpanzees) may even acquire these skills by direct observation with subsequent trial-and-error behavior, together with insightful problem solving, they do not seem to do these things naturally. Tool-using behavior preeminently involves praxic functions of manipulation, functions which are mediated by brain regions closely adjacent to those involved in language (Kimura, 1993). It might, therefore, be thought that the two behaviors coevolved synergistically. Note, however, that while both involve complex sequential activity, observation and imitation, rather than language, is of more use in transmitting tool skills to another (e.g., showing how to tie a knot is more effective than telling). Nevertheless, language, even more than tool use, archetypically is a human faculty.

LANGUAGE, SPEECH, AND COMMUNICATION

Speech, language, communication, and vocalization are not to be used interchangeably. Vocalization, often emotional, may be of communicatory value to conspecifics; language includes channels of communication additional to the oral-articulatory mode; speech as a form of communication is apparently unique (and maybe the only truly unique facility) to our species, and as one mode of realizing language it involves possibly unique peripheral (supralaryngeal tract) and central adaptations. We also retain older, nonverbal modes of communicating emotions by vocalizations, expressions, or gesture. Although such communication is clearly limbic in origin, the limbic system also modulates speech. Although language is discrete, categorical, essentially discontinuous, and volitional, emotional communications (human and nonhuman) tend to be more analog, graded, continuous, and automatic. Speech has to be learned, even though up to a certain age we are predisposed to acquire it rapidly, whereas emotional expressions are universal and apparently hardwired. Nevertheless, there is an inherited component to language (our capacity to acquire it), together with a learned component. This is true even of our expressions. Language is arbitrary in its coding, propositional, open-ended and infinitely variable, and removed from its referent, unlike our nonverbal communication, which typically refers only to what is immediately present. It is not clear how necessary language is to thought, though global aphasics can still behave as logical, rational human beings. Nevertheless, language is an undoubted aid to thought efficiency as well as the main medium of communication for information exchange between individuals and groups. Indeed, there must have been strong selective pressures to develop such a medium to communicate information about both the physical and the social landscapes in the contexts of hunting, gathering, enemies, and allies. The medium clearly would also have the potential for transmitting false information and deception, and thus would have contributed to the development of social or Machiavellian intelligence, the conscious mind, and the individuation of the self.

Evolutionary gradualists favor gradual selective pressures for adaptation to underlie the acquisition of new repertoires, although punctualists like Gould and Eldredge (1993) place more emphasis on discrete discontinuities caused by stochastic mutations. With language, we see these two competing tendencies realized on the one hand in Chomsky's (1980) perspective and, on the other hand, in the continuity viewpoint, espoused here, where language is believed to have evolved from prior primate behaviors.

According to Chomsky, all languages, although superficially very different, evince common and genetically determined principles that are unique to humans. He sees language as generated by a specialized modular organ that is informationally separated from other cognitive systems (i.e., without biological precedent) and that did not, therefore, gradually evolve from hominid precursors or homologues. Although most would agree that the ability to deploy syntactic rules has a genetic basis, current evolutionary thinking favors the gradual accumulation of numerous, small interacting mutations (whether or not such change is at times comparatively rapid, according to the model of punctuated equilibrium; see Gould & Eldridge, 1993). Moreover, if there is indeed any truth in the idea of a language module, it is likely to be instantiated in a network itself, interwoven more or less inextricably with other such cognitive modules, neural systems, or both (Mesulam, 1998). As such, the idea of Fodorian (Fodor, 1983) modularity loses much of its force.

Pinker (1997) also viewed grammar as the most significant manifestation of language and as autonomous and modular. However, he viewed language as evolving from a general purpose problem solver, evolved by our hunter–gatherer ancestors in a world of catching, finding, preparing, and cooking, as they analyzed and categorized experiences in the context of the physics of space, time, number, and the nature of objects. The mind is not, according to Pinker, a single, coherent unity but an interacting community of distinct modules (including language), each specialized for a particular function. He makes no attempt, however, to relate such modules to biology or to possible neural networks. Müller (1996) was impressed by the likely homologies between human language and hominid communication; he noted the idea of radical mutations is incompatible with higher mammalian evolution and invokes continuity, if not also gradualism. He noted that the occurrence of new emergent properties of behavior from increased neural complexity shows that apparent absence of behavioral continuity does not imply structural discontinuity. Bradshaw (1997) similarly observed that brain structures, now subserving language, may indeed merely have kept pace volumetrically with a general increase in brain size; the consequence, however, may have been to permit the appearance of grammar, such structures previously merely handling the prefrontally mediated, general conditionality rules of behavior (e.g., If x occurs, then do y.) which nevertheless underlie true grammar. Thus an increase in a structure's size, in pace with the rest of the brain, can lead to apparent qualitative changes of function.

The hereditary nature of certain language disorders and the possible identification of causative genes (Fischer, Vargha-Khadem, Watkins, Monaco, & Pembrey, 1998), the existence in the community of individuals with well-preserved language in the presence of otherwise severe cognitive deficits (e.g., Williams syndrome), and the otherwise good cognitive skills but very poor language and social functioning skills of people with autism, do not really support the idea of a discrete, independently acquired, language module; usually the distinctions between preserved and decremented functions are not as clear cut as they at first seem (Vargha-Khadem, Watkins, Alcock, Fletcher, & Passingham, 1995). A rare exception may be a family where about half of its members are affected by a severe speech and language disorder apparently transmitted as an autosomal dominant trait. The family known as KE has been widely publicized as suffering primarily from a defect in the use of grammatical suffixation rules, thus supposedly supporting the existence of genes specific to grammar. Fisher et al. (1998), however, noted that the phenotype is broader in nature, with virtually every aspect of grammar and language affected, extending to a severe oral dyspraxia.

Müller (1996) proposed that language develops epigenetically, via complex interactions with the internal and external environments, noting the continued plasticity of the developing, and even mature, nervous system. Corballis (1996) emphasized the role of regulatory genes in this context, controlling the period of postnatal development to maximize environmental influences and learning in multiple brain loci; with regulatory genes, we just do not need to invoke newly appearing language genes, and existing circuits can even adapt to such newly invented processes as reading. Schoenemann and Wang (1996) essentially agreed, seeing our huge brain increase as relating to the complexity of our environment and mental world (physical and social), which led in turn to the need to invent a conventionalized communicatory system from pre-existing neurocognitive circuits. From such a newly entered niche, fresh selective pressures would now operate. Language is not part of a general purpose problem solver (whatever Pinker, 1997, may claim) nor conversely is it a separately evolved quasi-independent module. Its roots lie early, rather than late, and the sudden flowering of art and culture in the European Upper Paleolithic 35,000 years ago was not due to the sudden saltatory appearance of language but was a purely local, cultural phenomenon involving a critical societal mass. Language, like mathematics its cousin, nevertheless permitted as it and society developed, the cognitive handling of ever more complex concepts by categorizing and labelling at progressively higher hierarchical levels. Thus language, chemical formulae, mathematics, and concepts generally in semantic memory involve hierarchical organization, much as administration of a large commercial organization involves hierarchical coordination of processes and information; the chief executive is not alone responsible for sales, purchasing, advertising, distribution, salaries, or personnel; the personnel director is not responsible for staffing in a single plant; the plant manager is not responsible for appointing a programmer in the design section, who is however, responsible for implementing a whole new hierarchy of programs, routines, and commands. The elements in a complex organic molecule lose their independent identity in the new emergent properties of the molecule, which may play a complex role in the workings of entire neural systems within a human brain. It may be a peculiarly human capability to be able to keep track, via such short-hand labels, assisted by language, and in a reductionist fashion, of so many descriptive or explanatory levels. Such developments nevertheless occurred, along with advances in tool behavior and nonutilitarian art, which all interacted, autocatalytically, in the development of society. Language thus served as an enhanced communicatory medium in handling the challenges of both an increasingly complex society and an increasingly complex physical world; it also served as a unique cognitive tool for modeling future eventualities, privately or publicly.

A possible bridge with primate communication may be with MacNeilage's (1998) proposal that lip-smacks, serving as facio-visual communicative gestures, may have modulated calls and imposed an elementary syllabic structure. Primate orofacial communicative gestures may thus have merged with phonation. Rizzolatti et al. (1996) also noted that the phonetic gestures of the speaker may be more important than the actual sounds and are represented for and recovered by the listener as invariant motor commands via an identified circuit (involving the superior temporal sulcus and the inferior frontal gyrus, both on the left) devoted in nonhuman primates to the recognition of hand and mouth gestures; the latter area they believe to be homologous to our Broca's motor speech area in the prefrontal cortex. Rizzolatti and Arbib (1998) extended these ideas, seeing the monkey homologues of Broca's area as representing a system that matches observed events to similar, internally generated actions, thus forming a link between observer and action. Such an observation-execution matching system would provide in primates generally, including ourselves, a bridge from *doing* to *communicating*, as the link between actor and observer becomes a link between sender and receiver of messages. Rizzolatti and Arbib (1998) thus propose that the development of the human speech circuit may stem from the fact that the precursor of Broca's area was initially endowed with a mechanism, manuo-brachial and oro-facial, for recognizing actions made by others, with speech an evolution of the latter's gestures. Syllabification, via vocalization punctuated by lip-smacks, may have completed the picture. This chapter, however, is not the place to debate whether or not a complex system of manual gestures preceded true speech.

Aboitiz and Garcia (1997) took a similar approach, albeit wider and maybe more conventional, to the question of primate homologues of our brain mechanisms underlying speech and language. They propose that the neural correlates of language are embedded in a large-scale neurocognitive network comprising widespread connections between temporal, parietal, and prefrontal cortices—a network involved in the temporal organization of behavior and of motor sequences and in working memory, where the immediate aspects of cognitive processing are elaborated. The establishment of cortico-cortical connections in temporoparietal cortex, they say, enabled the development of multimodal associations, with Wernicke's area originating as a convergence where such conceptual associations acquired a phonological correlate. They further speculate whether these phonological representations projected to infero-parietal areas and on to the incipient homologue of Broca's area, to form a working memory circuit for processing, producing, and learning complex articulations. With subsequent evolutionary development and input from prefrontal regions, a neural substrate for language may gradually have evolved, via adaptation of existing structures and, especially, development of extensive connections between them. Spatial mechanisms in the right hemisphere may merely have involved rearrangement of connections from the largely left-hemisphere ground plan for language. (Given the extreme antiquity in the vertebrates, however, of a right-hemisphere representation of spatial and emotional functions, see Bradshaw & Rogers, 1993, it could instead be argued that left-hemisphere-mediated call systems may have come later.) Thus, a number of scenarios have been proposed for the gradual emergence of language, but all involve homologous structures in earlier primates that have been preadapted for, or have adapted toward, the subsequent assumption of human speech and language. When may this have occurred? The hypoglossal canal in the primate skull transmits the nerve that supplies the tongue muscles. Kay, Cartmill, and Balow (1998) reported that this canal is absolutely and relatively larger in modern humans, Neanderthals, and early, modern *Homo sapiens* (of 400,000 years ago) than in African apes, *Australopithecus* and *H. habilis*. Thus human vocal abilities may have appeared much earlier than the first archaeological evidence of symbolic behavior, to which this discussion now turns.

THE EVOLUTION OF INTELLECT: EVIDENCE FROM ART

Although language is preeminently symbolic, there are no fossil phonemes. Art, though not as utilitarian as speech, retains a presence in the archaeological record.

Nonutilitarian behavior may moreover be a window to the psyche, reflecting the play of a disengaged intellect. We may not be the only species to engage in such behavior. Captive capuchin monkeys, given clay, will mold it into odd-shaped balls and decorate them with paint and leaves; then, like children, they will lose interest, suggesting that, as perhaps with latter-day rock art (Bradshaw, 1997), the interest lies in the action rather than the product (Barnett, 1997; Westergaard & Suomi, 1997). From a human aesthetic viewpoint, a range of abilities is apparent. Lenain (1995) noted apes' capacities for introducing variations that appear formally relevant and esthetic; their sense of order; their evidence of form, rhythmicity, and balance; and their taste for color contrasts. Similarly, Boysen, Berntson, and Prentice (1987) noted that chimpanzees do not mark randomly but pay attention to the boundaries of the paper and of predrawn squares. Clearly, at least 5 million years ago the seeds were germinating of an artistic sense.

Prior to the creative explosion of art and artifacts in the western European Upper Paleolithic of around 35,000 years ago, there is a relative dearth of evidence for such activity, either in the earlier assemblages of artifacts from supposedly modern *Homo sapiens sapiens,* or from our extinct cousins, the Neanderthals, or earlier *Homo erectus* (Chase & Dibble, 1987). Nevertheless, the pleasing symmetry of the Acheulian biface hand axes constructed by *H. erectus,* our probable ancestor, the apparent use of ochre, and the various manuports and *objets trouvés* (unusual pebbles and crystal) found in habitation layers of 800,000 years ago, all suggest an aesthetic sense and a concept of symbolism extending back a million years or more. Moreover Bednarik (1997a, 1997b) reviews the evidence that *H. erectus* in the Lower Paleolithic marked portable objects (although, see D'Errico & Villa, 1997, for a note of caution); produced petroglyphs; employed ochre; probably recognized iconicity (how objects resemble each other); created wooden objects and composite weapons; drilled bone, ivory, and shell to make beads; and may have undertaken short sea voyages—all with a brain volume considerably smaller than ours. There is even recent evidence for music among the Neanderthals, with the discovery of what appears to be a bone flute over 43,000 years old (Jelinek, 1997). This interpretation, however, has been disputed; d'Errico, Villa, Llona, and Idarraga (1998), among others, see the modifications observed on the Divje Babe cave-bear femur as produced by carnivore teeth, with the most ancient musical instruments known to date still being Aurignacian flutes of *H. sapiens sapiens* around 30,000 years ago. There is similar debate whether our extinct Neanderthal cousins, with a brain volume similar to ours, may also have engaged in ritual burial (see Gargett, 1989). Art, symbolism and representation, is one way of drawing attention to objects or properties of the environment, or the current preoccupation of the agent; more immediately, attention may be directed by pointing, or it may be withheld or misrepresented.

POINTING, DIRECTING ATTENTION, WITHHOLDING INFORMATION AND DECEPTION

Gaze and direction of attention are important sources of primate social information. Chimpanzees and orangutans spontaneously follow human gaze direction; macaques do not, but will follow the gaze direction of their conspecifics (Emery, Lorincz, Perrett, Oram, & Baker, 1997). Pointing with the index finger, arm extended in the direction of an interesting object, remaining fingers curled under the hand, thumb to side, is vital to human communication and universal to all human cultures (Butterworth, 1997). Its emergence in infancy has been traditionally linked with the early development of perspective taking, intersubjectivity, and empathy. It is important for telling, indicating, and asking, and aims to draw another's attention. Dogs point with the whole body to signal prey direction to the pack, but is the behavior truly intentional, and would it occur without an audience? Babies point to redirect the attention of other babies, although neither can as yet speak. Their behavior seems to represent a declaration of interest and a wish to share the experience of an object. They start pointing at the same time as making speechlike cooing; age at commencement of pointing may be a good predictor of progress in understanding language. Pointing is more likely with the right hand, which, with the latter's control by the left or language hemisphere, implies connections with language mechanisms. (It is, of course, inappropriate to ask, in babies who have not yet developed manipulative skills, whether such dextral pointing reflects handedness.)

Chimpanzees do not readily point with the index finger and without tuition rarely point by gesturing with hands or arms. There are of course differences in the resting morphology of the index finger in humans and chimpanzees (Povinelli & Davis, 1994). Nevertheless, animals with extensive human experience may extend the hand to refer humans to objects, while rarely doing so to other apes or extending the index finger (Call & Tomasello, 1994). However, Leavens, Hopkins, and Bard (1996) do describe spontaneous index-finger pointing in three laboratory chimpanzees who had not received language training; the behavior generally occurred in the presence of a human, referred to environmental objects, and appeared intentionally communicative.

Although deception is widespread among animals, evidence of intentional or planned deception is limited largely to primates (Mitchell & Anderson, 1997). Deceptive pointing is even rarer than communicative. However, Mitchell and Anderson (1997) reported that, when placed in experimental circumstances similar to those previously used with children and chimpanzees, capuchin monkeys (Cebus apella) showed communicative and deceptive deixis (pointing) where they benefitted by indicating, accurately or falsely, the location of hidden foods. However, the authors invoked response inhibition and conditional discrimination learning, rather than possession of a true theory of mind in this infra-ape species. Pointing, attentional redirection, and deception, however, all imply an incipient theory of mind and the possibility of a Machiavellian intelligence.

MACHIAVELLIAN INTELLIGENCE AND THEORY OF MIND

Although group membership may provide many benefits, an individual's own interests are rarely identical and necessitate constant reassessment of one's standing in a changing network. Social skills permit the formation of alliances and the switching of tactics when necessary or beneficial. We, therefore, spend much time gathering social information and ascertaining the intentions of others and their current attentional state. Intense social competition, where our conspecifics may be our own worst enemies, results in manipulation and deception, the balancing of competitive and cooperative options, reciprocity and deceit, plot and counterplot, and gamesmanship to permit the weak to beat the strong. Social or Machiavellian intelligence (Humphrey, 1976; Whiten, 1991), a characteristic of higher primates, involves the ability to outwit peers and competitors by predicting their likely responses to our own changes in behavior, relationships, or alliances (Dunbar, 1993) and by interpreting their behavior by inferring their likely desires, beliefs, knowledge, or intentions. A possible criterion for the achievement of such a theory of mind, perhaps normally present in us by 5 years of age, is an understanding that another could have a false belief about a physical or social situation. Deliberate deception of others, therefore, may indicate possession of a theory of mind and the application of Machiavellian intelligence. Although the best evidence that an animal is capable of deception would be for it to be able to recognize deception in another (Mills, 1997), it must also be noted that the criteria for *deliberate* are not easily established.

Relative to apes, we are cognitively superior not only in problem solving, motor skills, and communication but also in social-event perception, shared attention, imitation, pantomime, cooperation, deception, and reciprocal communication of intentions. Although monkeys may apparently deceive and cooperate, they may not understand why their actions have certain effects on objects and other individuals; this insight may only have emerged some 16 million years ago with the separation of the orangutan lineage from that of the other primates. In Byrne's (1995) view, this watershed in the evolution of human intelligence includes the capacity to mind read or attribute mental states to others and, allowing for forward planning, toolmaking, imitation, and teaching, is a necessary precursor for the ultimate evolution of language. (Dunbar, 1996, took this further and viewed language evolution as a socially relevant form of information exchange [gossip] for purposes of social bonding and to keep track of multiple social relationships in increasingly large and unwieldy groups; indeed Joffe and Dunbar, 1997, noted a linear relationship between social group size and size of the primate neocortex.) Either way, Machiavellian or social intelligence, the need simultaneously to track the actions of others, played a major role in the evolution of language and consciousness. It may be absent or defective in autism, Asperger's syndrome, or schizophrenia (Baron-Cohen, 1995) and may be mediated, according to brain-imaging studies with theory-of-mind tasks, by medial prefrontal structures (Baker et al., 1996), which otherwise are known to be involved in personality, social behavior, and our intrinsic humanity.

Could a chimpanzee ever experience an autistic or schizophrenic state? Does it possess conscious self-awareness or a theory of mind? Heyes (1998) disputed the empirical evidence that apes have mental-state concepts like *want* or *know* or *believe*, suggesting that such apparent behavior could always have occurred by chance or as a product of nonmentalistic processes such as associative learning; he regards as noncompelling the argument that the theory-of-mind hypothesis, in infrahuman species, is the more parsimonious. However, to quote Cartmill (1995): "in the last analysis perhaps the best reason for thinking that some animals have minds like ours is simply that they seem to recognize that we have minds like theirs" {p. 77).

In conclusion, human intellectual capacity can be viewed at levels ranging from the elemental (performance measures, neurophysiological correlates) to the global (praxis, tool use, language, esthetics). There is a long evolutionary prehistory, however, to behaviors we tend to view as preeminently human, and a distinction between hardwired and adaptive behaviors, as with language, is not always easily made. While some degree of synergistic coevolution seems to have been inevitable, the behaviors reviewed here do not seem to be mediated by an evolved general purpose problem solver; nor, however, should they be viewed as independent and modular. The prefrontal cortex plays a significant role in many of the behaviors, the dorsolateral prefrontal cortex perhaps being the substrate of fluid problem-solving intelligence of an abstract nature and the cingulate and orbitofrontal cortex the substrate of Machiavellian (or social) behaviors or intellect.

REFERENCES

Aboitiz, F. (1996). Does bigger mean better? Evolutionary determinants of brain size and structure. *Brain, Behaviour and Evolution, 47,* 225–245.

Aboitiz, F., & Garcia, R. (1997). The evolutionary origin of the language areas in the human brain. A neuroanatomical perspective. *Brain Research Reviews, 25,* 381–396.

Baker, S. C., Rogers, R. D., Owen, A. M., Frith, C. D., Dolan, R. J., Frackowiak, R. S. J., & Robbins, T. W. (1996). Neural systems engaged by planning: A PET study of the Tower of London task. *Neuropsychologia, 34,* 515–526.

Barnett, A. (1997, August 30). A monkey could make it. *New Scientist*, 19.

Baron-Cohen, S. (1995). *Mindblindness: An essay on autism and theory of mind*. Cambridge, MA.: MIT Press.

Bechara, A., Damasio, H., Tranel, D., & Damasio, A. R. (1997). Deciding advantageously before knowing the advantageous strategy. *Science, 275*, 1293–1296.

Bednarik, R. G. (1997a). The origins of navigation and language. *The Artefact, 20*, 16–56.

Bednarik, R. G. (1997b). The role of Pleistocene beads in documenting hominid cognition. *Rock Art Research, 14*, 27–39.

Bigler, E. D., Johnson, S. C., Jackson, C., & Blatter, D. (1995). Aging, brain size and IQ. *Intelligence, 21*, 109–111.

Blinkov, S. M., & Glezer, I. I. (1968). *The human brain in figures*. New York: Basic Books.

Boysen, S. T., Berntson, C. G., & Prentice, J. (1987). Simian scribbles: A reappraisal of drawing in the chimpanzee (*Pan troglodytes*). *Journal of Comparative Psychology, 101*, 82–89.

Boysen, S. T., Berntson, G. G., Shreyer, T. A., & Hannan, M. B. (1995). Indicating acts during counting by a chimpanzee (*Pan troglodytes*). *Journal of Comparative Psychology, 109*, 47–51.

Bradshaw, J. L. (1997). *Human evolution: A neuropsychological perspective*. Hove, England: Psychology Press/Taylor Francis.

Bradshaw, J. L., & Rogers, L. J. (1993). *The evolution of lateral asymmetries, language, tool use and intellect*. San Diego, CA: Academic Press.

Brannon, E. M., & Terrace, H. S. (1998). Ordering the numerosities 1 to 9 by monkeys. *Nature, 282*, 746–749.

Brooks, D. J. (1995). The role of the basal ganglia in motor control: Contributions from PET. *Journal of the Neurological Sciences, 128*, 1–13.

Butterworth, G. (1997). Starting point. *Natural History, 5*, 14–16.

Byrne, R. W. (1995). *The thinking ape: Evolutionary origins of intelligence*. Oxford: Oxford University Press.

Cabeza, R., & Nyberg, L. (1997). Imaging cognition: An empirical review of PET studies with normal subjects. *Journal of Cognitive Neuroscience, 9*, 1–26.

Call, J., & Tomasello, M. (1994). Production and comprehension of referential pointing by orangutans (*Pongo pygmaeus*). *Journal of Comparative Psychology, 108*, 307–317.

Calvin, W. H. (1994, October). The emergence of intelligence. *Scientific American*, 79–85.

Caro, T. M., & Hauser, M. D. (1992). Is there teaching in nonhuman animals? *The Quarterly Review of Biology, 67*, 151–174.

Cartmill, M. (1995). Significant others. *Natural History, 6*, 74–77.

Cattell, R. B. (1963). Theory of fluid and crystallized intelligence: A critical experiment. *Journal of Educational Psychology, 54*, 1–22.

Chase, P. G., & Dibble, H. L. (1987). Middle Palaeolithic symbolism: A review of current evidence and interpretations. *Journal of Anthropological Archaeology, 6*, 263–296.

Chomsky, N. (1980). Rules and representations. *Behavioral and Brain Sciences, 3*, 1–61.

Corballis, M. (1996). How to grow human. *Behavioral and Brain Sciences, 19*, 633–634.

Damasio, A. (1994). *Descartes' error: Emotion, reason and the human brain*. New York: Putnam.

Deacon, T. W. (1986a). Human brain evolution: 1. Evolution of language circuits. In H. J. Jerison & I. Jerison (Eds.), *Intelligence and Evolutionary Biology* (pp. 363–380). New York: Springer.

Deacon, T. W. (1986b). Human brain evolution: 11. Embryology and brain allometry. In H. J. Jerison & I. Jerison (Eds.), *Intelligence and Evolutionary Biology* (pp. 381–415). New York: Springer.

Deacon, T. W. (1990). Problems of ontogeny and phylogeny in brain-size evolution. *International Journal of Primatology, 11*, 237–282.

Deary, I. J., & Caryl, P. G. (1997). Neuroscience and human intelligence differences. *Trends in Neurosciences, 20*, 365–371.

Dehaene, S., Dehaene-Lambertz, G., & Cohen, L. (1998). Abstract representations of numbers in the animal and human brain. *Trends in the Neurosciences, 21,* 355–361.

D'Errico, F., & Villa, P. (1997). Holes and grooves: The contribution of microscopy and taphonomy to the problem of art origins. *Journal of Human Evolution, 33,* 1–31.

D'Errico, F., Villa, P., Llona, A. C. P., & Idarraga, R. (1998). A Middle Palaeolithic origin of music? Using cave-bear bone accumulations to assess the Divje Babe 1 bone 'flute.' *Antiquity, 72,* 65–79.

Dunbar, R. I. M. (1993). Coevolution of neocortical size, group size and language in humans. *Behavioral and Brain Sciences, 16,* 681–735.

Dunbar, R. I. M. (1996). *Grooming, gossip and the evolution of language.* London: Faber.

Emery, N. J., Lorincz, E. N., Perrett, D. I., Oram, M. W., & Baker, C. I. (1997). Gaze following and joint attention in rhesus monkeys (*Macaca mulatta*). *Journal of Comparative Psychology, 111,* 286–293.

Fisher, S. E., Vargha-Khadem, F., Watkins, K. E., Monaco, A. P., & Pembrey, M. E. (1998). Localisation of a gene implicated in severe speech and language disorder. *Nature Genetics, 18,* 168–170.

Fodor, J. A. (1983). *The modularity of the mind: An essay on faculty psychology.* Cambridge, MA: MIT Press.

Foti, D. J., & Cummings, J. L. (1997). Neurobehavioral aspects of movement disorders. In R. L. Watts & W. C. Koller (Eds.), *Movement disorders: Neurologic principles and practice* (pp. 15–30). New York: McGraw-Hill.

Gardner, H. (1983). *Frames of mind: The theory of multiple intelligence.* New York: Basic Books.

Gargett, R. H. (1989). Grave shortcomings: The evidence for Neanderthal burial. *Current Anthropology, 30,* 157–177.

Geschwind, N. (1965). Disconnexion syndromes in animals and man. *Brain, 88,* 585–644.

Gould, S. J., & Eldredge, N. (1993). Punctuated equilibrium comes of age. *Nature, 366,* 223–227.

Harvey, P. H. (1986). Allometric analysis and brain size. In H. J. Jerison & I. Jerison (Eds.), *Intelligence and evolutionary biology* (pp. 199–210). New York: Springer.

Hauser, M. D. (1988). Invention and social transmission: New data from wild vervet monkeys. In R. Byrne & A. Whiten (Eds.), *Machiavellian intelligence: Social expertise and the evolution of intellect in monkeys, apes and humans* (pp. 327–343). Oxford: Oxford University Press.

Hauser, M. D. (1997a). Ape people. *Nature, 390,* 246–247.

Hauser, M. D. (1997b). Artifactual kinds and functional design features: What a primate understands without language. *Cognition, 64,* 285–308.

Hauser, M. D., & Carey, S. (1998). Building a cognitive creature from a set of primitives: Evolutionary and developmental insights. In C. Allen & D. Cummins (Eds.), *The evolution of mind* (pp. 51–106). Oxford: Oxford University Press.

Heyes, C. M. (1998). Theory of mind in nonhuman primates. *Behavioral and Brain Sciences, 21,* 101–148.

Holloway, R. L. (1995). Toward a synthetic theory of human brain evolution. In J. P. Changeux & J. Chavaillon (Eds.), *Origins of the human brain* (pp. 42–54). Oxford, England: Clarendon Press.

Horn, J. L., & Cattell, R. B. (1967). Age differences in fluid and crystallized intelligence. *Acta Psychologica, 26,* 107–129.

Huffman, M. A. (1997). Current evidence for self-medication in primates: A multidisciplinary perspective. *Yearbook of Physical Anthropology, 40,* 171–200.

Humphrey, N. K. (1976). The social function of intellect. In P. P. G. Bateson & R. A. Hinde (Eds.), *Growing points in ethology* (pp. 307–317). Cambridge: Cambridge University Press.

Jelinek, J. (1997). An unexpected spectacular find. *Rock Art Research, 14*(1), 59–66.

Jensen, A. R. (1987). Individual differences in the Hick paradigm. In P. A. Vernon (Ed.), *Speed of information processing and intelligence* (pp. 101–175). Norwood, NJ: Ablex.

Jerison, H. J. (1986). Evolutionary biology of intelligence: The nature of the problem. In H. J. Jerison & I. Jerison (Eds.), *Intelligence and evolutionary biology* (pp. 1–12). New York: Springer.

Joffe, T. H., & Dunbar, R. I. M. (1997). Visual and socio-cognitive information processing in primate evolution. *Proceedings of the Royal Society of London B, 264,* 1303–1307.

Karten, H. J. (1991). Homology and evolutionary origins of the neocortex. *Brain, Behaviour and Evolution, 38,* 264–272.

Kay, R. F., Cartmill, M., & Balow, M. (1998). The hypoglossal canal and the origin of human vocal behavior. *Proceedings of the National Academy of Sciences, 95,* 5417–5419.

Kien, J. (1991). The need for data reduction may have paved the way for evolution of language ability in hominids. *Journal of Human Evolution, 29,* 157–165.

Kimbel, W. D., Walter, R. C., Johnason, O. C., Reed, K. E., Aronson, J. L., & Assefa, Z. (1996). Late Pliocene *Homo* and Oldowan tools from the Hadar formation (Kada Hadar Member), Ethiopia. *Journal of Human Evolution, 31,* 549–561.

Kimura, D. (1993). *Neuromotor mechanisms in human communication.* Oxford: Oxford University Press.

Kranzler, J. H., & Jensen, A. R. (1989). Inspection time and intelligence: A meta-analysis. *Intelligence, 13,* 329–347.

Kutas, M., & Federmeier, K. D. (1998). Minding the body. *Psychophysiology, 35,* 135–150.

Leavens, D. A., Hopkins, W. D., & Bard, K. A. (1996). Indexical and referential pointing in chimpanzees (*Pan troglodytes*). *Journal of Comparative Psychology, 110,* 346–353.

Leiner, H. C., Leiner, A. L., & Dow, R. S. (1995). The underestimated cerebellum. *Human Brain Mapping, 2,* 244–254.

Lenain, T. (1995). Ape painting and the problem of the origin of art. *Human Evolution, 10,* 205–215.

MacNeilage, P. F. (1998). The frame/content theory of evolution of speech production. *Behavioral and Brain Sciences, 21,* 499–546.

Marzke, M. W., Toth, N., Schick, K., Reece, S., Steinberg, B., Hunt, K., Linscheid, R. L., & An, K. (1998). EMG study of hand muscle recruitment during hard hammer percussion manufacture of Oldowan tools. *American Journal of Physical Anthropology, 105,* 315–332.

Mesulam, M. M. (1998). From sensation to cognition. *Brain, 121,* 1013–1052.

Mills, C. (1997, July/August). Unusual suspects. *The Sciences,* 32–36.

Mitchell, R. W., & Anderson, J. R. (1997). Pointing, witholding information and deception in capuchin monkeys (*Cebus apella*). *Journal of Comparative Psychology, 111,* 351–361.

Müller, R. (1996). Innateness, autonomy, universality? Neurobiological approaches to language. *Behavioral and Brain Sciences, 19,* 611–675.

Pantelis, C., & Brewer, W. (1996). Neurocognitive and neurobehavioural patterns and the syndromes of schizophrenia: Role of frontal-subcortical networks. In C. Pantelis, H. E. Nelson, & T. R. E. Barnes (Eds.), *Schizophrenia: A neuropsychological perspective* (pp. 317–343). Chichester, UK: Wiley.

Pinker, S. (1997). *How the mind works.* London: Allen Lane.

Povinelli, D. J., & Davis, D. R. (1994). Differences between chimpanzees (*Pan troglodytes*) and humans (*Homo sapiens*) in the resting state of the index finger: Implications for pointing. *Journal of Comparative Psychology, 108,* 134–139.

Reed, T. E., & Jensen, A. R. (1991). Arm nerve conduction velocity (NCV), brain NCV, reaction time and intelligence. *Intelligence, 15,* 33–47.

Rizzolatti, G., & Arbib, M. A. (1998). Language within our grasp. *Trends in Neurosciences, 21,* 188–194.

Rizzolatti, G., Fadiga, L., Matelli, M., Bettinardi, V., Paulesu, E., Perani, D., & Fazio, F. (1996). Localization of grasp representations in humans by PET: 1. Observation versus execution. *Experimental Brain Research, 111,* 246–252.

Schmahmann, J. D. (1997). *The cerebellum and cognition.* New York: Academic Press.

Schoenemann, P. T., & Wang, W. S. (1996). Evolutionary principles and the emergence of syntax. *Behavioral and Brain Sciences, 19,* 646–647.

Semaw, S., Renne, P., Harris, J. W. K., Feibel, C. S., Bemor, R. L., Fesseha, N., & Mowdray, K. (1997). 2.5 million years old stone tools from Gona, Ethiopia. *Nature, 385,* 333–336.

Semendeferi, K., Damasio, H., Frank, R., & Van Hoesen, G. W. (1997). The evolution of the frontal lobes: A volumetric analysis based on three-dimensional reconstructions of magnetic resonance scans of human and ape brains. *Journal of Human Evolution, 32,* 375–388.

Shallice, T. (1988). *From neuropsychology to mental structure.* Cambridge: Cambridge University Press.

Shapiro, K. L., Arnell, K. M., & Raymond, J. E. (1997). The attentional blink. *Trends in Cognitive Sciences, 1,* 291–296.

Sternberg, R. J., & Kaufman, J. C. (1998). Human abilities. *Annual Review of Psychology, 49,* 479–502.

Stuss, D. T., Eskes, G. A., & Foster, J. K. (1994). Experimental neuropsychological studies of frontal lobe functions. In F. Boller & J. Grafman (Eds.), *Handbook of Neuropsychology* (Vol. 9, pp. 149–185). New York: Elsevier.

Vargha-Khadem, F., Watkins, K., Alcock, K., Fletcher, P., & Passingham, R. (1995). Praxic and nonverbal cognitive deficits in a large family with a genetically transmitted speech and language disorder. *Proceedings of the New York Academy of Sciences, 92,* 930–933.

Vernon, P. A., & Mori, M. (1992). Intelligence, reaction times and peripheral nerve conduction velocity. *Intelligence, 16,* 273–288

Visalberghi, E., & Fragaszy, D. M. (1990). Do monkeys ape? In S. T. Parker & K. R. Gibson (Eds.), *"Language" and intelligence in monkeys and apes: Comparative developmental perspectives* (pp. 247–273). Cambridge: Cambridge University Press.

Vogel, G. (1997). Scientists probe decisions behind decision-making. *Science, 275,* 1269.

Westergaard, G. C., & Suomi, S. J. (1997). Modification of clay forms by tufted capuchins (*Cebus apella*). *International Journal of Primatology, 18,* 455–467.

Whiten, A. (1991). The emergence of mindreading: Steps towards an interdisciplinary enterprise. In A. Whiten (Ed.), *Natural theories of mind: Evolution, development and simulation of everyday mindreading* (pp. 195–207). Oxford, England: Blackwell.

Wickett, J. C., & Vernon, P. A. (1994). Peripheral nerve conduction velocity, reaction time and intelligence: An attempt to replicate Vernon & Mori (1992). *Intelligence, 18,* 129–131.

Wickett, J. C., Vernon, P. A., & Lee, D. H. (1994). *In vivo* brain size, head perimeter and intelligence in a sample of healthy adult females. *Personality and Individual Differences, 16,* 831–838.

Wynn, K. (1998). Psychological foundations of number: Numerical competence in human infants. *Trends in Cognitive Sciences, 2*(8), 296–303.

5

※

The Primate Origins of Human Intelligence

Richard W. Byrne
University of St Andrews, Scotland

Intelligence, as Fowler's *Modern English Usage* expressed it in 1926, is what most of us flatter ourselves that we can find in the looking glass. And at least when it comes to species intelligence, we would be right. Species, or biological, intelligence concerns the differences between animal species in mental or behavioral aptitudes. In all other ways, however, its meaning is parasitic on the everyday human usage. For example, the aptitudes that cause us to label some species of animal as relatively intelligent are almost inevitably human ones—and would still be, even if the nonhuman species were to possess the aptitudes in greater measure than we do, though usually they display only a pale shadow of the human level. We simply wouldn't recognize intelligence if it were not "our sort." Also, like human intelligence, species intelligence is inherently comparative: "better than some other species" is always implied. Finally, and once again just as with human intelligence, there is a long-standing and unresolved debate as to whether the intelligence of an animal species is best described as a single, general purpose attribute, an all-pervasive "g" factor, or as a set of special purpose skills, or modular "intelligences" (Rozin, 1976; Tooby & Cosmides, 1992). The former accords well with people's everyday preference for distinguishing between clever and dumb animals, whereas the latter makes it easier to make contact with the biological approach to animal form (morphology), in which a particular function is sought for each specific adaptation.

If the term *species intelligence* is so heavily anthropocentric, does it have any usefulness for biologists? Or is species intelligence one of those everyday distortions that serves only to assert human dominion over nature, and this time in a particularly circular and self-fulfilling way? That depends on how it is used. Undoubtedly, most of the everyday smart or dumb judgments we make about animals are fatuous. For example, I used to think that dogs were obviously smarter than sheep—not an unusual judgment in a country where black and white sheepdogs are famous for their control of large flocks of sheep and their exquisitely precise understanding of shepherds' whistles. I was then chastened to discover that in parts of northern India, shepherds also use systems of whistles to control sheep, but in this case dogs are not the intervening force: The sheep understand the commands themselves! Dogs are much easier for humans to appreciate than sheep: They have mobile faces whose expressions reliably reveal their emotions, they are biologically predisposed to do what their owners (as surrogate pack leaders) want, and they are fast moving and alert in demeanor. When such superficial biases are set aside, there are surprisingly few artificial tasks that discriminate reliably between animal species (Warren, 1973).

Where species differences in intelligence become valuable is in the search for the evolutionary path of—specifically—human intelligence (Byrne, 1995). Searching for the origins of human aptitudes, it is entirely appropriate to focus myopically on human aptitudes in animals. Comparison is no longer invidious; making comparisons between species is the bread-and-butter of evolutionary method. In doing so, there are good pragmatic reasons to study the diversity of behavioral skills that make up intelligence as a whole, rather than assuming that they are a reflection of any single underlying entity. One cannot at the start of this enterprise be sure that intelligence is highly modular, but if it is not, nothing has been lost by studying aptitude in different domains separately. If those separate attributes turn out to be highly correlated, one can later simplify description by invoking an underlying, general capacity. This focus on behavioral skills also serves as a healthy reminder that one can only record observable behavior: going beyond that becomes theory laden.

Suppose one has studied some behavioral aptitude in a range of species. How can these data be converted into knowledge about the ancient past? The method is called *evolutionary reconstruction*, and it depends on having a taxonomy of a group of living species that accurately reflects their evolutionary history of relatedness (phylogeny). Evolution proceeds by branching as new species are formed. New species result from the isolation of populations of an existing species (as on an archipelago) and also by specialization of subpopulations in exploiting different microhabitats (Ridley, 1993). Each branching leaves its descendants with a distinctive legacy of features as a direct result of their shared ancestry. Some of these shared features are primitive ones, retained from much earlier stages in the branching process, but some are novel and specific to the most recent common ancestor: the so-called *derived* features. Shared, derived features enable the pattern of branching to be reconstructed, and the result is a phylogenetic taxonomy. This, like a family tree, reflects the history of the process of descent (Hennig, 1966; Ridley, 1986). Each branch point in the taxonomy implies the definite existence of an extinct ancestor of a group of living species; groups of this kind are called *clades*. Identifying clades of living species is, in a sense, a method of discovering extinct species. Moreover, we can be certain that these extinct species did give rise to the living forms we see today, whereas fossils—despite their comforting solidity—may be of "dead end" species that became extinct without leaving issue. It is therefore important to identify genuine clades from impostors, groups that share other sorts of similarity. Groups of species also can, for example, look similar because of shared primitive features. The great apes—chimpanzee, bonobo, gorilla, orangutan—used to be treated as a clade, *Pongidae*, but in fact they are distinguished from humans only by their retention of primitive features such as small brains and long body hair. The proper clade includes humans, and the term *great ape* might be better used now in this inclusive sense. Also, as taxonomists have long realized, adaptation to a common environmental problem can make unrelated species become similar; for example, birds and bats share wings because both are adapted to exploit the air. To minimize these problems, complex and distinctive structures are needed, ideally ones having little direct effect on the animal and thus not under active selection. Fortunately, it seems that much of the sequence of DNA in cell nuclei is no longer expressed and meets this tall order rather well. Furthermore, with the assumption that neutral mutation occurs at a more or less constant rate, the extent of molecular difference can be taken as a clock and calibrated with known fossil dates. Figure 5.1 shows the estimated divergence dates from humans of various primates, our closest living relatives.

With a reliable phylogeny derived from DNA sequence data, a series of ancestors of increasing remoteness in evolutionary time from our species of interest, in this case humans, has been automatically discovered. In the second part of the process of evolutionary reconstruction, one needs to flesh out the characteristics of the ancestor implied by each clade. For this, one can use all the shared features, primitive and derived, of living species in the clade. Because the source of this evidence is living, behavioral traits can be studied just as well as morphological ones. The comparative study of the behavior of living mammals, especially the primates, provides the data for reconstructing the evolution of human intellectual capacities that existed before the last ancestor humans share with any living animal. The remainder of this chapter reviews this evidence for what it can reveal about the nature of the intelligence humans display today.

The Primates

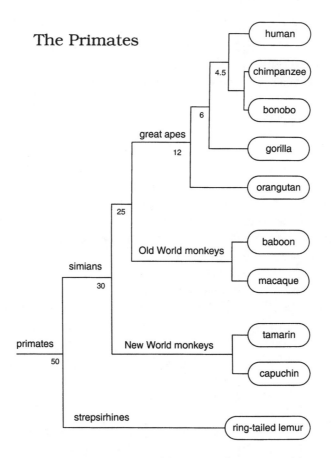

FIG 5.1. A partial phylogenetic taxonomy of the primates, showing some of the major groups and well-studied species. The numbers at branch points are the approximate estimated dates of divergence, in millions of years, based on the calibration of setting the orangutan human divergence to 12M. This is justified by the existence of Dryopithecine ape fossils at that date which show some derived characters of the orangutan, whereas the date of 16M more commonly used for this is overly conservative because no possible orangutan ancestors are known that early (Meike Köhler, pers. comm. 1998).

EARLIEST ORIGINS: BEFORE 50M

The two lineages of modern primates that converge at 50M (million years ago) are unlike each other in many respects. In cases like this, the most reasonable assumption is that their common ancestor showed the more primitive trait, the typical mammalian version. On this basis, our earliest primate ancestors were relatively small and not very social animals, with brains just as small as would be expected from this body size, nocturnal but with considerable binocular vision, four legged but with a five-fingered hand whose fingernails allowed dextrous gripping. If we wanted to think of a modern animal that was something like this, a rat or a tree shrew would do, except that the dextrous hand would give superior manipulative ability and binocular vision would allow adept grasping, as is found in modern strepsirhine primates like lemurs. There are a number of fossils of early primates from this period that do indeed resemble some modern lemurs (Simons, 1972), and one of these may even be the ancestor of all modern forms. Like all modern mammals (Mackintosh, 1983), these earliest primates must have possessed the ability to respond to correlations in the environment (classical, Pavlovian conditioning) and to modify their behavior flexibly on the basis of experience (instrumental, Skinnerian conditioning). As with these modern mammals, the efficiency of their learning would be greatly increased by biological predispositions to learn connections appropriate for survival (Roper, 1983), such as associating a feeling of nausea with the most recent new food tasted.

INCREASING SOCIAL SOPHISTICATION: 50M TO 25M

Our ancestors of 30M were very different animals. Living by day rather than largely by night, forming long-lasting social groups, this species was larger—perhaps the size of a domestic cat—yet its brain was twice as large as would be expected in a typical mammal of that size. We know this because these traits pervade its descendants, the living monkeys and apes. Early attempts to compare learning abilities of these simian primates with those of other mammals in the psychologist's laboratory found no qualitative differences but considerably greater speed of learning in simians (Passingham, 1981). Subsequent field studies have found many more dramatic differences, some apparently qualitative and all centered around social skill. Best documented are the skills of some monkeys, but there is no doubt that apes are basically similar.

Monkeys and apes compete largely by means of alliances, rather than brute strength (Harcourt, 1988). Allies are often found among kin, and in some species social rank is effectively inherited from the mother because her constant support allows a growing youngster to win every encounter with individuals subordinate to its mother (Chapais, 1992). In addition, friendships show occasional uses of deception to attain individual goals at the expense of other group members (Byrne & Whiten, 1992), and some tactics are quite subtle (Byrne & Whiten, 1990). Examples include suppressing copulation calls when mating with disallowed individuals (and thus achieving secrecy); suddenly staring into the distance when pursued (and thus distracting the pursuers); a juvenile screaming as if hurt when near an adult with food (and thus gaining the food when the mother attacked the other adult); withholding food-advertisement calls when discovering small amounts of food (and thus monopolizing the food).

Sometimes individuals seem to be punished if the deception is detected, although it is often hard to know whether the aggression is because of the deceit or simply in order to achieve the goal. In the most compelling case, rhesus monkeys who were detected with food they did not advertise by calling received more aggression than discoverers of food who were vocal (Hauser & Marler, 1993). These tactics actually work by manipulating the mental states of the target individuals, but in general it is possible that they are acquired as a result of learning from past coincidences, without any understanding of their mechanism (Byrne, 1997c). However, for this to be a plausible explanation, very rapid—perhaps one-trial—learning must be envisaged. All the evidence points to a simian specialization in rapid learning ability in social contexts, with imperfect transfer to learning speed in artificial, laboratory tasks.

Along with this enhanced learning ability, simian primates are larger brained than most mammals of their size (Jerison, 1973; Passingham, 1981), and the main site of their brain expansion is the neocortex. It is therefore highly suggestive that the size of the neocortex, relative to the rest of the brain, correlates across species with the average group size (Dunbar, 1992), a measure that gives some indication of the size of the social learning task typically confronting a member of that species. (In contrast, no such correlations are found with measures of environmental complexity—range size or day-journey length—above or below that expected for a given body size.) The implication is that neocortical enlargement is the physical underpinning of social sophistication. This is supported by the relative frequency with which deception has been reported in a species; this too is correlated with the neocortex ratio of that species (Byrne, 1993, 1996).

It is therefore believed that some pressure to aggregate into long-lasting social groups—perhaps a result of the increased predation on our diurnal and rather small simian ancestors—selected for increased ability to manage the complex social interactions that group living presented (Byrne & Whiten, 1988, 1997; Humphrey, 1976). The net result was a considerable increase in brain size, allowing memorization of the rapidly increasing number of relationships and personal idiosyncrasies in these enlarged groups and rapid development of manipulative tactics to ensure maximization of individual gains within group living. The earliest origins of our mental swiftness and memory capacity seem likely to have been the social demands confronting our ancestors of over 25M.

UNDERSTANDING HOW THINGS WORK: 12M

Few species of apes exist today, although a much wider range of fossil species are known. Good evidence of mental or psychological capacities is lacking for the many closely related species of gibbon or lesser ape, so interest focuses on the nonhuman great apes. Of these, the common chimpanzee has been extensively studied in the field and in captivity, but the bonobo or pygmy chimpanzee, the gorilla, and the orangutan have been relatively neglected. Several times a remarkable aptitude has been first discovered in the chimpanzee and only later detected in other great ape species, so that even now it would be premature to identify clear mental differences between them. This section, therefore, concentrates on the human ancestors of 12M, from which time humans share ancestry with all four species of nonhuman great ape.

In contrast to their social sophistication, monkeys sometimes seem relatively incurious about the natural world, unable to profit from even obvious signs. Vervet monkeys that discover the track of a python or a dead antelope in a tree, which is normally a certain cue to the nearby presence of a leopard, show no increased wariness, even though these species are among their major predators (Cheney & Seyfarth, 1988). Chimpanzees, encountering recently made nests when they are ranging in the dangerous area that overlaps the range of another group, examine the nests minutely and visibly increase their wariness (Goodall et al., 1979). Correlated with this monkey-chimpanzee difference in using information from objects is a difference in using objects themselves—as tools. Under natural conditions, the only primate to use tools routinely is the chimpanzee (Boesch & Boesch, 1990; Goodall, 1964, 1986; McGrew, 1992; Nishida, 1986). Tool use by most animals is a matter of a single habit, such as the anvil rocks of sea otters or probing spines of Galapagos woodpecker finches (Beck, 1980). Chimpanzees use tools for a wide range of purposes, including pestle-pounding to gain palm tree pulp, chiseling open bees' nests, hammering hard nuts on a stone anvil, drinking from a leaf sponge, soliciting sex by leaf-tearing, wiping off blood or feces with a leaf, clubbing large predators, aiming stones when throwing and so forth. Moreover, chimpanzees make many of their tools; for example, the flexible stems used to fish for insects inside a termite mound or an ant nest in a tree bole are made by picking a suitable stem, stripping off the leaves, and biting the end to remove irregularities. Different tools are made for different purposes: 9 in. flexible stems for insect fishing, slender but rigid 2 ft. wands for ant dipping, and thick rods for chiseling. In captivity, monkeys can develop tool use (Visalberghi & Trinca, 1987; Westergaard & Fragaszy, 1987), but the problem space they must explore is highly restricted because they are presented with a relatively limited range of materials that relate in straightforward ways to the tasks required of them.

Although chimpanzees do readily invent novel forms of tool use, the most interesting tool-using traditions are social customs, dependent on cultural transmission for their maintenance (McGrew, 1998). This is clear because in different places the techniques differ slightly and in ways that do not relate to ecological conditions—the task and tool materials are the same. In some areas, tools used in insect fishing are repaired by biting the end, in other areas both ends are used, and in others the tool is discarded when one end becomes frayed. In a scatter of sites across Africa, safari ants are eaten by dipping a stick into the moving column; in the west, a short probe is used with one hand and the ants are bitten off with the teeth, but in the east a long rod is dipped into the column with one hand, and then the other hand sweeps up the rod to remove a much greater number of ants. Stone-tool use to break nuts is only found in west Africa, though the nut species are widespread. Chimpanzees—in populations that discard blunted probes, use short dipping sticks and do not know how to break hard nuts—would clearly benefit from the techniques seen elsewhere.

Once thought the exclusive province of chimpanzees, elaborate traditions of toolmaking and tool use are now known from one population of orangutans (Fox, Sitompul, & Van Schaik, 1999). Moreover, the plant-feeding methods of mountain gorillas feature many of the same aptitudes that make chimpanzee tool traditions so remarkable, though no tools are used (Byrne & Byrne, 1991, 1993). These gorillas rely on abundant, nutritious herbs that are, unfortunately, difficult or painful to eat: nettles, thistles, hook-covered clambering plants, and soft piths encased in woody exteriors. The techniques used to deal with these difficulties are elaborate in that they require correct sequencing of several different stages; require accurate coordination of the two hands performing different roles at each stage; they are flexible, with stages omitted if they are unnecessary in any given case; and show hierarchical embedding, with subprocesses that can be iterated to a criterion. The methods for different plants are not alike, but several of them share these general features. Although anthropological interest has always focused on the tools chimpanzees make and use, the manner in which they construct and employ the tools is very similar to gorilla plant feeding in its structural complexity (Byrne, 1999). Both species show very strong behavioral laterality for these skillful tasks but not in other, less complex aspects of their manual behavior. With only one population of gorillas known to show these techniques, no distinctive traditions can be followed, but the pattern of variance within the skills themselves strongly suggests that the general approach, or layout, is socially acquired in each case. Details of grip, movement, and hand preference vary idiosyncratically, but the organization of the skills is remarkably standardized despite the complexity of the skills and the range of apparently viable alternative methods. On current evidence, it is most likely that chimpanzee tool traditions and gorilla plant preparation skills are learned by imitation of the overall organization or program, just as humans learn motor skills from others (Byrne & Russon, 1998). Nothing in the behavior of monkeys suggests a similar ability.

To be able to build up novel motor skills that are elaborate in organization and to copy the layout of these skills from other, more skillful practitioners, implies an understanding of how behavior causes change to be effected in the physical world. This is also seen in experiments where cooperation is required. An apparatus was designed so that two parties, sitting on either side, must collaborate for both to be delivered rewards (Mason & Hollis, 1962). One individual can see which one of two handles needs to be pulled; the other can reach and pull the handle. Monkeys and apes readily learn either role, over a number of trials. However, when rhesus monkeys were switched to the other person's role, they had again to learn this—as if from scratch (Povinelli, Parks, & Novak, 1992). Chimpanzees tested under identical circumstances knew immediately how to take the other person's role (Povinelli, Nelson, & Boysen, 1992). Whether the apes' superior understanding is a matter of understanding physical cause and effect, or mental intentions and knowledge, is here a moot point. However, great apes do show an ability to appreciate causes that lie purely in the mental realm: the clearest evidence concerns intention and other-person knowledge.

Adult humans routinely attempt to distinguish intentional acts from accidents, and this forms a basis of most legal codes. In one recent experiment (Call & Tomasello, 1998), chimpanzees, orangutans, and children learned that marking a box by placing a counter on top of it for 10 seconds indicated that this box had a reward inside. Then the experimenter began making "accidents," in which another box was also marked for exactly the same time, but in this case the counter was apparently knocked onto the box and after 10 seconds noticed and removed. Children, chimpanzees, and orangutans did not hesitate: they picked the deliberately marked box rather than the accidentally marked one, even on the first trial. Indeed, over time, they became slightly more likely to open the accidentally marked box—perhaps because the oddity of making regular accidents prompted further exploration.

In using language, we routinely take account of the prior knowledge of our audience. Great apes share something of this ability. Chimpanzees will give warning calls if they see a predator (actually a veterinarian with a dart gun) approach a close ally; however, they distinguish between cases when their ally is unable to see the predator, when they call zealously, and when the ally is well able to see the predator, in which case the observer often remains silent (Boysen, 1998). This distinction is based on understanding that an individual that can see a risk must therefore know about it and is evidently fundamental to real communication, in which audience knowledge is taken into account. However, monkeys in the same experimental situation make no such distinction, calling as avidly in either case (Cheney & Seyfarth, 1990a).

That great apes, but not monkeys, can sometimes evaluate the intentions and knowledge of others is consistent with the findings on observational records of deception. As noted, most records of deception could be explained as a product of very rapid associative learning by individuals who may not be able to assess others' knowledge: as functional but not necessarily intentional deception. However, a subset of records could not plausibly be understood this way and instead implied the ability to understand other-person knowledge (Byrne & Whiten, 1991). These records were not distributed at random, or in rough proportion to the number of cases from each species, but were tightly clumped in one taxonomic group: the great apes (Byrne & Whiten, 1992). They come from gorillas, bonobos, and orangutans, as well as chimpanzees; therefore, this seems to be an aptitude general in great apes.

The implication is that an individual of the common ancestor species at 12M already had some appreciation of how behavior affects the physical world, how familiar actions can be organized into more novel and sometimes complex plans, and the knowledge and intentions of other individuals, in so far as they differ from its own. This qualitative increase in understanding 'how things work' is not associated with any further enlargement of relative neocortex or brain volume (Byrne, 1996). However, because the great apes are indeed large animals, their brains are absolutely larger than those of any monkeys, so it is possible that causal understanding requires the brain volume to cross some threshold value. The alternative is presumably a representational reorganization, new "software" formats allowing more complex and even invisible parameters, such as intentions, to be computed.

To what environmental problem these cognitive skills were an adaptive solution is also unclear. Certainly, social complexity is not a strong candidate because the great apes do not show systematically more elaborate societies than monkeys. One possibility is that the problems of food acquisition favored individuals with the most cost-effective techniques (Byrne, 1997b). This is plausible because great apes are heavy animals, yet because they are adapted to hanging in tree canopies, their locomotion on the ground is energetically less efficient than that of monkeys; furthermore, throughout their range, they must compete for food with monkey species that have the guts able to deal with less ripe fruit and less tender leaves. Clearly, great apes must have some compensatory advantage, and the suggestion is that this is given by skilled food preparation, itself enabled by their ability to build up complex structures of behavior. Alternative theories have stressed instead the challenge of locomotion in the three-dimensional space of fragile vines and often rotten branches (Povinelli & Cant, 1995) or the skills needed to construct night nests (Fruth & Hohmann, 1996) as possible adaptive causes of the cognitive advances found in the great apes.

THE LAST COMMON ANCESTORS: 4.5M

Our closest relatives are the two species of chimpanzee; based on the best current estimates from molecular taxonomy (Waddell & Penny, 1996), their ancestors split from ours only 4.5M, little earlier than the earliest fossils identified as hominids (i.e., ancestors only of ourselves), those of *Ardipithecus ramidus*. Unfortunately, reconstruction of the psychology of this last common ancestor species is particularly difficult. The two chimpanzee species themselves shared ancestry until much more recently, about 1M, yet now they differ in many ways (de Waal, 1997). Common chimpanzees are routine toolmakers with elaborate social customs of tool use and effective group hunters of relatively large prey, living in loose communities somewhat dominated by coalitions of males and with occasional infanticide and intercommunity lethal aggression. Bonobos show none of these traits but instead live in more cohesive groups in which nonreproductive sex (found in a variety of different patterns in all great apes) seems to dominate social bonding, and females play a much more equal role in group activities. For every character where there is such a difference, the state of the common ancestor at 1M is indeterminate; this makes it very difficult to use evolutionary reconstruction to decide on the nature of our common ancestor at 4.5M. In particular, tool manufacturing and coordinated group hunting are traits long held crucial in human ancestry, so it is most frustrating not to know if their parallel development in common chimpanzees was by convergence or descent from a hunting and toolmaking ancestor. Furthermore, one captive bonobo (named Kanzi) has proved able to achieve remarkable linguistic success, given an enriched but essentially normal human upbringing and the use of a board of word icons with which to express himself (Savage-Rumbaugh & Lewin, 1994). (Chimpanzees lack the breath control, lip and tongue control, and to some extent larynx configuration to speak.) Kanzi can understand spoken English at normal speech rates, reliably identifying words on the basis of single phoneme differences, and can use complex syntax such as embedded relative clauses to decipher meaning (Savage-Rumbaugh et al., 1993; Savage-Rumbaugh, Williams, Furuichi, & Kano, 1996; Savage-Rumbaugh, Shanker, & Taylor, 1998). This performance can be demonstrated under controlled testing, with novel, or even absurd, sentences. His production lags far behind but nevertheless serves to convey a rich range of meanings in an organized way. The fact that such a degree of language comprehension can be developed in a chimpanzee raises the possibility that language itself is not a genetically programmed adaptation but a program that is learned by each child under normal human rearing (Byrne, 1995; Lock, 1980; Savage-Rumbaugh et al., 1998). Whether or not Kanzi's remarkable skills will prove special to bonobos, or to the naturalistic regime of rearing he has experienced, is not yet known, nor are any comparable skills established for bonobos in the wild. However, these are the least well studied and rarest great apes, and the future may change many of our current beliefs about them. At present, we cannot reliably attribute any greater cognitive skills to our ancestors of 4.5M than those of

12M, but the chimpanzee-human clade may well prove to show unique cognitive adaptations of some sort.

BUILDING THE COMPOSITE PICTURE

To translate, from the series of partially reconstructed ancestors to the historical path of our ancestry before we branched off from any living relative, requires two caveats. First, it must be remembered that changes from one form to the other were not progressive improvements toward an eventual human ideal. Evolution by natural selection does not work that way (Dawkins, 1986); it merely tends to ensure that species that survive are optimized for exploiting current environments (optimized locally, not globally and ideally, given the extent of variation available in past generations). Second, evolutionary reconstruction is a good deal more ambiguous about why changes occurred than what did occur. Correlational evidence can be used to evaluate plausible speculations, but as with any history we may never know for sure what caused a change.

Although our stock before 50M was typically mammal-like, these earliest primate ancestors should not be underestimated. With binocular vision and dextrous, five-fingered hands they would likely have been investigative animals and would certainly have quickly learned to use environmental correlates to maximize feeding efficiency and survival (classical conditioning). The results of their exploration would similarly have guided their future actions (instrumental conditioning), and to the limited extent that they were social their exploration and learning would have benefitted from a focus narrowed to the essentials by the experience of others (stimulus enhancement). Biological predispositions to learn would additionally have guided these generalized mechanisms of learning, making it easier to learn events important for survival. Although a rather unspecialized mammal, our ancestral population was even at this date adapted for survival by flexibility, not surprisingly, perhaps, when one considers that it was little different from the mammals that competed alongside the dinosaurs for tens of millions of years, and then survived the Cretaceous-Tertiary extinction event at 65M (caused by the effects of a meteorite impact in what is now the Caribbean, perhaps compounded by volcanism in the Indian Deccan).

The lineage that gave rise to monkeys and apes had by 30M developed traits that today are closely associated with living in long-lasting groups. These include complex sociality based on social knowledge, an extensive network of social relationships kept in place by demonstrations of commitment, manipulative social behavior that enables an individual to profit without unduly disrupting group living, and relatively large brain size resulting chiefly from neocortex enlargement. The humanness of this simian picture must not blind one to the fact that long-lasting group living is costly to individuals; members of the same species are the closest competitors for food that an individual faces, and the only competitors for mates. Presumably, there was a good environmental reason for the trend to greater sociality, and the pattern of group living in modern primates suggests that avoidance of predation is the major benefit (van Schaik, 1983). A few modern monkey species—and some of our hominid ancestors—faced a particular challenge of terrestrial predators on African savannahs, but the prevalence of group living among all monkey and ape groups suggest an earlier, forest origin to complex sociality (Dunbar, 1988). The nocturnal existence of the earliest primates had by this time given way to diurnal and arboreal living; an arboreal primate in daytime is conspicuous, inevitably increasing predation risk and the benefit of group living. The psychological skills of these simian ancestors would have seemed oddly concentrated in the social domain, as in the case of modern monkeys (though sheer speed of learning is enhanced in other contexts), and not associated with any deep understanding of the causes of other individuals' behavior, even in the social domain. The implication for human origins is that in human evolution complex sociality predated the ability to understand other people as causal agents with independent minds.

Only the great apes, including ourselves, have developed these latter skills, whose origin therefore appears to be before 12M. This ancestor population was again of forest-living individuals, adapted to forage delicately by hanging, despite their considerable bulk, but correspondingly less able to travel efficiently on the ground. They would have possessed a much more general ability to understand causality, both physical (how actions achieve changes to objects) and mental (how varying intentions and knowledge affect individuals' behavior). There is no sign that this species was any more social than its ancestors of 25M; therefore, the enhanced understanding of mechanism seems unlikely to have a social origin. A possible alternative is that, in the face of severe feeding competition from monkeys, the surviving great apes were those able to bring to bear enhanced manual skills by acquiring complex and efficacious techniques for food processing. This package of abilities included organizing structures of actions hierarchically into novel programs, understanding and hence copying aspects of the skilled behavior of others, and seeing how actions achieve their effects. On this thesis, which remains controversial at present, the understanding of other minds was secondarily derived from an understanding of a rather more visible behavioral causality. In addition, some of the descendants of this population, notably one species of chimpanzee and humans, have shown considerable abilities at toolmaking, elaborate traditions of tool use, and some degree of coordinated hunting. Whether these are derived traits of the most recent common ancestor at 4.5M, or simply within the potential of any great ape and elicited by particular ecological circumstances, is not yet known.

In any case, the last common ancestor at 4.5M was equipped with a number of cognitive aptitudes that form the bedrock of later, distinctively human adaptations. These apes were already large-brained and able to keep track of extensive and complex social relationships; quick to learn and able to exploit other individuals in ways sufficiently complex as to be labeled political and Machiavellian; able to understand how actions change objects in the world, and how their own and others' actions can be organized into hierarchical programs to achieve novel goals; and that other individuals sometimes have knowledge and goals different from their own. Animals like this would be able to see the purpose of true communication, in which speaker and hearer try to model the other's knowledge, and would be able to build up hierarchically embedded structures of action that are so crucial to human language. This is to say that the legacy of great ape cognition is peculiarly suitable for the development of language.

REFERENCES

Beck, B. B. (1980). *Animal tool behavior.* New York: Garland Press.

Boesch, C., & Boesch, H. (1990). Tool use and tool making in wild chimpanzees. *Folia Primatologica, 54,* 86–99.

Boysen, S. T. (1998, August). *Attribution processes in chimpanzees. Heresy, hearsay or heuristic?* Paper presented at the XVIIth Congress of the International Primatological Society, University of Antananarivo, Madagascar.

Byrne, R. W. (1993). Do larger brains mean greater intelligence? *Behavioural and Brain Sciences, 16,* 696–697.

Byrne, R. W. (1995). *The thinking ape: Evolutionary origins of intelligence.* Oxford: Oxford University Press.

Byrne, R. W. (1996). Relating brain size to intelligence in primates. In P. A. Mellars & K. R. Gibson (Eds.), *Modelling the early human mind* (pp. 49–56). Cambridge, England: Macdonald Institute for Archaeological Research.

Byrne, R. W. (1997a). Machiavellian intelligence. *Evolutionary Anthropology, 5,* 172–180.

Byrne, R. W. (1997b). The technical intelligence hypothesis: An additional evolutionary stimulus to intelligence? In A. Whiten & R. W. Byrne (Eds.), *Machiavellian intelligence II: Extensions and evaluations* (pp. 289–311). Cambridge: Cambridge University Press.

Byrne, R. W. (1997c). What's the use of anecdotes? Attempts to distinguish psychological mechanisms in primate tactical deception. In R. W. Mitchell, N. S. Thompson, & L. Miles (Eds.), *Anthropomorphism, anecdotes, and animals: The emperor's new clothes?* (pp. 134–150). New York: SUNY Press.

Byrne, R. W. (1999). Cognition in great ape ecology. Skill-learning ability opens up foraging opportunities. *Symposia of the Zoological Society of London, 72,* 333–350.

Byrne, R. W., & Byrne, J. M. E. (1991). Hand preferences in the skilled gathering tasks of mountain gorillas (*Gorilla g. beringei*). *Cortex, 27,* 521–546.

Byrne, R. W., & Byrne, J. M. E. (1993). Complex leaf-gathering skills of mountain gorillas (*Gorilla g. beringei*): Variability and standardization. *American Journal of Primatology, 31,* 241–261.

Byrne, R. W., & Russon, A. E. (1998). Learning by imitation: A hierarchical approach. *Behavioral and Brain Sciences, 21,* 667–721.

Byrne, R. W., & Whiten, A. (1988). *Machiavellian intelligence: Social expertise and the evolution of intellect in monkeys, apes and humans.* Oxford, UK: Clarendon Press.

Byrne, R. W., & Whiten, A. (1990). Tactical deception in primates: the 1990 data-base. *Primate Report, 27*, 1–101.

Byrne, R. W., & Whiten, A. (1991). Computation and mindreading in primate tactical deception. In A. Whiten (Ed.), *Natural theories of mind* (pp. 127–141). Oxford, England: Basil Blackwell.

Byrne, R. W., & Whiten, A. W. (1992). Cognitive evolution in primates: Evidence from tactical deception. *Man, 27*, 609–627.

Byrne, R. W., & Whiten, A. (1997). Machiavellian intelligence. In A. Whiten & R. W. Byrne (Eds.), *Machiavellian intelligence II: Extensions and evaluations* (pp. 1–23). Cambridge: Cambridge University Press.

Call, J., & Tomasello, M. (1998). Distinguishing intentional from accidental actions in orangutans (*Pongo pygmaeus*), chimpanzees (*Pan troglodytes*), and human children (*Homo sapiens*). *Journal of Comparative Psychology, 112*, 192–206.

Chapais, B. (1992). The role of alliances in social inheritance of rank among female primates. In A. H. Harcourt & F. B. M. de Waal (Eds.), *Coalitions and alliances in humans and other primates* (pp. 29–59). Oxford: Oxford University Press.

Cheney, D. L., & Seyfarth, R. M. (1988). Social and non-social knowledge in vervet monkeys. In R. W. Byrne & A. Whiten (Eds.), *Machiavellian intelligence: Social expertise and the evolution of intellect in monkeys, apes and humans* (pp. 255–270). Oxford, UK: Clarendon Press.

Cheney, D. L., & Seyfarth, R. M. (1990a). Attending to behavior versus attending to knowledge: examining monkeys' attribution of mental states. *Animal Behavior, 40*, 742–753.

Cheney, D. L., & Seyfarth, R. M. (1990b). *How monkeys see the world: Inside the mind of another species*. Chicago: University of Chicago Press.

Cords, M. (1997). Friendships, alliances, reciprocity and repair. In A. Whiten & R. W. Byrne (Eds.), *Machiavellian intelligence II: Extensions and evaluations* (pp. 24–49). Cambridge: Cambridge University Press.

Dawkins, R. (1986). *The blind watchmaker*. London: Longman.

de Waal, F., & van Roosmalen, A. (1979). Reconciliation and consolation among chimpanzees. *Behavioral Ecology and Sociobiology, 5*, 55–56.

de Waal, F. B. M. (1989). *Peacemaking among primates*. Cambridge, MA: Harvard University Press.

de Waal, F. B. M. (1997). *Bonobo: The forgotten ape*. Berkeley: University of California Press.

Dunbar, R. I. M. (1988). *Primate social systems*. London: Croom Helm.

Dunbar, R. I. M. (1991). Functional significance of social grooming in primates. *Folia Primatology, 57*, 121–131.

Dunbar, R. I. M. (1992). Neocortex size as a constraint on group size in primates. *Journal of Human Evolution, 20*, 469–493.

Fox, E., Sitompul, A., & Van Schaik, C. P. (1999). Intelligent tool use in wild Sumatran orangutans. In S. T. Parker, H. L. Miles, & R. W. Mitchell (Eds.), *The mentality of gorillas and orangutans* (99–116). Cambridge: Cambridge University Press.

Fruth, B., & Hohmann, G. (1996). Nest building behavior in the great apes. In W. C. McGrew, L. F. Marchant, & T. Nishida (Eds.), *Great ape societies* (pp. 225–240). Cambridge: Cambridge University Press.

Goodall, J. (1964). Tool-using and aimed throwing in a community of free-living chimpanzees. *Nature, 201*, 1264–1266.

Goodall, J. (1986). *The chimpanzees of Gombe: Patterns of behavior*. Cambridge, MA: Harvard University Press.

Goodall, J., Bandora, A., Bergmann, E., Busse, C., Matama, H., Mpongo, E., Pierce, A., & Riss, D. (1979). Intercommunity interactions in the chimpanzee population of the Gombe National Park. In D. Hamburg & E. R. McCown (Eds.), *The great apes* (pp. 13–54). Menlo Park, CA: Benjamin Cummings.

Harcourt, A. (1988). Alliances in contests and social intelligence. In R. W. Byrne & A. Whiten (Eds.), *Machiavellian intelligence: Social expertise and the evolution of intellect in monkeys, apes and humans* (pp. 132–152). Oxford, UK: Clarendon Press.

Hauser, M. D., & Marler, P. (1993). Food-associated calls in rhesus macaques (*Macaca mulatta*): II. Costs and benefits of call production and suppression. *Behavioral Ecology, 4,* 206–212.

Hennig, W. (1966). *Phylogenetic systematics.* Urbana: Illinois Press.

Humphrey, N. K. (1976). The social function of intellect. In P. P. G. Bateson & R. A. Hinde (Eds.), *Growing points in ethology* (pp. 303–317). Cambridge: Cambridge University Press.

Jerison, H. J. (1973). *Evolution of the brain and intelligence.* New York: Academic Press.

Lock, A. (1980). *The guided reinvention of language.* London: Academic Press.

Mackintosh, N. J. (1983). General principles of learning. In T. R. Halliday & P. J. B. Slater (Eds.), *Animal behavior, volume 3: Genes, development and learning* (pp. 149–177). Oxford, England: Blackwell Scientific Publications.

Mason, W. A., & Hollis, J. H. (1962). Communication between young rhesus monkeys. *Animal Behavior, 10,* 211–221.

McGrew, W. C. (1992). *Chimpanzee material culture: Implications for human evolution.* Cambridge: Cambridge University Press.

McGrew, W. C. (1998). Culture in non-human primates? *Annual Review of Anthropology, 27,* 301–328.

Nishida, T. (1986). Local traditions and cultural transmission. In B. B. Smuts, D. L. Cheney, R. M. Seyfarth, R. W. Wrangham, & T. T. Struhsaker (Eds.), *Primate Societies* (pp. 462–474). Chicago: University of Chicago Press.

Passingham, R. E. (1981). Primate specializations in brain and intelligence. *Symposia of the Zoological Society of London, 46,* 361–388.

Povinelli, D. J., & Cant, J. G. H. (1995). Arboreal clambering and the evolution of self-conception. *Quarterly Journal of Biology, 70,* 393–421.

Povinelli, D. J., Nelson, K. E., & Boysen, S. T. (1992). Comprehension of role reversal in chimpanzees: Evidence of empathy? *Animal Behavior, 43,* 633–640.

Povinelli, D. J., Parks, K. A., & Novak, M. A. (1992). Role reversal by rhesus monkeys, but no evidence of empathy. *Animal Behavior, 44,* 269–281.

Ridley, M. (1986). *Evolution and classification: The reformation of cladism.* London: Longman.

Ridley, M. (1993). *Evolution.* Oxford, England: Blackwell Scientific Publications.

Roper, T. J. (1983). Learning as a biological phenomenon. In T. R. Halliday & P. J. B. Slater (Eds.), *Animal behavior, volume 3: Genes, development and learning* (pp. 178–212). Oxford, England: Blackwell Scientific Publications.

Rozin, P. (1976). The evolution of intelligence and access to the cognitive unconscious. In J. M. Sprague & A. N. Epstein (Eds.), *Progress in psychobiology and physiological psychology* (pp. 245–277). New York: Academic Press.

Savage-Rumbaugh, E. S., Murphy, J., Sevcik, R. A., Brakke, K. E., Williams, S. L., & Rumbaugh, D. M. (1993). Language comprehension in ape and child. *Monographs of the Society for Research in Child Development, 58,* 1–252.

Savage-Rumbaugh, E. S., Williams, S. L., Furuichi, T., & Kano, T. (1996). Language perceived: *Paniscus* branches out. In W. C. McGrew, L. F. Marchant, & T. Nishida (Eds.), *Great ape societies* (pp. 173–184). Cambridge: Cambridge University Press.

Savage-Rumbaugh, S., & Lewin, R. (1994). *Kanzi. The ape at the brink of the human mind.* New York: John Wiley.

Savage-Rumbaugh, S., Shanker, S. G., & Taylor, T. J. (1998). *Apes, language and the human mind.* New York: Oxford University Press.

Simons, E. L. (1972). *Primate evolution.* New York: Macmillan.

Smith, H. J., Newman, J. D., & Symmes, D. (1982). Vocal concomitants of affiliative behavior in squirrel monkeys. In C. T. Snowdon, C. H. Brown, & M. R. Petersen (Eds.), *Primate communication* (pp. 30–49). Cambridge: Cambridge University Press.

Smuts, B. B. (1985). *Sex and friendship in baboons*. New York: Aldine Hawthorn.

Tooby, J., & Cosmides, L. (1992). The psychological foundations of culture. In J. H. Barkow, L. Cosmides, & J. Tooby (Eds.), *The adapted mind* (pp. 19–136). New York: Oxford University Press.

van Schaik, C. P. (1983). Why are diurnal primates living in groups? *Behavior, 87,* 120–147.

Visalberghi, E., & Trinca, L. (1987). Tool use in capuchin monkeys: Distinguishing between performing and understanding. *Primates, 30,* 511–521.

Waddell, P. J., & Penny, D. (1996). Evolutionary trees of apes and humans from DNA sequences. In A. J. Lock & C. R. Peters (Eds.), *Handbook of Symbolic Evolution* (pp. 53–73). Oxford, UK: Clarendon Press.

Warren, J. M. (1973). Learning in vertebrates. In D. A. Dewsbury & D. A. Rethlingshafer (Eds.), *Comparative psychology: A modern survey* (pp. 471–509). New York: McGraw-Hill.

Westergaard, C. G., & Fragaszy, D. (1987). The manufacture and use of tools by capuchin monkeys (*Cebus apella*). *Journal of Comparative Psychology, 101,* 159–168.

6

Pumping Up Intelligence: Abrupt Climate Jumps and the Evolution of Higher Intellectual Functions During the Ice Ages

William H. Calvin
University of Washington

The title is not a metaphor, although past tense might be better as this chapter is about how each of the many hundred abrupt coolings of the last several million years could have served as a pump stroke, each elevating intelligence a small increment—even though natural selection was not operating on intelligence per se.

Although we often use the term *intelligence* to encompass both a broad range of abilities and the efficiency with which they are enacted, it also implies flexibility and creativity, an "ability to slip the bonds of instinct and generate novel solutions to problems" (Gould & Gould, 1994, p. 70). Those three pillars of animal intelligence—association, imitation, and insight—are also impressive (Byrne, 1994), as are the occasional symbolic (Deacon, 1997) and reasoning (Gould & Gould, 1998) abilities. But Piaget (1929, 1952) said that intelligence is what you use when you don't know what to do, when neither innateness nor learning has prepared you for the particular situation.

97

Intelligence is improvisational. Still, most of the time, not much improvisation is necessary; the individual has encountered somewhat similar situations before, has a repertoire of actions, and simply starts one and gropes, using feedback's progress reports to guide to the goal. No major planning is needed in most cases, and thus not much in the way of intellectual wherewithal. This suggests a focus on those few behaviors that require an elaborate multistage plan prepared during "get set." An example would be the ballistic movements (hammering, clubbing, throwing, kicking, spitting) where the speed of feedback is so inadequate (they are often over and done by the time that progress reports can start modifying the movement), where only near-perfect plans will succeed.

What the mind is often seeking during "get set," I suspect, is *coherence*—finding a conceptual combination of sensory input, memories, and movement plans that fit together particularly well—though, because of novelty, most will rate less than "the perfect ten" of exact, unambiguous fits. Similar to this is Barlow's (1987) suggestion that intelligence is all about making a guess that discovers some new underlying order. Guessing well neatly covers a lot of ground relevant to higher intellectual functions: finding the solution of a problem or the logic of an argument, happening upon an appropriate analogy, creating a pleasing harmony or witty reply, or guessing what is likely to happen next.

HIGHER INTELLECTUAL FUNCTIONS

Because they all involve pattern finding and all emphasize human abilities not widely shared with the other apes, this discussion is restricted to the higher intellectual functions. *Intelligence* is used as a term denoting the speed and scale of individual performance of them, not unlike the manner in which much of the variance of the general factor "g" can be accounted for (Jensen, 1992) by the subtests that emphasize speed of performance and the number of items that must be borne in mind simultaneously—as in those multiple choice analogies: A is to B as C is to D, E, or F, which require six concepts to be simultaneously managed. Closely related is our ability to remember phone numbers long enough to dial them. Many people can retain a seven-digit number for 5 to 10 seconds but will resort to writing it down if faced with an out-of-area number or an international one of even greater length. When getting close to your limit, you try to collapse several items into one chunk in order to make more room (Simon, 1983).

Definitions of *higher intellectual function* vary; I tend to use the phrase to refer to the structured mental abilities such as the following:

- *syntax*, the structuring schemes of phrases and clauses used to disambiguate sentences longer than a few words. For example, "I think I saw him leave to go home" has nested embedding involving four verbs. (Syntax is an evolutionary puzzle because there aren't obvious intermediate forms in development or aphasia between short structureless protolanguage sentences and recursive embedding.)

- *planning*, those speculative structured arrangements. For example, "Maybe we can go to the country this weekend if I get my work finished, but if I have to work Saturday, then maybe we can go to a movie on Sunday instead." (Squirrels hoarding nuts isn't planning but an innate behavior triggered by longer nights releasing more melatonin from the pineal. Holding an intention for a few hours isn't planning either and neither are foraging behaviors that could be explained more simply by choosing between familiar migration routes. Perhaps we should reserve the term for something that requires multiple stages of the move to be assembled in advance of action, rather than organizing the later stages after getting the initial moves in motion, which goal-plus-feedback can accomplish.)
- *chains of logic*, our prized rationality. But the emphasis here is on novel chains, not routine ones. The most mindless of behaviors may be segued, the completion of one calling forth the next: courtship behavior may be followed by intricate nest building, then a segue into egg laying, then incubation, then the stereotyped parental behaviors. (Köhler's chimps, that piled up boxes to reach the hanging banana, might qualify under the novel chaining requirement, if simpler explanations can be eliminated.)
- *games with arbitrary rules*, such as hopscotch. (Both *Pan* species, chimpanzees and bonobos, have a version of blind man's bluff, but it is not structured.)
- *music* of a structured sort, such as harmony and counterpuntual themes (perhaps not rhythm per se but certainly rhythms within rhythms).

Obviously, if one relaxes the nested-or-chained structural requirement, there are various primate behaviors that are possible evolutionary precursors. I am focusing here on structuring because humans exhibit such a large increment in ability over our *Pan* cousins across these five areas—and because I am interested in whether or not there is a common core of neural machinery that is shared by all such structured behaviors, one where improvements in any one of the five might improve the other four "for free."

Evolutionary arguments often commit the reification fallacy (a gene for intelligence). Indeed, we often assume that an abstraction like language implies a concrete entity such as a language module (separate, of course, from any planning module, thus creating a balkanization of the mind). Yes, there is localization of function—and we certainly tend to name a cortical area according to the first of its functions we discover—but multiple functions are commonplace (see chap. 6 of *Cerebral Code* (1996a) for a discussion of how a neocortical area could alternate between being a narrow specialist and performing as a general-purpose scratch board).

LANGUAGE IN THE MULTIPLE USE CONTEXT

Multiple uses of a structural entity are common, and a familiar example is the curb cut where the steplike curb is locally smoothed into a gentle ramp. What paid for curb cuts was, of course, wheelchair requirements. But as soon as a curb cut is in place, 99% of its traffic is for secondary uses such as bicycles, suitcases, baby carriages, and grocery carts—none of which would have paid for it.

A secondary free use may, of course, later pay for further improvements (just imagine the skateboarders holding a bake sale to pay for widening), suggesting that the evolutionary history of higher intellectual function might first emphasize one structured use and later others. If the notion of a free lunch offends, note that it is commonly assumed that music is a spare-time use of the language-related parts of the brain, that there was likely little natural selection for four-part harmony via barbershop quartets.

Language is the most defining feature of human intelligence: without the orderly arrangement of verbal ideas permitted by syntax, humans might be little more clever than *Pan*. For a glimpse of life without syntax, consider the Sacks (1989) description of Joseph, an 11-year-old boy who was deaf. Because he could not hear spoken language and had never been exposed to fluent sign language, Joseph did not have the opportunity to learn syntax during the critical years of early childhood:

> Joseph saw, distinguished, categorized, used; he had no problems with perceptual categorization or generalization, but he could not, it seemed, go much beyond this, hold abstract ideas in mind, reflect, play, plan. He seemed completely literal—unable to juggle images or hypotheses or possibilities, unable to enter an imaginative or figurative realm.... He seemed, like an animal, or an infant, to be stuck in the present, to be confined to literal and immediate perception, though made aware of this by a consciousness that no infant could have. (p. 40)

Language cortex isn't just the traditional Broca and Wernicke areas but much of the lateral aspects of the temporal and frontal lobes, plus the parietal lobe areas near the left sylvian fissure (see, e.g., Ojemann, 1991). Language localizations have a strong overlap with nonlanguage sequential functions, such as sound strings and hand-arm sequencing (most aphasics have some form of hand-arm apraxia; see Kimura, 1993).

And this overlap brings an important point: the use that initially paid for the structuring abilities seen in the higher intellectual functions need not be any one of them. The original wheelchair analog could, for example, be the structured planning needed for some nonintellectual function, such as the ballistic hand-arm movements used for hammering, clubbing, and throwing.

Throwing is a particularly interesting possibility because targets are located at many different distances and elevations, making each hunting throw a novel situation, quite unlike the more stereotyped dart throws and basketball free throws where long practice can "find the right groove." There is also a premium on being right the first time, as dinner is likely to flee if you miss.

Apes have elementary forms of the rapid arm movements that humans are experts with—hammering, clubbing, and throwing—and one can imagine hunting and toolmaking scenarios that, in some settings, were important additions to the basic hominid gathering and scavenging strategies. The evolutionary rewards for individuals having better-than-average projectile hunting skills could thus set the stage for free secondary uses, such as longer time scale planning, logical trains of thought, and perhaps even music and syntax. Some of these, once they had a chance to show their stuff, are exposed enough to natural selection to pay for further improvements—and thus improve throwing accuracy, *pari passu* (Calvin, 1983, 1993, 1996b).

FINDING THE RIGHT LEVEL

Although it seems to have played little role so far in our modern concepts of intelligence, the concept of *levels of organization* is a common one in the sciences. Much of guessing well involves finding the right level at which to address a problem, neither too literal nor too abstract—or, sometimes, inventing a new level on the fly.

Levels are best defined by certain functional properties (Calvin & Bickerton, 2000), not anatomy. As an example of four levels, fleece is organized into yarn, which is woven into cloth, which can be arranged into clothing. Each of these levels of organization is transiently stable, with ratchetlike mechanisms that prevent backsliding: Fabrics are woven, to prevent their disorganization into so much yarn; yarn is spun, to keep it from backsliding into fleece.

A proper level is also characterized by causal decoupling from adjacent levels (Pagels, 1988); it's a study unto itself. For example, you can weave without understanding how to spin yarn (or make clothing). Chemical bonds illustrate a proper level: Mendeleyev discovered the patterns of the table of elements and thereby predicted the weights and binding properties of undiscovered elements, without knowing anything about the underlying patterns of electron shells (or the overlying patterns of stereochemistry).

Mental life can pyramid a number of levels, thereby creating structure. Some of the major tasks of early childhood involve discovering four levels of organization in the apparent chaos of the surrounding environment:

- Infants discover phonemes and create standard categories for them; 6-month-old Japanese infants can still tell the difference between the English /l/ and /r/ sounds but after another 6 months of regular exposure to the Japanese phoneme, the babies will treat the occasional English sounds as mere imperfect versions of the Japanese phoneme (Kuhl, Williams, Lacerda, Stevens, & Lindblom, 1992) and thus be set up for later confusing the English words *rice* and *lice*.
- With a set of basic speech sounds, babies start discovering longer duration patterns amid strings of phonemes, averaging nine new words every day during the preschool years.
- Between 18 and 36 months of age, children start to discover still longer patterns of words called phrases and clauses, learning rules such as add *-s* for plural and add *-ed* for past tense.
- After syntax, they go on to discover Aristotle's rule about narratives having a beginning, middle, and end (and they then demand bedtime stories with a proper ending).

Indeed, we find it very rewarding to discover half-hidden patterns all through life: that's the basis for the popularity of crossword and jigsaw puzzles, and it's why science is so much fun.

Pyramiding four levels in a mere 4 years is impressive. But levels can also be created spontaneously, as one seeks an analogy or makes a novel abstraction. To spend more time at the more abstract levels in this house of cards, the prior levels have to be sufficiently shored up to prevent backsliding over one's concentration span.

FROM STRATIFIED STABILITY TO DARWINISM

If there's no little person inside the head to stack up those higher stories of the house of cards, then what self-organizes a higher level? In the simpler physical systems, noise (as in diffusion) can provide the raw material for self-organizing structures (such as crystals). As Bronowski (1973) observed: "The stable units that compose one level or stratum are the raw material for random encounters which produce higher configurations, some of which will chance to be stable." (p. 348). If there is an organizational principle in the universe that is even more elementary than Darwin's, it is Bronowski's.

But, as Darwin first realized, competitions between stable alternatives can improve the results, providing a quality bootstrap under certain conditions. Not all of what is loosely called "Darwinian" qualifies, however, because many pruning processes do not have a result that copies and competes. As I have discussed elsewhere (Calvin, 1996a, 1997), there appear to be six essential features of a recursive Darwinian process:

- It involves a *pattern*. Classically, this is a string of DNA bases called a gene, but the pattern could be a melody or the brain activity associated with a thought.
- *Copies* are somehow made of this pattern, as when cells divide or one whistles an overheard tune. Indeed, the unit pattern is defined by what is semi-reliably copied (e.g., the gene's DNA sequence is semi-reliably copied while whole chromosomes or organisms usually are not).
- Patterns occasionally *change*. Point mutations from cosmic rays may be the best known alterations, but far more common are copying errors and (as in meiosis) "shuffling the deck."
- Copying *competitions* occur for occupation of a limited environmental space. For example, several variant patterns called bluegrass and crabgrass compete for my backyard.
- The relative success of the variants is influenced by a *multifaceted environment*. For grass, it's the nutrients, water, sunshine, how often it's cut, and so forth. We sometimes say that the environment selects or that there is selective reproduction or selective survival. Darwin called this biasing *natural selection*.
- The next generation is based on which variants survive to reproductive age and successfully find mates. The high mortality among juveniles makes their environment much more important than that of adults. This means that the surviving variants place their own reproductive bets from a shifted base, rather than the original center of variants at conception (this is what Darwin called an *inheritance principle*). In this next generation, a spread around the currently successful is again created. Many new variants will be worse than the parental average, but some may be even better fitted to the environment's collection of features.

From all this, one gets that surprising Darwinian drift toward patterns that almost seem designed for their environment. In the cardboard version of Darwinian, particular parts such as natural selection are often confused with the entire Darwinian process, but no one essential by itself will suffice. Without all six essentials, the process will shortly grind to a halt.

For example, neural patterning in development (all of that culling of cells and synapses) is an example of a sparse case: just a pattern carved by a multifaceted environment. There is no replication of the pattern, no variation, no population of the pattern to compete with a variant's population, and there's nothing recursive about achieving quality because there's no inheritance principle. It's very useful but it's not a quality bootstrap.

MAKING DARWINISM FAST ENOUGH

Speed is of the essence in behavior, however, and one might reasonably worry about whether or not a neocortical version of the Darwinian process can operate quickly enough to provide an answer within the windows of opportunity afforded by either hunting or social repartee. There are at least four catalysts that can greatly speed up evolutionary processes:

- *Systematic recombination* (crossing over, sex) generates many more variants than do copying errors and the much rarer point mutations. There's also nonsystematic recombination, such as bacterial conjugation or the conflation of ideas.
- *Fluctuating environments* (seasons, climate changes, diseases) change the name of the game, shaping up more complex patterns capable of doing well in several environments. For such jack-of-all-trades selection to occur, the climate must change much faster than efficiency adaptations can track it.
- *Parcellation* (as when rising sea level converts the hilltops of one large island into an archipelago of small islands) typically speeds evolution. It raises the surface-to-volume ratio (or perimeter-to-area ratio) and exposes a higher percentage of the population to the marginal conditions on the margins.
- Local extinctions (as when an island population becomes too small to sustain itself) speed evolution because they create *empty niches*. The pioneers that rediscover the niche get a series of generations with no competition and with enough resources even for the odder variants that would never grow up to reproduce under any competition. For a novel pattern, that could represent the chance to establish itself before the next climate change, for which it might prove better suited than the others.

There are also catalysts acting at several removes, as in Darwin's example of how the introduction of cats to an English village could improve the clover in the surrounding countryside: The cats would eat the mice that attack the bumble bee nests and, thereby, allow more flowers to be cross-pollinated. Although a Darwinian process will run without these catalysts, using Darwinian creativity often requires some optimization for speed.

Explaining how neocortical circuitry can implement the six essentials and the four catalysts on a milliseconds-to-minutes time scale, thereby facilitating intelligent "get set" groping, lies beyond the scope of this article (see Calvin, 1996a, 1998b). However, these ten facets of a rapid evolutionary process will be useful in considering how we got our big brains so quickly (2.5 million years is quick). What sped up the slow biological evolution of the rapid neural evolutionary machinery underlying the higher intellectual functions?

HOMINID EVOLUTION AND THE ICE AGES

The earliest known changes in hominids, seen soon after the australopithecines diverged from the other *Pan* cousins approximately 5 million years ago, were rearrangements of hips and knees for upright posture. Brain size (an admittedly inadequate indicator of functional capacities) didn't change very much, remaining in the great ape ballpark. But a number of interesting things all started to happen between 3 and 2 million years ago.

- The archaeologists have traced stone tools back that far: the simplest types, the split pebbles, which make such good cutting edges for getting through animal hides, go back to approximately 2.5 million years, with much more elaborate ones developing by 1.5 million years ago. Although various mammals use found objects for tasks such as opening shells, simple toolmaking (shatter a rock and select the sharp edges) seems to have been on the rise by 2.5 million years ago.
- The onset of the ice ages has been moved back to about the same time by the paleoclimatologists. Since then, ice sheets have slowly built up. They melt off somewhat more quickly (the rise in sea level takes about 8,000 years) and remain at a minimum for another similar period. The major meltoffs occurred approximately every 40,000 years—until about 0.7 million years ago, when a 100,000-year cycle became more prominent. It isn't clear what temperature has to do with African-based hominid evolution, as the average temperatures there only drop about 5°C during the colder periods, enough to create some glaciers on the equatorial volcanos but hardly enough to create a wintertime for animals living in the Rift Valley. All of the ice sheets that formed at higher latitudes were surely unseen by our African ancestors. The drought that came with coolings surely affected Africa, however.
- And brain size finally starts to change approximately 2.4 million years ago as the australopithecine lineage split off a distinctive *Homo* lineage with increased cranial capacity, and it kept increasing in size; nothing of the kind is known for other animals. Many animal lineages also split between 3 and 2 million years ago: chimp-bonobo, gibbon-siamang, mastodon-ele-

phant (accelerated speciation is best studied, however, in the antelope and pig lineages).

What do these three things have to do with one another, or with intelligence? Cause and effect? Or merely three independent trains set in motion by the major rearrangement of ocean currents and climate that followed the damning up of the Old Panama Canal about 3 million years ago, when North and South American finally joined together and forced the equatorial currents that equilibrated the Atlantic and Pacific Oceans into a long detour around the southern continents?

THE MARK TWAIN TRANSITION TIME PRINCIPLE

The writer Mark Twain once observed that "A round man cannot be expected to fit into a square hole right away. He must have time to modify his shape." Evolution can often track climate changes, selecting for variants with more or less body insulation. Indeed, up until a decade ago, we thought that the ice ages were glacially slow, that slow changes in the earth's orbit caused gradual cooling, which caused more ice to gradually form and sea level to gradually lower. No animal lived long enough to realize that climate changes were happening because the change during the lifetime of any one generation was so minuscule.

What happens if the climate changes abruptly, so that adaptations over the generations cannot track it and the habitat is largely disrupted (no more customary plants or prey, a different setting for reproduction, etc.) all within one generation's time on earth?

There is a general answer to this (Calvin, 1996b) and a much more specific one. The general answer is that the circumstance provides a selective pressure for versatility, one that counters the usual lean-mean-machine tendencies that reduce unneeded anatomy and behavior in the name of efficiency. Evolutionary theory suggests a tendency towards the latter if the environment remains the same for long enough. But when the habitat changes so drastically in such short a time, only reserve capacity in behavior can solve the problems. Lean mean machines don't survive the downsizings very well. The more versatile may have what it takes.

The more specific answer, however, is grass.

Abrupt Climate Change

Inferring ancient climates can be done from layers of sediments that accumulate in lake and ocean floors. From cores, one can study such proxy climate indicators as pollen types and oxygen isotope ratios, and how they change over time. But there's a problem: worms and bottom-scavenging fish stir the bottom, mixing together hundreds (if not thousands) of years of sediments. Like a moving average of a stock-market index, a smoothed record of paleoclimate can miss some dramatic fluctuations that made and lost fortunes.

When year-by-year high-resolution records became available from Greenland ice cores, where records like tree rings can be seen, we became aware that climate could—and frequently did—change quite rapidly. We now know that this is not merely a peculiarity of Greenland, that these were worldwide events in many cases. Unlike the high latitude ice sheets, these abrupt climate shifts affect the tropics as well.

Atop those glacially slow rhythms, abrupt coolings and warmings have often occurred. Abrupt means decade transition times; *often* means every few thousand years. These flips may last for centuries (or even 1,500 years) before flipping back, just as abruptly. Obviously, this is not the abrupt climate change that volcanos and Antarctic ice sheet collapse can cause; it's bistable. Ocean circulation seems to have several modes, and when it switches between modes, the abruptness of the transition profoundly affects ecosystems. In the tropics, average annual temperatures fall 3 to 5°C. In Europe, the decrease is 5 to 9°C, and some high latitude locations cool more than twice as much.

The magnitude of the temperature change isn't the big problem. It's how fast it occurs, Mark Twain's problem. If these coolings were to occur slowly, with temperature ramping down over 500 years, one might expect high altitude plants and animals to slowly move down the hillsides into the valleys below. Each generation of hominids could have continued to make a living in much the way their parents taught them, though their diet mix would shift over the centuries. But with major changes within a decade, other events supervene.

First comes drought (there is much less evaporation from tropical oceans, which also reduces a major greenhouse gas; water vapor). Then, similar to what we saw in the 1997 and 1998 El Niño, vast fires occur even in tropical forests. After that comes a succession of plants leading, over a few centuries, from grass to forests (of species better suited to the new annual temperature).

For many terrestrial species, this is a trial and, eventually, an opportunity. Because of vanishing resources, the habitat becomes patchy. There are refugia, where a somewhat traditional way of life can be maintained, but they don't support very many. These subpopulations inbreed because the resources are too scarce to support a journey to find another subpopulation, but they tend to mix during the downsizing itself, as stray individuals locate remaining subpopulations. Some subpopulations may form entirely from strays.

Thus an abrupt cooling is likely to provide three (recombination, climate stress, parcellation) of the catalysts that speed up evolutionary processes. The fourth, reexpanding into empty niches, may occur during an abrupt warming (which is accompanied by increased rainfall), where pioneers discover new territories of untapped resources and have many offspring survive, even the odder ones.

Why Us?

The foregoing is likely true for many mammalian species, not just our ancestors. The remaining great apes likely went through this cycle many times. What was special about hominids?

Eating grass indirectly as meat. The first few years after the great forest fires is a boom time for the remaining grazing animals, with all the grass and succulent shoots. But the waterholes are scarce, and thus whole herds bunch together to visit the remaining waterholes. They lose a few peripheral individuals to the predators that lay in wait there.

What was so special about hominid predators lingering around the waterholes? For one, upright posture. The grazing animals have innate search images for four-legged predators; they keep their distance. But bipeds can get much closer (as my colleague Arnold Towe notes, if you drop down on all fours, grazing animals move away promptly). Upright posture may, if efficient enough, allow hominids to run animals to exhaustion. But clearly, at some stage, projectile predation became a part of the picture (Calvin, 1993). Even something so simple as flinging a tree branch can be effective in the context of a tightly packed herd at a waterhole: the herd immediately starts to wheel around and flee, but the branch lands somewhere in their midst and trips an animal or two. Attempts to get back up are delayed by other animals stampeding past, and injuries will often occur. In any event, the hunters will often have time to run up to a downed animal before it can escape. Chimpanzees love to fling branches, and they also covet fresh meat, but they don't seem to have made the connection, perhaps because of lacking savannah waterholes frequented by herds. Following a cool-crash-and-burn downsizing, there are plenty of temporary savannahs.

GROWTH CURVES

Chattering between two climate states thus has the potential to speed up evolution, and cool, crash, and burn cycles provide some opportunities that our upright australopithecine ancestors might have exploited. What, however, makes this an important driver for hominid evolution and intelligence, as opposed to a bookshelf full of varied suggestions on what might have been behind it all?

Compared, say, with invention of the carrying bag? The basic idea of a carrying bag must have been very important for both gathering and for small-game hunting. But one cannot reinvent the carrying bag for extra credit. Some inventions can be repeated; for example, the aquatic mammals have all discovered that a small reduction in body hair buys them greater swimming efficiency. Another reduction buys them even more. No matter where along the growth curve they are, another increment has additional rewards. (There is, however, a limit: you can only become so naked.) Some growth curves are also steeper than others, faster at driving evolution than slower candidates (which might, like many on that bookshelf of plausible candidates, have done the job in the long run). So the steepness and extent of growth curves are important considerations in sorting out where our intelligence came from.

There are two aspects of the eat grass indirectly scenario that have long growth curves, and they involve things where we humans have considerably enhanced abilities over the great apes. They can also be pumped in one percent increments to produce many-fold improvements. That abstraction is not called intelligence but could be the wheelchairlike curb cut that gave higher intellectual functions their entry-level jobs.

COOPERATION AND GROUP SELECTION

The good-of-the-group-gene possibility was dismissed a few decades ago (see Sober & Wilson, 1998) on the theoretical grounds that it would, like a leaking tire, backslide. Even if somehow concentrated into a subpopulation yielding a majority of cooperators, you'd still expect that tendencies to share could be swamped by all the nonreciprocating freeloaders, who would out-reproduce the sharers.

If this were the prime consideration, of course, we would also have to conclude that car tires would never work because they all, sooner or later, go flat. We just pump them back up occasionally, and the cool-crash-and-burn cycle suggests both a concentration mechanism and a pump that might allow widespread cooperation to become established for long enough to invent other solutions to the freeloader problem.

There is a certain amount of random recombination of populations during the downsizing, as noted earlier. It is not unlike randomly selecting a jury of 12 from a jury pool of many hundreds. Even if the jury pool is representative (half male, 90% right-handed, appropriate racial mixtures), some individual juries are dramatically different (all of one sex or race, all left-handed, and so forth). That's just one of the well-known phenomena of probability theory (drawing small samples without replacement). Therefore, even if innate tendencies toward cooperation were only prominent in 10% of the population, after parcellation many subpopulations would have none and some might have a majority.

These island subpopulations are not competing with one another like football teams, thanks to those resource-free gaps; they are fighting the environment in the cool-crash-and-burn case, and most subpopulations disappear with time. When conditions allow populations to reexpand, there will be, after expansion into interbreeding continental populations, a higher proportion of those genes that helped some subpopulations survive the downsizing.

This, too, is susceptible to the "Why us?" objection as it would seem to apply to many mammalian species, and the answer may lie in what is shared. Groups with a majority of cooperation genes might spend less time arguing (and thereby wasting time that could be spent in locating more food) and fighting (thereby both losing time and risking injury) during the downsizing. This is particularly attractive because of the long growth curve for cooperation, as noted earlier. Or what's shared is language, where in order to realize its benefits, you might need a sizeable proportion of those with beginner's traits.

Or, as Derek Bickerton has proposed (see Calvin & Bickerton, 2000), cognitive capacities (mental categories for giver, recipient, beneficiaries, type of action, and so on) to keep rough track of freeloading tendencies might allow "Who owes what to whom" to find another use, namely saying "Who did what to whom." Solving the cheater problem in reciprocal altruism could thus be the wheelchair that paid for the argument-structure scheme of handing syntax, until structured language started earning its own way. This by itself would constitute a large step up in intelligence.

PRECISION THROWING AS CURB CUT

Another ape-to-human improvement with a long growth curve is precision throwing, which is so handy for expanding hunting abilities beyond that seen in the other predators. Hunting herd animals also have a link to cooperation because any one prey animal is usually too much for one hunter to eat; one simply has to give away most of it as the chimpanzees do (tolerated scrounging) and hope for reciprocation when someone else gets lucky. Frans de Waal (1996) observed:

> If carnivory was indeed the catalyst for the evolution of sharing, it is hard to escape the conclusion that human morality is steeped in animal blood. When we give money to begging strangers, ship food to starving people, or vote for measures that benefit the poor, we follow impulses shaped since the time our ancestors began to cluster around meat possessors. At the center of the original circle, we find a prize hard to get but desired by many ... this small, sympathetic circle grew steadily to encompass all of humanity—if not in practice then at least in principle.... Given the circle's proposed origin, it is profoundly ironic that its expansion should culminate in a plea for vegetarianism. (p. 146)

And, of course, hunting was one of the only solutions to an environment where, for a few centuries, you either had to eat grass or eat an animal that ate grass.

The side-of-the-barn accuracy needed for flinging branches into waterhole herds may not have much of a growth curve by itself (it doesn't matter which one you trip), but it could have gotten hunters onto the bottom of the precision-throwing growth curve. Being able to hit smaller herds has an even higher payoff. So does throwing from farther away (herds eventually become wary), which also reduces risk to the hunter. One can use other projectiles, such as rocks. One can become accurate enough to hit lone animals. Then there are spears and their augmentation by launching sticks, and so forth. Each improvement has an additional payoff: more days that you and your dependents can eat nice, sterile, high-calorie, low-toxicity fresh meat. (Cooking has made the world much safer for vegetarians and scavengers.)

It's easy to see how natural selection could have repeatedly improved throwing, but what does it have to do with higher intellectual function? As noted, all of the ballistic movements require much detailed planning during "get set" as feedback is too slow. While many ballistic movements have some payoffs even when stereotyped, the hominid hunter cannot function like the frog throwing its tongue when a fly is heading into its "gun sight." There is no standard throw because of the approach distance problem; each throw is a somewhat novel problem in both elevation and range, even if using a standard projectile size and weight.

And, beyond planning and versatility demands, there is the problem of timing jitter (Calvin, 1983). If you throw at a rabbit-sized target a car-length away, and release 5 ms too soon, you'll overshoot the target. At two car lengths away, the launch window shrinks eight-fold. Redundant motor programs, each with independent noise, can solve this double-the-distance problem by using 64 times as many motor programs in parallel.

Even the four-fold increase in the number of neocortical neurons during hominid evolution cannot solve this jitter problem (by itself, it would only buy a 25% increase in approach distance). Many-fold increases in parallelism can only be done by temporarily borrowing helpers from association cortex during "get set."

I have developed this jitter-reduction idea elsewhere (Calvin, 1983, 1993, 1996b). What's important for intelligence is to recall Kimura's (1993) result from aphasics, that most also suffered from hand-arm sequencing problems when confronted with novel sequencing tasks (apraxia), and to recall Ojemann and Mateer's (1979) result from the perisylvian core of language cortex, about the overlap of nonlanguage sensory and motor-sequencing tasks. If there is a common neural sequencing machinery for mouth and face, hand and arm, and sensory and motor, language cortex is an obvious candidate (Calvin & Ojemann, 1994).

This can explain how a curb cut paid for by natural selection for precision throwing might greatly augment planning on other time scales. The structured aspect of the higher intellectual functions could easily arise from the nested embedding aspect of throwing: the shoulder motion is atop the forward motion of the trunk; planning the elbow rotation needs to similarly work from the velocity of the upper arm; the wrist flip needs to be planned in light of the prediction of all those compounded motions controlling the lower arm's velocity, and so forth. All of the coordination must be done in advance, tweaking the parameters to find one of the dozens of possible combinations that will hit the target amidst a sea of solutions that will miss. This is nested embedding of much the same sort as shown in those binary diagrams of phrase structure, the other major way of doing syntax (see Calvin & Bickerton, 2000). As humans assemble words to find a coherent sentence to speak, they grapple with a problem analogous to novel hand-arm sequencing.

Whatever paid for it in natural selection terms (and I assume it was different things at different times), such a multiple-use neural sequencer would have major implications for the structured higher intellection functions, and thus for intelligence.

THE PUMP RUN BY BISTABLE CLIMATE

Pumping up intelligence is thus a real possibility—even though the natural selection that paid for it may be as remote as wheelchairs are from skateboards. Higher intellectual functions may have some silent, nonintellectual partners, those novel ballistic movements.

Ignoring compound interest considerations for a moment, how many strokes on the pump, and of what size, would be sufficient to produce the many-fold increases in the mental functions that separate the *Pan* and *Homo* species? There were several dozen biphasic cooling-warming events (each lasting between 70 and 1,500 years) in the last ice age alone, between 117,000 years and 11,000 years ago. There were dozens of ice ages and, although the high-time-resolution records do not extend to cover them yet, cores with thousand-year resolution can pick up the longer-lasting cooling events. They have now been traced back to 1.1 million years ago. From what we know of the oceanographic mechanisms (see Broecker, 1997, 1999; Calvin, 1998a), I would guess that some will be found between 2 and 3 million years ago—but not in the period before the Isthmus of Panama forced the major detours in ocean currents.

Therefore, there are hundreds of events of similar type each time: abrupt cooling, crashing populations, and burning ecosystems. This suggests that a one percent increment each time might be sufficient. However, there were likely many more events (and thus even smaller increments might suffice) because the typical abrupt cooling or warming chattered between modes like an old fluorescent light tube before finally settling down in the new mode. Typically, there would be a century where the temperature and rainfall whipped back and forth between modern and ice-age values a few times, where vast storms churned large quantities of dust into the atmosphere (the isotopic signature of the dust in the Greenland cores suggests that much came from the Great Gobi Desert). Such flickering climate would have run the population contraction-expansion cycle a few times within a single madhouse century.

This type of pumping and multiple use shows how big steps up in functionality (say, from unstructured protolanguage to structured syntax) can arise from a series of small changes in nonintellectual functions. It may be that something else from that bookshelf of plausible suggestions will prove to run the evolutionary ratchet more quickly than my combination of grass, throwing, and cooperation. But if we are to ever give an explanation for how an ape can turn into a human, we will likely have to address the profound challenges and unusual opportunities given our ancestors by the fickle climate.

ACKNOWLEDGMENTS

During the two decades that this theory has been under construction, I have profited from numerous suggestions. The most recent extensions of the theory have benefitted much from a stay at the Rockefeller Foundation's Bellagio Center, one at the Whiteley Center at Friday Harbor Laboratories, and from workshops sponsored by the Preuss Foundation and the Mathers Foundation and by the Center for Human Evolution at the Foundation for the Future.

AFTERWORD: THE FUTURE'S INTELLIGENCE TEST FOR HUMANS

It has been 8,200 years since an abrupt cooling of even half the magnitude discussed here (the Little Ice Age starting about 700 years ago was an order of magnitude smaller). Everything we know about the geophysical mechanisms (see Broecker, 1999; Calvin, 1998a) suggests that another one could easily happen—indeed, that our greenhouse-effect warming could trigger an abrupt cooling in several different ways.

Because such a cooling would occur too quickly for us to make readjustments in agricultural productivity and associated supply lines, it would be a potentially civilization-shattering affair, likely to cause a population crash far worse than those seen in the wars and plagues of history.

The best understood part of the flip-flop tendencies involves what happens to the warm Gulf Stream waters, with the flow of about a hundred Amazon Rivers, once they split off Ireland into the two major branches of the North Atlantic Current. They sink to the depths of the Greenland-Norwegian Sea and Labrador Sea because so much evaporation takes place (warming up the cold dry winds from Canada, and eventually Europe, so that it is unlike Canada and Siberia) that the surface waters become cold and hypersaline—and therefore more dense than the underlying waters. At some sinking sites, giant whirlpools

15 km in diameter can be found, carrying surface waters down into the depths. Routinely flushing the cold waters in this manner makes room for more warm waters to flow far north.

But this sinking mechanism can fail if fresh water accumulates on the surface, diluting the dense waters. The increased rainfall that occurs with global warming causes more rain to wall into the oceans at the high latitudes. Ordinarily, rain falling into the ocean is not a problem, but at these sites in the Labrador and Greenland-Norwegian Seas, it can be catastrophic—so can meltwater from the nearby Greenland ice cap, especially when it comes out in surges. By shutting down the high-latitude parts of this Nordic heat pump, these consequences of global warming can abruptly change Europe's climate. If Europe's agriculture reverted to the productivity of Canada's (at the same latitudes but lacking a preheating for winds off the Pacific Ocean), 22 out of 23 Europeans would starve.

The surprise is that it isn't just Europe that gets hit hard. Most of the habitable parts of the world have similarly cooled during past episodes. Another failure would cause a population crash that would take much of civilization with it, all within a decade.

Ways to postpone such a climatic shift are conceivable, however—cloud-seeding to create rain shadows in critical locations is just one possibility. Although we can't do much about everyday weather or greenhouse warming, we may nonetheless be able to stabilize the climate enough to prevent an abrupt cooling.

Devising a long-term scheme for stabilizing the flushing mechanism has now become one of the major tasks of our civilization, essential to prevent a drastic downsizing whose wars over food would leave a world where everyone hated their neighbors for good reasons. Human levels of intelligence allow us both foresight and rational planning. Civilization has enormously expanded our horizons, allowing us to look far into the past and learn from it. But it remains to be seen whether humans are capable of passing this intelligence test that the climate sets for us.

REFERENCES

Barlow, H. B. (1987). Intelligence: The art of good guessing. In R. L. Gregory (Ed.), *Oxford companion to the mind* (pp. 381–383). Oxford: Oxford University Press.

Broecker, W. S. (1997). Thermohaline circulation, the Achilles heel of our climate system: Will man-made CO_2 upset the current balance? *Science, 278,* 1582–1588.

Broecker, W. S. (1999, January). What if the conveyor were to shut down? Reflections on a possible outcome of the great global experiment. *GSA Today, 9*(1),1–7.

Bronowski, J. (1973). *The ascent of man.* Boston: Little Brown.

Byrne, R. W. (1994). The evolution of intelligence. In P. J. B. Slater & T. R. Halliday (Eds.), *Behaviour and evolution* (pp. 223–265). Cambridge: Cambridge University Press.

Calvin, W. H. (1983). A stone's throw and its launch window: Timing precision and its implications for language and hominid brains. *Journal of Theoretical Biology, 104*, 121–135.

Calvin, W. H. (1987). The brain as a Darwin machine. *Nature, 330*, 33–34.

Calvin, W. H. (1993). The unitary hypothesis: A common neural circuitry for novel manipulations, language, plan-ahead, and throwing? In K. R. Gibson & T. Ingold (Eds.), *Tools, Language, and Cognition in Human Evolution* (pp. 230–250). New York: Cambridge University Press.

Calvin, W. H. (1996a). *The cerebral code.* Cambridge, MA: MIT Press.

Calvin, W. H. (1996b). *How brains think.* New York: Basic Books.

Calvin, W. H. (1997). The six essentials? Minimal requirements for the Darwinian bootstrapping of quality. *Journal of Memetics - Evolutionary Models of Information Transmission*, 1, at *http://www.fmb.mmu.ac.uk/jom-emit/1997/vol1/calvin_wh.html*

Calvin, W. H. (1998a). The great climate flip-flop. *The Atlantic Monthly, 281*(1), 47–64.

Calvin, W. H. (1998b). Competing for consciousness: A Darwinian mechanism at an appropriate level of explanation. *Journal of Consciousness Studies, 5*(4), 389–404.

Calvin, W. H. (1998c, November). The emergence of intelligence. *Scientific American Presents, 9*(4), 44–51

Calvin, W. H., & Bickerton, D. (1999). *Lingua ex machina: Reconciling Darwin and Chomsky with the human brain.* Cambridge, MA: MIT Press.

Calvin, W. H., & Ojemann, G. A. (1994). *Conversations with Neil's brain: The neural nature of thought and language.* Reading, MA: Addison-Wesley.

Deacon, T. (1997). *The symbolic species: The co-evolution of language and the brain.* New York: W. W. Norton.

de Waal, F. (1996). *Good natured: The origins of right and wrong.* Cambridge, MA: Harvard University Press.

Gould, J. L., & Gould, C. G. (1994). *The animal mind.* New York: Scientific American Library.

Gould, J. L., & Gould, C. G. (1998). Reasoning in animals. *Scientific American Presents, 9*(4), 52–59.

Jensen, A. R. (1992). Understanding *g* in terms of information processing. *Educational Psychology Review 4*, 271–308.

Kimura, D. (1993). *Neuromotor mechanisms in human communication.* Oxford: Oxford University Press.

Kuhl, P. K., Williams, K. A., Lacerda, F., Stevens, K. N., & Lindblom, B. (1992). Linguistic experience alters phonetic perception in infants by 6 months of age. *Science 255*, 606–608.

Ojemann, G. (1991). Cortical organization of language. *Journal of Neuroscience, 11*, 2281–2287.

Ojemann, G., & Mateer, C. (1979). Human language cortex: Localization of memory, syntax, and sequential motor-phoneme identification systems. *Science, 205*, 1401–1403.

Pagels, H. (1988). *The dreams of reason.* New York: Basic Books.

Piaget, J. (1929; 1952). *The origins of intelligence in children.* New York: International Universities Press.

Sacks, O. (1989). *Seeing voices.* Berkeley: University of California Press.

Simon, H. A. (1983). *Reason in human affairs.* Palo Alto, CA: Stanford University Press.

Sober, E., & Wilson, D. S. (1998). *Unto others: The evolution and psychology of unselfish behavior.* Cambridge, MA: Harvard University Press.

7

---‿✸‿---

Evolution of the
Generative Mind

Michael C. Corballis
University of Auckland

Until as recently as the 1960s, it was widely supposed that the common ancestor of humans and our closest relative, the chimpanzee, dated from some 20 or 30 million years ago. This seemed to allow plenty of time for the apparent physical and mental differences between our two species to have evolved. Over the last 30 years, however, the analysis of molecular data, beginning with the work of Sarich and Wilson (1967) comparing the albumens of living primate species, has forced a reappraisal of our similarities to other apes and of the dates of divergence between the different species. Comparisons of DNA sequences have confirmed the major conclusions of this earlier work, showing that humans are much closer to the chimpanzee than was previously suspected. The modern consensus is that the hominid and chimpanzee clades diverged only 5 or 6 million years ago (Cann, 1987; Waddell & Penny, 1996), and by one estimate the chimpanzee has about 99.6% of its amino acid sequences and 98.4% of its DNA nucleotide sequences in common with our own species (Goodman, 1992).

Yet humans are still inclined to believe that we are superior in intellect to our primate cousins, perhaps vastly so. To be sure, chimpanzees and other primates show some ability to fashion and use tools, may possess at least the rudiments of a theory of mind (Byrne, 1995), and lead social lives of moderate complexity. Chimpanzees and other great apes have been shown to be capable of symbolic representation, although they have yet to demonstrate language at a level beyond that of a 2-year-old human child. But where humans have spread themselves over the globe, and briefly beyond it, the natural environments of chimpanzees and gorillas are restricted to ever-shrinking pockets of Africa—to the extent that both are endangered species. It is beyond imagination to stretch the toolmaking abilities of any nonhuman primate to the automobile, the laptop computer, or even a pair of scissors. There is nothing in chimpanzee society to compare to the social and political intricacy of a modern state, or even a village. And even the most extravagant claims about the linguistic capacities of a chimpanzee fall far short of suggesting that we might ever sit down with our primate cousins and have a decent family chat.

Of course, some of our human exploits represent the accumulation of knowledge and know-how over many generations, with contributions from many individuals. Indeed, as individuals, very few of us would know how to begin to design a computer or an automobile, and few of us would even manage to survive if placed in the natural environment of the chimpanzee or gorilla without any of our usual supports—such as clothes, implements, or written instructions. But even if we subtract out the accumulated benefits of what we are pleased to call civilization, it appears that humans do possess a biologically determined quality of mind that separates us from the great apes.

HUMAN INTELLIGENCE: UNITARY OR MULTIFACETED?

Although we may wish to call that quality of mind *intelligence*, it is by no means clear how to define it. One issue is whether our distinctive intelligence is unitary or multifaceted. To Descartes (1647/1985), writing in the 17th century, nonhuman animals, even apes, were essentially robots, their behavior subject to fixed mechanical laws, whereas humans possessed a freedom of action that could not be reduced to mechanical principles. This freedom, especially evident in the unlimited variability of human language, depended on God-given nonmaterial influences operating via the pineal gland. The idea that the human mind is somehow beyond the control of natural laws—that we possess free will—is still widely accepted, at least among people at large,[1] although it is not especially helpful to cognitive scientists trying to understand how the mind works.

Chomsky, who has professed a neo-Cartesian perspective (Chomsky, 1966), agrees that the infinite variability of human language does indeed distinguish the human mind from the animal mind and depends not on divine intervention but rather on computational principles. Given a set of rules, and a vocabulary of symbols, there is no limit to the number of well-formed sentences that we can generate. A simpler example of a rule-governed activity is counting—given

---

[1]A recent survey in New Zealand, in which religious observance is not especially high, revealed that just over half of the population believe in some form of life after death.

simple rules for incrementing numbers, and ten digits, we can count any number of objects, a facility that gives rise to the concept of infinity (Chomsky, 1988). A common view, then, is that the human mind is a generalized computer, able to apply general computational principles to a great variety of different domains. This generalized capacity explains why humans can do so many things that cannot easily be explained as specific adaptations, such as playing chess, constructing buildings, proving Euclidean theorems, or flying to the moon.

Evolutionary Psychology and the Modularity of Mind

But this view of the human mind is not universally accepted. It has also been argued that the mind is not a generalized computer at all but rather a set of specialized modules (Fodor, 1983). The modular view of the mind was set in evolutionary context by advocates of what has come to be termed *evolutionary psychology* (Cosmides & Tooby, 1987, 1994; Pinker, 1997). According to this perspective, the modern human mind comprises a set of adaptive specializations that have evolved during the Pleistocene—the period from approximately 1.6 million years ago until approximately 10,000 years ago. In the pre-agricultural world of the Pleistocene, our hominid forebears are thought to have existed primarily as hunter–gatherers. From about 13,000 years ago, beginning with the domestication of wild plants and animals in the Near East, human societies gradually began to assume different and varied characteristics, although a few hunter–gatherer societies remain today (Diamond, 1997). However, the extraordinary cultural diversity that has emerged over the past 13,000 years is considered too recent to have had any significant impact on our biological makeup. In stressing our common biological heritage, evolutionary psychology is therefore often in conflict with recent traditions of postmodernism and cultural relativism in psychology and the social sciences (Pinker, 1997).

One of the arguments for viewing the mind in terms of specific adaptations rather than a generalized problem solver is based on a reasoning task developed by Wason (1966), in which people are shown cards with symbols on them and asked how they verify certain statements about those symbols. For example, they might be shown four cards, displaying the symbols A, K, 2, and 7, and asked which two cards they should turn over to check the truth of the following claim: If a card has a vowel on one side, then it has an even number on the other side. Most people adopt the strategy of choosing the cards displaying the A and the 2. It is indeed rational to turn over the A, but turning over the 2 is suboptimal in the sense that whatever is on the other side cannot disconfirm the statement. The better strategy in that sense is to turn over the 7 because the presence of an A on the other side would falsify the statement.

However, people typically do adopt the optimal strategy on exactly analogous tasks that refer to social settings. For example, suppose the cards A, K, 2, and 7 are replaced by cards bearing the labels *beer*, *Coke*, *22*, and *17*, respectively, and it is explained that there are beverages on one side and people's ages on the other. If asked which two cards they need to turn over to check the truth of the statement "If a person is drinking beer, he or she must be over 20 years old," most people (including, no doubt, underage drinkers) easily understand that the critical cards are those bearing the labels *beer* and *17* (Cox & Griggs, 1982). Tooby and Cosmides (1989) inferred that this kind of reasoning does not depend on a general purpose reasoning device but applies specifically to social contracts of the sort that were likely to have been important to a hunter–gatherer community, where cooperation and trust were important. In particular, we are especially adept at strategies for detecting cheaters, such as the underage drinker or the spouse who takes a lover. In other words, there is a cheater-detection module.

Tooby and Cosmides' argument rests on the discontinuity between performance on the Wason task in abstract settings, such as with the cards *A*, *K*, *2*, and *7*, and performance in social settings, such as with the cards *beer*, *Coke*, *22*, and *17* set in the context of drinking in a pub. Oaksford and Chater (1994), however, have argued that the supposed irrationality of choosing the *2* rather than the *7* in the abstract version is based on Popperian logic, which proceeds by falsification rather than verification, and that a unified perspective emerges if one considers instead a Bayesian approach. We may consider the more general form of the proposition that is tested to be "If p then q"; in the Wason example, the *2* then becomes q and the *7* becomes *not-q*. According to Popperian logic, it is rational to examine *not-q*, because if this is accompanied by p, the proposition is falsified. According to the Bayesian approach, however, the relative gain in information derived from investigating q and *not-q* depends on the a priori probabilities of p and q. In particular, if the a priori probabilities are low, then the ordering of the four options in terms of information gain is $p > q > \text{not-}q > \text{not-}p$, suggesting that the subjects in the original Wason experiment could be construed to be behaving rationally. Oaksford and Wason provide what they call a *rational analysis* of the Wason selection task, based on Bayesian theory, in which there is no need to postulate a specialized module or to appeal to selection pressures operating in the Pleistocene. People, they argue, are Bayesians, not Popperians, and their selection strategies can be understood in terms of a unified theory.

Oaksford and Chater's argument has been criticized in turn by Laming (1996), who argued that Bayesian analysis actually does support the view that turning over the *2* in the original Wason task is irrational; therefore, there is indeed a distinct discrepancy between how people respond in abstract and how they respond in social settings. But whichever view is correct, there is an inherent implausibility to the idea that social intelligence depends on domain-specific modules. As Moore (1996) argued, social intelligence is simply too broadly applicable across different domains for the modular argument to be credible.

Another problem with evolutionary psychology is that evidence about the structure of the mind is based on experiments carried out on present-day humans, albeit sometimes in different cultural settings, and the evolutionary component has to be derived from a purely conceptual process of reverse engineering to what is known (or guessed) about social pressures operating during the Pleistocene. Pinker (1997) has been especially prolific in relating present-day dispositions to conditions on the African savanna: Humans like to eat potato chips because fatty foods were scarce but nutritionally valuable during the Pleistocene; we like landscapes with trees because trees provided shade and escape from carnivores on the African savanna; our liking for green suburban lawns harks back to the green hills of East Africa; our love of flowers derives from their distinctiveness as markers for edible fruit, nuts, or tubers amid the greenery; and so on. But there are no fossils to document the origins of these behaviors, and the potential for post hoc theorizing is virtually limitless.

A stronger argument for modularity comes from developmental disorders that appear to affect cognition in very specific ways. These include autism, Asperger syndrome, dyslexia, specific language impairment (SLI), and Williams syndrome. For example, children with SLI seem to have a very specific deficit in grammar, but otherwise normal intelligence, which has been taken as evidence for a grammar module (e.g., Gopnik, 1990; Pinker, 1994). Similarly, Baron-Cohen (1995) argued that autism results from a specific deficit in a theory of mind module, located in the orbitofrontal cortex, leaving language relatively unimpaired. Williams syndrome results from a microdeletion on the long arm of chromosome 7, affecting the expression of several genes, and children with this disorder appear to have normal syntax and theory of mind but serious deficits in spatio-constructive skills, numerical cognition, problem solving, and planning (Bellugi, Wang, & Jernigan, 1994). Because at least some of these developmental disorders are clearly of genetic origin, the specificity of the deficits not only encourages the idea that the mind is modular but also suggests that specific genes may underlie each module.

But even this evidence is not unequivocal. Karmiloff-Smith (1998) argued that the developing brain can achieve the same ends through different developmental routes. She raises the possibility that SLI, which seems to imply a specific linguistic deficit, may actually result from a subtle deficit in acoustic processing in early childhood. Again, although children with this impairment appear to process faces normally, suggesting an intact face-processing module, closer analysis shows that they achieve their good scores by processing faces in a feature-by-feature manner, whereas normal controls process faces in a predominantly holistic fashion. Moreover, although language processing is superficially normal in children with Williams syndrome, more detailed analysis shows some very specific syntactic deficits, including difficulties in processing embedded relative clauses and difficulties in forming agreement between phrase-structure elements. They also appear to learn the lexicon differently than normally developing children.

The Neuroconstructivist Approach

Instead of assuming that the mind consists of independent, genetically coded modules, Karmiloff-Smith advocated what she called a *neuroconstructivist* approach to development, in which developmental disorders arise at a level of processing lower than that of cognitive modules. Thus genetic anomalies might disrupt acoustic processing, thresholds for neural firing, levels of inhibition, and so forth, and set the course of cognitive development along different paths. Instead of a rigid, innately determined modularity, the mechanisms underlying development are not so much domain-specific (or modular) as merely domain-relevant. Domain specificity is achieved only through the interaction of these domain-relevant mechanisms with environmental influences and may take different routes as a function of low-level deficits. According to this view, different developmental disorders do not imply strict modularity but lie on a continuum.

Other theorists have also sought compromises between domain-general and domain-specific conceptions of the human mind. Even Fodor (1983), the arch-modularist, has maintained that the modules, although independent of one another, do interact with a central component that operates in holistic fashion; input modules feed into this central component, and output modules take information selectively from it. Although this central component may be identified with consciousness, or perhaps even general intelligence, Fodor despairs of being able to understand or even study it. Cognitive scientists, he believes, should be satisfied merely to study the input and output modules. In somewhat more positive vein, Sperber (1994) suggested that there is a module of metarepresentation (MMR) that acts as a kind of general clearing house for the other modules.

In general, there appears to be a growing unease with what one might call hard-core modularity, in which the human mind is composed largely if not wholly of independent, encapsulated modules (see also Karmiloff-Smith, 1992). Moreover, there seems little doubt that there are both general and specific aspects of intelligence. Indeed, debates over their interrelations are somewhat reminiscent of earlier arguments in factor analysis about whether there is a single, general factor underlying all aspects of intelligence, as initially proposed by Spearman (1904), or whether there are multiple factors, as later proposed by Thurstone (1947). We can now recognize that there is truth to both positions.

There are indeed specific intelligences, but these tend to be positively correlated, so there is a general factor underlying them. This leads to a hierarchical concept of intelligence, in which general intelligence, or *g*, is understood to be broken down into increasingly specific components (e.g., Carroll, 1993). From an evolutionary perspective, we might suppose that there is some aspect, at least, of the general component that distinguishes our species from other primates and explains our adaptability to diverse environments and our extraordinary control over natural forces.

Clues From Language

Although I argue that this general capacity goes beyond language itself, it is in the use of language that humans seem most obviously to differ from other species, and it is therefore prudent to begin by asking what it is about language that distinguishes it from other forms of communication. Although great apes can apparently master the use of symbols to represent objects and actions, there is no evidence, even after several decades of systematic research, that they are capable of anything resembling the grammar of human language. There has been no demonstration of the use of tense, number, mood, articles, or the recursion that gives rise to indefinitely extendable sentences such as "This is the cat that killed the rat that ate the malt that lay in the house that Jack built," or of the embedding of clauses that allows that same sentence to be registered as "The malt, which was eaten by the rat that was killed by the cat, lay in the house that Jack built."[2] As Pinker (1994) remarked, chimpanzees "just don't 'get it'" (p. 340).

Bickerton (1995) suggested that chimpanzees and other great apes are capable only of what he calls *protolanguage*, which is essentially language without grammar. Protolanguage is the language of 2-year-old children, or of people who were not exposed to linguistic input during childhood, or of Broca's aphasics, or of the pidgins that were used by traders in negotiating with those who spoke different languages. What the chimpanzee lacks, therefore, is the ability, normally acquired by children between the ages of 2 and 4, to convert protolanguage into a true language, with a generative grammar that essentially allows the speaker an unlimited variety of possible utterances and the flexibility to speak of past, present, or future. The generative component is especially important because it takes communication beyond any specific circumstances that might have led to its evolution. That is, we might see generativity as the key to the human mind,

---

[2]Too much embedding can create difficulties, however, as in the following rendition: "The malt that the rat that the cat killed ate lay in the house that Jack built."

precisely because it allows us to create and understand meanings that are entirely novel.[3]

GENERATIVITY AS A GENERAL CAPACITY

But can we extrapolate from language to other human activities? Some have argued that we cannot. Indeed, the Chomskyan notion of generativity is a purely structural notion, unrelated to other cognitive or motor functions, or even to semantic or pragmatic aspects of language. According to Chomsky (1966), "man has a species-specific capacity, a unique type of intellectual organization which cannot be attributed to peripheral organs or intellectual organization and which manifests itself in what we may refer to as the 'creative aspect' of ordinary language—its property being both unbounded in scope and stimulus-free" (pp. 4–5). Similarly, Pinker (1994) held that grammar is a module, specific to language, and indeed that language itself is distinct from thought.

We have already seen that there is reason to doubt the existence of a specific grammar module (Karmiloff-Smith, 1998), and there are also reasons to doubt that language can be wholly separated from thought. It is true that there are aspects of thought, such as the manipulation of visual images, that seem complementary to language, in that they are iconic rather than symbolic, analog rather than propositional, and perhaps right rather than left hemispheric (e.g., Corballis, 1997), but there are also many respects in which the properties of thought mimic those of language—not surprisingly, since one of the functions of language is to convey our thoughts. To be sure, the linear, temporal nature of vocal language imposes constraints that may not apply to thought itself (although some thoughts are so constrained), but this difference may be fairly superficial. For example, the manual sign languages invented by deaf people all over the world are not constrained in this fashion and make use of the three dimensions of space, as well as that of time, in order to convey grammatical structure. Yet there is now little doubt that sign languages acquired in early childhood have all the hallmarks, including generative grammar, of natural language (Armstrong, Stokoe, & Wilcox, 1995).

THE GENERATIVITY OF THOUGHT

Contrary to Pinker and others, cognitive linguists such as Fauconnier (1997) and Langacker (1991) argued that generativity in human language is indeed

---

[3]I recently visited a publishing house in the south of England, and the publisher greeted me with the following extraordinary statement: "Ribena is trickling down the chandeliers." Although surprised, I had no difficulty understanding what he meant, and was indeed able to confirm that it was true. This illustrates the extraordinary flexibility of language to express ideas that are utterly novel in terms of one's past experience.

derived from cognitive abilities and may have evolved from perceptual or motor abilities. Bickerton (1995) argued similarly that generative language is
part of thought itself and indeed comprises that aspect of thought that is
uniquely human. Many theories of semantic memory, for example, not only
emphasize the propositional nature of knowledge representation and thought
but also distinguish between propositional and analogue modes (e.g., Anderson, 1995; Paivio, 1986), and Wilcox (1998) argued that meaning generation
is at the root of generativity, in language as in thought. Certainly, thought is
just as generative as language, and indeed it is difficult to believe that generative language could have evolved independently of the generativity of
thoughts that underlie it. We generate ideas, and then we generate sentences
to express them. It is true that we can generate thoughts that defy verbal expression, just as we can generate nonsense sentences that express no coherent
thoughts, but this need not contradict the view that the underlying generative
process is common to both thought and language.

One aspect of thought that displays a recursive property analogous to that
of language is the ability to attribute states of mind or mental perspectives to
others. For example, we can often appreciate that another person is observing
us, or knows what we are thinking, and this so-called theory of mind lends itself to precisely the kind of recursion that is expressible in language, such as "I
know that he can see me" or "I know that she knows that I am thinking about
her." Theory of mind is a ubiquitous aspect of our social lives. It allows us to cooperate, show empathy, imitate, teach, and of course lie and deceive—and
also bestow human qualities on our pets and our machines. It no doubt
evolved as a dimension of the complex of skills required to maintain the deli-
cate balance between social and individual needs.

Another mental activity with a marked generative component is remembering past events. The constructive nature of episodic memory is well documented (e.g., Bartlett, 1932; Neisser, 1967) and has important implications in
eyewitness testimony (Loftus & Ketcham, 1991) and in the evaluation of
claims of childhood abuse (Loftus & Ketcham, 1994). Given the unreliability
of episodic memory, one may wonder if evolution has sold us a lemon. A somewhat different perspective emerges, however, if episodic memory is viewed as
part of a more general ability to travel mentally in time, into the future as well
as the past. If memory for the past sometimes involves the construction of
events that are distortions of what actually occurred, the elaboration of future
scenarios is even more obviously invented, although with some grounding in
experience. In terms of adaptation to a variable and changing world, the generative component may be more important than strict adherence to the
facts—hence our predilection for fantasy and fiction. It has been proposed
that episodic memory itself, as well as the more general capacity for mental

time travel, are uniquely human (Suddendorf & Corballis 1997; Tulving, 1993).[4]

To some degree, then, language, theory of mind, episodic memory, and mental time travel all illustrate the recursiveness and generativity of the human mind. All may also depend on the expansion in hominid evolution of the prefrontal cortex (Deacon, 1997). They are to some extent codependent. Premack and Premack (1994) and Byrne (1995) argued that theory of mind is a necessary precursor to language, and Byrne (1995) also suggested that the great apes possess at least the rudiments of a theory of mind, but not of generative language. Certainly, our speech often directly conveys mental concepts ("I think that … "; "I wonder if … "). Further, much of our conversation has to do with events in the past, as well as plans for the future, implying that language and mental time travel are intimately connected.

Although connected, these generative aspects of the mind are also dissociable. For example, people with severe deficits in episodic memory, such as the well-known amnesic known as H.M. (Corkin, 1984), do not show corresponding language deficits. Moreover, we have seen that there are apparent double dissociations between language and theory-of-mind deficits, with autism characterized as a specific impairment of a theory-of-mind module and SLI a specific impairment of a grammar module. However, as Karmiloff-Smith (1998) pointed out, there is reason to believe that these and other developmental disorders are not truly independent, and even if the adult human brain is organized in modular fashion, it does not necessarily follow that the modules developed independently, nor need it follow that they evolved independently. More generally, double dissociations can be predicted from highly interactive systems that are manifestly nonmodular (e.g., Plaut, 1995; Van Orden, Jansen op de Haar, & Bosman, 1997).

Development as the Key to Generativity

Greenfield (1991) gave a developmental account of how hierarchical representation might emerge in different activities that are at first undifferentiated but later become increasingly independent, or even modularized. The beginnings of

---

[4]There is recent evidence that scrub jays have memory, not only of *where* they stored food but also of *when* they stored it (Clayton & Dickinson, 1998). Since episodic memory is supposed to store information about events that are located in time and space, this evidence might suggest that scrub jays have episodic memory. However, according to Tulving (1993), a further characteristic of episodic memory is that it is accompanied by a special kind of consciousness called *autonoetic* consciousness, which involves an awareness of self, and there is of course no evidence that scrub jays are capable of such consciousness, nor is it obvious how one might obtain such evidence. Indeed, as Griffiths, Dickinson, and Clayton (1998) pointed out, the question of whether nonhumans are capable of episodic memory in the sense defined by Tulving may be unanswerable.

generativity are manifest in hierarchical construction, so in language development, for example, there is a point at which children begin to combine words into phrases and then use those phrases as units. In children up to the age of 2, a common neural substrate roughly corresponding to Broca's area appears to underlie the hierarchical organization of elements in at least two different activities, speech and tool use. Greenfield noted parallels between the ways in which children combine words and the ways in which they combine objects, such as nuts and bolts or nesting cups. Just as children learn to combine words into phrases and then treat those phrases as units, so they learn to combine nesting cups by placing one inside another and then treat the nested combination as a unit.

The developmental evidence reviewed by Greenfield actually stopped short of the developmental stage at which language emerges from protolanguage, and thus achieves the level of generativity evident in, for example, a skilled craftsman. She nevertheless suggested that the relationship between language and the construction of objects may persist into adulthood and is one of homology rather than analogy. She cited the evidence of Grossman (1980) that Broca's aphasics not only had grammatical deficits but were also deficient in reproducing hierarchical tree structures composed of lines. However, she also refers to unpublished evidence that, in a sample of children with mental retardation, some were skilled in hierarchical construction but deficient in grammar, while others showed the reverse pattern. She relates these findings to neurophysiological evidence that, beyond the age of 2, there is increasing differentiation in the region of Broca's area, such that an upper region subserves the manipulation of manual objects and an adjacent lower region subserves grammar. In many cases of brain injury, both regions will be damaged, resulting in combined deficits, but in some cases one or the other region might be damaged, resulting in dissociated deficits.

This view suggests that it might be growth itself, and in particular the growth of the frontal lobes, that provides the key to generativity, with the increasing differentiation of that growth underlying the emergence of the different domains that exhibit generativity. Chomsky (e.g., 1971, 1986) repeatedly argued that children's understanding of phrase structure must be innate because there is no way it could be learned by an associative mechanism, but this view is increasingly challenged. Elman (1993) showed that associative mechanisms might acquire hierarchical structure if they change structurally as they learn. For example, a network that starts with a rapidly fading memory, but increases its memory capacity over time, initially only learns short strings of words but is gradually able to deal with longer strings and handle previously learned strings (phrases) as units. A more general challenge to the Chomskyan view of language, based on developmental and associative principles, is provided by Elman, Bates, Johnson, Karmiloff-Smith, Parisi, and Plunkett (1996).

Generativity, and the hierarchical structure that supports it, might therefore depend on the acquisition of skill in the course of growth. Greenfield (1991) reviewed the evidence for frontal-lobe involvement in both language and tool use, whereas Wheeler, Stuss, and Tulving (1997) argued further that the prefrontal cortex is critical to episodic memory and mental time travel, which also exhibit generativity. We have also seen that the prefrontal cortex seems to be critically involved in theory of mind (Baron-Cohen, 1995). Although it is likely that differentiation within frontal circuits depends on innate constraints that are fairly loosely specified—domain relevant rather than domain specific, in Karmiloff-Smith's (1998) words—it is also likely that the nature of the input is important.

There is some evidence that the left hemisphere of the brain undergoes a growth spurt between the ages of 2 and 4, and this is precisely the age range during which children normally acquire syntax (Thatcher, Walker, & Guidice, 1987). If growth itself is the key to the development of hierarchical, recursive structures, then this could explain why grammar is acquired at this stage of development, and why it is normally subserved by the left hemisphere. The extent to which the structure of grammar is innately given or derived from the input remains a matter of contention, but there is surely at least a case for supposing that the input is much more important than the Chomskyan school has allowed (Elman et al., 1996; Sampson, 1997). Language may be special simply because language is a major input during these critical years and normally the only input that possesses the complex, hierarchical structure that a rapidly growing cortex can exploit to full advantage. But a young Mozart, exposed to music during this period, might equally develop a complex, generative understanding of music. This may explain why the representation of music in professional musicians, who presumably were exposed to music at an early age, is not only left hemispheric, but appears to be represented in the left hemisphere in areas that lie very close to the different language-mediating areas (Sergent, Zuck, Terriah, & MacDonald, 1992)

There is a final argument for postulating growth mechanisms of this sort, which is distinct from the notion that the human mind is composed of multiple modules, each under independent genetic control that evolved during the Pleistocene. The latter view—the so-called "Swiss army knife" model of the human mind—does not seem to square with extraordinarily close genetic similarity between ourselves and the other great apes (Goodman, 1992). Genetically speaking, a much simpler solution is to alter the growth pattern of the brain and allow environmental input to structure brain circuits during periods of rapid growth. All that was needed to create a human from the common ancestor of humans and chimpanzees may have been a little tinkering with the growth plan. Perhaps the major change was simply a prolongation of growth itself, but this may have been accompanied by interhemispheric gradients, so that growth spurts occur at different stages on the two sides of the brain. A mechanism of this sort could explain the cerebral asymmetries that seem so much a feature of the human brain (Corballis, 1991a, 1991b).

THE EVOLUTION OF GENERATIVITY

Thus far, I have used the term generativity to refer to those activities that involve the combination of elements in a rule-governed but unbounded fashion. Language is the obvious example, but many other activities, such as mathematics, manufacture, music, dance, creating past or future scenarios, or even imagining impossible scenes, like a cow jumping over the moon, have these properties. From an evolutionary perspective, however, it is reasonable to suppose that generativity emerged from simpler capacities.

At the most primitive level, generativity requires some active impulse that creates novelty, often in a seemingly open-ended manner. It is this impulse that we are inclined to identify with free will, or creativity. However, we need not go along with Descartes and suppose that it is uniquely human. Most animals engage in playful activity that seems to have a large random component, which anyone who owns a kitten or a playful dog can verify. This kind of random activity plays a role that is analogous to that of mutation in evolutionary adaptations: It increases the repertoire of actions that might prove adaptive.

But to use this creative energy to construct something also requires building blocks. In the case of language, the building blocks are the basic elements of language, such as morphemes, words, and phrases, that are combined in hierarchical fashion to form the infinite variety of sentences that we can produce and understand. In the case of manufacture, the building blocks include just those—building blocks—and also the enormous variety of elements that are combined in various ways to produce useful objects. These elements include bricks, boards, nails, screws, nuts, bolts, knobs, hooks, handles, wheels, axles, lids, blades, batteries, transistors, wires, sockets, plugs, keys, locks, switches, bulbs, springs, and many more. In the case of episodic memory, they include all the events, places, people, and so on, that have populated our lives and that allow us to create past and future scenarios. The capacity for generativity is vastly increased if the elements are mental rather than physical, so that one need not be constrained by the here and now. It is presumably for this reason that a number of authors have emphasized the importance of symbols (e.g., Deacon, 1997), or names (Terrace, 1985), in the evolution of generative language. Thus, Noble (1998) goes so far as to write that "generativity is not the defining feature of language.... Rather, 'generativity' derives from a more fundamental defining feature, which is that language is the use of signs as symbols" (p. 1199). The use of internal elements of representation is not unique to language nor are the elements necessarily symbolic. The reconstruction of past events, or the imaginative construction of future ones, obviously involves the manipulation of internal representations, unconstrained by the immediate stimulus environment. Even effective manufacture also requires that one knows what one wants even if it is not physically present. How often do you have to return to the hardware store to buy some component that you need to finish the job?

But for the kind of unbounded generativity that is evident in language and the free play of human imagination, building blocks are not enough; we also need rules that allow them to be combined in lawful and meaningful ways. It seems likely that the prefrontal cortex is critical to the recursive application of rules that seem so basic to language and construction (Greenfield, 1991). We have also seen that the frontal lobes are critical to episodic memory (Wheeler et al., 1997), although there is also evidence that the hippocampus is critical (Vargha-Khadem, Gadian, Watkins, Connelly, Van Paesschen, & Mishkin, 1997), leading Pillemer (1998) to suggest that there may actually be two kinds of memory. One is an older, image-based memory, dependent on the hippocampus and other medial temporal-lobe structures, while the other is based on narrative and is mediated by the frontal lobes. Conway (1999) suggested that these components may not be independent, but rather that the more recent frontal-lobe networks may act to modulate the output of the older image-based system. In terms of the perspective offered here, we may suppose that the stored images set up by the hippocampal system provide the building blocks, while the frontal-lobe system provides the generative rules that allow the images to be organized in coherent narrative sequences.

According to Deacon (1997), the human prefrontal cortex is about twice the size that would be predicted in an ape with a brain the size of a human brain. If one compares the relative sizes of brain regions between different primate species, the human prefrontal cortex is the most divergently enlarged, while the olfactory bulbs are the most divergently reduced—we have progressed, you might say, from stink to think. If the frontal lobes are indeed critical to the generative application of rule systems, not only in language but also in a variety of other mental and physical activities as well, then this enlargement might indeed hold the key to what is special about the human mind. It would, of course, be wrong to simply jump to this conclusion before examining the evidence from our nearest relatives, the great apes.

Generativity in the Great Apes

There seems little doubt that great apes can acquire internal representations, even ones that are symbolic. Although there is considerable question as to whether great apes can be taught anything resembling language (Bickerton, 1995; Pinker, 1994), they can be taught quite extensive vocabularies of symbols that represent objects or actions. This appears to be true of the four different species of great ape, namely the orangutan (Miles, 1990), the gorilla (Patterson, 1978), the common chimpanzee (Premack & Premack, 1983), and the pygmy chimpanzee (Savage-Rumbaugh & Lewin, 1994). These vocabularies can be used to formulate simple requests, but there is some doubt as to whether an ape can actually construct a sentence (Terrace, Pettito, Sanders, & Bever, 1979). There is perhaps a fairly general (but not universal) consensus that great apes are capable of protolanguage but lack the grammatical component, and perhaps even the potential for grammar, that is required for true generative language (Bickerton, 1995).

This does not necessarily mean that generativity itself is denied to the chimpanzee or the other great apes because the generativity of thought may well have been a precursor to the generativity of language. Byrne (1995), for example, argued that the great apes do indeed possess a theory of mind, suggesting that this faculty was also present in the common ancestor of ourselves and the other great apes. He suggests that this was in fact a necessary precursor for the subsequent evolution of language in the hominid line.

Nevertheless, the question of whether or not great apes, or any other primates for that matter, possess a theory of mind has been highly contentious ever since it was raised by Premack and Woodruff (1978). A commonly cited example of theory of mind is tactical deception, in which one animal deliberately sets out to deceive another. Deception in itself is not sufficient, however, because it might occur directly through natural selection, such as in camouflaged coloring or eyespots on a butterfly wing, or through associative learning, as when an animal discovers simply through trial and error that a certain deceptive action is rewarding. Byrne and Whiten (1990) collected anecdotes of tactical deception and applied careful criteria to determine which are intentional, implying theory of mind. The main criterion they used was novelty, indicating that the deception was computed rather than merely habitual. Byrne and Whiten conclude from their survey that, among the primates, only the great apes (chimpanzee, gorilla, and orangutan) display intentional tactical deception—that is, deception that manifestly involves an appreciation of what the deceived animal is thinking, or what it can see.

This evidence is not wholly convincing since it is based on anecdote, and the number of examples is small—only 18 cases out of the 253 that were submitted met the criteria. Attempts to provide experimental rather than anecdotal evidence for theory of mind in animals have not been wholly satisfactory because few of the theory-of-mind tests developed for children have been successfully adapted for comparative research. Povinelli, Nelson, and Boysen (1990) developed one technique in which a chimpanzee watches two people in a room, one of whom places a food bait in one of four receptacles that are hidden from the chimpanzee's view. The other person is out of the room when the action occurs. The two people then each point to a receptacle, all four of which are now visible to the chimpanzee, and the animal must choose the receptacles that contains the bait. The animals performed above chance, which Povinelli et al. took to mean that the animals could tell which of the two people knew where the food was. However, performance was initially at chance, suggesting that the chimpanzees may have simply learned which of the two people provided the reliable information, without necessarily attributing knowledge to that person. Povinelli (1994) has since acknowledged that this study, and others like it, do not provide unequivocal evidence that chimpanzees can attribute mental states to others. Heyes (1998) suggested versions of the experiment that she considers might provide the critical evidence, but to my knowledge they have not been attempted and may still not be decisive (e.g., Suddendorf, 1998).

Superficially, at least, chimpanzees do seem to appreciate what another animal can see, given that chimpanzees frequently make eye contact and follow the gaze of others. For example, Povinelli (1998) recorded that if a person makes eye contact with a chimpanzee, and then shifts his or her gaze to some location behind the chimpanzee, the animal then looks over the person's shoulder to where the person's gaze is directed. But this does not mean that the chimpanzee understands that the person is looking at something there; it may simply be a hard-wired response that has proven adaptive in locating threats or interesting objects, or even in engaging in acts of deception. Indeed, at least some of the evidence for tactical deception in great apes, documented by Byrne and Whiten (1990), may reflect this hard-wired sensitivity to direction of gaze, and the learned understanding that certain acts are more safely performed while the watcher's gaze is elsewhere. Povinelli's more recent research suggests that chimpanzees actually have little understanding what others see. A chimpanzee will beg for food as often to a blind-folded person as to a sighted one, evidently not understanding that the blind-folded person cannot see, yet this is a task that even 2½-year-old children can perform (Povinelli, 1998). Contrary to the earlier claims of Povinelli et al. (1990), the evidence now largely weighs against the idea that chimpanzees can understand the minds of others.

Research on theory of mind of mind in chimpanzees appears to have suffered something of the fate that earlier befell research on language in chimpanzees; after a period of initial promise, there is now a more realistic appraisal that borders on pessimism. Even Premack has concluded that apes do not have a fully fledged theory of mind (Premack & Dasser, 1991). Heyes (1998) provided a review of the experimental evidence, reiterating and expanding her earlier challenge (Heyes, 1993) to experimenters to prove that the evi-

dence cannot be explained in nonmentalist terms. A more generous interpretation of the evidence might be that the chimpanzee's ability to attribute
mental states is roughly comparable to that of the 2-year-old child and does
not have the full recursive power that becomes evident in human children
only when they reach the age of about 4. At the age of 2, children do show
some measure of empathy, engage in pretense, and recognize themselves in a
mirror, and great apes, but not monkeys, seem to display similar capabilities
(see Suddendorf, 1999, for review).

At the age of about 4, however, children reach a new level of flexibility in the
attribution of mental states. It is not until then that they show themselves able
to attribute false beliefs, sometimes considered the acid test of theory of mind
(Wimmer & Perner, 1983). For example, 3-year-old children shown that a
candy box contains pencils, not candy, will aver that another child not privy to
this demonstration will nevertheless believe the box to contain pencils, and indeed declare themselves to have known this all along (Gopnik & Astington,
1988). Even 4-year-olds tend to claim that they have always known what in fact
they learned earlier on that same day (Taylor, Esbensen, & Bennett 1994).
There is little evidence on how great apes can perform on these tests, but
Premack (1988) reported an unsuccessful attempt to demonstrate the attribution of false belief in a chimpanzee.

Another test that is sometimes said to require theory of mind is the mirror
test, in which some mark, such as red dye, is surreptitiously placed on an animal's face, and the animal is then shown its own reflection in a mirror. Among
the nonhuman primates, only the great apes will then touch the marked locations, suggesting self-recognition (Gallup, 1977). But while this suggests that
the animal has a sense of its own body, it need not mean that it has a concept of
its own mind. At least some children as young as 18 months can also pass the
mirror test, but this appears to depend on online viewing. Two- and 3-year-old
children will remove a marker surreptitiously placed on their heads if they are
allowed to view themselves on live video but not if the video is delayed. Even a
2-second delay may be sufficient to disrupt the action. It is only by about the age
of 4 that children understand that a delayed image is indeed an image of themselves (Povinelli, 1998). Povinelli suggested that 2-year-olds may understand
that the delayed image is just like themselves, but is not actually themselves. He
goes on to suggest that the chimpanzee's understanding of its reflection in the
mirror, like the 2-year-old's, is essentially a kinesthetic self-concept, formed
from the immediate correlation of the animal's movements with those viewed
in the mirror, but includes no sense of continuity over time. The development of
a self-concept that continues through time at approximately age 4 may also underlie the emergence of true autobiographical memory at about that age (Nelson, 1993). Povinelli suggested that this concept of *self*, along with the ability to

truly understand the minds of others, is uniquely human, denied even to our closest relative, the chimpanzee.

Although monkeys do not pass the mirror test, there is neurophysiological evidence for a mapping between the perception and production of manual action that may well be a precursor to theory of mind. Rizzolatti and his colleagues (e.g., Rizzolatti, Fadiga, Gallese, & Fogassi, 1996) discovered what they call *mirror neurons* in ventral premotor area F5 of the monkey, so-called because they respond not only when the animal makes a given grasping response but also when the animal sees the same response made by another. Area F5 is analogous to Broca's speech area in humans, and Arbib and Rizzolatti (1997) suggested that these neurons may be preadaptations for language because they map intentional actions between individuals—or between agent and patient, to use the terminology of semantic theory. Equally, they might be considered a preadaptation for theory of mind, providing a kind of motor empathy between individuals.

Even so, this internal mapping between action and perception may be no more than perceptuomotor, selected perhaps in the context of food-sharing transactions. Mirror neurons need not tell the animal anything of the mental perspective of the animal making the perceived gesture. What may be missing is the recursive component that seems to be critical to theory of mind, and which may have depended on further elaboration of frontal circuits that did not take place until much later, perhaps only in the hominid line following the split from the chimpanzee line. That is, the monkey or chimpanzee can know, but does not appear to know that it knows, or know that others know. Once this kind of recursion becomes possible it leads to a generativity that resembles that in language, and indeed that is often expressed in language. It is this intricate mental perspective taking, often with several levels of recursion, that makes human relationships so complex. We cannot only know that others know, but we can know that they know that we know something. And so it goes.

In general, then, the evidence on theory of mind in apes appears to be converging on a conclusion that is at least roughly analogous to the consensus that has emerged in relation to language in apes. Great apes, and chimpanzees in particular, appear to perform on tests of mental attribution and self concept at about the level of a 2-year-old child, but lack the sophisticated, recursive mental capacity—or what Suddendorf (1999) termed *metamind*—that emerges around the age of 4. True generativity, displaying the unboundedness of human language and creative thought, may therefore not have emerged in hominid evolution until some time after the hominid line split from the line that led to the modern chimpanzee, some 5 million years ago.

Before considering how generativity might have evolved in the hominids, it is useful to review the preadaptations that might have set the stage. Primates are characteristically visual creatures and have excellent voluntary control over their limbs, with hands and arms well adapted to such activities as grooming, picking fruit, manipulating objects, making tools, gesturing, and throwing. The mirror neurons, referred to previously, also suggest a preadaptation to map actions that are visually perceived onto those that are performed by the animal itself. It is no surprise, then, that the most successful attempts to teach symbolic communication to great apes has involved either manual gestures or visual shapes rather than vocal speech. It is also clear that great apes can deal with combinations of visual symbols, both in production and comprehension, although this ability is extremely limited compared with humans. Kohler's (1927) classic experiments on problem solving in chimpanzees likewise suggest a limited ability to manipulate internal representations of objects in order to solve an external problem. It seems likely that the ability to form internal representations of objects, as well as internal representations of manual actions, may have served as a preadaptation for the later evolution of generative thought. That is, the building blocks may be in place, along with a limited ability to combine them, but there is as yet no evidence for the recursive, generative metamind that characterizes our own species from about the age of 4 years.

Bipedalism and the Freeing of the Hands

The most important characteristic that distinguished the early hominids from the other great apes was bipedalism, or the ability to walk freely on two legs rather than four. Whatever the selective pressures that led to this adaptation, it would have had an important consequence: It freed the hands from any direct involvement in locomotion. This would have enhanced the capacity for manipulation and perhaps for imitating objects and actions with the hands and arms, and even with the whole body. These activities would have further increased the capacity for the establishment of internal representations, allowing rehearsal of shapes and actions by mimicking them. Donald (1991) postulated a mimetic culture in the early hominids that preceded the emergence of true language, in which our forebears made extensive use of mime to communicate with one another.

Bipedalism may have also led to pointing as a means of highlighting objects and directing attention to them. Among primates, pointing seems to be uniquely human (Butterworth & Grover, 1988). Human infants seem to understand pointing at approximately 12 months of age, and can themselves point at approximately 14 months (Shaffer, 1984). Although chimpanzees can be taught to look in the direction of a pointing finger, they do not themselves point (Woodruff & Premack, 1979). I have argued that manual gestures, including pointing, were the basis for the subsequent evolution of generative language

(Corballis, 1991b, 1992, 1999), but they would also have served to sharpen and expand the internal representations of objects and actions. In short, the human body, with the arms and hands freed from locomotory duty, and the upright stance allowing more open confrontation, assumed a theatrical role, and this in turn allowed many aspects of the external world to be embodied as internal representations.

Although Donald (1991) argued that the mimetic culture was eventually succeeded by a symbolic one, and that mimesis persists in a nonlinguistic form in activities such as dance and mime, I have argued for a gradual transition from gestural to vocal language (Corballis, 1991b, 1992, 1999). The vocal cries of primates are largely under subcortical control, and relatively resistant to modification, so it is therefore, it is likely that propositional communication evolved largely in the manual modality, although perhaps punctuated by vocalizations. Arbib and Rizzolatti (1997) also argued, on the basis of the mirror neurons, that language originated in manual gestures. A further compelling argument in favor of the gestural theory is that modern humans acquire manual sign languages as readily as they acquire vocal ones and go through essentially the same developmental stages in doing so (Armstrong, Stokoe, & Wilcox, 1995). The most impressive evidence of this comes from sign languages invented by the deaf, but sign languages have also been developed by hearing communities (e.g., Kendon, 1988), and all of us tend to resort to manual gestures when trying to communicate with those who speak a different tongue. If people are prevented from speaking, moreover, their signing begins to assume grammatical components (Goldin-Meadow, McNeill, & Singleton, 1996).

In the course of evolution, however, vocalizations would have assumed a more prominent role, accompanied by increasing cortical control and changes in the vocal tract to permit a greater variety of sounds. Indeed Lieberman (1998) argued that vocal speech did not emerge until the arrival of our own species, *Homo sapiens*, some 150,000 years ago. Contrary to Lieberman's, however, my own view is that language itself did not appear de novo at this point but had already evolved in a primarily gestural form, and that what early *H. sapiens* effected was a switch to a predominantly vocal mode.

The Increase in Brain Size

It seems likely that the capacity for recursion and generativity began to develop with the emergence of the genus *Homo* something over 2 million years ago. It was at this stage of hominid evolution that brain size began to increase beyond that of the earlier australopithecines, whose brain size did not differ appreciably from that of modern great apes (Martin, 1990). Another emergent property that might have been critical to the evolution of generativity is the prolongation of infancy, allowing much of the growth of the brain takes place after birth; the brain of the newborn chimpanzee is about 60% of its ultimate weight, compared with about 24% for the human infant. As we have seen, environmental input during growth may be critical to the development of hierarchical structures in language and manufacture (Greenfield, 1991), and perhaps to generativity in general. There is evidence that this prolongation of infancy was not present in *Australopithecus africanus* or *Homo habilis* (Smith, 1986) but was present in *Homo ergaster*[5] by some 1.6 million years ago (Brown, Harris, Leakey, & Walker, 1985). *Homo ergaster*, the African contemporary of *Homo erectus*, is likely to have been an ancestor of modern humans and may well have developed generative language, perhaps in a predominantly manual rather than a vocal mode.

The Switch to Vocal Language

Although the transition from manual to vocal language may have been gradual, the emergence of an autonomous vocal language may not have come about until very recently in hominid evolution, perhaps with the appearance of *Homo sapiens* about 150,000, to 100,000 years ago. Although it is true that most of us make quite extensive use of gestures to embellish speech, we can produce fully grammatical language through speech alone and make ourselves understood with little impediment. This is well illustrated by such devices as the telephone, radio, and encounters after dark. The final transition from gesture to speech would have freed the hands and arms once again, this time from a role in propositional language, and allowed people to explain techniques of manufacture while at the same time demonstrating them. Thus pedagogy was born. I have suggested that this may explain why the development of tools remained largely static for some 2 million years but then quite suddenly began to develop a new sophistication with the emergence of our own species (Corballis, 1991b, 1992, 1999). The explosion in manufacture is often dated from the profusion of artifacts, ornaments, and cave drawings in Europe and the Near East at about 35,000 years ago (e.g., Pfeiffer, 1985) but probably goes back to at least 90,000 years ago in Africa (Yellen, Brooks, Cornelissen, Mehlman, & Stewart, 1995)— very close to the African origin of our species.

This advance in manufacture, which continues to develop exponentially, would have added to the inventory of building blocks and construction rules that continue to clutter our minds. Because manual signs are more iconic than spoken words, the switch to vocal language may also have hastened a trend to arbitrary, symbolic representation, perhaps allowing a greater flexibility of thought and

---

[5]Brown et al. (1985) refer to this species as *Homo erectus*, but I have followed the reclassification suggested by Groves (1989).

generativity. And finally, the emergence of writing would have allowed knowledge to be stored, vastly increasing the sum total of human resources.

CONCLUSIONS

Evolutionary psychologists have argued that the human mind differs from that of the great apes largely because of the existence of specialized modules that appeared during the Pleistocene and evolved along independent trajectories. It is also claimed that these modules have a genetic basis, even to the point that each module may depend on different genes. This rather simplistic, highly reductionist view seems unlikely on a number of counts. First, the argument seems circular: Characteristics of human thought or action are linked to selective pressures operating in the Pleistocene, but there seems no way to independently verify that such pressures actually existed. One might caricature evolutionary psychology as declaring: "It is, therefore it was selected for." Second, the notion of reverse engineering from behavior to module to gene seems biologically naive. It is unlikely that modules were selected for independently of each other and independently of the existing genotype. Moreover, to suppose that the growing number of postulated modules represent independent genetic modifications defies the high degree of genetic similarity between humans and chimpanzees, who were not blessed with the Pleistocene experience and the peculiar selective pressure that are supposed—or conjectured—to have accompanied it. It is unlikely that new genes, such as the grammar genes postulated by Pinker (1994), were simply plugged in as extras. Finally, the idea that the human mind was created by simply adding a large number of independent and highly specialized modules flies in the face of the commonsense view, articulated by Descartes (1647/1985), that the human mind is distinguished from that of an ape by a unitary quality that adds an open-endedness and flexibility to our thoughts, words, and actions. The human mind is more like a general-purpose computer, we seem to feel, than a bank of specialized computational devices, able to turn the power of reason to virtually any problem, be it mechanical, social, or computational.

In this chapter, I have argued that the commonsense view may be closer to the truth than the currently fashionable modular view. Many if not all of the qualities of mind that seem to set humans apart, such as language, manufacture, theory of mind, and episodic memory and mental time travel, seem to have in common the properties of recursiveness and generativity. In children, these properties seem to emerge between the ages of 2 and 4 and may be formed through the interaction between growth of the brain, especially the prefrontal cortex, and environmental input. A growing brain may be not only more responsive to environmental modification than a static one, but also growth may allow it to build the hierarchical and recursive structures necessary for unbounded generativity. In evolution, the increase in brain size and the prolongation of postnatal brain growth that was necessary for this development may have taken place over the past 2 million years. Genetically, the changes could be accomplished by changes to a small number of genes regulating the timing and pattern of growth, rather than by the relatively large number of genes implied by the modular theory.

But this is not to say that the distinctive intelligence implied by our capacity for generativity is unitary. If not modular, it is at least lumpy. Depending on the environmental input during the critical periods of growth, and perhaps on genetic differences in the patterns of brain growth, individuals may differ with respect to the various mental abilities that depend on the flexible manipulation of elements. Some individuals may develop superior language abilities, others may acquire superior social skills through a highly developed theory of mind, yet others may excel in mechanical or musical skills. Yet all of these acquisitions may depend on a common mechanism, a growth-dependent sensitivity to environmental structuring. This account may well be consistent with hierarchical factor models of human intelligence (e.g., Carroll, 1993).

Although I have argued that the generative component emerged in the hominid line after the split from the line that led to the modern chimpanzee, it was clearly highly dependent on preadaptations. The great apes do seem capable of forming symbolic representations, and even of combining them in simple ways. Some authors, such as Deacon (1997) and Noble and Davidson (1996), have argued that the key to the human mind lies in the invention of symbolic representations themselves, and it is of course possible that symbols did acquire new properties in hominid evolution that permitted a freer play of combination and invention. Even so, it seems to me more likely that the key to the emergence of generativity had to do with combinatorial structures rather than with the building blocks. I have also argued that the preadaptations were primarily visuomotor and led to forms of communication and construction that were built on manual and bodily activities rather than on vocal sounds.

An alternative evolutionary scenario that seeks a compromise between modularity and the intuition that there is a general purpose aspect to the human mind has been proposed by Mithen (1996). There are three phases to this scenario. Phase 1 represents the early hominid era when the mind was characterized by general intelligence. Phase 2 is the hunter–gatherer phase, during which independent modules evolved; these are the adaptive specializations postulated by the evolutionary psychologists. Phase 3 represents the emergence of the modern human mind, beginning perhaps 60,000 years ago, when communication channels opened among the modules, and between the modules and general intelligence, so that the mind achieved a fluidity and creativity not previously possible. A difficulty with this scenario is that it undermines the argument for modularity itself. The idea of independent modules is based on evidence from modern humans and reverse engineered back to the hunter–gatherer phase. If the present-day modules are not encapsulated after all, what ground do we have supposing that they were independent, encapsulated entities during the Pleistocene?

Even so, any scenario is heavily reliant on speculation, and the ideas presented in this chapter are probably no less speculative than Mithen's. At least there seems fairly general agreement that hominid evolution can be divided into three broad phases. In my account, the early hominid phase was dedicated largely to the development of protolanguage and an expansion of representations based on bodily gestures, brought about by bipedalism and the freeing of the hands and arms from locomotion. The later, hunter–gatherer phase may have seen the emergence of more generative modes of thought and language, made possible by alterations to the pattern of growth, so that much of the growth of an enlarged brain took place after birth in order to receive progressive imprints from experience. The final, modern phase may have seen the eventual replacement of bodily gestures and forms of representations by a speech code, which freed the hands, and the imagination, for a wider range of generative action.

REFERENCES

Anderson, J. A. (1995). *Cognitive psychology and its implications* (4th ed.). San Francisco, CA: W. H. Freeman.

Arbib, M. A., & Rizzolatti, G. (1997). Neural expectations: A possible evolutionary path from manual skills to language. *Communication & Cognition, 29,* 393–424.

Armstrong, D. F., Stokoe, W. C., & Wilcox, S. E. (1995). *Gesture and the nature of language.* Cambridge: Cambridge University Press.

Baron-Cohen, S. (1995). *Mindblindness: An essay on autism and theory of mind.* Cambridge, MA: MIT Press.

Bartlett, F. C. (1932). *Remembering.* Cambridge: Cambridge University Press.

Bellugi, U., Wang, P. & Jernigan, T. L. (1994). Williams syndrome: An unusual neuropsychological profile. In S. Broman & J. Grafman (Eds.), *Neurodevelopmental disorders: Implications for brain function* (pp. 23–56). Hillsdale, NJ: Lawrence Erlbaum Associates.

Bickerton, D. (1995). *Language and human behavior.* Seattle, WA: University of Washington Press.

Brown, F., Harris, J., Leakey, R., & Walker, A. (1985). Early Homo erectus skeleton from west Lake Turkana, Kenya. *Nature, 316,* 788–792.

Butterworth, G., & Grover, L. (1988). The origins of referential communication in human infancy. In L. Weiskrantz (Ed.), *Thought without language* (pp. 5–24). Oxford, UK: Clarendon Press.

Byrne, R. W. (1995). *The thinking ape: Evolutionary origins of intelligence.* Oxford: Oxford University Press.

Byrne, R. W., & Whiten, A. (1990). Tactical deception in primates: The 1990 database. *Primate Report, 27,* 1–101.

Cann, R. L. (1987). In search of Eve. *The Sciences, 27,* 30–37.

Carroll, J. B. (1993). *Human cognitive abilities: A survey of factor-analytic studies*. New York: Cambridge University Press.

Chomsky, N. (1966). *Cartesian linguistics: A chapter in the history of rationalist thought*. New York: Harper & Row.

Chomsky, N. (1971). *Problems of knowledge and freedom*. New York: Pantheon Books.

Chomsky, N. (1986). *Knowledge of language: Its nature, origin, and use*. New York: Praeger.

Chomsky, N. (1988). *Language and problems of knowledge: The Managua lectures*. Cambridge, MA: Cambridge University Press.

Clayton, N. S., & Dickinson, A. D. (1998). Episodic-like memory during cache recovery in scrub jays. *Nature, 395*, 272–274.

Conway, M. (1999). Unique memories: Creating the mind's "I." *Nature, 397*, 575–576.

Corballis, M. C. (1991a). Memory, growth, evolution, and laterality. In W. Hockley & S. Lewandowsky (Eds.), *Relating theory to data*. Hillsdale, NJ: Lawrence Erlbaum Associates.

Corballis, M. C. (1991b). *The lop-sided ape*. New York: Oxford University Press.

Corballis, M. C. (1992). On the evolution of language and generativity. *Cognition, 44*, 197–226.

Corballis, M. C. (1997). Mental rotation and the right hemisphere. *Brain & Language, 57*, 100–121.

Corballis, M. C. (1999). The gestural origins of language. *American Scientist, 87*(2), 138–145.

Corkin, S. (1984). Lasting consequences of bilateral medial temporal lobectomy. Clinical course and experimental findings in H. M. *Seminars in Neurology, 4*, 249–259.

Cosmides, L., & Tooby, J. (1987). From evolution to behavior: Evolutionary psychology as the missing link. In J. Dupre (Ed.), *The latest on the best: Essays on evolution and optimality* (pp. 277–306). Cambridge: Cambridge University Press.

Cosmides, L., & Tooby, J. (1994). Origins of domain specificity: The evolution of functional organization. In L. A. Hirschfeld & S. A. Gelman (Eds.), *Mapping the mind: Domain specificity in cognition and culture* (pp. 88–116). Cambridge: Cambridge University Press.

Cox, J. R., & Griggs, R. A. (1989). The effects of experience on performance in Wason's selection tasks. *Memory and Cognition, 10*, 496–502.

Deacon, T. (1997). *The symbolic species*. Harmondsworth, England: Allen Lane, The Penguin Press.

Descartes, R. (1985). *The philosophical writings of Descartes* (J. Cottingham, R. Stoothoff, & D. Murdock, Eds. and Trans.). Cambridge: Cambridge University Press. (Original work published 1647)

Diamond, J. (1997). *Guns, germs, and steel: The fates of modern human societies*. Cambridge, MA: Harvard University Press.

Donald, M. (1991). *Origins of the modern mind*. Cambridge, MA: Harvard University Press.

Elman, J. L. (1993). Learning and development in neural circuits: The importance of starting small. *Cognition, 48*, 71–99.

Elman, J., Bates, E., Johnson, M., Karmiloff-Smith, A., Parisi, D., & Plunkett, K. (1996). *Rethinking innateness: A connectionist perspective on language*. Cambridge, MA: MIT Press.

Fauconnier, G. (1997). *Mappings in thought and language*. Cambridge: Cambridge University Press.

Fodor, J. A. (1983). *The modularity of mind*. Cambridge, MA: MIT Press.

Gallup, G. G., Jr. (1977). Self-recognition in primates: A comparative approach to the bidirectional properties of consciousness. *American Psychologist, 32*, 329–338.

Goldin-Meadow, S., McNeill, D., & Singleton, J. (1996). Silence is liberating: Removing the handcuffs on grammatical expression in the manual modality. *Psychological Review, 103*, 34–55.

Goodman, M. (1992). Reconstructing human evolution from proteins. In S. Jones, R. Martin, & D. Pilbeam (Eds.), *The Cambridge encyclopaedia of human evolution* (pp. 307–312). Cambridge: Cambridge University Press.

Gopnik, A., & Astington J. W. (1988). Children's understanding of representational change and its relation to the understanding of false belief and the appearance-reality distinction. *Child Development, 59,* 26–37.

Gopnik, M. (1990). Feature-blind grammar and dysphasia. *Nature, 344,* 715.

Greenfield, P. M. (1991). Language, tools, and the brain: The ontogeny and phylogeny of hierarchically organized sequential behavior. *Behavioral & Brain Sciences, 14,* 531–595.

Griffiths, D., Dickinson, A., & Clayton, N. (1998). Episodic memory: What can animals remember about their past? *Trends in Cognitive Science, 3,* 74–80.

Grossman, M. (1980). A central processor for hierarchically structured material: Evidence from Broca's aphasia. *Neuropsychologia, 18,* 299–308.

Groves, C. P. (1989). *A theory of human and primate evolution.* Oxford, UK: Clarendon Press.

Heyes, C. M. (1993). Anecdotes, training, trapping, and triangulation: Do animals attribute mental states? *Animal Behaviour, 46,* 177–188.

Heyes, C. M. (1998). Theory of mind in non-human primates. *Behavioral & Brain Sciences, 21,* 101–148.

Karmiloff-Smith, A. (1992). *Beyond modularity: A developmental perspective on cognitive science.* Cambridge, MA: MIT Press.

Karmiloff-Smith, A. (1998). Development itself is the key to understanding developmental disorders. *Trends in Cognitive Science, 10,* 389–398.

Kendon, A. (1988). *Sign languages of aboriginal Australia.* Cambridge: Cambridge University Press.

Kohler, W. (1927). *The mentality of apes* (E. Winter, Trans.). London: Routledge & Kegan Paul.

Laming, D. (1996). On the analysis of irrational data selection: A critique of Oaksford and Chater. *Psychological Review, 103,* 364–373

Langacker, R. W. (1991). *Concept, image, and symbol: The cognitive basis of grammar.* Berlin, Germany: Mouton de Gruyter.

Lieberman, P. (1998). *Eve spoke: Human language and human evolution.* New York: W.W. Norton.

Loftus, E., & Ketcham, K. (1991). *Witness for the defense: The accused, the eyewitness, and the expert who puts memory on trial.* New York: St. Martin's Press.

Loftus, E., & Ketcham, K. (1994). *The myth of repressed memory: False memories and allegations of sexual abuse.* New York: St. Martin's Press.

Martin, R. D. (1990). *Primate origins and evolution: A phylogenetic reconstruction.* Princeton, NJ: Princeton University Press.

Miles, H. L. (1990). The cognitive foundations for reference in a signing orangutan. In S. T. Parker & K. Gibson (Eds.), *"Language" and intelligence in monkeys and apes: Comparative developmental perspectives* (pp. 511–539). New York: Cambridge University Press.

Mithen, S. (1996). *The prehistory of the mind.* London: Thames & Hudson.

Moore, C. (1996). Evolution and the modularity of mindreading. *Cognitive Development, 11,* 605–621.

Neisser, U. (1967). *Cognitive psychology.* New York: Appleton-Century-Crofts.

Nelson, K. (1993). The psychological and social origins of autobiographical memory. *Psychological Science, 4,* 7–14.

Noble, W. (1998). Can lateralization cause language? *Current Psychology of Cognition, 17,* 1198–1201.

Noble, W., & Davidson, I. (1996). *Human evolution, language, and mind.* Cambridge: Cambridge University Press.

Oaksford, M., & Chater, N. (1994). A rational analysis of the selection task as optimal data selection. *Psychological Review, 101,* 608–631.

Paivio, A. (1986). *Mental representation: A dual coding approach.* New York: Oxford University Press.

Patterson, F. (1978). Conversations with a gorilla. *National Geographic, 154,* 438–465.

Pfeiffer, J. E. (1985). *The emergence of humankind.* New York: Harper & Row.

Pillemer, D. B. (1998). *Momentous events, vivid memories.* Cambridge, MA: Harvard University Press.

Pinker, S. (1994). *The language instinct.* New York: William Morrow.

Pinker, S. (1997). *How the mind works.* New York: Norton.

Plaut, D. (1995). Double dissociations without modularity: Evidence from connectionist neuropsychology. *Journal of Clinical and Experimental Neuropsychology, 17,* 291–331.

Povinelli, D. J. (1994). Comparative studies of mental state attribution: A reply to Heyes. *Animal Behaviour, 48,* 239–241.

Povinelli, D. J. (1998). Can animals empathize? Maybe not. *Scientific American, 9*(4), 67–75.

Povinelli, D. J., Nelson, K. E., & Boysen, S. T. (1990). Inferences about guessing and knowing by chimpanzees (*Pan troglodytes*). *Journal of Comparative Psychology, 104,* 203–210.

Premack, D. (1988). "Does the chimpanzee have a theory of mind?" revisited. In R. W Byrne & A. Whiten (Eds.), *Machiavellian intelligence* (pp. 160–179). Oxford, UK: Clarendon Press.

Premack, D., & Dasser, V. (1991). Perceptual origins and conceptual evidence for theory of mind in apes and children. In A. Whiten (Ed.), *Natural theories of mind: Evolution, development and simulation of everyday mindreading* (pp. 253–266). Oxford, England: Basil Blackwell.

Premack, D., & Premack, A. (1983). *The mind of an ape.* New York: W.W. Norton.

Premack, D., & Premack, A. J. (1994). How "theory of mind" constrains language and communication. *Discussions in Neuroscience, 10,* 93–105.

Premack, D., & Woodruff, G. (1978). Does the chimpanzee have a theory of mind? *Behavioral & Brain Sciences, 4,* 515–526.

Rizzolatti, G., Fadiga, L., Gallese, V., & Fogassi, L. (1996) Premotor cortex and the recognition of motor actions. *Cognitive Brain Research, 3,* 131–141.

Sampson, G. (1997). *Educating Eve: The "language instinct" debate.* London: Cassell.

Sarich, V., & Wilson, A. C. (1967). Immunological time scale for hominid evolution. *Science, 158,* 1200–1203.

Savage-Rumbaugh, S., & Lewin, R. (1994). *Kanzi: An ape at the brink of the human mind.* New York: Wiley.

Sergent, J., Zuck, E., Terriah, S., & MacDonald, B. (1992). Distributed neural network underlying musical sight-reading and keyboard performance. *Science, 257,* 106–109.

Shaffer, H. R. (1984). *The child's entry into a social world.* New York: Academic Press.

Smith, B. H. (1986). Dental developments in *Australopithecus* and early *Homo. Nature, 323,* 327–330.

Spearman, C. (1904). General intelligence, objectively determined and measured. *American Journal of Psychology, 15,* 201–293.

Sperber, D. (1994). The modularity of thought and the epidemiology of representations. In L. A. Hirschfeld & S. A. Gelman (Eds.), *Mapping the mind: Domain specificity in cognition and culture* (pp. 39–67). Cambridge: Cambridge University Press.

Suddendorf, T. (1998). Simpler for evolution: Secondary representation in apes, children, and ancestors. *Behavioral & Brain Sciences, 21,* 131.

Suddendorf, T. (1999). The rise of the metamind: Beyond the immediately present. In M. C. Corballis & S. E. G. Lea (Eds.), *The descent of mind* (pp. 218–260). Oxford: Oxford University Press.

Suddendorf, T., & Corballis, M. C. (1997). Mental time travel and the evolution of the human mind. *Genetic, Social, and General Psychology Monographs, 123,* 133–167.

Taylor, M., Esbensen, B. M., & Bennett, R. T. (1994). Children's understanding of knowledge acquisition: The tendency for children to report that they have always known what they have just learned. *Child Development, 65,* 1581–1604.

Terrace, H. S. (1985). In the beginning was the "name". *American Psychologist, 40,* 1011–1028.

Terrace, H. S., Pettito, L. A., Sanders, R. J., & Bever, T. G. (1979). Can an ape create a sentence? *Science, 206,* 891–902.

Thatcher, R. W., Walker, R. A., & Guidice, S. (1987). Human cerebral hemispheres develop at different rates and ages. *Science, 236,* 1110–1113.

Thurstone, L. L. (1947). *Multiple factor analysis.* Chicago, IL: University of Chicago Press.

Tooby, J., & Cosmides, L. (1989). Evolutionary psychology and the generation of culture, part 1. *Ethology and Sociobiology, 10,* 29–49.

Tulving, E. (1993). What is episodic memory? *Current Directions in Psychological Science, 2,* 67–70.

Van Orden, G. C., Jansen op de Haar, M., & Bosman, A. M. T. (1997). Complex dynamic systems also predict dissociations, but they do not reduce to autonomous components. *Cognitive Neuropsychology, 14,* 131–165.

Vargha-Khadem, F., Gadian, D. G., Watkins, K. E., Connelly, A., Van Paesschen, W., & Mishkin, M. (1997). Differential effects of early hippocampal pathology on episodic and semantic memory. *Science, 277,* 376–380.

Waddell, P. J., & Penny, D. (1996). Evolutionary trees of apes and humans from DNA sequences. In A. Lock & C. R. Peters (Eds.), *Handbook of human symbolic evolution* (pp. 53–73). Oxford: Oxford University Press.

Wason, P. (1966). Reasoning. In B. M. Foss (Ed.), *New horizons in psychology.* London: Penguin.

Wheeler, M. A., Stuss, D. T., & Tulving, E. (1997). Toward a theory of episodic memory: The frontal lobes and autonoetic consciousness. *Psychological Bulletin, 121,* 331–354.

Wilcox, S. (1998). Structural generativity, meaning generation, and the origins of language. *Current Psychology of Cognition, 17,* 1215–1220.

Wimmer, H., & Perner, J. (1983). Beliefs about beliefs: Representation and constraining function of wrong beliefs in young children's understanding of deception. *Cognition, 13,* 103–128.

Woodruff, G., & Premack, D. (1979). Intentional communication in the chimpanzee: The development of deception. *Cognition, 7,* 333–362.

Yellen, J. E., Brooks, A. S., Cornelissen, E., Mehlman, M. J., & Stewart, K. (1995). A Middle Stone Age worked bone industry from Katanda, Upper Semliki Valley, Zaire. *Science, 268,* 553–556.

8

Unraveling the Enigma of Human Intelligence: Evolutionary Psychology and the Multimodular Mind

Leda Cosmides
John Tooby
University of California

EVOLUTIONARY PSYCHOLOGY AND THE ENIGMA OF INTELLIGENCE

Evolution brought brains and minds into a world initially devoid of intelligent life. The evolutionary process designed the neural machinery that generates intelligent behavior, and important insights into how this machinery works can be gained by understanding how evolution constructs organisms. This is the rationale that underlies research in evolutionary psychology.

Evolutionary psychology was founded on interlocking contributions from evolutionary biology, cognitive science, psychology, anthropology, and neuroscience. It reflects an attempt to think through, from first principles, how current knowledge from these various fields can be integrated into a single, consistent, scientific framework for the study of the mind and brain (Cosmides & Tooby, 1987; Pinker, 1997; Tooby & Cosmides, 1992b).

Perhaps more than any other issue, questions about the nature and evolution of human intelligence and rationality have played a central organizing role in the development of evolutionary psychology. Indeed, how evolutionary psychologists answer questions about the evolutionary basis of intelligence demarcates it from more traditional behavioral science approaches. As a starting point, evolutionary psychologists share with other cognitive scientists a commitment to discovering exactly how mental operations are realized computationally and physically in the mind and brain. To this, they add a perspective that attempts to incorporate knowledge about the brains and natural behavior of each species that has been studied, and a recognition that the evolutionary process constructed the computational systems present in the minds of organisms primarily through natural selection (Cosmides & Tooby, 1987; Pinker, 1997; Tooby & Cosmides, 1992b).

To make progress in understanding the phenomenon of evolved intelligence, we have been led to distinguish two related meanings of intelligence. We call these *dedicated intelligence* and *improvisational intelligence*. Dedicated intelligence refers to the ability of a computational system to solve a predefined, target set of problems. Improvisational intelligence refers to the ability of a computational system to improvise solutions to novel problems. Ordinary use of the term *intelligence* is inconsistent: People sometimes use it to mean something similar to improvisational intelligence. But the term is also often applied to systems that are highly successful at solving their respective problems, regardless of whether the problem is novel or the solution improvised. People remark on the intelligence of such things as the bat's sonar navigation system, more accurate bombs, the rice cooker with sensors and fuzzy logic circuits that decide when the rice is done, and Sojourner, the semiautonomous rover that explored the surface of Mars. Distinguishing between these two types of intelligence is indispensable for understanding how evolution constructed intelligent circuitry in organisms.

Traditionally, many behavioral and social scientists have, implicitly or explicitly, believed the following:

1. Humans are endowed with improvisional intelligence.
2. Most human behavior is explained by the operation of improvisional intelligence.
3. Most of our interesting and important psychological operations are the output of a system for improvisional intelligence.
4. Improvisional intelligence is achieved by an architecture that is essentially a blank slate connected to general-purpose (content-independent, domain-general) reasoning and learning circuits.
5. Improvisional intelligence is easy, at least in concept, to understand and to design, and might soon be built into artificial systems.

6. Specialized programs, because they are inflexible, would hamper or reduce the intelligence of a system.
7. Therefore, humans evolved intelligence by giving up instincts and innate structure and substituting general-purpose learning, reasoning, and intelligence instead.

In contrast, we have come to the following conclusions:

1. Humans are endowed with improvisational intelligence, but
2. Humans are also endowed with a large and heterogeneous set of evolved, reliably developing, dedicated problem-solving programs, each of which is specialized to solve a particular domain or class of adaptive problems (e.g., grammar acquisition, mate acquisition, food aversion, way-finding).
3. Each such neural program exhibits a well-engineered, problem-solving intelligence when applied to the targeted set of problems it evolved to solve. However, these adaptive specializations cannot, by their nature, display improvisional intelligence, at least individually.
4. A very large proportion of human thought and action owes its intelligent patterning to dedicated problem-solving intelligence rather than improvisional intelligence.
5. The larger the number of dedicated intelligences a system has, the broader the range of problems it could solve.
6. For reasons rooted in the nature of computation and in the way natural selection works, improvisional intelligence is difficult to implement and to evolve, and presents deep theoretical challenges. In short, the puzzle of how improvisional intelligence is computationally and evolutionary possible is a profound one.
7. Nevertheless, improvisional intelligence might have been achieved through (a) bundling an increasing number of specialized intelligences together and (b) embedding them in an encompassing architecture that has a *scope syntax*: an elaborate set of computational adaptations for regulating the interaction of transient and contingent information sets within a multimodular mind.

In short, evolutionary psychologists have arrived at a series of sometimes heterodox conclusions about what intelligence means, how it is constructed, and what role intelligence plays in the human psychological architecture. The remainder of the chapter sketches out the logic that has led to these conclusions (see also Cosmides & Tooby, 1987, in press; Tooby & Cosmides, 1992a, 1992b; Tooby & DeVore, 1987). In order to retrace these steps, we will need to address a series of fundamental questions, such as What is intelligence? What is computation? and What is an adaptive problem?

The Robot Challenge

The fields of cognitive psychology and artificial intelligence grew up together, and their animating questions became deeply intertwined. The pioneering work of mathematicians and early computer scientists, such as Alan Turing, John Von Neuman, Alan Newell, and Herbert Simon, set off a race to create intelligent machines, where intelligence was defined with respect to a cultural standard of general problem solving. The goal of developing a causal account of how thought can be produced by a mechanical system was shared by both cognitive psychologists and computer scientists. As many thought of it, the primary difference between the two fields was whether the mechanical system in question was a carbon-based brain or a silicon-based computer, and researchers debated whether this difference in physical substrate was trivial or would constrain, in important ways, the kinds of computations that each system could perform. In this atmosphere, many discussions of intelligence were framed by what one can think of as the robot challenge: What criteria would a robot have to meet before it was said to exhibit humanlike intelligence? What programs would the robot need in order to achieve these criteria?

Steven Pinker (1997) formulated one of the clearest analyses of the robot challenge. In Pinker's view, intelligence is "the ability to attain goals in the face of obstacles by means of decisions based on rational (truth-obeying) rules" (p. 62), where *rational* and *truth-obeying* are understood not in the narrow logician's sense but in the broader sense of rules that correspond to reality, at least in the statistical sense. In arguing for this definition, he points out that (i) without a specification of a creature's goals, the concept of intelligence is meaningless (is a toadstool brilliant because it is good at remaining exactly where it is?); (ii) we would be hard pressed to credit an organism with much intelligence if, in attempting to overcome obstacles to achieve goals, its actions were unconnected to reality (e.g., wanting to split a log, it hacks at empty space); and (iii) overcoming obstacles implies the ability to shift to different plans of action, depending on the nature of the obstacle. Different means are chosen to achieve the same end, depending on the particulars of the situation one is facing. According to Pinker, any system exhibiting this property—robot, space alien, or earth species—would count as having "rational, humanlike thought." Pinker's definition elegantly captures many intuitions that people have about intelligence—at least of the human variety—and provides a clear foundation for thinking about the question. It also encapsulates much of what we mean when we speak of improvisional intelligence.

Indeed, views such as this have organized the thinking of philosophers and scientists for many centuries. What kind of mental machinery does an organism need to manifest this form of intelligence? Evolutionary psychologists argue that there are actually many different possible answers to this question (Cosmides & Tooby, in press; Pinker, 1994, 1997; Tooby & Cosmides, 1992b). However, this is not the traditional view. Noting that humans—unlike many other animals—are able to pursue so many different goals, overcoming so many different obstacles using so many different means, many thinkers have assumed that the nature of the mental machinery that creates intelligence in humans must be free of anything that might constrain it; that is, it must be a blank slate. The flexibility of human intelligence—that is, our ability to solve many different kinds of problems—was thought to be conclusive evidence that the circuits that generate it are general purpose and content free. *Homo sapiens* was thought of as the one animal endowed with reason, a species whose instincts were erased by evolution because they were rendered unnecessary by (or were incompatible with) culture, the ability to learn, and intelligence. This conception of the nature of human intelligence has been a central pillar of what we have called the standard social science model (SSSM), that is, the worldview that has dominated the social and behavioral sciences for the past century (for an extended dissection of this paradigm, see Tooby & Cosmides, 1992b).

The Standard Social Science Model

The SSSM maintains that the human mind is a blank slate, virtually free of content until written on by the hand of experience. According to the 13th-century philosopher Aquinas, there is "nothing in the intellect that was not previously in the senses." Working within this framework, the 17th- and 18th-century British Empiricists and their successors produced elaborate theories about how experience, refracted through a small handful of innate mental procedures, inscribed content onto the mental slate.

Over the years, the technological metaphor used to describe the structure of the human mind has been consistently updated, from blank slate to switchboard to general purpose computer. But the central tenet of these Empiricist views has remained the same: All of the specific content of the human mind originally derives from the "outside"—from the environment and the social world—and the evolved architecture of the mind consists solely or predominantly of a small number of general purpose mechanisms that are content-independent and that are referred to using terms such as *intelligence, learning, induction, imitation, rationality,* and *the capacity for culture.*

So according to this view, the same mechanisms are thought to govern how one acquires a language, learns to recognize emotional expressions, responds to the possibility of incest, responds to an attack or flattery, or adopts ideas about friendship and reciprocity (indeed everything but perception, which is often accepted as being specialized and at least partly innately structured). The mechanisms that govern reasoning, learning, and memory are hypothesized to operate uniformly, according to unchanging principles, regardless of the content they are operating on or the larger category or domain involved. (For this reason, we call such hypothesized mechanisms *content-independent* or *domain-general*.) Such mechanisms, by definition, have no preexisting content built in to their procedures; they are not designed to construct certain contents more readily than others; and they have no features specialized for processing particular kinds of content more than others. Because these hypothetical mental mechanisms have no content of their own to impart, it logically follows that all the particulars of what we think and feel are derived externally, from the physical and social world. In this view, the evolutionary process explains the evolution of the human body, human intelligence, and the capacity for learning culture, but the blank slate nature of the human mind interposes a barrier between biology and human mental content that renders evolution essentially irrelevant to human affairs. Unlike other animals, our evolution washed us clean of instincts and innate mental organization. So, the issue of the nature of human intelligence, and the role that it plays in the operation of the human mind, is not a minor one. Beliefs about intelligence ramify far beyond psychology, into every aspect of the behavioral and social sciences. Although there have been intense controversies about the significance of individual differences in intelligence and its measurement, its larger theoretical role as the central concept explaining how humans differ from other species, acquire culture, and generate the majority of their behavior has seemed almost self-evident to scholars.

Nevertheless, we think that three decades of converging research in cognitive psychology, evolutionary biology, anthropology, and neuroscience have shown that this plausible and persuasive view of the human mind is incorrect. Evolutionary psychology represents an alternative proposal about how to organize our understanding of the human mind and the nature of human intelligence. According to this alternative perspective, all normal human minds reliably develop a standard collection of reasoning, emotional, and motivational circuits or programs. These programs were functionally designed over evolutionary time by natural selection acting on our hunter–gatherer (and more distant) ancestors. They are individually tailored to the demands of particular evolutionary functions and often come equipped with what philosophers would once have called "innate ideas." There are far more of them than anyone had suspected, and they respond far more sensitively to the particulars of human life than anyone had imagined. Humans appear to have evolved circuits specialized for the domains of friendship, incest avoidance, coalitions, landscape preference, status, number, aggression, mating, language, intuiting what others are thinking, judging personality, and hundreds of other functions. These circuits organize the way we interpret our experiences, inject certain recurrent concepts and motivations into our mental life, give us our passions, and provide cross-culturally universal frames of meaning that allow us to understand the actions and intentions of others and to acquire the locally variable components of culture (for relevant reviews, see, e.g., Barkow, Cosmides, & Tooby, 1992; Gallistel, 1990; Hirchfeld & Gelman, 1994; Pinker, 1994, 1997).

The Organismic Challenge

The robot challenge grew out of the concerns of cognitive scientists interested in machine intelligence. But we would like to propose two definitions of intelligence that grow out of the concerns of evolutionary biologists, behavioral ecologists, and others who study animal behavior. The world is full of millions of species, all of whom have succeeded in surviving and reproducing in a world of fierce antagonists, entropy, and harsh environmental reverses. No existing robot or computer comes close to solving the stringent problems routinely faced by members of the living world. Facts about the living world constitute the organismic challenge: What criteria would an organism have to meet before it was said to exhibit some form of intelligence? What kind of programs would the organism need in order to achieve these criteria?

As special as human intelligence may be—and we do believe that it is zoologically unprecedented—one does see other animals overcome obstacles to attain goals, and their decisions take into account real facts about the world. The goals pursued may be different from ours; the range of possible goals pursued by members of any one species may be more limited, and the variety of means any one species employs in attaining them may be more limited as well. Nevertheless, everyone recognizes that the animals that surround us routinely overcome obstacles to attain goals, even if (to nonbiologists) the status of other organisms, such as plants, fungi, protists, and prokaryotes, is less clear.

Although nonbiologists are frequently unaware of the subtlety, intricacy, elegance, and sophistication expressed in the behavior of nonhumans, there is now a wealth of data available that needs to be assimilated into a general consideration of natural intelligence. Over the last 30 years, there has been an explosion of research in field biology, the rapid development of new experimental methods, and dramatic advances in adaptationist evolutionary biology that together provide a panorama of superb computational problem solving applied to a immense array of adaptive problems by a multiciplicity of species. For example, having wandered far in search of food in terrain that is often devoid of landmarks, desert ants return home, directly, by a straight line route, a feat they accomplish through vector integration (Gallistel, 1990; Wehner & Srinivasan, 1981). During classical conditioning, pigeons, rats, and other animals perform computations that are equivalent to a nonstationary multivariate time series analysis: From noisy, changing data, they figure out the contingencies between events in the world (Gallistel, 1990). Migratory birds extract configural relationships from the constellations and use them to navigate across thousands of miles. Rats, which evolved to be opportunistic omnivores, have such sophisticated strategies for testing novel foods that they routinely outwit exterminators attempting to poison them (Kalat & Rozin, 1973; Rozin & Kalat, 1971). Zebras continue to feed if they detect that the nearby lion has fed recently, and bother to interrupt their feeding only if they have insufficient evidence that this is the case. Male mice often kill unrelated baby mice, an act that causes the dead infants' mothers to reach estrus far earlier than they would if they had continued to nurse the unrelated male's offspring. They do not, however, kill their own pups: A male's first intravaginal ejaculation starts a neural timer that counts off the days of a typical pregnancy, and he stops committing infanticide several days before the birth of babies that could, in principle, be his own (Perrigo, Bryant, & vom Saal, 1990). A male dunnock will feed the chicks of the female he has been mating with in proportion to the probability that her babies are his as opposed to the coresident male's (Burke, Davies, Bruford, & Hatchwell, 1989; Davies, 1989). A stickleback fish will risk his life in defense of his nestful of eggs in proportion to the number of eggs in it (Pressley, 1981). Desert rodents manage their larder of seeds, taking into account the age of the seeds, their stage of germination, their nutritional value, the humidity in each area of the cache, the cost of acquisition, and many other variables (Gendron & Reichman, 1995; Post, McDonald, & Reichman, 1998). Chimpanzees engage in Machiavellian political intrigues, involving shifting coalitions and alliances (de Waal, 1982). In all these cases, the animals are using information about changes in the state of the world or the value of a resource to adjust their behavior in ways that achieve adaptive outcomes.

WHAT IS INTELLIGENCE?

To analyze these forms of intelligence, which are so abundantly manifest in the animal world, and to explore how they might relate to the emergence of human intelligence, it is necessary to introduce two definitions that distinguish two meanings of intelligence that apply to organisms. Because these forms of intelligence arose naturally, through the process of evolution, we think a number of insights might come from grounding the analysis of intelligence within the causal framework of evolutionary biology. For one thing, there are constraints on what kinds of machinery natural selection can design, and this will affect the form that intelligence takes. In particular, developing a conception of intelligence that can be applied widely to organisms allows us to zero in on those aspects of human intelligence that may be zoologically unique. Therefore, we would like to define two forms of intelligence as follows:

Intelligence$_1$. A computational system or program is intelligent$_1$ when it is well designed for solving a target set of adaptive computational problems. We will call this *dedicated intelligence*.

Intelligence$_2$. A computational system is intelligent$_2$ to the extent that it is well designed for solving adaptive computational problems, and has components designed to exploit transient or novel local conditions to achieve adaptive outcomes. We will call this *improvisational intelligence*.

To understand what these definitions mean, we need to say more precisely what we mean by *computational, designed, adaptive problem, adaptive outcome, transient, novel,* and *local.* These terms are defined with respect to one another, within a causal framework provided by Darwin's theory of evolution by natural selection.

What Is a Computational System?

Organisms are composed of many parts. Some of these parts are computational. By computational, we mean that they are designed to (i) monitor the environment for specific changes and (ii) regulate the operation of other parts of the system functionally on the basis of the changes detected. For example, the diaphragm muscle, which causes the lungs to contract and expand, is not computational. But the system that measures carbon dioxide in the blood and regulates the contraction and extension of the diaphragm muscle is. The plastic cover on a thermostat is not computational, nor are the parts of a furnace that generate heat. But the thermocouple that responds to ambient temperature by toggling the switch on the furnace, and the connections between them, form a computational system. Muscles are not computational, but the visual system that detects the presence of a hungry-looking lion, the inference mechanisms that judge whether that lion has seen you or not, and the circuits that cause your muscles to either run to a nearby tree (if the lion has seen you) or freeze (if it hasn't seen you) do compose a computational system. The language of information processing can be used to express the same distinction: One can identify the computational components of a system by isolating those aspects that were designed to regulate the operation of other parts of the system on the basis of *information* from the internal and external environment.

By "monitoring the environment for specific changes," we mean the system is designed to detect a change in the world. That change can be internal to the organism (such as fluctuations in carbon dioxide levels in the blood or the activation of a memory trace) or external to the organism (such as the onset of a rainstorm or the arrival of a potential mate). Changes in the world become *information* when (i) they interact with a physical device that is designed to change its state in response to variations in the world (i.e., a transducer), and

(ii) the changes that are registered then participate in a causal chain that was designed to regulate the operation of other parts of the system. A photon, for example, does not become information until it causes a chemical reaction in a retinal cell, which was designed for this purpose and is part of a causal system that was itself designed to regulate an organism's behavior on the basis of inferences about what objects exist in the world and where they are.

A set of features is not computational unless they were *designed* to exhibit these properties. For example, the outer cells of a dead tree stump expand in the rain, and as this happens, the inner portions of the stump might become compressed. But these dead cells were not designed for detecting changes in weather. More important, although their swelling does cause a change in the inner part of the stump, it is not *regulating* the operation of the stump. Regulation means more than merely influencing or changing something. It means systematically modifying the operation of a system so that a *functional* outcome is achieved. In the case of a thermostat, that function was determined by the intentions of the engineer who designed it. In the case of an organism, that function was determined by natural selection, which acted to organize the properties of the organism.

A causal process does not need the human properties of foresight and intention to be capable of designing something. The selection of parts on the basis of their functional consequences is the crux of the concept of design (e.g., we say a thermocouple has been designed because the two different metals, each with different heat-conducting properties, did not come together by chance; they were selected for the thermocouple *because* this has functional consequences if one's purpose is to regulate something's temperature). From this perspective, it does not matter whether the causal system that does the selection is a volitional agent or a feedback process. A system can be said to be designed whenever the cause of its having the parts and properties that it has—rather than others—is that they have functional consequences, i.e., that they solve a problem of some kind (see, e.g., Nozick, 1993, p. 118). By this criterion, natural selection designs organisms. Chance events, such as mutations, cause alternative parts (design features) to be introduced into a population of organisms, but natural selection is not a chance process. Natural selection is a systematic feedback process that retains or discards parts because of their consequences on the functional performance of the system.

How Natural Selection Designs Organisms

The heart of Darwin's insight is the recognition that organisms are self-reproducing machines (Dawkins, 1976, 1986; Williams, 1966). From a Darwinian perspective, the defining property of life is *reproduction*, or more fully, the presence in a system of devices (organized components) that cause the system to construct new and similarly reproducing systems. These organized components can be thought of as design features: They are present because they participate in the causal process whereby the organism produces new organisms with a similar structure, (i.e., with a similar design). One can consider design features at many scales from, for example, the visual system, the eye, and the retina, down to the retinal cells, their organelles, and the photoreactive pigments that trigger the firing of the cell.

Individuals die, but their design features live on in their descendants—if they have any. When an organism reproduces, replicas of its design features are introduced into its offspring. But the replication of the design of the parental machine is not always error free. As a result, randomly modified designs (i.e., mutants) are introduced into populations of reproducers. Because living machines are already exactingly organized so that they cause the otherwise improbable outcome of constructing offspring machines, random modifications will usually introduce disruptions into the complex sequence of actions necessary for self-reproduction. Consequently, most newly modified but now defective designs will remove themselves from the population—a case of negative feedback.

However, a small residual subset of design modifications will, by chance, happen to constitute improvements in the system's machinery for causing its own reproduction. Such improved designs (by definition) cause their own increasing frequency in the population—a case of positive feedback. This increase continues until (usually) such modified designs outreproduce and thereby replace all alternative designs in the population, leading to a new species-standard design. After such an event, the population of reproducing machines is different from the ancestral population: The population- or species-standard design has taken a step uphill toward a greater degree of functional organization for reproduction than it had previously. Over the long run, down chains of descent, this feedback cycle pushes designs through state-space toward increasingly well-engineered—and otherwise improbable—functional arrangements. These arrangements are functional in a specific sense: The elements are well organized to cause their own reproduction in the environment in which the species evolved.

For example, if a more sensitive retina, which appeared in one or a few individuals by chance mutation, causes predators to be detected more quickly, individuals who have the more sensitive retina will produce offspring at a higher rate than those who lack it. Those of their offspring that inherit that more sensitive retina will also evade predators better and therefore produce offspring at a higher rate, and so on down the generations. By promoting the reproduction of its bearers, the more sensitive retina thereby promotes its own spread over the generations, until it eventually replaces the earlier model retina and becomes a universal feature of that species' design. This spontaneous feedback process—natural selection—causes functional organization to emerge naturally and inevitably, without the intervention of an intelligent designer or supernatural forces. Genes are simply the means by which design features replicate themselves from parent to offspring. They can be thought of as particles of design: elements that can be transmitted from parent to offspring and that, together with an environment, cause the organism to develop some design features and not others. Because design features are embodied in individual organisms, there are usually only two ways they can propagate themselves: by solving problems that increase the probability that offspring will be produced by either the organism they are situated in, or by that organism's kin. An individual's relatives, by virtue of having received some of the same genes from a recent common ancestor, have an increased likelihood of having the same design feature as compared to other conspecifics. This means that a design feature in an individual that causes an increase in the reproductive rate of that individual's kin will, by so doing, tend to increase its own frequency in the population. A computational element that causes an individual to be motivated to feed her sisters and brothers, if they are starving, is an example of a design circuit that increases kin reproduction. When the individual's siblings reproduce, they might pass on this same circuit to their children. Hence, design features that promote both direct reproduction and kin reproduction, and that make efficient trade-offs between the two, will replace those that do not. How well a design feature systematically promotes direct and kin reproduction is the bizarre but real engineering criterion determining whether a specific design feature will be added to or discarded from a species' design. Therefore, we can potentially understand why our brains are constructed in the way they are, rather than in other perfectly possible ways, when we see how its circuits were designed to cause behavior that, in the world of our ancestors, led to direct reproduction or kin reproduction.

Computational and Noncomputational Adaptive Problems

We can now define the concept of adaptive behavior with precision. Adaptive behavior, in the evolutionary sense, is behavior that tends to promote the reproduction of the design feature into the next generation (which usually means increasing the net lifetime reproduction of an individual bearing the design feature or that individual's genetic relatives). By promoting the replication of the genes that built them, circuits that—systematically and over many generations—cause adaptive behavior become incorporated into a species' neural design. In contrast, behavior that undermines the reproduction of the individual or his or her blood relatives removes the circuits causing those behaviors from the species, by removing the genes that built those circuits. Such behavior is *maladaptive*, in the evolutionary sense.

So, evolutionists continually analyze how design features are organized to contribute to lifetime reproduction, not because of an unseemly preoccupation with sex, but because reproduction was the final causal pathway through which a functionally improved design feature caused itself to become more numerous with each passing generation, until it became standard equipment in all ordinary members of the species.

Enduring conditions in the world, such as the presence of predators, the need to share food to buffer against bad luck in food acquisition, or the vulnerability of infants, constitute *adaptive problems*. Adaptive problems have two defining characteristics. First, they are conditions or cause-and-effect relationships that many or most individual ancestors encountered, reappearing again and again during the evolutionary history of the species. Second, they are problems whose solution increased the reproduction of individual organisms or their relatives—however indirect the causal chain, and even if the effect on the organism's own offspring or the offspring of kin was relatively small. Most adaptive problems have to do with relatively mundane aspects of how an organism lives from day to day: what it eats, what eats it, who it mates with, who it socializes with, how it communicates, and so on.

A subset of adaptive problems are computational. Adaptive computational problems are those problems that can be solved by design features that monitor some aspect of the environment (either internal or external) and use the information detected to regulate the operation of other parts of the organism. Those parts of an organism that were designed to regulate its behavior on the basis of information are computational. To say these parts were designed for this purpose means that their contribution to this regulatory process was one of the functional consequences that caused them to be incorporated into the species's architecture by natural selection. There can, of course, be computational systems that regulate the operation of subsystems that are not behavioral, at least in the colloquial sense (e.g., the system in a mother that detects how much an infant is sucking at the breast and adjusts milk production on the basis of this information would be a computational system).

What Does *Well-Designed* Mean?

An enduring adaptive problem constantly selects for design features that promote the solution to that problem. Over evolutionary time, more and more design features accumulate that fit together to form an integrated structure or device that is well engineered to solve its particular adaptive problem. Such a structure or device is called an *adaptation*. Indeed, an organism can be thought of as largely a collection of adaptations, such as the functional subcomponents of the eye, liver, hand, uterus, or circulatory system. Each of these adaptations exists in a species' design now because it contributed ancestrally to the process of self and kin reproduction.

So natural selection builds adaptations—that is, problem-solving machinery —to solve evolutionarily long-standing adaptive problems, and some of these problems are computational in nature. One can identify an aspect of an organism's physical or psychological structure—its phenotype—as an adaptation by showing that (i) it has many design features that are improbably well suited to solving an ancestral adaptive problem, (ii) these phenotypic properties are unlikely to have arisen by chance alone, and (iii) they are not better explained as the by-product of mechanisms designed to solve some alternative adaptive problem or some more inclusive class of adaptive problem. Finding that an architectural element solves an adaptive problem with reliability, precision, efficiency, and economy is prima facie evidence that one has located an adaptation (Williams, 1966). Ultimately, the objective measure of engineering quality is how much better than random a system is at meeting its functional goals. Intuitively, however, we can appreciate the quality of evolved systems by comparing them, where feasible, to human efforts.

Using this standard, evolved systems are not optimal or perfect (whatever that may mean), but they are very good by human engineering standards. We can say this with confidence because human engineers—even when they have enormous research budgets and can devote decades to a single project—have not been able to match the quality of what evolution produces. Skeptics of the power of natural selection have based their skepticism on verbal assertion rather than any comparison of the performance of human-engineered and evolutionarily engineered systems (e.g., Gould & Lewontin, 1979). Natural selection has produced exquisitely engineered biological machines—grammar acquisition, object recognition, word-meaning induction, the regulation of walking, tactile perception, olfaction, color constancy systems, solar energy capture—whose performance is unrivaled by any machine yet designed by humans.

WHAT IS DEDICATED INTELLIGENCE?

It should now be clear what we mean by our proposed definition of targeted intelligence, as applied to organisms: A neural program manifests *dedicated intelligence* when it is well designed for solving a targeted set of adaptive computational problems. (This is similar to the concept of ecological rationality developed in Tooby & Cosmides, 1992b).

Researchers know about thousands of systems of dedicated intelligence in humans and other species, designed for the regulation of food choice, mate choice, alliance maintenance, predator-escape, contagion avoidance, thermoregulation, fluid intake, social status, sex changes, aphid farming, landmark recognition, grammar acquisition, child survival, deception detection, aggression, patch selection in foraging, incest avoidance, dead-reckoning, coalition formation, offspring recognition, birth regulation, sex ratio manipulation, fungus-growing, web-building, blood pressure management, celestial navigation, competitive infanticide, snake avoidance, toxin assessment, and everything else necessary to maintain the innumerable alternative ways of life exhibited by earth's species.

By intention, this definition of dedicated intelligence is agnostic on several issues. For example:

- *It does not rest on any specific conception of the nature of the computational machinery that produces solutions to adaptive problems.* Natural selection has come up with an immense diversity of solutions to various adaptive problems, and there are no grounds for prejudging the methods by which adaptive computational problems might be solved (Tooby & Cosmides, in press). This contrasts with some approaches to assessing problem-solving performance (e.g., Kahneman, Slovic, & Tversky, 1982). In the judgment and decision-making community, for example, researchers often define a subject as rational only if he or she adheres to the experimenter's preferred procedure for decision making, where the procedure is usually some formalism derived from mathematics, probability theory, or logic, such as Bayes' Rule, or *modus tollens*. This is like grading sharpshooters on the basis of their form in holding the rifle, instead of on how often they hit the target.
- *It does not depend on the presence of a brain.* By this definition, there can be intelligent systems distributed throughout an organism's body, which is fortunate, because all bodies contain highly sophisticated computational regulatory processes. They need not all be localized with one another in a central computational organ. Thus, this definition includes organisms equipped with distributed cognition (e.g., decentralized systems composed of sensors and springs in the limbs of an organism that adjust their motion sensitively to details of the terrain, Clark, 1997). Indeed, phylogenetically, distributed intelligence undoubtedly appeared before it became concentrated into brains. It would be arbitrary to tie the definition of intelligence to the distribution of its physical basis rather than to its regulatory performance.
- *It does not depend on the existence of a mentally represented goal.* Not all behavior that looks goal directed involves representations of goals. For example, ticks have a circuit directly linking chemoreceptors to motor neurons, so that the smell of butyric acid causes the tick to drop from a tree (Uexkull, 1905/1957). Because butyric acid is emitted only by mam-

mals, this circuit usually results in the tick landing on a mammalian host, whose blood it then drinks. The design of this circuit makes the tick's behavior appear goal directed. Yet it involves no explicit representation of a goal state. Nevertheless, this computational system clearly exhibits dedicated intelligence. The simplicity of this system is not the issue. Computation without explicit goals can involve any level of complexity. For example, it seems unlikely that either vision or spontaneous early grammar acquisition involve explicitly represented goals, but both involve very intricate computational processes. So, a system can exhibit targeted intelligence whether or not it explicitly represents goal states, and humans appear to have intelligent programs of both kinds. Of course, explicitly represented goal states are a necessary feature of improvisional intelligence, as we discuss.

- *The requirement that intelligent machinery be adaptively well designed introduces criteria such as economy, efficiency, precision, and reliability into the analysis of intelligence.* Not only is there a biological justification for this, but this matches our intuitions as well. Consider two desert ants, equipped with two different navigational designs, facing the problem of returning to the nest. One travels the shortest distance, thereby saving energy and reducing the amount of time she spends above ground, where she is at risk of being predated upon. The other meanders across the landscape without doing anything functional on this longer path, although she also eventually reaches home. Biologically, one design is better than the other (because it has solved the problem more efficiently), which parallels our intuition that the first ant has behaved more intelligently than the second. The cost of running the computational system is also part of the analysis, and so the ultimate currency for comparing alternative designs for fulfilling the same function is the net fitness produced over the set of conditions being considered.

- *The definition refers to adaptations, programs, or systems, not to entire organisms.* It provides criteria for judging whether any particular subsystem exhibits dedicated intelligence but cannot be used to assess the intelligence of the organism as a whole using a single-dimensional variable. For example, a bee has foraging algorithms that are very well engineered for foraging among flowers (Heinrich, 1981), but it lacks the ability to navigate by the stars or (we suspect) to create or track false beliefs in social competitors. Similarly, strokes can knock out a person's ability to speak grammatically, yet leave intact their ability to think spatially. Both species and individual organisms will embody distinct complexes of specific abilities. Therefore, this definition is incompatible with a framework that necessarily views intelligence as a unitary phenomenon and attempts to array species along a continuum of more or less intelligent. Also, by applying the criterion of how well designed a computational system is at solving a particular class of adaptive problem, this definition does not prejudge whether an organism's improvisional intelligence is achieved via a bundle of dedicated computational modules or by a single, general purpose system.

- *This definition distinguishes between the design of a system and the outcome achieved by a particular organism in a particular instance.* One cannot judge intelligence or how well engineered a dedicated computational system is by its performance on a single occasion for the same reason that the value of a betting system cannot be evaluated by what happens on a single bet. The quality of the dedicated intelligence in a computational system is a function of the performance of the system summed across the range of environments considered relevant to the evaluation. For natural selection, the range of relevant environments is the distribution of conditions faced by the ancestors of the species during their evolution. For example, savannah predators often ambushed their prey from trees. A well-designed computational system that evolved to function in that environment might routinely cause prey to spend a few extra calories walking around a tree that is too dense to see through, even though in 999 out of 1,000 cases the tree is predator free. Descendants of such prey, such as humans, might still find visually impenetrable, overhead foliage mildly disquieting, even in a postindustrial world where there are no longer leopards or saber-toothed tigers. Nevertheless, that computational system is still manifesting intelligence$_1$.

- *The degree of dedicated intelligence displayed by a neural program is relative to the ecological structure of the world the organism inhabits and to the problem-solving goals posed by its associated adaptive problem.* Once a target set of outcomes is specified (what behaviors solve the adaptive problem), any number of alternative computational designs can be compared by examining how well each performs in reaching the goal. The better a design is at reaching the goal, the more dedicated intelligence it shows. On this view, the intelligence of a program design would consist of its relative operational success compared with known alternative computational designs. This makes the assessment of intelligence relative to specified goals. Obviously, the best design will depend on which goal is selected. Different methods will perform best according to different definitions of success. "Goals" in this sense, include all of the different issues of costs and benefits relevant to alternative computational systems and decision consequences. For example, which kinds of errors are costly and which kinds are cheap (what, for example, is the cost of being afraid of a nonvenomous snake versus the cost of being unafraid of a venomous one)? What is the cost (in time, metabolic energy, processing load, and so on) of one system of computation as opposed to another? Also, the best design will depend on the distribution of background conditions within which problem solving is to take place. Different designs will perform best in different problem-solving environments.

Natural problem solving tends to take place in complex environments with certain stable or statistically recurring features. To understand why a particular computational method will prove more effective in one environment than another, one needs to answer such questions as the following: What is always true in the task environment, what is statistically true, and what is never true? What do detectable cues predict about the undetectable features of the environment? What information is routinely available? How stable are the variable dimensions of the task environment? And so on. Moreover, the best design will depend on the ecological distribution of different problem types that the problem-solving system encounters. Because computational strategies ordinarily involve trade-offs, different methods will perform best against different composite problem populations. Thus, the answer to the question, Which design is most intelligent?, is not and cannot be invariant and universal. The intelligence of a design is always relative to the goal to be reached (or the total array of values and trade-off functions), to the background conditions that it operates in, to the total problem population to which it will be applied, and to other factors as well. We have called the well fittedness of computational designs to environments *ecological rationality* (Tooby & Cosmides, 1992a; see also Gigerenzer, Todd, & ABC Research Group, 1999).
On the other hand, this definition of dedicated intelligence differs from more traditional views in a series of ways. For example:

- *It privileges adaptive problems over other kinds of problems.* Adaptive problems are the enduring cause-and-effect relationships that select for some design features over others. If we are to understand in what way mechanisms in our minds were designed to be intelligent, we need to relate these designs to the structure of the problems they were constructed to solve. In contrast, the pursuit of nonadaptive outcomes by an organism is a by-product of computational machinery designed by natural selection for the realization of adaptive outcomes. A male robin red breast may not look particularly intelligent when it overcomes obstacles to attack a tuft of red features, nor does a human male when he spends time looking for pornographic pictures rather than courting actual women (Dawkins, 1982). But the computational systems that organize the behavior of the robin and the man such that they pursue these goals exhibit intelligence$_1$ nevertheless. These mechanisms lead to such odd outcomes because there are things in the world other than rival robins and living women that satisfy the input conditions for the monitoring devices employed by the computational systems that (respectively) regulate aggression in robins and courtship in humans (see Sperber, 1994, on the actual versus proper domain of an adaptation).

- *It is easily applied to organisms but does not apply as easily to human-made machines.* Because natural selection applies generally to anything capable of self-reproduction and mutation, this approach to intelligence can be used to recognize instances of intelligence$_1$ in any species. Because human-made artifacts are not themselves replicators, this definition cannot be directly applied to them. An analogue of this definition can be applied, if one is willing to specify a function for the machine. Alternatively, one could choose to look at artifacts as extensions of the human phenotype, as Dawkins (1982) does, which would then make their intelligence dependent on how well they served evolved goals. As Richard Dawkins has argued, machines are created to realize the goals of the organisms that designed them, and any intelligence exhibited by a machine was derived from the adaptations of the organisms that created it (Dawkins, 1982). In a similar vein, Dennett (1987) has argued that machines manifest "derived intentionality": a goal-directedness derived from the goals and intentions of the organism that made it, which manifests "original intentionality."

- *Because it privileges adaptive problems, it is difficult to apply the concept of dedicated intelligence to a system that executes complex behaviors to solve arbitrarily chosen problems.* Consider, for example, a person with autism who spends all his time memorizing the telephone book. Is this intelligent behavior or not? True, he is overcoming obstacles to achieve a goal, but it is an odd goal, unconnected to the solution of any ancestral adaptive problem, and it is pursued at the expense of nearly all other goals. This is the kind of situation for which the term *idiot savant* was coined: Such a person exhibits some features of intelligence but not others. On the other hand, if you discovered that this person was in fact a visitor from another planet, and that prior visitors had encrypted the coordinates of his home planet in the phone book, the same behavior would seem more intelligent, in part because returning home is an instance of an intelligible adaptive problem.

HOW IS DEDICATED INTELLIGENCE ACHIEVED?

All animals, including humans, are endowed with computational systems that manifest intelligence$_1$. Although this point is subject to a great deal of debate, we would argue that the human mind is very similar to the minds of other animal species. That is, it is bristling with a large number of specialized computational systems, each of which is well designed for solving a different adaptive problem. Functional specialization is one of the primary means by which computational systems achieve their problem-solving power, thereby manifesting intelligence$_1$.

Functional Specialization

Why should this be true? A basic engineering principle is that the same device is rarely capable of solving two different problems equally well. We have both screwdrivers and saws because each solves a particular problem better than the other. It would be futile to cut planks of wood with a screwdriver or to turn screws with a saw.

For exactly the same reason, natural selection has divided our body into organs such as the heart and the liver. Pumping blood throughout the body and detoxifying poisons are two very different problems. Consequently, your body has evolved a different machine for solving each of them. The design of the heart is specialized for pumping blood; the design of the liver is specialized for detoxifying poisons. Your liver can't function as a pump, and your heart cannot detoxify poisons.

The same principle applies to the mind. When carefully considered, it leads to the conclusion that the mind has many independent, evolved programs. One reason for this becomes clear if you put yourself in the position of a superhuman engineer. Imagine you are trying to design an organism like ourselves—one that has values and uses them to make choices. What would your organism be like if you gave it only one set of choice criteria?

Let's say your science project is to design a model human female, and you want her to be able to choose nutritious foods. Natural selection has engineered into humans an elaborate set of neural circuits organized to choose nutritious food on the basis of taste, smell, and digestive consequences. Knowing this, you decide to give your science project the same programs. But if this is the only set of choice criteria she has, what kind of *mate* would she end up choosing? A goat cheese pizza or a giant chocolate bar? Although superior to a bad date, they will not measure up as a parent to her children. To solve the adaptive problem of finding the right mate, her mental machinery would have to be guided by qualitatively different standards and values than when she is choosing the right food, or the right word, or the right path to get home.

We humans solve many different adaptive problems well. To accomplish these feats, *there must be at least as many independent evolved mental programs as there are adaptive domains in which the standards for successful behavior are qualitatively different.* We think that one can identify hundreds or perhaps even thousands of these domains, ranging from thermoregulation, parenting, and food choice to mate choice, friendship maintenance, language acquisition, romantic love, pollutant avoidance, predator defense, sexual rivalry, status attainment, projectile accuracy, and kin welfare. Since environments cannot provide organisms with definitions of problem-solving success, independent problem solvers must be built in to the brain for each incommensurate value domain. For this and many other reasons, the brain must be composed of a large collection of evolved circuits, with different circuits specialized for solving different problems. In this view, the brain is necessarily a diverse collection of dedicated computers networked together.

Functional specialization can take many forms. For choice behavior, knowledge of the appropriate criteria must somehow be embodied in the program, either as a database or implicitly, in the nature of the cues to which the procedures that cause attraction, repulsion or disinterest respond. But information about proximal goals is not the only kind of functional specialization that one sees in the mind. Biological machines are tailored to the structure of the environments in which they evolved, and information about the stably recurring properties of these ancestral worlds can be embodied in the very way their procedures work. For example, one function of vision is object recognition, and this is easier if the same object—e.g., a banana—appears to have the same color—yellow—from one situation to the next, regardless of changes in the wavelengths of the light illuminating it. This is called *color constancy*, and our visual system does it very well. Natural selection has created color constancy circuits that automatically compensate for the wild changes in illumination that occur on the surface of the earth as the sun traverses the sky and under variations in cloud cover and forest canopy (Shepard, 1992). As a result, that banana looks yellow to us at high noon and at sunset, even though, objectively speaking, it is swamped by red light at sunset, such that it is a source of far more red than yellow light. Natural—that is, ancestrally recurrent—changes in terrestrial illumination pose no problems for these circuits, because they are calibrated to them: Their procedures were shaped by them and embody knowledge about them. But these circuits cannot compensate for evolutionarily novel changes in illumination, such as the unearthly spectrum cast by the sodium vapor lights that illuminate many parking lots at night. The cars that we think of as red and green and blue all look a muddy brown when they are illuminated by these golden lights because our color constancy mechanisms were not shaped by, and embody no knowledge of, the spectral properties of sodium (Shepard, 1992).

Evolved Crib Sheets

This principle applies not just to perception but to all of our learning and reasoning circuits as well. In this view, many dedicated intelligences are equipped with design features that function as crib sheets. They come to a problem already "knowing" a great deal about it. This allows them to be far more intelligent than they otherwise would be if they embodied no equivalent to innate knowledge. For example, a newborn's brain has response systems that expect faces to be present in the environment; babies less than 10 minutes old turn their eyes and head in response to facelike patterns but not to scrambled versions of the same pattern (Johnson & Morton, 1991). Neural maturation brings other evolved circuits on line subsequently. [as the phrase doesn't add anything for those in the know, and is likely to be obscure to those 'not in the know', we'd rather leave it out]. Infants have strong assumptions, deriving from the evolutionary past, about how the world works and what kinds of things it contains, even at 2½ months (the point at which they can see well enough to be tested). They assume, for example, that the world will contain rigid objects that are continuous in space and time, and they have preferred ways of dividing the world into separate objects (Spelke, 1990). Indeed, an infant's mind is designed to *privilege* some hypotheses about what counts as an object over others. Ignoring shape, color, and texture (all of which they can see), they treat any surface that is cohesive, bounded, and that moves as a unit as a single object. Another privileged hypothesis is that solid objects are impenetrable (Baillargeon, 1986). So when one solid object appears to pass through another, these infants are surprised, just as you or I would be.

A baby with a completely open mind—one lacking any privileged hypotheses—would be undisturbed by such displays. Why shouldn't a toy train travel smoothly through a solid block of wood? If the superhuman engineer were to remove these privileged hypotheses from the baby's mind, the baby would be left without informative guidance in the world in which we actually live. By definition, a blank-slate system must entertain all possible hypotheses equally: that it was born into a world in which objects are like mercury droplets, no one has a face, and surfaces that move together are physically unconnected to each other. These are properties of imaginable universes but not of the one in which we evolved. There is nothing in our evolutionary past that would cause our brains to be organized in such a futile way.

So babies have dedicated intelligences built into them with strong commitments about the nature of the universe and niche they actually evolved in, instead of being prepared to deal with all worlds, whether they exist or not. In watching objects interact, babies less than a year old distinguish causal events from noncausal ones that have similar spatio-temporal properties (Leslie, 1988, 1994); they distinguish objects that move only when acted upon from ones that are capable of self-generated motion (making the inanimate/animate distinction) (Gergely, Nadasdy, Csibra, & Biro, 1995; Mandler & McDonough, in press; Premack & Premack, 1997), and they assume that the self-propelled movement of animate objects is caused by invisible internal states—goals and intentions (Baron-Cohen, 1995). Toddlers have a well-developed mind-reading system (i.e., a system for intuiting what is on others' minds), which uses eye direction and movement to infer what other people want, know, and believe. This system is domain-specific: It is designed only for understanding the behavior of animate beings. It is content-dependent: It is activated by stimuli that have properties ancestrally associated with animate beings, such as eyes or self-propelled motion (seeing a boulder rarely excites curiosity about its hopes, ambitions, or beliefs). And it is functionally-specialized: It is designed to compute beliefs, desires, and intentions, not color, trajectory, or weight. Indeed, the mind-reading system is so functionally specialized that it can be selectively impaired (i.e., impaired while other cognitive abilities are intact). This can be clearly seen in certain people with autism (Baron-Cohen, 1995; Leslie, 1987).

The Structure of a Dedicated Intelligence

The structure of a dedicated intelligence reflects the long-enduring structure of the adaptive problem it solves. Natural selection coordinates the structure of a recurrent adaptive problem (including the features of the environment in which it occurs) with the structure of an adaptive problem solver such that the interaction of the two produces the solution to the problem. If selection has created a well-engineered adaptation, then elements that are necessary to solve the problem but lacking from the world are supplied by the structure of the problem-solving device. Equally, that which is reliably supplied by the environment will tend to be left out of the device, because too much redundancy will be unnecessarily costly. So, strictly speaking, one should not look for the complete solution to the adaptive problem in the mechanism itself; the solution emerges from the complementary interaction of the mechanism and the world. For example, the visual system supplies exactly the information about the world (in the form of assumptions built into scene analysis) that the retina is incapable of supplying (Marr, 1982). Linguistic evidence available to the child supplies too few constraints to allow grammar acquisition to proceed, so the language acquisition device makes assumptions about grammar that are present in the structure of all known human languages (Pinker & Bloom, 1990). To understand the operation and organization of our dedicated intelligences, it is necessary to understand what regularities reliably permeated the structure of natural problem environments—the environment of evolutionary adaptedness, or EEA (Tooby & Cosmides, 1990, 1992b). Obviously then, the malfunctioning of our dedicated intelligences frequently comes about when a situation lacks cues and relationships that tended to be stably true in the past, and on which the intelligence relies for its successful operation. This is why one must talk about the ecological rationality of evolved computational devices; no intelligent architecture can operate properly outside of the context for which it was designed (Gigerenzer et al., in press; Tooby & Cosmides, 1992a).

Dedicated Intelligences Expand Our Abilities

In the past, many researchers have assumed that violations of the blank-slate assumption would limit intelligence. However, autism graphically illustrates what happens when an evolved intelligence is missing. A person with autism may have a normal IQ, be better than normal at embedded figures tasks (like *Where's Waldo?*), and be able to make sophisticated inferences about machines. Yet this same person cannot make simple inferences about other people's beliefs and desires. If a normal 3-year-old sees a character, Charlie, looking at one of four candies and is asked, "Which candy does Charlie want?", the child will point to the one Charlie's eyes are trained on. But a person with autism will answer randomly, even though he can tell you exactly which candy Charlie is looking at (Baron-Cohen, 1995). The person with autism can detect eye direction but, unlike you or me, he cannot use it to infer what someone wants. This shows that whatever the mental tool kit is that comes with having a normal IQ and normal abilities to reason about the physical world, it is not sufficient for reasoning about the mental world. Because the mind of a person with autism is missing a dedicated intelligence designed to make inferences about the mental world, he does not know that eye direction can indicate desire. Similarly, having an intact mind-reading system is insufficient for reasoning about the physical world: Adults with Williams syndrome are good at inferring other people's mental states, yet they are profoundly retarded and have difficulty learning even very simple spatial tasks (Tager-Flusberg, Boshart, & Baron-Cohen, 1998).

Domain-specialized inferential tools and knowledge bases are found not just in the learning systems of infants and toddlers, but in those of adults as well. For example, it is now well established (if not universally assented to) that the learning mechanisms that govern the acquisition of a language are different from those that govern the acquisition of food aversions, and both of these are different from the learning mechanisms that govern the acquisition of snake phobias. Each program has knowledge of its particular domain built into its structure, which allows it to perform its function far more efficiently than any blank-slate system could. The language acquisition device knows, for example, that the names of objects are nouns (Pinker, 1994). The snake phobia system knows what snakes look like, knows what fear looks like on other's faces, and has a procedure specialized for using fear on other's faces to change the intensity of fear you feel in the presence of snakes (Mineka & Cook, 1993; Ohman, Dimberg, & Ost, 1985). The food aversion system knows that nausea is usually caused by foods recently ingested, that it is more likely to be caused by novel foods than by familiar foods, and uses the contingency between food ingestion and nausea to regulate the subsequent attractiveness of food items (Garcia, 1990; Seligman, 1971). How did these systems get these specialized procedures and knowledge? Those mutations that, for example, built in the knowledge of what snakes looked like and what a fear-face looked like, increased the efficiency with which one learns which snakes should be avoided; hence, they were selected for.

The mind is not packed with specialized programs merely because they afford small differences in efficiency. Different problems *require* different dedicated intelligences. Knowledge about beliefs and desires, which allows one to infer the behavior of other people, will be misleading if it is applied to rocks and lakes. Knowing that concrete objects are nouns will not allow you to avoid venomous snakes. Two devices are better than one when the crib sheet that helps solve problems in one domain is misleading—or useless—in another. This is why many dedicated intelligences are designed to be activated in one domain and not others: To be useful, they must be activated only in those domains that match the assumptions they work under.

The more dedicated intelligences an architecture has, the more problems it can solve. A brain equipped with a multiplicity of specialized inference engines will be able to generate more successful types of problem-solving behavior than an architecture that is stripped of specializations. In this view, the flexibility and power often attributed to blank slates and content-independent algorithms is illusory. All else being equal, a content-rich system will be able to infer far more than a content-poor one.

Why Content-Rich Is Better Than Content-Poor

This view of the mind is radically at variance with the model of the mind that is the centerpiece of the standard social science model. Its advocates have attributed everything—from hopscotch to romance to rivalry—to the evenhanded operation of "learning", "intelligence", "reasoning", and "decision making." Regrettably, those simply remain names for mysterious hypothetical processes, not well-validated theories of how things actually happen computationally. To fill this gap, cognitive scientists proposed that the mind comes endowed with general-purpose computational circuits that are jacks-of-all-trades. Prime candidates were so-called *rational* algorithms: programs that implement formal methods for inductive and deductive reasoning, such as the laws of probability, mathematics, or formal logic. Others have proposed comprehensive pattern associator architectures that compute correlations or contingencies. These methods are inviting precisely because they are content free. Given the seemingly inexhaustible diversity of human action, it seemed reasonable to conclude that the mind be initially free of all content, so that variations in experience could drive the accumulation of the rich particularity so notable in the individual human mind.

What do we mean by a content-free program? Consider *modus ponens* and *modus tollens*, two domain-general rules of logic. Whenever "If P then Q" is true and P is true, *modus ponens* allows you to validly conclude that Q is also true. *Modus tollens* licenses a different inference: When "If P then Q" is true, but Q is false, it allows you to conclude that P is also false. These rules are content independent: They allow you (or an automaton, such as a computer or a neural circuit) to deduce true conclusions from true premises, no matter what is substituted in for P and Q. Let's say that P = you snooze and Q = you lose. If it is true that "If you snooze, you lose" then you can conclude that anyone who snoozed lost (*modus ponens*), and anyone who won didn't snooze (*modus tollens*). They will produce new knowledge whenever a true premise is combined with a true if-then statement—anything from "If it rains, the ground gets wet" to "If you can keep your head while all those around you are losing theirs, then you'll be a man, my son." Bayes's rule, a widely used equation for computing the probability that a hypothesis is true given data about that hypothesis, is also content independent. It can be applied equally to medical diagnosis, deciding whether Paul McCartney was dead before *Abbey Road* was recorded, playing Baccarat against James Bond, or any other subject matter.

Unfortunately, devices limited to executing Bayes's rule, modus ponens, and other "rational" procedures derived from mathematics or logic are computationally very weak compared with an evolved system of dedicated, content-specialized intelligences (Tooby & Cosmides, 1990, 1992b). The theories of rationality embodied by such traditional rational procedures, in order to be able to make valid inferences for all possible contents in all possible domains, have no built-in assumptions about the long-term ecological structure of the world or the problem domain (Gigerenzer et al., in press). They can be applied to a wide variety of domains, however, only because they lack any information that would be helpful in one domain but not in another. Having no evolved problem spaces or specialized procedures tailored to a domain, there is little they can deduce about it; having no privileged hypotheses, there is little they can induce before their operation is hijacked by combinatorial explosion—the cost of considering, searching, or processing all of the combinatorial possibilities. These jacks of all trades are, necessarily, masters of none. They achieve generality only at the price of broad ineptitude. Domain-specific algorithms do not need to make the same trade-off: Each can be master of a different domain. The difference between domain-specific methods and domain-independent ones is akin to the difference between experts and novices: Experts can solve problems faster and more efficiently than novices because they already know a lot about the problem domain.

Dedicated intelligences—such as the ones that govern how we reason and learn about faces, objects, language, snakes, mind reading, nausea, and so on—have the following five properties (Pinker, 1994):

1. they are complexly structured for solving a specific type of adaptive problem;
2. they reliably develop in all normal human beings;
3. they develop without any conscious effort and in the absence of any formal instruction;
4. they are applied without any conscious awareness of their underlying logic; and
5. they are distinct from whatever more general abilities to process information or behave intelligently that may exist.

In short, they have all the hallmarks of what scholars would once have called an instinct (Pinker, 1994). To reconnect cognitive science with evolutionary biology, these functionally specialized, content-rich intelligences can be considered reasoning instincts and learning instincts. They make certain kinds of inferences just as easy, effortless, and natural to humans as spinning a web is to a spider or dead reckoning is to a desert ant. In short, instincts manifest intelligence$_1$: They are well designed for solving adaptive computational problems.

For most of this century, the consensus has been that even if other animals are ruled by "instinct," humans have lost their instincts and had them replaced with "reason," "intelligence," or "learning." This evolutionary erasure and substitution is the explanation for why humans are more flexibly intelligent than other animals. William James (1892), however, argued against this commonsense view. He maintained that human behavior is more flexibly intelligent than that of other animals because we have more instincts than they do, not fewer. If instincts are like tools in a toolbox, then the larger the number that the mind is endowed with, the more abilities it has. James' view fits presciently with work in modern computer science, in which each additional subroutine expands the computer's ability to solve problems.

There is no reason to think that instincts are what we have in common with other species, whereas what is uniquely human is noninstinctual. Not only are instincts or dedicated intelligences often specific to each species, but many of our instincts give rise to abilities that are unique to humans, such as language. As Darwin put it, humans manifest language because we evolved "an instinctive tendencies to acquire an art" (see Pinker, 1994, p. 20).

Finally, we think that having a brain that is well endowed with computational systems that manifest intelligence$_1$ is a precondition for the evolution of intelligence$_2$, improvisional intelligence. To pick one necessary contribution, dedicated intelligences prevent combinatorial explosion and create a context in which design features that increase flexibility—a dangerous addition—can continue to have adaptive functional consequences.

BEYOND DEDICATED INTELLIGENCE: THE HOMINID ENTRY INTO THE COGNITIVE NICHE

When contextualized within the extraordinary diversity of the living world, humans stand out, exhibiting a remarkable array of strange and unprecedented behaviors—from super tankers to ice skating to sculpture—that are not found in other species. What is at the core of these differences? Arguably, one central and distinguishing innovation in human evolution has been the dramatic increase in the use of contingent information for the regulation of improvised behavior that is successfully tailored to local conditions—an adaptive mode that has been labeled the *cognitive niche* (Tooby & DeVore, 1987). If you contrast, for example, the food acquisition practices of a bison with that of a !Kung San hunter, you will immediately note a marked difference. For the bison, grasslands are undoubtedly a rich tapestry of differentiated food patches and cues; nevertheless, the bison's decisions are made for it by dedicated intelligences designed for grass and forage identification and evaluation—adaptations that are universal to the species and that operate with relative uniformity across the species range. In contrast, the !Kung hunter uses, among many other nonspecies-typical means and methods, arrows that are tipped with a poison found on only one local species of chrysomelid beetle, toxic only during the larval stage (Lee, 1993).

This method of food acquisition is not a species-typical adaptation: Not all humans use arrows, poison their arrows, have access to a beetle species from which poison can be derived, or even hunt. Nor are any of the component relationships—between beetle larva and poison, between arrows and poison, or even between arrows and hunting—stable from a phylogenetic perspective. Each relationship on which this practice is based is a transient and local condition, and these contingent facts are being combined to improvise a behavioral routine that achieves an adaptive outcome: obtaining meat. Whatever the neural adaptations that underlie this behavior, they were not designed specifically for beetles and arrows but exploit these local, contingent facts as part of a computational structure that treats them as instances of a more general class (e.g., living things, projectiles, prey).

Most species are locked in coevolutionary, antagonistic relationships with prey, rivals, parasites and predators, in which move and countermove take place slowly, over evolutionary time. Improvisation puts humans at a great advantage: Instead of being constrained to innovate only in phylogenetic time, they engage in ontogenetic ambushes against their antagonists—innovations that are too rapid with respect to evolutionary time for their antagonists to evolve defenses by natural selection. Armed with this advantage, hominids have exploded into new habitats, developed an astonishing diversity of subsistence and resource extraction methods, caused the extinctions of many prey species in whatever environments they have penetrated, and generated an array of social systems, artifacts, and representational systems far more extensive than that found in any other single species.

This contrast—between transient, local, contingent facts and relationships that hold over the species range—is at the heart of what makes humans so different. To evolve, species-typical behavioral rules must correspond to features of the species' ancestral world that were both globally true (i.e., that held statistically across a preponderance of the species' range) and stably true (i.e., that remained in effect over enough generations that they selected for adaptations in the species). These constraints narrowly limit the kinds of information that such adaptations can be designed to use. The set of properties that had a predictable relationship to features of the species' world that held widely in space and time is a very restricted one. In contrast, for situation-specific, appropriately tailored improvisation, the organism only needs information to be applicable, or "true," temporarily, locally, or contingently. If information only needs to be true temporarily, locally, and situationally to be useful, then a vastly enlarged universe of context-dependent information becomes potentially available to be employed in the successful regulation of behavior. This tremendously enlarged universe of information can be used to fuel the identification of an immensely more varied set of advantageous behaviors than other species employ, giving human life its distinctive complexity, variety, and relative success. Hominids entered the cognitive niche, with all its attendant benefits and dangers, by evolving a new suite of cognitive adaptations that are evolutionarily designed to exploit this broadened universe of information, as well as the older universe of species-extensive true relationships.

The hominid occupation of the cognitive niche is characterized by a constellation of interrelated behaviors that depend on intensive information manipulation and that are supported by a series of novel or greatly elaborated cognitive adaptations or dedicated intelligences. This zoologically unique constellation of behaviors includes locally improvised subsistence practices; extensive context-sensitive manipulation of the physical and social environment; "culture," defined as the serial reconstruction and adoption of representations and regulatory variables found in others' minds through inferential specializations evolved for the task; language as a system for dramatically lowering the cost of communicating propositional information; tool use adapted to a diverse range of local problems; context-specific skill acquisition; multi-individual coordinated action; and other information-intensive and information-dependent activities (Tooby & Cosmides, 1992b).

Although some have argued that social competition was the sole driving force behind the evolution of human intelligence (as in the Machiavellian hypothesis; Humphrey, 1984; Whiten & Byrne, 1997), we do not think this is a sufficient explanation for what is distinctive about human intelligence (for an alternative, see Tooby & DeVore, 1987). We certainly do believe that humans have evolved dedicated intelligences specialized for social life and social cognition (e.g., Cosmides, 1989; Cosmides & Tooby, 1989, 1992), but what is truly distinctive about human life encompasses far more than the social. For example, the causal intelligence expressed in hunter-gatherer subsistence practices appears to be as divergent from other species as human social intelligence. So, improvisational intelligence is not simply dedicated social intelligence—something we also know from the fact that individuals with autism can lose social intelligence while maintaining high levels of causal intelligence.

WHAT IS IMPROVISATIONAL INTELLIGENCE?

Earlier, we defined intelligence$_2$ as intelligence$_1$ plus enhancements. More specifically, we said that a system is intelligent$_2$ to the extent that it is well designed for solving adaptive computational problems *and has components designed to exploit transient local conditions to achieve adaptive outcomes*. Whether in social interactions, hunting, toolmaking, programming, poetry, legal argumentation, athletics, or anything else, people recognize the presence of a distinctively human kind of intelligence when people reach goals more effectively through the tailoring of their conduct to take into account the distinctive features of the situation they are in. The rigid application of rules, regardless of whether they seem appropriate to the circumstances, and regardless of their success at reaching goals, strikes humans of whatever culture as diagnostic of a lack of intelligence.

Dedicated intelligence seems directly related to adaptive problems (nutrition, relationships, perception), while it is less obvious that the same is true for improvisational intelligence. The reason for this is that, in improvising to reach an adaptive outcome (e.g., Zorro defeating his enemies), one may need to pursue any of an endless array of intermediate goal states without intrinsic reward characteristics (e.g., Zorro playing the fool to keep his identity hidden). Hence, a system that evolves toward improvisional intelligence will produce, as a by-product, a system that can also compute how to pursue a large body of seemingly arbitrary goal states that are not necessarily adaptive. This is why improvisional intelligence appears to resemble the traditional concept of a general-purpose intelligence, despite the differences in conceptions of the machinery that achieves this outcome. This also makes it obvious why two problems that confront the evolution of improvisational intelligence are (i) the need to keep its use coupled to adaptive goals, and (ii) producing inferences that are correct (or, at least, useful) sufficiently often to pay for its cost.

The benefits of successful improvisation are clear: The ability to realize goals through exploiting the unique opportunities that are inherent in a singular local situation yields an advantage over a system that is limited to applying only those solutions that work across a more general class of situation. What 10 years of ordinary battle on the plains of Troy could not accomplish, one Trojan horse could. The improvisational exploitation of unique opportunities also fits our folk intuitions about what counts as intelligence. As members of the human species, instances of intelligence excite our admiration precisely to the extent that the behavior (or insight) involved is novel, and not the result of the "mindless" application of fixed rules. Indeed, it would seem that every organism would be benefitted by having a faculty that caused it to perform behaviors fitted to each individual situation. But: If it is generally useful, why haven't many other species evolved this form of intelligence (Tooby & DeVore, 1987)? Indeed, how is this form of intelligence computationally and evolutionarily possible at all?

To see why the existence of this form of intelligence is puzzling, let us first consider what is meant by conditions that are transient and local and the difficulty of building adaptations to the transient.

For an allele to spread to fixation throughout a species, it is not enough for the design feature it builds to confer an advantage in a single lifetime or a single locale. The incorporation of a trait into a species' design by selection is a large-scale, cumulative process, involving the summation of events that take place across the entire species' range and across a large number of generations. For selection to propel an allele consistently upwards, the relevant relationships between the environment, the organism, and the adaptive benefit must be stable—they must persist across many generations. For this reason, the functional designs of species-typical computational adaptations should, in general, both reflect and exploit conditions that hold true over long periods of time and over most or all of the species range. For example, eye direction statistically signals knowledge acquisition in organisms with eyes, and so monitoring eye direction is informative for making inferences about what another organism knows (i.e., seeing is knowing; Baron-Cohen, 1995). The mechanisms that make these inferences are components of a system that achieves adaptive outcomes by exploiting conditions that are stable with respect to the phylogenetic history of our species, even though these conditions are experienced as transient and local by individual human beings.

This stability can, of course, be of a statistical nature. Undoubtedly there are many cases in which a predator fails to recognize something it is looking at (otherwise camouflage would not have evolved in so many prey species). But the correlation between eye direction and object recognition can be weak, as long as it is positive; all that is necessary for selection to favor an eye direction detector is that using eye direction to infer knowledge confer a reproductive advantage—however slight—over not using it. Reliably occurring variations also count as stable relationships that selection can exploit. As we discussed, the human color constancy system is designed to compensate for wide variations in terrestrial illumination. True, the spectral properties of the light you experience are transient over the course of a day, and differ from location to location. But they are evolutionarily recurrent variations. They are not transient and local in the sense intended in the definition of intelligence$_2$. And the color constancy system exhibits intelligence$_1$ but not intelligence$_2$. It produces color constancy when illuminant conditions fall within the envelope of variations that were stably present during the evolution of this system (intelligence$_1$), but it cannot exploit conditions that are evolutionarily transient and local, such as the spectral properties of the sodium vapor lamp, to produce the adaptive outcome of color constancy. Thus, *transient* and *local* are here defined with respect to the history of a species, not the history of an individual.

THE ENIGMA OF IMPROVISIONAL INTELLIGENCE

The costs and difficulties of the cognitive niche are so stringent that only one lineage in 4 billion years has wandered into the preconditions that favored the evolution of this form of intelligence. Natural computational systems that begin to relax their functional specificity run into, and are inescapably shaped by, savagely intense selection pressures. One of the greatest problems faced by natural computational systems is combinatorial explosion (for discussion, see Cosmides & Tooby, 1987; Tooby & Cosmides, 1992b). Combinatorial explosion is the term for the fact that alternatives multiply with devastating rapidity in computational systems, and the less constrained the representational and procedural possibilities are, the faster this process mushrooms, choking computation with too many possibilities to search among or too many processing steps to perform. Every marginal increase in the generality of a system exponentially increases the computational cost, greatly limiting the types of architectures that can evolve, and favoring, for example, the evolution of modules only in domains in which an economical set of procedures can generate a sufficiently large and valuable set of outputs. This means that domain specificity—and dedicated intelligences—will be the rule rather than the exception in natural computational systems. And while it answers the question of why a broad, general form of intelligence is so extraordinarily rare among animal species, it deepens the question of how it could be possible at all.

Elsewhere, we have written at length about the trade-offs between problem-solving power and specialization: general-purpose problem-solving architectures are very weak but broad in application, whereas special-purpose prob-lem-solving designs are very efficient and inferentially powerful but limited in their domain of application (Cosmides & Tooby, 1987; Tooby & Cosmides, 1992b). Thus, on first inspection, there appear to be only two biologically possi-ble choices for evolved minds: either general ineptitude or narrow compe-tences. This choice appears to rule out general intelligence. Yet, hominids did manage to evolve an architecture that allowed them to enter the cognitive niche, exploiting conditions that, from a phylogenetic perspective, are transient and local, to achieve adaptive outcomes. What is the way out of this puzzle?

We cannot simply return to the traditional view. The traditional argument that because human intelligence appears unprecedentedly broad in application, the human cognitive architecture's core problem-solving engines must them-selves be general purpose, cannot be reconciled with what is now known about the complexity of natural problems and the shortcomings of such architectures.

Nor have we yet confronted the core of the problem. From evolutionary and computational perspectives, it is far from clear how local improvisation could evolve, operate, or even be a nonmagical, genuine cognitive possibility. The central evolutionary enigma behind improvisional intelligence can be stated as follows: A computational system, by its nature, can only apply rules or proce-dures to problems and must do so based on its categorization of individual prob-lems into more general classes (i.e., there must be a causal process whereby appropriate procedures are activated in a given situation).[1] Adaptations, by their nature, can only see individual events in the life of the organism as in-stances of the large-scale evolutionarily recurrent categories of events that built them (Tooby & Cosmides, 1990). Therefore, if computational systems can only respond to situations as members of classes to which computational rules apply, and if evolution only builds computational adaptations that see individual situ-ations as members of large-scale, evolutionarily recurrent classes of events, how can there be a brain whose principles of operation commonly lead it to impro-vise behaviors that exploit the *distinctive* features of a situation? By the nature of how selection works, how could species-typical computational rules evolve that allow situation-specific improvisation at all, much less at a sufficiently low cost?

These are all difficult problems, and we suspect that no one presently has a full account of how improvisional intelligence could evolve and what subcomponents it requires for its operation. However, we think there are some tentative answers that look promising.

To start, there is an alternative to domain-general ineptitude or narrow intel-ligence. Cognitive specializations, each narrow in their domain of application,

---

[1]By rules or procedures, we only mean the information-processing principles of the computational system, without distinguishing subfeatural or parallel architectures from others.

can be bundled together in a way that widens the range of inputs or domains that can be successfully handled. This avoids the weakness of an architecture that consists of content-independent procedures, while avoiding the narrowness of a single domain-specific inference engine. It gets the benefits of specialized problem-solving power but progressively widens the scope of the problems that can be solved with each additional specialization that is added.

Moreover, such an architecture can be further improved; compatible content-independent engines can be embedded within this basic design because their defects when operating in isolation can be offset by implanting them in a guiding matrix of specializations (e.g., Cosmides & Tooby, 1996b; Gigerenzer et al., 1999). For example, the specializations provide the input content and the problem spaces, choking off combinatorial explosion, and provide a large repertoire of efficient specialized inference rules to augment the general inference rules. Of course, other architectural features are required to solve the problems raised by the interactions of these heterogeneous systems, as discussed later in this chapter (Tooby & Cosmides, 1990, 1992a, 1992b). This seems to us to be a necessary if partial solution to the question of how human intelligence can be not only broad in its range of application but also sufficiently powerful when applied (Sperber, 1996; Tooby & Cosmides, 1990, 1992b).

Second, a promising answer to the question of how evolved mechanisms, which are built only by species-wide regularities, can evolve to represent the distinctive or unique aspects of individual situations might be as follows: All situations are decomposed according to evolved interpretive rules that do see its elements only as instances of evolutionarily recurrent categories. (There seems to be no other possibility.) However, any given situation can be represented as unique in its particular combination of evolutionarily recurrent elements. The elements are computationally meaningful as instances of evolved categories, which allows evolved problem-solving rules to be applied to them. Indeed, the more evolved categorization systems that intersect on the same situation, the more situation interpretations are possible, and the more alternative manipulations can be considered and sifted according to evaluation systems that recognize valuable outcomes. (So, for example, we have the choice of viewing a man as a physical object, as an animal, as an agent with mental states, as a son, a potential sex partner, a shape, a member of a species, and so on.) Thus, the behavioral course decided upon might be uniquely tailored to the local situation, not because the elements are interpreted as novel but because the configuration taken as a whole is a novel combination of familiar elements. On this view, improvisional intelligence would benefit from a familiarity with the elements involved in unique situations, and should be stalled when genuinely new elements appear (which seems to be accurate).

Third, improvisional intelligence does not appear to be an autonomous ability, disconnected from the rest of the architecture and not relying on any other computational or informational resource. On the contrary. Not only does it depend on a base of dedicated intelligences but it also must be supplied with a dense accumulation of information relevant to the situation being faced. This is why we emphasized that the hominid entry into the cognitive niche depended on the huge increase in the use of *contingent* information for the regulation of improvised behavior that is successfully tailored to local conditions. The intensive use of information that is only temporarily or locally true creates what we have called the *scope problem*. Hence, we think another aspect to improvisional intelligence is a series of computational adaptations—what we have called *scope syntax*—to solve the problems introduced by the exploitation of contingent information. We think that any system that humans would recognize as having intelligence$_2$ will have a scope syntax.

WHAT IS THE SCOPE PROBLEM?

When hominids evolved or elaborated adaptations that could use information based on relationships that were only "true" temporarily, locally, or contingently, this opened up a new and far larger world of potential information than was available previously. Context-dependent information could now be used to guide behavior to a far greater extent than had been possible before. This advance, however, was purchased at a cost: The exploitation of this exploding universe of potentially representable information creates a vastly expanded risk of possible misapplications. This is because information that is useful within a narrow arena of conditions can be false, misleading, or harmful outside of the scope of those conditions[2]. Imagine, for example, that the following piece of contingent information is true: "The mushrooms [*here*] are edible." This is useful if you are collecting food here. But if you are collecting food elsewhere, this same information could kill you: The mushrooms *here* might be edible, but the mushrooms 3 miles away may be poisonous. To be useful, there needs to be a way of representing the scope within which the information about mushrooms being edible is true; *here* is a scope marker. (We represented this scope marker with a word, but to be useful in guiding an individual's behavior, it only needs to take the form of a conceptual tag attached to the information.) Or consider a different kind of contingent information, this time pertaining to someone's beliefs: "[*Bo believes that*] his arrows are back at camp." You can use this piece of contingent information to predict where Bo will go to look for his arrows, even if, in re-

---

[2]Indeed, the world outside of the local conditions may be commonly encountered, and depending on how narrow the envelope of conditions within which the information is true, scope-violating conditions are likely to be far more common than the valid conditions.

ality, someone stole them and hid them near the stream. If you want to retrieve the arrows yourself, you do not go to the camp. *Bo believes that* acts as a scope marker, which represents the boundaries within which the information about arrows can be usefully applied. This scope marker makes a very limited guarantee: it tells you the information will be useful for predicting Bo's behavior, but it can't promise that it will be useful for other purposes, such as fetching arrows. (Leslie [1987] calls data formats with slots for an agent [*Bo*], an attitude [*believes*] and a proposition [*his arrows are back at the camp*] a *meta*representation, because it is a representation that is about another representation—in this case, one that is in Bo's head.)

The cognitive niche depends on a computational strategy in which information is used even though the information is only applicable temporarily or locally. But this computational strategy can be successful only if the boundaries within which each representation remains useful are specified. Are the beetle larvae that are used to poison arrows toxic at all times of the year? Once harvested and applied, how long does the poisoned arrow tip remain poisonous? If it is poisonous to humans, gazelles, and duikers, is it also poisonous to lions, cape buffalo, and ostriches? If these relationships are true here, are they true on foraging territories on the other side of the Okavango? If the first several statements from my father in answer to these questions turned out to be true, will the remainder be true also? Moreover, because these aspects of the world are (by definition) transient and local, their boundaries must be continually monitored and reestablished.

Information only gives an advantage when it is relied on inside the envelope of conditions within which it is applicable. Hence, when considering the evolution of adaptations to use information, the costs of overextension and misapplication have to be factored in, as well as the costs and nature of the defenses against such misapplication. Expanding the body of information used to make decisions is harmful or dangerous if the architecture does not and cannot detect and keep track of which information is applicable, where it is applicable, and how the boundaries of applicability shift.

Moreover, the problem is not simply that information that is usefully descriptive only within a limited envelope of conditions will (by definition) be false or harmful outside of the scope of those conditions. The scope problem is aggravated by the fact that information is integrated and transformed through inferences. Information is useful to the extent it can be inferentially applied to derive conclusions that can then be used to regulate behavior. Inferences routinely combine multiple inputs through a procedure to produce new information, and the value of the resulting inferences depends sensitively on the accuracy of the information that is fed into them. For example, the truth of the conclusion that it will be better to move to an area where there is more game is dependent on the proposition that there is more game in the new location and on the implicit or explicit assumption that the necessary poisons for hunting can be obtained there as well.

Not only does inference combinatorially propagate errors present in the source inputs, but the resulting outputs are then available to be fed in as erroneous inputs into other inferences, multiplying the errors in successive chains and spreading waves. For example, if one wrong entry is made in a running total, all subsequent totals—and the decisions based on them—become wrong. This process has the potential to corrupt any downstream data set interacted with, in a spreading network of compounding error. The more the human cognitive architecture is networked together by systems of intelligent inference, and the more it is enhanced by the ability to integrate information from many sources,[3] the greater the risk is that valid existing information sets will be transformed into unreconstructable tangles of error and confusion. In short, the heavily inference-dependent nature of human behavior regulation is gravely threatened by erroneous, unreliable, obsolete, out-of-context, deceptive, or scope-violating representations.

Thus, it is not just the great increase in the use of contingent information that is important in understanding the human entry into the cognitive niche but the equally great increase in the permitted interaction among representations and representational systems. This increase is a double-edged sword: It offers great benefits in allowing many new inferences to be made, but it also aggravates the problem of data corruption—what scope syntax is designed to cope with. This increase in permissible interactions requires adaptations for translating information across mechanism boundaries and into common formats that make this interaction possible. The breadth of inferential interaction is important in understanding the distinctive aspects of the cognitive niche. Many representations in the human mind are not limited in their scope of application. They can be acted on by inference procedures that evolved to process information from other domains (as when inference procedures that evolved for making stone tools are applied to bone, a material of animal origin; Mithen, 1996), and they are allowed to inferentially interact with each other to a zoologically unprecedented degree (as when one's knowledge of bison anatomy and behavior affects how one fashions a tool for hunting them; Mithen, 1996). This is a pivotal element making such an architecture advantageous: Information can be made far more useful, if different items can be integrated into the same inferential structure, to produce new derivations. This phenomenon has been given various names—conceptual blending (Turner, 1996), conceptual integration (Sperber, 1994), domain sharing, or cognitive fluidity (Mithen, 1996). But

---

[3]i.e., to be de-encapsulated.

so far it is easier to point to examples of it than to provide a causal account of the machinery that produces it (for an interesting possibility, see Sperber, 1994).

In any case, the evolution of intelligence will depend critically on the economics of information management (see, e.g., Boyd & Richerson, 1985) and on the tools for handling information—that is, the nature of the adaptations that evolve to handle these problems. The net benefit of evolving to use certain classes of information will depend on the cost of its acquisition, the utility of the information when used, the damage of acting on the information mistakenly outside its area of applicability, and the cost of its management and maintenance. Because humans are the only species that has evolved this kind of intelligence, humans must be equipped with adaptations that evolved to solve the problems that are special to this form of intelligence.

HOW INTELLIGENCE$_2$ IS ACHIEVED

Scope Syntax, Truth, and Naïve Realism

For these reasons, issues involving not only the accuracy but also the scope of applicability of the information that the individual human acquires and represents became paramount in the design and evolution of the human cognitive architecture. We believe that there are a large number of design innovations that have evolved to solve the specialized programming problems posed by using local and contingent information, including a specialized scope syntax, metarepresentational adaptations, and decoupling systems. Indeed, we think that the human cognitive architecture is full of interlocking design features whose function is to solve problems of scope and accuracy. Examples include truth-value tags, source tags (self versus other; vision versus memory, etc.), scope tags, time and place tags, reference tags, credal values, operators embodying propositional attitudes, content-based routing of information to targeted inference engines, dissociations, systems of information encapsulation and interaction, independent representational formats for different ontologies, and the architecture and differential volatility of different memory systems.

Large amounts of knowledge are embodied in intelligent$_1$, domain-specific inference systems, but these systems were designed to be triggered by stimuli in the world. This knowledge could be unlocked and used for many purposes, however, if a way could be found to activate these systems in the absence of the triggering stimuli—that is, if the inference system could be activated by imagining a stimulus situation that is not actually occurring: a counterfactual. For example, by imagining a situation in which I left a knife near the counter's edge while the baby is toddling about the house, useful inferences about space, rigid object mechanics, biomechanics, intuitive biology, and intuitive psychology are unlocked, and a scenario unfolds before the mind's eye: "At counter's edge, the knife is within the baby's reach; she [will] see it, reach for it, and hurt herself" (*will* is a scope marker).

Given that our perceptions of the world are themselves mental representations, altering the architecture such that it can generate representations with the appropriate triggering features might not be too difficult to engineer—especially if the eliciting circumstance is itself a visual, tactile, kinesthetic, or proprioceptive percept, such as my seeing my hand about to put the knife on the counter (Tooby & Cosmides, 1990a). But for reasoning from this counterfactual situation to be useful, something else is needed. The premise—"the knife is at the counter's edge"—cannot be stored as something that has actually happened (if it has not), and the conclusion—"the baby hurt herself"—must be tagged as something that *could* happen but that *has not* happened.

In other words, one critical feature of a system capable of suppositional reasoning is the capacity to carry out inferential operations on sets of inferred representations that incorporate suppositions or propositions of conditionally unevaluated truth value, *while keeping their computational products isolated from other knowledge stores* (i.e., decoupled from them) until the truth or utility of the suppositions is decided, and the outputs are either integrated or discarded. This capacity is essential to planning, interpreting communications, employing the information communication brings, evaluating others' claims, mind reading, pretense, detecting or perpetrating deception, using inference to triangulate information about past or hidden causal relations, and much else that makes the human mind so distinctive. In what follows, we will try to sketch out some of the basic elements of a scope syntax designed to defuse problems intrinsic to the human mode of intelligence. By a scope syntax, we mean a system of procedures, operators, relationships, and data-handling formats that regulate the migration of information among subcomponents of the human cognitive architecture (for a fuller treatment, see Cosmides & Tooby, in press; also Leslie, 1987; Sperber, 1985).

To clarify what we mean, consider a simple cognitive system that we suspect is the ancestral condition for all animal minds and the default condition for the human mind as well: naïve realism. For the naïve realist, the world as it is mentally represented is taken for the world as it really is, and no distinction is drawn between the two. Indeed, only a subset of possible architectures are even capable of representing this distinction, and in the origin and initial evolution of representational systems, such a distinction would be functionless. From our external perspective, we can say of such basic architectures that all information found inside the system is assumed to be true, or is treated as true. However, from the point of view of the architecture itself, that would not be correct, for it would imply that the system is capable of drawing the distinction between true and false, and is categorizing the information as true. Instead, mechanisms in the architecture simply use the information found inside the system to regulate behavior and to carry out further computations. Whatever information is present in the system simply is "reality" for the architecture. Instead of tagging information as true or false—which seems so obvious to us—such basic architectures would not be designed to store false information. When new information is produced that renders old information obsolete, the old information is updated, overwritten, forgotten, or discarded. None of these operations require the tagging of information as true or false. They only involve the rule-governed replacement of some data by other data, just like overwriting a memory register in a personal computer does not require the data previously in that register be categorized as false. For most of the behavior-regulatory operations that representational systems evolved to orchestrate, there would be no point to storing false information, or information tagged as false. For this reason, there is no need in such an architecture to be able to represent that some information is true; its presence, or the decision to store it or remember it, is the cue to its reliability. In such a design, true equals accessible.

With this as background, and leaving aside the many controversies in epistemology over how to conceptualize what truth "really" is, we can define what we will call *architectural truth:* Information is treated by an architecture as true when it is allowed to migrate (or be reproduced) in an unrestricted or scope-free fashion throughout an architecture and is allowed to interact with any other data in the system that it is capable of interacting with. All data in semantic memory, for example, is architecturally true. The simplest and most economical way to engineer data use is for "true" information to be unmarked, and for unmarked information to be given whatever freedom of movement is possible by the computational architecture. Indeed, any system that acquires, stores, and uses information is a design of this kind. The alternative design, in which each piece of information intended to be used must be paired with another piece of information indicating that the first piece is true, seems unnecessarily costly and cumbersome. Because the true-is-unmarked system is the natural way for an evolved computational system to originate, and because there are many reasons to maintain this system for most uses, we might expect that this is also the reason why humans, and undoubtedly other organisms, are naïve realists. Naïve realism seems to be the likely starting point phylogenetically and ontogenetically, as well as the default mode for most systems, even in adulthood.

The next step, necessary only for some uses, is to have representations embedded within other data structures: metarepresentations (in a relaxed rather than narrow sense). For example, a cognitive architecture might contain the following structure: *The statement that "astrology is a science" is true.* This particular data structure includes a proposition (or data element) and an evaluation of the truth of the proposition (or data element).[4] However, such structures need not be limited to describing single propositions. Although it is common, in talking about metarepresentations and propositional attitudes, to depict a single representation embedded in an encompassing proposition, a single proposition is only a limiting case. A set of propositions or any other kind of data element can be bundled into a single unit that is taken, as a data packet, as an argument by a scope operator to form a metarepresentation. For example, the metarepresentation *Every sentence in this chapter is false* describes the truth value of a set of propositions as easily as *The first sentence in this chapter is false* describes the truth value of a single proposition. Indeed, sometimes integrated sets of propositions governed by a superordinate scope operator might become so elaborated, and relatively independent from other data structures, that they might conveniently be called *worlds*. We think large amounts of human knowledge inside individuals exists inside data structures of this kind.

A sketch of the kind of cognitive architecture and operators we have in mind begins with a primary workspace that operates in a way that is similar, in some respects, to natural deduction systems (see Gentzen, 1935/1969; Rips, 1994; Cosmides & Tooby, 1996a), although it may include axiom-like elements and many other differences as well. Its general features are familiar: There is a workspace containing active data elements, and procedures or operators act on the data structures, transforming them into new data structures. Data structures are maintained in the workspace until they are overwritten, or if not used or primed after a given period of time, they fade and are discarded. Products may be permanently stored in appropriate subsystems if they meet various criteria indicating they merit long-term storage or warrant being treated as architecturally true. Otherwise, the contents and intermediate work products of the workspace are volatile and are purged, which is one adaptation for protecting the integrity of the reliable data stores elsewhere in the architecture (e.g., the fact that dreams are volatile is probably a design feature to avoid corruption of memory stores; Symons, 1993). Data structures may be introduced from perception, memory, supposition, or from various other system components and modules. Some of the procedures and tags available in the workspace correspond to familiar logical operators and elements, such as variable binding, instantiation, if introduction and if elimination, the recognition and tagging of contradictions, *modus ponens*, and so on. Some of the procedures are ecologically rational (Tooby & Cosmides, 1992a; Cosmides & Tooby, 1996b); that is, they correspond to licensed transformations in various adaptive logics (which may diverge

---

[4]There is no need, in particular, for the data structure to be a sentencelike or quasi-linguistic proposition. For most purposes, throughout this paper, when we use the term *proposition* we are not committing ourselves to quasi-linguistic data structures—we will simply be using it as a convenient short-hand term for a data element of some kind.

substantially from licensed inferences in the content-independent formal logics developed so far by logicians). Indeed, many procedures consist of routing data structures through adaptive specializations such as cheater detection or hazard management algorithms (Cosmides, 1989; Cosmides & Tooby, 1997), with outputs placed back into the workspace—a process that resembles either calling subroutines or applying logical transformations, depending on one's taste in formalisms.[5] Deliberative reasoning is carried out in this workspace, while many other types of inference are carried out automatically as part of the heterogeneous array of intelligent$_1$ specializations available in the architecture. Some areas of this workspace are usually part of conscious awareness, and most are consciously accessible.

Scope Representations

The data sets in this system exist in structured, hierarchical[6] relations, which we will represent as indented levels. Data elements in the left-most position are in what might be thought of as the ground state, which means they are licensed to migrate anywhere in the architecture they can be represented. Through inference procedures, they can mate promiscuously with any other ground-state data elements, producing conclusions that are their inferential offspring. Usually, ground-state elements are permitted to interact with subordinate levels as well. In other words, they are architecturally true, or scope free. Other elements are subordinated under ground state elements through scope operators. Therefore, we might represent an architecturally true statement in the left-most position:

(1) Anthropology is a science.

When in the left-most position, the statement is unmarked by the architecture. As such, it is free to be stored or to be introduced into any other nondecoupled process in the architecture. A subordinated statement may be scope limited, such as the following:

---

[5]Various operators and features of the workspace provide the intuitions that logicians have elaborated into various formal logics—the elaboration taking place through the addition of various elements not found in the workspace, the attempt to simultaneously impose self-consistency and conformity to intuition, and the removal of many content-specific scope operators. For the human architecture itself, there is no requirement that the various procedures available to the workspace be mutually consistent, only that the trouble caused by inconsistency be less than the inferential benefits gained under normal consistions. Task-switching and scope-limiting mechanisms also prevent the emergence of contradictions during ordinary functioning, which makes the mutual consistency of the architecture as an abstract formal system not relevant. Mental logic hypotheses for human reasoning have been rejected empirically by many on the assumption that the only licensed inferences are logical. We believe that the content sensitivity of human reasoning is driven by the existence of domain-specific inference engines, which coexist beside operators that parallel more traditional logical elements.

[6]As well as heterarchical relations, governed by rules for data incorporation from other sources.

(2) The statement is false that:

(3)   Anthropology is a science.

In this case, the scope operator (2) binds the scope within which the information of the data structure (3) can be accessed, so that (3) is not free to be promoted to the ground state or to be used elsewhere in the system. In contrast, the function of an explicit true tag in a statement description operator (i.e., *The statement is true that p*) would be to release the statement from previous scope restriction, promoting it to the next left-most level, or, if it was originally only one level down, changing its status to unmarked, or architecturally true.[7] Time and location operators operate similarly:

(4) In ≠ Tobe (!Kung for "autumn"),

(5)   the mongongo nuts become edible and plentiful.

or

(6) At Nyae Nyae,

(7)   there are chrysomelid beetles suitable for making arrow poison.

Scope operators define, regulate, or modify the relationships between sets of information, and the migration of information between levels. They involve a minimum of two levels, a superordinate (or ground) level and a subordinate level. In these cases, the subordinate propositions cannot be reproduced without their respective scope tags, which describe the boundary conditions under which the information is known to be accurate, and which therefore license their use in certain inferences, but not others. As with classical conditioning, we expect that additional mechanisms are designed to keep track of the reality of the scope boundaries; for example, observing a lack of contingency outside the boundaries may eventually release the restriction. Thus, (6–7) may be transformed into (7) for an individual whose travels from camp to camp are typically inside the beetle species' range. Conversely, architecturally true statements like (1) can be transformed by a scope operation into something scope limited, as new information about its boundary conditions are learned. A time-based scope transformation would be as follows:

(8) It is no longer true that

(9)   anthropology is a science.

Scope operators regulate the migration of information into and out of subordinated data sets, coupling (allowing data to flow) and decoupling them according to the nature of the operator and the arguments it is fed. They bind propositions into internally transparent but externally regulated sets.

In so doing, they provide many of the tools necessary to solve the problems posed by contingent information. By imposing bounds on where scope-limited

---

[7]Promotion is equivalent to Tarskian disquotation, with respect to the next level in the architecture.

information can travel (or what can access it), it allows information to be retained by the system and used under well-specified conditions, without allowing it to damage other reliable data sets through inferential interaction. We will call representations that are bound or interrelated by scope operators *scope-representations* or *S-representations*.

Since computational features evolve because they enhance behavioral regulation, it is worth noting that these innovations markedly increase the range of possible behaviors open to the organism. In particular, one major change involves *acting as if*. The organism would be highly handicapped if it could only act on the basis of information known to be true, or have its conduct regulated by architecturally true propositions, although this was likely to be the ancestral state of the organism. With the ability *to act as if p*, or *to act on the basis of p*, the organism can use information to regulate its behavior without losing any scope-represented restrictions on the nature of the information, or without necessarily losing a continuing awareness that the information acted on is not or might not be true. Conditions where such a behavioral-representational subsystem are useful include the many categories of actions undertaken under conditions of uncertainty (e.g., *We will assume they got the message about the restaurant.*; or *We will act as if there is a leopard hiding in the shadows of the tree.*); actions with respect to social conventions or deontic commitments (which are by themselves incapable of being either true or not true, at least in an ordinary sense; e.g., *Elizabeth is the rightful Queen of England.*; *It is praiseworthy to make the correct temple sacrifices.*); adapting oneself to the wishes of others; hypothesis testing, and so on.[8] Pretense (Leslie, 1987) and deception (Whiten & Byrne, 1997) are simply extensions of this same competence, in which the agent knows the representations on which he or she is acting are false. (Deception and pretense are limiting cases in which the information is S-represented as false with 100% certainty. Typically, however, S-representations will be tagged with more intermediate credal values.) In order to get coordinated behavior among many individuals, and the benefits that arise from it, it is necessary to agree on a set of representations that will be jointly acted upon—a reason why social interaction so often involves the manufacture of socially constructed but unwarranted shared beliefs. Structures of representations can be built up that can be permanently consulted for actions, without their contents unrestrictedly contaminating other knowledge stores.

Credal values and modals (*it is likely that p; it is possible that p; it is certain that p*) allow the maintenance and transformation of scope-marked information bound

---

[8]Indeed, this kind of architecture offers a computational explanation of what kind of thing deontic ascriptions are: decoupled descriptions of possible actions and states of affairs, of suspended truth value, connected to value assignments of the possible actions.

to information about likelihood and possibility—regulatory information that often changes while the underlying propositions are conserved. Propositional attitude verbs (e.g., *think, believe, want, hope, deny*) are obviously a key category of scope operator as well (Leslie, 1987; Baron-Cohen, 1995).

Supposition, Counterfactuals, and Natural Deduction Systems

What makes such a system resemble, to a certain extent, natural deduction systems is the presence of scope operators, such as supposition, and the fact that these operators create subdomains or subordinate levels of representation, which may themselves have further subordinate levels, growing into multilevel, treelike structures. Supposition involves the introduction of propositions of unevaluated or suspended truth value, which are treated as true within a bounded scope and then used as additional content from which to combinatorially generate inferential products. The operator "if," for example, opens up a suppositional world (e.g., *I am in my office this afternoon. If students believe I am not in my office this afternoon, then they won't bother me. If I close my door, and leave my light off, they will believe I am not here.*) whose contents are kept isolated from other proposition sets, so that true propositions are not intermixed and hence confused with false ones (e.g., *I am not in my office*) or potentially false ones (e.g., *they won't bother me*). Any number of subordinate levels can be introduced, with additional subordinate suppositions or other scope operations.

A key feature of such a deduction system is the restricted application of inferences. Inferences are applied, in a rule-governed but unrestricted fashion within a level (e.g., *students believe I am not in my office this afternoon*, therefore, *they won't bother me*), but not across levels (e.g., there is no contradiction to be recognized between *I am in my office this afternoon* and the proposition *I am not in my office this afternoon* because they are at different levels in the structure; Leslie & Frith, 1990). Contents are architecturally true with respect to the level they are in and may enter into inferences at that level, while remaining false or unevaluated with respect to both the ground state of the architecture and other intermediate superordinate levels. Certain propositional attitudes (e.g., believe as opposed to know) also decouple the truth value of the propositions (*I am not in my office*) that are embedded in encompassing statements, a process that can be dissected computationally. Paradoxically, an architecture that only processes true information is highly limited it what it can infer, and most forms of human discovery by reasoning involve supposition. While some cases are famous, such as Newton's thought experiment in (10), normal cases of suppositions are so numerous that they permeate our thoughts in carrying out routine actions in our daily lives (11).

(10) *Suppose I threw this rock hard enough that the earth fell away in its curvature faster than the rock's downward ballistic took it?*

(11) What if I hold my airline ticket in my teeth while I pick up the baby with my right arm and our bags with my left arm?

Supposition (e.g., *12*) is a scope operation that suspends truth values for all successive computations that result from taking the supposition as a premise, which in this case is only (*13*).

(12) Suppose my wife, Desdemona, was unfaithful with Cassio.

(13)   Then Cassio, who I thought was my friend, has betrayed me.

Suppositions and their entailments remain internally interrelated and generative but isolated from the rest of the data in the architecture. If (*13*) was allowed to escape its scope restriction to enter into ground state-originating inferences, the effects would be disastrous. Othello would have (*13*) as part of his uncritically accepted semantic store of propositions, without it being warranted (or "true" within the decoupled world of Shakespeare's *Othello*).[9] Nevertheless, S-representations like (*12–13*) allow many types of useful and revelatory reasoning to proceed—everything from proof by contradiction to the construction of contingency plans. Additionally, suppositions contain specifications of when subordinate deductions can be discharged. This occurs when other processes produce a true proposition that duplicates that supposition. Evidence establishing (*12*) as true discharges the supposition, promoting (*13*) to architectural truth and stripping it of its scope restrictions.

Actions can also discharge suppositions—a key point. Consider a hominid considering how to capture a colobus monkey in a tree. An architecture that cannot consider decoupled states of affairs is limited in the behaviors it can take (e.g., close distance with monkey). This may often fail because of the nature of the situation. Consider, for example, a situation in which a branch from the monkey's tree is close to the branch of a neighboring tree. In this situation, the hominid confronts the following contingencies: If he climbs the trunk, then the monkey escapes by the branch. If he climbs across the branches, then the monkey escapes by the trunk. Before taking action, if the hominid suppositionally explores the alternative hunt scenarios, then he will detect the prospective failure. Moreover, given alternative inferential pathways leading to failure, the hominid, armed with the inferential power of supposition (and various other inferential tools, such as a model of the prey mind and a theory of mechanics), may then begin to consider additional courses of action suppositionally, reasoning about the likely consequences of each alternative. *Suppose there were no branch on the neighboring tree, then it could not be used as an escape route. Suppose, before I initiate the hunt by climbing up the trunk, I break that branch. Then it could not be used as an escape route. If I then go up the trunk, the monkey cannot escape. The hunt will be a success. End search for successful outcome. Transform*

---

[9]Such an architecture explains how humans process fictional worlds without confusing their environments and inhabitants with the real world.

suppositional structure into a plan. Conveniently for planning and action, the conditions for discharging a supposition specify the actions that need to be taken to put that aspect of the plan into effect, and the tree structure of suppositions provides the information about the order of the causal steps to be taken. Hominids armed with suppositional reasoning can undertake new types of successful behaviors that would be impossible for those whose cognitive architectures lacked such design features. It allows them to explore the properties of situations computationally in order to identify sequences of improvised behaviors that may lead to novel, successful outcomes. The restricted application of inferences to a level, until suppositions (or other scope limitations) are discharged, is a crucial element of such an architecture. The states of affairs under the scope of a specific supposition are not mistaken for states of affairs outside that supposition: superordinate and subordinate relationships are kept clear until their preconditions can be discharged (as when an action is taken).

Like a clutch in an automobile, supposition and other scope operators allow the controlled engagement or disengagement of powerful sets of representations, which can contain rich descriptions, with domain-specific inference engines, which can be applied when their preconditions are met. These operators provide vehicles whereby information which may or may not be counterfactual can be processed without the output being tagged as *true* and stored as such.

Because contingent information can change its status at any time with any new change in the world, it is important to have tools available that can take architecturally true information and scrutinize it. For example, the workspace that contains proposition p may benefit from demoting p into the scope-representation, *It appears that p*. Proposition p can still provide the basis for action but can now be subjected to inferential processes not possible when it was simply a free representation at ground state. Demotion into a scope-representation brings a representation out of architectural truth and into a new relationship with the primary workspace.[10] Because of this feature of the human cognitive architecture, humans can contingently refrain from being naïve realists about any specific data structure, although presumably we will always be naïve realists about whatever happens to be in the ground state in the workspace at any given time.[11]

---

[10]It is interesting in this regard that children's ability to distinguish appearance from reality (e.g., on seeing a sponge that looks like a rock, they can say that although it looks like a rock, it is really a sponge) matures at about the same time as their ability to represent false beliefs (about 4 years). This is sometimes interpreted as evidence for the maturation of a theory of mind (Baron-Cohen, 1995). It might, however, reflect the maturation of a more encompassing scope syntax, of which M-representations are a part.

[11]We think that ground-state representations are present in consciousness but are not automatically the objects of consciousness; that is, we are not automatically reflectively conscious of these data structures, although they can easily be made so. Data structures in the ground state must be demoted to become the object of inferential scrutiny. Indeed, we think that the function of the architectural component that corresponds to one referent of the word *consciousness* is to be a buffer to hold isolated from the rest of the architecture the intermediate computational work products during the period when their truth value and other merits are unevaluated. This explains why consciousness is so notoriously volatile.

Some operators are recursive, and some types of subordinated data structures can serve as the ground for further subordinated structures, leading potentially to a tree structure of subordinated and parallel relations whose length and branching contingencies are restricted only by performance limitations of the system. For example:

(14) *Anna was under the impression that*

(15)   *Clifford has claimed that*

(16)   *most anthropologists believe that*

(17)   *the statement is false that:*

(18)   *anthropology is a science.* [and]

(19)   *quantum physicists have demonstrated that:*

(20)   *science is only an observer-dependent set of arbitrary subjective opinions.*

Extensive thinking about a topic can produce structures too elaborate to be placed, in their entirety, into the workspace, and which are therefore considered in pieces. The cultural development of memory aids such as writing have allowed an explosion of conceptual structures that are larger than what our ancestors would have routinely used.

Scope operators greatly augment the computational power of the human cognitive architecture, compared with ancestral systems lacking such features. One advantage of an architecture equipped with scope operators is that it can carry out inferential operations on systems of inferences of unevaluated or suspended truth value, while keeping their computational products isolated from other knowledge stores until the truth or utility of the elements can be decided. It they were not kept isolated, their contents would enter into inferences with other data structures in the architecture, often producing dangerously false but unmarked conclusions (e.g., *science is only a set of arbitrary subjective opinions* would be disastrous guidance for someone who has to choose a medical strategy to arrest an epidemic in a developing country). Fortunately, (14) decouples the uncertain information in (15–20) from the rest of the architecture but allows the information to be maintained, and reasoned about, within various lawful and useful restrictions specified in the scope operators. The structure (14–20) is free to migrate through the system as a bound unit, entering into whatever licensed inferences it can be related to, but its subordinate elements are not.

Within subordinate levels (15–20), similar scope operations structure the inferences that are possible. The operator *demonstrate* assigns the value "true" to the subordinate element (20: *science is only…*), allowing its contents to be promoted to the next level. Within that level, it is treated as true, although it is not true above that level or outside of its scope-circumscription. The operator that governs that level—*claim*—prevents it from migrating independently of the metarepresentation it is bound to (*Clifford has claimed that…*). Both (16) plus entailments and (19) plus entailments are true within the world of Clifford's claims and are free to inferentially interact with each other, along with (20) and any other of Clifford's claims that turn up. Indeed, one can say that a representation is true with respect to a particular level in a particular data structure; any level can function as a ground level to subordinate levels. It is scope-conditionally true for a data structure when it is permitted by the architecture to interact with any other information held within the same or subordinate levels of that data structure.

Source, Error Correction, and the Evolution of Communication

Different scope operators obviously have different regulatory properties and, hence, different functions. *Claim, believe,* and *demonstrate,* for example, require source tags as arguments, as well as conveying additional information (e.g., publicly assert as true that p; privately treat as architecturally true that p; and have publicly established the truth that p, respectively).[12] Source tags are very useful because often, with contingent information, one may not have direct evidence about its truth but may acquire information about the reliability of a source. If the sources of pieces of information are maintained with the information, then subsequent information about the source can be used to change the assigned truth status of the information either upwards or downwards. For example, one may not assign much credal value to what most anthropologists believe (16), or one may discover that Clifford in particular is highly unreliable (15), while having a solid set of precedents in which Anna's impressions (such as 14) have proven highly reliable, despite the fact that she herself is unwilling to evaluate her impressions as trustworthy. Sources may include not only people but also sources internal to the architecture, such as vision, episodic memory, a supposition, previous inference, and so on. Thus, humans can have the thought "My eyes are telling me one thing, while my reason is telling me another."

In general, our minds are full of conclusions without our having maintained the grounds or evidence that led us to think of them as true. For a massively inferential architecture like the human mind, each item can serve as input to many other inferential processes, whose outputs are inputs to others. To the extent that the information is sourced, or its grounds and derivation are preserved in association with the data, then new data about its evidential basis can be used to correct or update its inferential descendants. (If "Stock in Yahoo is a good investment" is tagged with its source—Gordon Gekko—it can be reevaluated when you learn that Gekko has been indicted for insider trading and stock manipulation.) To the extent that information is not sourced, or its process of infer-

---

[12]We are not claiming that every propositional attitude term, for example, is reliably developing or innate. We consider it more plausible that there is an evolved set of information-regulatory primitives that can be combined to produce a large set of scope operators and scope representations.

ential derivation is not preserved in association with it, then it cannot be automatically corrected when the grounds for belief are corrected. (Even more basically, Sperber has persuasively argued that the inferential nature of communication itself requires the online metarepresentational processing of language in order for interpretation to be successful [Sperber & Wilson, 1986; Sperber 1985, 1996, 2000].)

Indeed, our minds are undoubtedly full of erroneous inferential products that were not corrected when their parent source information was updated because they could no longer be connected with their derivation. Because source tags, and especially pathways of derivation, are costly to maintain, mechanisms should monitor for sufficient corroboration, consistency with architecturally true information, or certification by a trusted source. If, or when, a threshold is reached, the system should no longer expend resources to maintain source information, and it should fade. This is what makes trust so useful (one does not need to keep the cognitive overhead of scope-processing communication) but so dangerous (one cannot recover and correct all of the implanted misinformation). After all, what is important about an encyclopedia of (accurate) knowledge about the world is the facts themselves; not who told them to you, what their attitude toward them was, or when you learned them. Typically, once a fact is established to a sufficient degree of certainty, source, attitude, and time tags are lost (Sperber, 1985; Tulving, 1983; Shimamura, 1995); for example, most people cannot remember who told them that apples are edible or that plants photosynthesize. Moreover, an encyclopedia is most useful when the facts can cross-reference one another, so that each can support inferences that may apply to others, thereby adding further, inferred facts to the body of knowledge (e.g., *Mercury is a poison.*; *Tuna has high levels of mercury.*; therefore, *People who eat tuna are ingesting poison.*). This means that truth conditions must not be suspended for facts in semantic memory, and the scope of application for any truth-preserving inference procedures must be relatively unrestricted within the encyclopedia, such that facts can mate promiscuously to produce new, inferred facts.

CONCLUSION

Since Frege, philosophers have been aware that propositional attitudes suspend semantic relations such as truth, reference, and existence (Frege, 1892; Kripke, 1979; Richard, 1990). Frege noticed, for example, that the principle of substitution of coreferring terms breaks down when they are embedded in propositional attitudes (i.e., one can believe that Batman fights crime without believing that Bruce Wayne fights crime). Or, consider the following statement:

(25) *Shirley MacLaine believes that*

(26)   *she is the reincarnation of an Egyptian princess named Nefu.*

(25–26) can be true, without Nefu ever having existed, and without it being true that Shirley is her reincarnation. The propositional attitude verb *believe* suspends truth, reference, and existence in (26), fortunately decoupling (26) from the semantic memory of those who entertain this statement.

Rather than being quirks, problems, and puzzles, as philosophers have often regarded them, it seems possible that such suspensions are instead adaptations: design features of a computational architecture designed to solve problems posed by the many varieties of contingent information exploited by our ancestors, and the interrelationships among sets of contingent information. To benefit from contingent information without being destroyed by it, the human cognitive achitecture must be equipped with a scope syntax. It seems likely that scope-representations and operators are reliably developing, species-typical features of the human cognitive architecture, and that design features of this kind are necessary—though not sufficient—for any system that manifests improvisational intelligence.

In sum, the picture of intelligence that emerges from the collision of evolutionary biology and cognitive science differs in many ways from more commonly held conceptions of what intelligence consists of. Such an evolutionary analysis throws doubt on some views (i.e., intelligence as a set of content-independent rational methods), necessitates some distinctions (i.e., between dedicated and improvisional intelligence), and appears to solve some questions (Why is improvisional intelligence so zoologically rare?). Nevertheless, it also uncovers a further set of questions (i.e., How can computational procedures evolve that exploit the novel features of unique situations?) that deepen the enigma of human intelligence and indicate that building an accurate model of the computational machinery underlying human intelligence will require novel insights that only improvisional intelligence can supply.

REFERENCES

Baillargeon, R. (1986). Representing the existence and the location of hidden objects: Object permanence in 6- and 8-month old infants. *Cognition, 23*, 21–41.

Barkow, J., Cosmides, L., & Tooby, J. (Eds.). (1992). *The adapted mind: Evolutionary psychology and the generation of culture.* New York: Oxford University Press.

Baron-Cohen, S. (1995). *Mindblindness: An essay on autism and theory of mind.* Cambridge, MA: MIT Press.

Boyd, R., & Richerson, P. (1985). *Culture and the evolutionary process.* Chicago: University of Chicago Press.

Boyer, P. (1993). *The naturalness of religious ideas.* Berkeley: University of California Press.

Burke, T., Davies, N., Bruford, M., & Hatchwell, B. (1989). Parental care and mating behaviour of polyandrous dunnocks *Prunella modularis* related to paternity by DNA fingerprinting. *Nature, 338*, 249–251.

Clark, A. (1997). *Being there.* Cambridge, MA: MIT Press.

Cosmides, L. (1989). The logic of social exchange: Has natural selection shaped how humans reason? Studies with the Wason selection task. *Cognition, 31*, 187–276.

Cosmides, L., & Tooby, J. (1987). From evolution to behavior: Evolutionary psychology as the missing link. In J. Dupre (Ed.), *The latest on the best: Essays on evolution and optimality.* Cambridge, MA: The MIT Press.

Cosmides, L., & Tooby, J. (1989). Evolutionary psychology and the generation of culture, Part II. Case study: A computational theory of social exchange. *Ethology and Sociobiology, 10,* 51–97.

Cosmides, L., & Tooby, J. (1992). Cognitive adaptations for social exchange. In J. Barkow, L. Cosmides, & J. Tooby (Eds.), *The adapted mind: Evolutionary psychology and the generation of culture* (pp. 163–228). New York: Oxford University Press.

Cosmides, L., & Tooby, J. (1996a). A logical design for the mind? *Contemporary Psychology, 41*(5), 448–450.

Cosmides, L., & Tooby, J. (1996b). Are humans good intuitive statisticians after all? Rethinking some conclusions of the literature on judgment under uncertainty. *Cognition, 58,* 1–73.

Cosmides, L., & Tooby, J. (1997). Dissecting the computational architecture of social inference mechanisms. In *Characterizing human psychological adaptations.* Ciba Foundation Symposium: Vol. 208. Chichester, UK: Wiley.

Cosmides, L., & Tooby, J. (2000). Consider the source: The evolution of adaptations for decoupling and metarepresentations. In D. Sperber (Ed.), *Metarepresentation.* Vancouver Studies in Cognitive Science. New York: Oxford University Press.

Davies, N. (1989). The dunnock: Cooperation and conflict among males and females in a variable mating system. In P. Stacey & W. Koenig (Eds.), *Cooperative breeding in birds* (pp. 457–485). Cambridge: Cambridge University Press.

Dawkins, R. (1976). *The selfish gene.* New York: Oxford University Press.

Dawkins, R. (1982). *The extended phenotype.* San Francisco: W.H. Freeman.

Dawkins, R. (1986). *The blind watchmaker.* New York: Norton.

Dennett, D. (1987). *The intentional stance.* Cambridge, MA: MIT Press.

de Waal, F. (1982). *Chimpanzee politics: Power and sex among apes.* New York: Harper & Row.

Frege, G. (1892). On sense and reference. In P. Geach & M. Black (Eds.), *Translations of the philosophical writings of Gottlob Frege.* Oxford, England: Blackwell.

Gallistel, C. R. (1990). *The organization of learning.* Cambridge, MA: MIT Press.

Garcia, J. 1990. Learning without memory. *Journal of Cognitive Neuroscience, 2,* 287–305.

Gendron, R. P., & O. J. Reichman. (1995). Food perishability and inventory management: A comparison of three caching strategies. *American Naturalist 145,* 948–968.

Gentzen, G. (1969). Investigations into logical deduction. In M. E. Szabo (Ed.), *The collected papers of Gerhard Gentzen* (pp. 405–431). (Original work published 1935). Amsterdam: North Holland Publishing Co.

Gergely, G., Nadasdy, Z., Csibra, G., & Biro, S. (1995). Taking the intentional stance at 12 months of age. *Cognition, 56,* 165–193.

Gigerenzer, G., Todd, P., & The ABC Research Group. (1999). *Simple heuristics that make us smart.* New York: Oxford University Press.

Gould, S., & Lewontin, R. (1979). The spandrels of San Marco and the Panglossian program: A critique of the adaptationist program. *Proceedings of the Royal Society of London, 250,* 281–288.

Heinrich, B. (1981). *Bumblebee economics.* Cambridge, MA: Harvard University Press.

Hirschfeld, L., & Gelman, S. (Eds.). (1994). *Mapping the mind: Domain-specificity in cognition and culture.* New York: Cambridge University Press.

Humphrey, N. (1984). *Consciousness regained.* Oxford: Oxford University Press.

James, W. (1892). *The principles of psychology.* London: Macmillan.

Johnson, M., & Morton, J. (1991). *Biology and cognitive development: The case of face recognition.* Oxford, England: Blackwell.

Kahneman, D., Slovic, P., & Tversky, A. (Eds). (1982). *Judgment under uncertainty: Heuristics and biases.* Cambridge: Cambridge University Press.

Kalat, J., & Rozin, P. (1973). "Learned Safety" as a mechanism in long-delay taste-aversion learning in rats. *Journal of Comparative & Physiological Psychology, 83,* 198–207.

Krebs, J. R., & Dawkins, R. (1984). Animal signals: Mind reading and manipulation. In Krebs, J. R., & Davies, N. B. (Eds.). *Behavioural ecology: An evolutionary approach* (2nd ed., pp. 380–402). Oxford, England: Blackwell.

Kripke, S. (1979). A puzzle about belief. In A. Margalit (Ed.) *Meaning and use.* (pp. 239–283). Dordrecht, Holland: Reidel.

Lee, R. B. (1993). *The Dobe Ju/'hoansi.* (2nd ed.). New York: Holt, Reinhart & Winston.

Leslie, A. (1987). Pretense and representation: The origins of "theory of mind." *Psychological Review, 94,* 412–426.

Leslie, A. (1988). The necessity of illusion: Perception and thought in infancy. In L Weiskrantz (Ed.), *Thought without language* (pp. 185–210). Oxford, UK: Clarendon Press.

Leslie, A. (1994). ToMM, ToBy, and Agency: Core architecture and domain specificity. In L. Hirschfeld & S. Gelman (Eds.), *Mapping the mind: Domain specificity in cognition and culture.* New York: Cambridge University Press.

Leslie, A., & Frith, U. (1990). Prospects for a cognitive neuropsychology of autism: Hobson's choice. *Psychological Review, 97,* 122–131.

Mandler, J. M., & McDonough, L. (in press). Studies in inductive inference in infancy. *Cognitive Psychology.*

Marr, D. (1982). *Vision: A computational investigation into the human representation and processing of visual information.* San Francisco: Freeman.

Mineka, S., & Cook, M. (1993). Mechanisms involved in the observational conditioning of fear. *Journal of Experimental Psychology: General, 122,* 23–38.

Mithen, S. (1996). *The prehistory of the mind.* London: Thames & Hudson.

Nozick, R. (1993). *The nature of rationality.* Cambridge, MA: Harvard University Press.

Ohman, A., Dimberg, U., & Ost, L. G. (1985). Biological constraints on the fear response. In S. Reiss & R. Bootsin (Eds.), *Theoretical issues in behavior therapy* (pp. 123–175). New York: Academic Press.

Perrrigo, G., Bryant, W., & vom Saal, F. (1990). A unique neural timing mechanism prevents male mice from harming their own offspring. *Animal Behavior, 39,* 535–539.

Pinker, S. (1994). *The language instinct.* New York: Morrow.

Pinker, S. (1997). *How the mind works.* New York: Norton.

Pinker, S., & Bloom, P. (1990). Natural language and natural selection. *Behavioral and Brain Sciences 13,* 707–784.

Post, D., McDonald, M., & Reichman, O. (1998). Influence of maternal diet and perishability on caching and consumption behavior of juvenile easter woodrats. *Journal of Mammalogy, 79,* 56–162.

Premack, D., & Premack, A. (1997). Infants attribute value+- to the goal-directed actions of self-propelled objects. *Journal of Cognitive Neuroscience, 9,* 848–856.

Pressley, P. (1981). Parental effort and the evolution of nest-guarding tactics in the ghreespine stickleback, *Gasterosteus aculeatus* L. *Evolution, 35,* 282–295.

Richard, M. (1990). *Propositional attitudes: An essay on thoughts and how we ascribe them.* Cambridge, MA: Cambridge University Press.

Rips, L. (1994). *The psychology of proof: Deductive reasoning in human thinking.* Cambridge, MA.: MIT Press.

Rozin, P., & Kalat, J. (1971). Specific hungers and poison avoidance as adaptive specializations of learning. *Psychological Review, 78,* 459–486.

Seligman, M. (1971). Phobias and preparedness. *Behavior Therapy, 2,* 307–320.

Shepard, R. N. (1992) The three-dimensionality of color: An evolutionary accommodation to an enduring property of the world? In J. Barkow, L. Cosmides, & J. Tooby (Eds.), *The adapted mind: Evolutionary psychology and the generation of culture.* New York: Oxford University Press.

Shimamura, A. (1995). Memory and frontal lobe function. In M. S. Gazzaniga (Ed.), *The cognitive neurosciences* (pp. 803–813). Cambridge, MA: MIT Press.

Spelke, E. S. (1990). Principles of object perception. *Cognitive Science, 14,* 29–56.

Sperber, D. (1985). Anthropology and psychology: Towards and epidemiology of representations. *Man, 20,* 73–89.

Sperber, D. (1994). The modularity of thought and the epidemiology of representations. In L. Hirschfeld & S. Gelman (Eds.), *Mapping the mind: Domain specificity in cognition and culture* (pp. 39–67). New York: Cambridge University Press.

Sperber, D. (1996). *Explaining culture: A naturalistic approach.* Oxford, England: Blackwell.

Sperber, D. (2000). Metarepresentations in an evolutionary perspective. In D. Sperber (Ed.), *Metarepresentation.* Vancouver Studies in Cognitive Science. New York: Oxford University Press.

Sperber, D., & Wilson, D. (1986). *Relevance: Communication and cognition.* Oxford, England: Blackwell.

Symons, D. (1993). The stuff that dreams aren't made of: Why wake-state and dream-state sensory experiences differ. *Cognition, 47,* 181–217.

Tager-Flusberg, H., Boshart, J., & Baron-Cohen, S. (1998). Reading the windows to the soul: Evidence of domain-specific sparing in Williams syndrome. *Journal of Cognitive Neuroscience, 10,* 631–639.

Tooby, J., & Cosmides, L. (1989). Evolutionary psychology and the generation of culture, Part I: Theoretical considerations. *Ethology & Sociobiology, 10,* 29–49.

Tooby, J., & Cosmides, L. (1990). The past explains the present: emotional adaptations and the structure of ancestral environments. *Ethology and Sociobiology, 11,* 375–424.

Tooby, J., & Cosmides, L. (1992a). *Ecological rationality and the multimodular mind: Grounding normative theories in adaptive problems.* (Center for Evolutionary Psychology Technical Report 92–1). Center for Evolutionary Psychology, University of California, Santa Barbara.

Tooby, J., & Cosmides, L. (1992b). The psychological foundations of culture. In J. Barkow, L. Cosmides, & J. Tooby (Eds.), *The adapted mind: Evolutionary psychology and the generation of culture.* New York: Oxford University Press.

Tooby J., & DeVore, I. (1987). The reconstruction of hominid behavioral evolution through strategic modeling. In W. Kinzey (Ed.), *Primate models of hominid behavior* (pp. 183–237). New York: SUNY Press.

Tulving, E. (1983). *Elements of episodic memory.* Oxford: Oxford University Press.

Turner, M. (1996). *The literary mind.* New York: Oxford University Press.

Uexkull, J. von. (1957). A stroll through the world of animals and men: A picture book of invisible worlds. In C. H. Schiller (Ed. & Trans.), *Instinctive Behavior: The development of a modern concept,* (pp. 5–80). New York: International Universities Press.

Wehner, R., & Srinivasan, M. (1981). Searching behavior of desert ants, genus *Cataglyphis* (*Formicidae,* Hymenoptera). *Journal of Comparative Physiology, 142,* 315–338

Whiten, A., & Byrne, R. (1997). *Machiavellian intelligence II: Extensions and evaluations.* Cambridge: Cambridge University Press

Williams, G. C. (1966). *Adaptation and natural selection: A critique of some current evolutionary thought.* Princeton, NJ: Princeton University Press.

9

Is Human Intelligence an Adaptation? Cautionary Observations From the Philosophy of Biology

Owen Flanagan
Duke University

Valerie Gray Hardcastle
Virginia Tech University

Eddy Nahmias*
Duke University

WHAT IS AN ADAPTATION?

It is obvious that humans are intelligent creatures. We display capacities to learn and to know that surpass all other species—at least in many domains. Furthermore, it is clear that intelligence is somehow connected to our genetic endowment because everything we do is at least permitted by our genes. What is less clear is whether intelligence considered as a general species trait is a biological adaptation in the strict sense. The strict sense we have in mind says that for some trait T (intelligence in the present case) and for some species S, T is an adaptation if and only if T was selected and maintained in S because T led (and possibly still does lead) to reproductive success and stability for S in a particular

---

*We follow alphabetical order in listing authors. Authorship itself is equal.

environment. This requires that for T to be a biological adaptation it led—or better, contributed—to population growth and stability at a level supportable by the ecological niche S occupies. Furthermore, to provide a case that some trait T is an adaptation, there must be reason to believe that T is heritable, that offspring are more likely to have trait T, if their parents had it.

To preview what is to come, our main points are these. First, adequate adaptationist explanations are difficult to provide for most traits, but especially mental (brain-based) traits because soft tissue leaves little fossil evidence and because what the mind does and how it does it are so enmeshed with culture. Second, and relatedly, in order to provide even a plausible argument schema that some trait is an adaptation, the trait needs to be well defined. This is simply a commonplace demand on scientific explanations: the explanandum (that which is to be explained) needs to be rigorously specified so that the explanans (that which does the explaining) has a suitable target, one that contains a bull's-eye. Winged flight in insects and birds, resistance to toxic metals in certain strains of grass, photoreceptor cells in eyes, and the ability of certain bacteria to eat oil are specified in the right sort of way for an evolutionary explanation. Third, if we are to provide an adaptationist explanation of some phenotypic trait, it needs to be of the sort we have reason to think is largely determined by the genotype. The reason for this demand is simply due to the fact that adaptationist explanations only cover traits governed by the principles of population genetics; they do not cover traits acquired through social learning. Fourth, there is no sufficiently rigorous and low-level conception of intelligence used consistently by psychologists such that one could begin to look for the genes for such a trait. In fact, psychologists do not agree on the most basic outline of what constitutes human intelligence, so the phenotype is neither univocally nor rigorously characterized.

Our argument is not entirely negative, for we set a challenge—one that it may be possible to meet—for psychologists interested in intelligence and for the intelligence-testing community. In order to provide a case that intelligence is an adaptation, psychologists will need to specify what intelligence is at a lower level than they standardly do. They will need to specify some competence or set of competencies that led to reproductive success and population stability in the environments in which *Homo sapiens* first evolved and that were subsequently maintained in the population because they did so. This much will help to secure the hope that there is some underlying set of genes that has a pretty straightforward relation to the phenotype(s) of intelligence, now well specified, that led to differential reproductive success. If the phenotype is specified at too far a remove from the initial evolutionary environment, we will have good grounds for suspecting that the trait in question is powerfully tied to forces of cultural selection, a problem we will call the *social learning suspicion*.

There is no harm in asking of some trait T (the ability to read or write, to compose music, to do quantum physics or philosophy) what underlying competencies allow it. But in cases such as these there is overwhelming reason to believe that the phenotypic trait in question has been produced by forces of cultural selection—working no doubt in concert with some underlying biological competencies. Reading, writing, composing music, doing quantum physics and philosophy are surely adaptive; they satisfy curiosity and make life better than it would be without these things. But to be adaptive is not the same as being an adaptation.[1] There is no evidence, for example, that the brains of literate populations, such as those of Belgians, differ from those in populations where literacy is very low, such as Bangladesh. Furthermore, literacy, despite being adaptive, does not lead to greater reproductive success than illiteracy—in fact, at present at least, literacy is one of the best predictors of decreasing population growth. If literacy is subserved by a set of genes possessed differentially by literate and illiterate people, then that set of genes is decreasing in frequency! When it comes to being a world-class composer, philosopher, or quantum physicist, there is no statistically significant evidence that such people do better at dating and mating than fruit farmers or fishermen. Probably the opposite. Indeed, Nietzsche thought that the very idea of a married philosopher was a joke.

It is important to emphasize, as we have just indicated, that a trait can be adaptive without being an adaptation. To show that some trait T is an adaptation, it will need to be specified in the right sort of way, at the right (low) level. In the case of humans, who abide the forces of cultural as well as biological selection, the trait will need to be specified in such a way that there is no basis for legitimate suspicion that the trait is largely the product of culture. One way to do this is to locate some trait in ancestral species that is thought to display or subserve intelligence in humans, where the ancestors display the trait without much suspicion that this display is due to social learning. If the trait is not picked out in this way, then there will be good grounds for the social-learning suspicion (which can be raised without calling into question the claim that social learning, whatever exactly it is, is subserved by intelligence, whatever it is).

We consider three traits that might fit the desiderata of occurring at the right (low) level, that are good candidates for being underlying components of human intelligence, and that appear to be adaptations: induction, pattern recognition, and face reading of conspecifics.

---

[1]The term *adaptive* is used in various ways, (1) sometimes as a synonym for *adaptation*, (2) sometimes to refer to any trait that increases reproductive success, regardless of its historical origins, and (3) sometimes to refer to any trait that is useful given the goals and purposes of its bearer. The first use of *adaptive* is a mistake. In discussing humans, we usually use *adaptive* in the third way, to refer to traits that allow us to flourish in our particular environments.

INTELLIGENCE, AS CURRENTLY CHARACTERIZED

It is pretty easy to win our first point that the concept of intelligence as currently conceived by psychologists and the intelligence-testing community is not univocally characterized, nor is it defined at a level of grain sufficient to dispel the social-learning suspicion.

In *Metaphors of Mind*, Robert Sternberg (1990) reports on two conferences held in 1921 and 1986 respectively that were devoted to defining intelligence, and in which 27 different conceptions or attributes of intelligence were compared in terms of frequency. The capacity "to reason abstractly, to represent, to problem-solve, and to make decisions" tops both lists, with "that which is valued by culture" a distant second on the 1986 list. Interestingly "that which is valued by culture" (p. 50) had no supporters in 1921, whereas 29% ranked it highly in 1986. This might be taken as evidence of a shift toward a conception of intelligence as a largely culturally created trait, which is probably true to some extent. How far it is true is unclear, however, since a trait, such as a certain eye or hair color, can be culturally valued without itself being a product of culture.

This issue to one side, the attributes identified as constituting intelligence in whole or in part range from "an adaptation to meet the demands of the environment effectively, to elementary processes (perception, sensation, attention), to metacognition, to spatial or verbal abilities, to speed of mental processing, to the ability to deal with novelty, to mental playfulness" (p. 50). The fact that there are 27 distinct conceptions is enough to secure the claim that there is no univocal conception afoot. It is also worth noting, for our purposes, that there is little explicit mention of social intelligence in these surveys. This is surprising because recent books, such as Howard Gardner's *Frames of Mind: The Theory of Multiple Intelligences* (1983) and Daniel Goleman's *Emotional Intelligence* (1995), place heavy emphasis on the importance of human intrapersonal and interpersonal intelligence and emotional intelligence, respectively. And there are researchers (see Baron-Cohen, Tager-Flusberg, & Cohen, 1993) studying autism who believe that people with autism lack genes that code for the brain structures that subserve fitness-enhancing forms of social intelligence. Furthermore, as we will discuss below, human and ape face-reading abilities crucial for social intelligence have long been thought to be adaptations (Darwin, 1872).

We do not have space to demonstrate one by one that each of the multifarious conceptions of intelligence occurs at too high a level to represent a trait, or set of traits, that is a straightforward result of a genotype, and that each is open to the social-learning suspicion. There are two general reasons for thinking this. First, Sternberg (1990) was committed to showing that our understanding of intelligence operates largely in terms of metaphors, and metaphors are notoriously imprecise. Second, and relatedly, even when some attribute of intelligence is specified in a way that gestures toward a competence of the sort that might be at the right level, such as the ability to learn or speed of mental processing, there is still a problem of vagueness unless and until the domain of the ability to learn or the speed of processing information of certain kinds is specified. For humans the ability to learn to detect position by sonar signals is not included, but what is? Speed of processing information about stock market trends is surely not included, but what is?

Still, these traits—the ability to learn (and remember) and to process information quickly—assuming that we can specify rigorously what it is that they range over, are closer to the sort of traits we need if we want to give an evolutionary account of intelligence, because these traits, unlike the ability to do quantum physics (despite quite possibly involving these traits), look like traits that might be relatively straightforward phenotypic expressions of some set of genes.

Indeed, Joe Z. Tsien (2000), a neuroscientist at Princeton, recently set off a feeding frenzy among journalists with reports of work involving the creation of smarter than normal mice. Operating with prior knowledge that NMDA receptors in the brain are importantly implicated in memory, Tsien performed knockouts of NR1 genes to prevent production of (strong) NMDA receptors, producing "dumb" mice. He then introduced NR2B genes into fertilized mouse eggs, producing "smart" mice. Why are the NR2B mice smart? First, they learn what typical mice learn (e.g., how to get around in complex spaces) more accurately and quickly than normal mice or mice with NR1 knockouts. Second, they do so because NR2B increases the time NMDA receptors are open to information from 0.10s to 0.25s, enough of a difference to make a difference.

Other traits that occur at the right level, in the right sort of way, to be considered adaptations underlying intelligence also include the following:

- Induction: the ability to reason inductively. If some regularity R is observed to occur at a rate of m/n in situation S, then if one is in S infer that the probability of R is m/n.
- Pattern recognition: the ability to recognize and rerecognize complex patterns. If some pattern P—say a particular geometrical configuration—occurs at time t, and then reappears at t_1, but with a different spatial orientation, recognize P as the same pattern.
- Face recognition or face-reading: the abilities to recognize and rerecognize faces of conspecifics over time, to respond to certain facial expressions in appropriate ways, and perhaps to read facial expressions as indicative of certain behavioral tendencies.

These traits (especially the first two) are implicated in what most everyone, at least implicitly, defines as *intelligence*. Accuracy and speed of processing subserve each. The three are related, possibly at the genotypic level. Furthermore, all three appear to be adaptations, assuming, that is, that we can specify their range in ways that tie induction, pattern recognition, and face recognition to fitness enhancement in the species and selective environment in question. We hasten to add that in making the claims that there is no univocal conception of intelligence among psychologists and that the characterizations available rarely, if ever, specify intelligence at the right (low) level, we have not claimed that some, possibly many intelligence tests fail to test for the right low-level traits. This is a separate question, one about which we remain agnostic, while nonetheless noting that some tests with which we are familiar appear to test— sometimes straightforwardly—for inductive and pattern-recognition abilities.

IDEALLY COMPLETE ADAPTATION EXPLANATIONS

Robert Brandon, a prominent philosopher of biology, holds that five elements are required for a fully satisfactory (which is different from *satisfying*) adaptation explanation. According to Brandon (1990), an ideally complete adaptation explanation must provide the following:

1. evidence that the traits in question are heritable;
2. evidence showing that some variants of the traits were better adapted than others in the organisms' particular ecological niche;
3. evidence that selection has in fact occurred; that is, that a variant's being better adapted than others resulted in differential reproduction;
4. information about the population structure from both a genetic and a selective point of view (i.e., information about patterns of gene flow and patterns of selective environments); and
5. phylogenetic information concerning what has evolved from what (i.e.,which traits are primitive and which derived).

This is a tall order, and biologists can give few complete explanations for any biological traits, including some that are well specified, that are clearly linked to certain genes and have left behind extensive fossil evidence. Nevertheless, aspiring to explanatory ideals is important in matters of evolution precisely because doing so reigns in flip, "just so" Panglossian storytelling. There is a fine line between outlining a genuinely possible scenario for how some trait evolved and outlining one for which there is little evidence but plenty of wishful thinking. One can use Brandon's five points as a touchstone to discover which sort of story is being offered and how complete or incomplete it is.

The challenge in creating a good adaptation story for a trait becomes that much greater if we are seeking to explain a cognitive or behavioral trait for which there is little or no fossil evidence. Still, greater does not mean impossible, as one might initially think, for there are ways of getting around incomplete or nonexistent historical records. Explaining how sleep is an adaptation provides a good example of how an adaptive explanation for a nonfossilized psychobiological trait is supposed to work—despite the fact that no one has provided a complete explanation of sleep as an adaptation (Flanagan, 2000). However, we can indicate why it is plausible to think that sleep evolved by natural selection, despite the fact that we have no direct evidence concerning our ancestors' sleeping habits, including, in cases where our ancestors are extinct, whether they had such habits at all. There is more than a "just so" story to be told about the fitness-enhancing functions of sleep.

SLEEP IS AN ADAPTATION

We first need some evidence that sleep is heritable. We can get that by looking for differences in sleep habits and patterns across several species and for similarities within a single species. It turns out that modes of sleep and sleep cycling are distinctively species specific. Humans, dolphins, birds, giraffes, lions, falcons, chickens, cats, and mice all sleep, and they do so in species-specific ways. Sleep habits, especially among humans, are subject to some degree to social learning, the amount of daylight available, environmental demands, and so on. But the reliability of certain patterns within a species across environments is striking evidence for powerful genetic pressures to sleep and to sleep in a certain species-specific way. Certain congenital sleep disorders also suggest the heritability of sleep-related traits. Fatal familial insomnia, for example, is an inherited disease that damages the anterior thalamus, which is involved in sleep regulation.

Next, we need evidence showing that some variants of the traits are better adapted than others in the organisms' particular ecological niche. We can get this evidence by looking at the sleep patterns of different types of animals. Predators sleep longer than prey. Lions sleep up to 22 or 23 hours a day, lolling about in shaded areas that abut open grazing areas. Gazelles, which lions find tasty, sleep in short minute-long spurts while standing up. When there are exceptions, such as in the case of bats, certain squirrels, and hamsters, all of whom sleep a lot, there are also ecological variables that help explain the exceptions. For example, such animals retire to the safety of unwelcoming caves or deep burrows with escape routes. In general, sleep occurs at times, places, and in a manner in which an animal is least vulnerable.

Third, we need to show evidence that selection has occurred. The phylogenetic record reveals this much. There are some amphibians, bullfrogs and tree frogs, for example, that rest and thereby conserve energy but do not show typical physiological signs of sleep. However, many creatures do sleep, and sleep appears to be a solution to certain design problems nature has faced in different contexts along different evolutionary pathways. Thus, the lineages leading to birds led to birds that sleep, and the separate lineages leading from certain reptiles to mammals to humans led to mammals that sleep.

We falter in answering Brandon's fourth and fifth points. Here is where a fossil record would serve us well, if there could be such a thing for sleep, as well as evidence for the genes that produce it. We simply don't know much about the patterns of gene flow or the history of selective environments relative to sleep, nor do we possess phylogenetic information concerning what sleep might have evolved from—although, the hypothesis that it evolved from genes that subserve rest in reptiles and amphibians is not unreasonable. Furthermore, certain neurotransmitters correlate well with the sleep cycles not only in humans but also in other mammals. Serotonin and norepinephrine tanks are refilled during sleep (these are importantly implicated in the abilities to learn and pay attention), and especially during REM sleep the brain is awash with acetylcholine (which is implicated in memory fixation). Recent research indicates that hypocretins (orexins), which are coded for by specific genes (at least in mice), may control waking and sleep patterns (Siegel, 1999).

In any case, we do know enough, by looking at what creatures are doing around us now, to feel confident in asserting that sleeping enhances many animals' rates of survival and hence their rates of reproduction, and furthermore, that being able to sleep was selected by nature for exactly these reasons (see Flanagan, 2000 for the complete story).

IS INTELLIGENCE AN ADAPTATION?

Can we tell an analogous story for psychological traits relevant to human intelligence? Even if we can't define what we mean by intelligence in a sufficiently rigorous fashion to determine whether there could be genes for it, perhaps we can circle around answering the question of whether intelligence is an adaptation by looking at better defined psychological relatives of intelligence or, what is different, low-level forms of intelligence, capacities such as the ability to recognize patterns, to reason inductively, and to recognize and read faces of conspecifics.

For induction and pattern recognition, the story looks remarkably similar to the one we just told about sleep being an adaptation. We can find evidence that the capacities for pattern recognition and induction are heritable by looking at the differences in these cognitive capacities across species as contrasted with the similarities found within a single species. Like sleep, the abilities to recognize patterns and reason inductively are distinctively species specific. Humans, dolphins, birds, giraffes, lions, falcons, chickens, cats, and mice can each do these things, but they each do so in species-specific ways. Mice, for example, can remember the various patterns of exploration they followed when searching for food (Olton, 1978, 1979; Olton & Samualson, 1976). Pigeons can go one step further and remember arbitrary light sequences in order to get food (Straub, Seidenberg, Terrace, & Bever, 1979; Terrace, 1984). Chimps can reason analogically, matching half an apple with half a pail of water (Gillan, Premack, & Woodruff, 1981; Woodruff & Premack, 1981). As with sleep, the reliability of certain patterns in a particular species' environment provides us with evidence that the ability to recognize certain patterns and to reason over these patterns is indeed genetically influenced in a powerful way.

Next, we need evidence showing that some variants of the traits are better adapted than others in the organisms' particular ecological niche. We can get this by looking at the patterns of inductive inferences in different types of animals. Bees, for example, can recognize and follow the dances their scouts perform to indicate where the nearest flowers are growing. However, when scout bees found nectar in the middle of a lake (placed there by investigating biologists), and then reported their find back to the hive, the other bees refused to follow, arguing implicitly in their behavior that flowers don't grow in the middle of a lake (Linden, 1999). Within the confines of nectar-location cognition, bees can recognize and analyze very sophisticated patterns.

Zoologist Ben Beck has remarked that if you give a screwdriver to a chimpanzee, he will use it for everything but its intended purpose; if you give one to a gorilla, he will rear back in horror, then try to eat it, then later forget about it; if you give one to an orangutan, he will hide it until his keeper is gone and then use it to dismantle his cage (as quoted in Linden, 1999, pp. 6–7). Though chimps, gorillas, and orangutans are all part of the great ape family, how they reason and for what purposes vary widely.

Third, the phylogenetic record shows that selection has occurred. There are some creatures, sea slugs and grasshoppers, for example, that can learn via classical conditioning but cannot do much more. However, many animals do recognize patterns important for their survival and reason to some degree about what those patterns mean in terms of more food, more mating opportunities, fewer predators, or a safer place to rest. Pattern recognition and inductive reasoning appear to be solutions to certain design problems nature has faced in different contexts, along different evolutionary pathways. Thus, the lineages leading to birds led to birds that can distinguish among what seem, to the untrained ear, to be very similar bird calls, and the separate lineages leading from certain reptiles to mammals led to mammals that can recognize the faces of their conspecifics and, what is different, read what these facial expressions mean.

Now face recognition (or coding) and rerecognition may be a phenotype that is subserved by whatever subserves general-purpose pattern recognition, assuming that pattern recognition is a general-purpose competence. However, prosopagnosia (the loss of the ability to recognize faces) supplies a possibility proof that one can lose the ability to recognize a particular type of pattern without losing the ability to recognize patterns more generally. It has been suggested plausibly that face recognition and face reading are so important for social animals, such as humans and other primates, that nature selected for a modularized site for it, thus explaining why it can be knocked out without damage to our general pattern-recognition abilities. While pattern recognition in general represents a low-level ability that is an adaptation for many animals, face recognition, reading, or both may represent an adaptation specific to those species, notably primates, that evolved a complex social system in which the ability to recognize conspecifics and perhaps predict their behavioral tendencies is likely to increase reproductive success. We discuss this possibility further later in the chapter.

As with sleep, we again are unable to meet adequately Brandon's fourth and fifth criteria for pattern recognition, induction, and face recognition, or face-reading. Here again a fossil record would serve us well, if there could be such a thing for particular cognitive abilities. We don't know very much about the patterns of gene flow or the history of selective environments relative to our cognitive capacities (though more on this follows), nor do we have any phylogenetic information concerning the traits from which pattern recognition, induction, and face recognition or face-reading might have evolved (though the latter may have evolved from the first two abilities). Nevertheless, we do know enough by looking at what living creatures are doing around us to feel confident in asserting that these capacities enhanced their rate of survival and reproduction and that, furthermore, nature selected being able to reason in these ways for these reasons.

THE SPANDRELS OF INTELLIGENCE

It may now seem that we have been able to answer the question we originally posed. Did human intelligence evolve by natural selection? We just explained how one could give an adaptationist explanation for three properties we believe are allied with intelligence. However, we must hasten to point out that two of these capacities—induction and pattern recognition—are found pretty far down the tree of life. Sea slugs may not be able to recognize patterns, but many other creatures can. If we are concerned with the sort of intelligence that separates us from groundhogs, sparrows, and the great white shark, then we have not found it. Or perhaps we have found it and are expressing undue pessimism. How could that be? We said at the start that to make the case for human intelligence as an adaptation we need to specify the competencies in question at a low enough level to have a basis for believing that they are a pretty straightforward production of an underlying genotype. We also said that the range of the competencies will need to be well specified; that is, they will need to be specified in a way that describes how the competencies are standardly realized in the species in question. Except for face recognition and reading where we have explicitly specified the range of the competence, we have not done so for pattern recognition and induction. Nonetheless, we have indicated that these competencies do have species-specific ranges. Perhaps, therefore, we have located some difference between human and nonhuman pattern recognition and induction that does capture what is specific to human intelligence. The difference has to do with the types of patterns over which pattern recognition ranges and the types of regularities inductive reasoning can capture. Specifying the relevant ranges is no easy task. Our pattern recognition and inductive capacities do not range over certain phenomena that these competencies range over in other species. On the other hand, there surely seems to be something to the idea that, overall, our pattern recognition and inductive capacities have a very wide bandwidth.

Humans not only recognize patterns and then reason over them, we do so with a vengeance. We appear to be the quintessential reasoning machine. Moreover, we can compose great symphonies, invent computers, and cure horrible diseases; we can even wax philosophical about the nature of intelligence. Are these abilities adaptations? The best answer is probably not.

Evolutionary biologists normally use the term *adaptation* in a historical sense. A trait is an adaptation if and only if the trait spread across a population due to selection pressures for it. To say that a trait is an adaptation is to say something about the causal history of the trait. The ability to walk upright is presumed to be an adaptation, giving our Austrolapithicine ancestors the reproductive edge 5 or 6 million years ago. Today, being bipedal enables us to waltz, tango, and tap dance. However, Mother Nature does not care about these dancing capacities. The ability to tango is not an adaptation—it wasn't selected for—even though it may now be useful in the sense that it is fun, beautiful, a good way to get exercise, and socially approved. Being able to tango may help attract mates and thereby increase one's reproductive potential. However, that it does so now is not an argument that it served the same function back when bipedalism was being selected for. Nor, as with the case of literacy discussed earlier, is their any reason to think that the genes that subserve the ability to tango are different in tangoers and nontangoers because the underlying trait is almost certainly bipedalism simpliciter and because almost anyone can be taught to tango.

Most people think that the abilities to read and write are highly adaptive for humans, but the abilities to read and write were not selected for during the Pleistocene. The underlying competencies that subserve the ability to read and write may have emerged during the Pleistocene (though given the paleontological record we have of our forbearers, the ability likely developed much earlier, for there exist abstract representational remains that appear to have served communicative functions among earlier species of the genus *Homo*). However, these competencies were not selected for because literacy itself played any fitness-enhancing role as the ice melted. The abilities to read and write came as free riders on brains selected to do other things—hunt, forage, mate, and communicate facially and vocally with conspecifics. Thus, the capacities to read and write are not adaptations. Nor would the fact, if it were a fact (which it isn't), that literate people are more reproductively successful than nonliterate people indicate that there are at present any differential selection pressures pulling for brains that can learn to read and write. Brain-damaged persons aside, all human beings can become literate. When and where one is born determines whether literacy is acquired. The potential is invariably there—as it was even for our Pleistocene ancestors living at the end of the last Ice Age. Literacy will occur if it has been invented in one's locale and if the proper social, nutritional, and educational resources are in place. Except for malformed individuals, all humans since Homo sapiens evolved on the African savannah (and quite possibly the Neanderthals as well) have possessed the neural equipment to become literate.

Nevertheless, the fact that some trait is not itself an adaptation, but is an effect of an adaptation, does not in any way imply that it does not or cannot have effects. Suppose that literacy is made possible through some cultural change that tapped the previously untapped potential of brains selected for something else. Despite not being a biological adaptation, literacy has various effects on our bodily behavior. Even if it is not an adaptation that evolved because it contributed to our reproductive success, we are still quite properly inclined to say that literacy is highly adaptive. However, in this instance we mean that literacy contributes, for example, to human flourishing, to our general happiness, and to our well being.

There is one apparent snag in this argument. Literacy, despite not being a biological adaptation, did contribute to the development and proliferation of certain cultural practices, advances in health care and engineering, for example, that did lead (and still do lead) to vast population growth over the entire globe. Therefore, literacy contributed to differential population growth of Homo sapiens relative to other species. Doesn't that make literacy an adaptation? The answer is no. And the reason is that a trait T is an adaptation only if it is fitness enhancing and, in addition, is thus in virtue of being governed by the forces of natural selection. Literacy is fitness enhancing in the sense just described, but its emergence was governed by forces of cultural selection. Thus, we reach the same conclusion: Literacy is adaptive but not an adaptation.

In order to show that a particular aspect of human intelligence evolved by natural selection, we are going to have to show that it is not a simple by-product of some other trait that was selected for. We need to show, in other words, that intelligence isn't a spandrel. The term spandrel in architecture refers to the triangular spaces left over when arches are placed next to each other at right angles, such as when beginning to mount a dome, as in many great churches, or in a straight line, such as in the magnificent Roman aqueducts. Spandrels are inevitable by-products of arch and column designs (Gould & Lewontin, 1978).

Take, for example, the design of the heart and the fact that hearts make noise. The heart is a pump. The function of the heart is to pump blood in a regular and reliable manner throughout the body, thereby keeping the body oxygenated. A pump needs room to expand and contract. At no point in the process of heart design did Mother Nature think it would be good to make a noisy heart since making noise matters not one bit to the design of a well-functioning circulatory system. Heartbeats are simply what you get automatically from a blood pump housed in a body cavity. To be sure, the sounds of beating hearts can be used diagnostically to see if your heart is pumping the way it should, just as spandrels can be filled with beautiful artwork. However, neither the social practice of heart diagnostics nor artful design of spandrels were part of the original intentions of evolutionary selection or of Roman architects (in fact Romans did not decorate spandrels, Christians did). In this way, heartthrobs are an example of a biological spandrel. There were selection pressures on many of the details of the circulatory system, including many features of blood, but the features of the circulatory system relevant to survival and reproduction did not involve any direct or indirect concern with making noise. Nor did selection of a well-designed circulatory system concern itself with coloration. (Red [actually purple] blood is good to have if you are human. If you have green blood, you have a problem and should see a doctor. But this is not because red blood is an adaptation. Red blood comes as an inevitable side effect of the hemoglobin of blood cells selected for their capacity to oxygenate organs.) The color of blood is a biological spandrel; it is a by-product of the primary design intentions for blood.

Sometimes spandrels are utilized for biological purposes but not because they are, as it were, useful to the internal biological economy of organisms that possess the spandrel. The fact that heart sounds or blood coloration are not themselves adaptations does not detract from their usefulness in medical diagnosis. Our biology obviously allows for medical practices to develop, but there is no interesting sense of the concept of biological adaptation according to which we could credibly call such practices adaptations.

On the other hand, some traits that were originally selected for to serve a certain function end up being able—with some engineering modifications—to serve another function. Such traits are *exaptations* (Gould, 1991). Virtually all adaptations begin as exaptations simply because nature rarely produces a mutation that is a fully formed adaptation. Selection pressures work to modify and eventually to maintain some traits because they serve a new function as well as, or in place of, the function they were originally selected for. Feathered wings (when they constituted only 5% of a wing) were probably selected for thermoregulation, but now selective pressures work to maintain feathered wings because they enable flight as well as serving to regulate body temperature. Insect wings are the preferred example here because it is known that it was aerodynamically impossible for the first wing-buds to enable insects to get aloft. Initial selection was definitely not for flight.

It is standard in evolutionary biology to say that some characteristic is a nonadaptation only if it is a concomitant of a trait that was selected for and if, in addition, no concurrent positive selection or independent modification operates on the trait. Therefore, while the capacity to fly was a sequelae (literally *a follow-up*) of selection pressures for efficient thermoregulation, the feathered wings that enable flight are an adaptation because, despite being a sequelae, they were (and are) subject to positive selection and independent modification pressures. On the other hand, the human chin, the sound of a beating heart, and *Ulysses* are examples of sequelae that are true nonadaptations. They are spandrels, and it is pretty clear that even if they have been put to various uses—chins for sporting goatees, the sound of the heart to soothe crying infants and diagnose heart disease, and Joyce to confound college freshman—these uses have not called any selection pressures into play.

No one thinks that Mother Nature cares now, or when she built our brains, about the accomplishments of the great minds in the history of astronomy, quantum physics, mathematical logic, literary criticism, or, for that matter, evolutionary biology. To be sure, these monumental theoretical productions of great minds are good, important, and wonderful to consider, but this is a long way from saying that the specific capacities that produced them are functional in any interesting biological sense.

The reason we can confidently assert that the capacities to do science, higher mathematics, philosophy, and cognitive neuroscience are not adaptations is the same reason that the capacities to read and write are not adaptations. These are productions that require a heavy dose of culture and social learning. The brain has not, as best scientists can tell, changed significantly since *Homo sapiens* became a distinctive species 500,000 years ago. All the aforementioned activities are recent developments, and, simply stated, Mother Nature does not look ahead several hundred centuries when engaged in design by natural selection.

CREATIVE DECEPTION AND OTHER MINDS:
A CASE OF ADAPTATIONIST OVERSTEPPING

It should be clear that a particularly daunting task for evolutionary biologists is determining which traits should count as adaptations and which are effects of those selected traits. Are there any psychological traits allied with intelligence that we believe aren't spandrels? Yes. We have already discussed three: pattern recognition, induction, and face recognition or face reading.

We now want to discuss a higher-level cognitive ability that may be more specific to (or unique in) humans to determine whether we can use the methods we have developed to provide an adaptation explanation for it. This capacity might be called *mind reading*. Some theorists seem to think that mind reading is just a special, distinctively human (or possibly occurring in a few other primates) extension of our face-recognizing and face-reading competencies, but it is not. Mind reading, as it is expressed in human life, goes far beyond our basic face-recognition or face-reading capacities and involves attribution of complex mental states in ourselves and others. Mind reading may be an adaptation, but the existing arguments that it is an adaptation are weak.

There is an intellectual industry afoot today called *theory of mind* that seeks to describe and explain how it is that humans solve what philosophers traditionally call the *problem of other minds*. Theory of mind is sometimes aligned with—but need not be—evolutionary psychology. Evolutionary psychology seeks to explain characteristic human traits in adaptationist terms (Barkow, Cosmides, & Tooby, 1992). Many have accused evolutionary psychology, just as they accused sociobiology from which it descended, of being carelessly adaptationist, seeking to explain practices, such as teenage dating or male delinquency, for which there is reasonable basis for harboring the social-learning suspicion, as pure biological adaptations; of being what may come to the same thing, *panadaptationist* (assuming that all species-specific traits are adaptations); and of not recognizing the distinctions among adaptations, exaptations, and spandrels or between traits that are true biological adaptations and those that are simply adaptive.

One idea that psychologists have floated recently is that, ironically, our ability to deceive one another showcases intelligence of just the sort we prize in humans (Barkow et al., 1992; Bogdan, 1997; Byrne & Whiten, 1988). They hypothesize that creative deception of the sort only humans engage in stems from the complex social arrangements in which we find ourselves. Navigating our social structure requires a human sort of intelligence, and one index of the underlying intelligence is our capacity to deceive; that is, one way to investigate human intelligence profitably, given that no one has a good definition of it yet, is to isolate one component of it—our ability to cheat others—which is well specified.

One central, important feature of our social structure, for the proponents of this point of view, is that it involves reciprocal altruism—long-term mutual relations including the exchange of benefits. Unlike some types of cooperative behavior, like hunting for large game, reciprocal altruism requires that the altruist pays a price (in terms of reproductive success) at the time of the act and only receives the reciprocal benefit after a significant period of time (Mesterton-Gibbons & Dugatkin, 1992; Taylor & McGuire, 1988). Because of the time delay between altruistic acts, any population that did evolve altruistic behavior among nonkin could be invaded by cheats who receive benefits while never returning them, at great cost to the sucker altruists. Thus, reciprocity would most likely become an evolutionary stable strategy only in populations that could avoid invasion by cheats, presumably by detecting them and withholding altruistic acts. Even if such detection evolved, however, benefits remain for subtle cheats who return favors but find ways to receive more than they give. As is the case with full-blooded cheats, subtle cheats could take over a population of naïve altruists and altruism would dissipate. To maintain reciprocity, a population needs to be able to detect subtle cheats, deny them benefits, and perhaps even punish them. In anthropomorphic terms, reciprocity allows for the evolution not only of a communal marketplace but also of embezzlement and castigation.

Machiavelli noted that "one who deceives will always find those who allow themselves to be deceived." This commentary might be appropriate for our society, but when approaching deception from an evolutionary point of view, we can see that selection should weed out those who allow themselves to be deceived too often. The selective advantage of deception seems pervasive. At the same time, pressure to counter this deception should be equally pervasive.

In short, while reciprocal altruism allows for extensive cooperation beyond spatially limited kin altruism and beyond temporally limited mutual cooperation, it also promotes cheating, detection of cheating, and punishment for cheating. It thereby provides selective pressure for a host of cognitive abilities, beginning with the ability to recognize individuals who are altruists and those who are cheats and to remember which is which. Notice that these abilities likely rely on face recognition and might be thought to provide a basis for selection to further enhance this ability. In this case face recognition or face-reading, itself an adaptation, would serve as the exaptation for a secondary adaptation, the capacity to read other minds. In any case, the guiding idea is that reciprocal altruism sets up selective pressures on populations to develop a deep social intelligence.

Of course, we have been using the term *selection* in a way that is ambiguous in its distinction between natural selection and social selection, although evolutionary psychologists intend the former. This aside, subtle cheating does not necessarily evolve in a society of reciprocal altruists (nothing necessarily evolves); nevertheless, it would or, at least, might seem to offer a significant selective advantage if it did evolve. Anthropologists often discuss the complicated reciprocal systems of human societies (e.g., economies) in terms of the intelligence they require, but perhaps they have it backwards. Maybe reciprocal altruism selected for social intelligence.

All this armchair theorizing is well and good, but to develop an evolutionary explanation we need to know: Are there any animal social structures that actually involve reciprocal altruism? That turns out to be difficult to ascertain. To test for reciprocal altruism, ethologists must determine what counts as an altruistic act, assign to the act cost and benefit values measured in terms of fitness, and then attempt to observe when such acts are occurring, between whom they are occurring, and with what values. It also requires knowing the relatedness of the participants to differentiate it from kin altruism.

Robert Trivers (1971), an early proponent of reciprocal altruism as an adaptation, misses the mark with his own examples of cleaning symbiosis and bird alarm calls as purported instances of exchange with delayed reward. Cleaning symbiosis is better viewed as by-product beneficence between two species that have coevolved (like hosts and parasites). Bird alarm calls may not carry a cost to the caller, and even if they do, they may be accounted for by kin altruism. Trivers' third example of humans is of course much more effective but only if he is right that our reciprocal relations are the result of natural selection and not cultural invention.

In fact, few examples of reciprocal altruism have been well documented. The best evidence so far is for vampire bats, some marine mammals, and primates, especially apes (see articles by de Waal & Luttrell, 1988; Taylor & McGuire, 1988; Wilkinson, 1988). The rarity of this sort of reciprocity may well come from the obstacles it must overcome in order to become stable in a population. Nevertheless, even though reciprocal altruism is rare, it does exist. So the hypothesis is still possible. Perhaps reciprocal altruism sets up a feedback loop involving selective pressures for increasingly complicated deception and then for increasingly effective detection of deception. Perhaps, this arms race led to the evolution of the mind-reading abilities that we now see as distinctively human.

To test this hypothesis, we should look at evidence for deception to determine, first whether or not such deception appears in species with reciprocal altruism, and second whether or not some forms of deception require specific kinds of intelligence. Simple behavioral deception occurs often both between and within many species. We see this most clearly during mating rituals and in the conflict between predator and prey. There are obviously powerful selective forces for these types of deception, but because they can be hardwired, or learned behaviorally, they do not appear to require much in the way of cognitive power.

Primates, however, appear to practice more complex, cognitively based forms of deception. In addition, reciprocal relationships are more extensive in primates. It could be that this fact allows more opportunities for subtle cheating. The complicated fighting coalitions of baboons and food sharing of chimpanzees, for example, offer numerous and subtle opportunities for withholding reciprocity (fully or, more subtly, only in part). However, can one differentiate simple deception from the more creative forms of deception, which require actively predicting others' behavior (see Whiten & Byrne, 1988)? Where do we find this type of deception?

As with reciprocal altruism, testing for such creative deception is notoriously difficult. After all, the goal of deception is to be difficult to detect, and it usually involves an act from an animal's normal repertoire of behavior deployed deceptively. Even a "higher" primate—the primatologist—may miss it. (Indeed, the trainers are often the deceivers' targets.) Furthermore, acts of creative deception will probably be rare. If any particular act of creative deception were frequently successful, we might reasonably suspect that the act is a behavioral habit and consider the target a dupe, unworthy of being considered intelligent (see Dennett in Whiten & Byrne, 1988). Interesting creative deception should evolve in species that are also adept at detecting deception. As Samuel Butler reminds us: "The best liar is he who makes the smallest amount of lying go the longest way." David Hume's 'sensible knave' is a knave because he cheats, and he is sensible because he cheats only when the probability of being caught is low. Thrasymachus, Socrates' interlocutor in the first two books of Plato's *Republic*, defends cheating; indeed, he sees cheating as essential to success. But Thrasymachus is careful to point out that one must work to *seem* good, despite not being good.

In any case, and most significantly, to show that an animal understands the nature of deception, a researcher needs to determine that the deceptive tactic is not the result of contingencies of reinforcement that produce a behavioral habit simpliciter; that is, the tactic better not be wholly acquired through and wholly subserved by an unconsciously mediated process of operant conditioning (and this despite the fact that the capacity to learn via operant conditioning may well be an adaptation, indeed an adaptation that subserves intelligence). Determining this for sure is impossible to do in the wild because we cannot know everything to which the animal has been exposed. Indeed, it is nearly impossible under even the most controlled conditions.

Whiten and Byrne (1988) believe that chimpanzee behavior shows that they have some conception of deception itself, distinguishing between overt behavior and the deceptive intentions that sometimes underlie it. They classify most monkey deception as less creative than ape's (except for baboons, whose fighting alliances seem to be a case of reciprocal altruism). These conclusions have been questioned, however, both because they often rely on anecdotal evidence (as one critic said, "the plural of anecdote is not data") and because most of the examples can still be explained with a behaviorist interpretation, albeit a complicated one (see Commentary on Whiten & Byrne, 1988, p. 247).

Criticisms of Whiten and Byrne aside, a variety of researchers who observe apes across diverse environments and in different social groups are finding what they believe are examples of deception and that the most creative instances occur in apes (see also Byrne, 1995; de Waal, 1996; and Linden, 1999). Examples cited include apes (and baboons) pretending to be injured to avoid confrontations, covering up sexually induced outbursts to avoid angering a dominant, hiding fear grins in conflicts, and pretending to see predators to escape pursuit. Apes also offer the best evidence for detection of deception: becoming angry when they figure out they had been tricked (sometimes by their human trainers) and punishing their tormentors using so-called moralistic aggression (de Waal, 1996). If past unconscious reinforcement of a habitual response can be ruled out, these examples might indicate that the agent recognizes that the target has a desire and intends to act on it but that certain actions may prevent the target from carrying out these intentions.

How can we determine that these behaviors actually involve the agent intentionally causing a false belief (or its cognitive equivalent) in another? Not surprisingly, there is as yet no conclusive test for such high-level cognition in nonlinguistic creatures, but looking at the capacity for counter-deception offers a way into the puzzle. A well-known example concerns a subordinate chimp, Belle, who has been shown the location of some hidden fruit, which she knows the dominant chimp, Rock, would steal from her if he had access to it. Belle, even without past experience, either avoids the hidden fruit when Rock is present or leads the group away from the food. Rock then counters by pretending to be preoccupied, only to follow Belle to the right location (Byrne, 1995).

Perhaps our abilities to deceive and to detect cheaters highlights a human form of intelligence, something having to do with theory of mind or recognizing intentions. Perhaps. But before we can make such claims, we need to determine how close we are to giving an ideal adaptationist explanation for the phenomena. Two problems stand out almost immediately. First, the case of cheaters and cheater detection is not analogous to the case of sleep, for we don't have a rich comparative basis from which to draw inferences about the phylogenetic past. Opportunities to deceive and to detect deceivers are rare rather than abundant, as are the species that engage in creative deception. Hence, we cannot provide evidence showing that some variants of the traits are better adapted than others in the organisms' particular ecological niche, nor can we give evidence that selection has occurred, that a variant being better adapted than others resulted in differential reproduction. If we are going to run an evolutionary argument for cheater detection being selected as an adaptation, then we need somehow to point back to the original conditions—the original ecological niche—in order to trace information about the structure of the population and the flow of genes relative to the selective environments and to derive phylogenetic information concerning what evolved and from what it evolved, which traits are primitive and which derived. Because we can't meet Brandon's second and third conditions, we need to meet his fourth and fifth conditions. However, we can't do that any more than we could with the lower level traits discussed earlier.

Finally, we need to attend to Brandon's first criterion, that only heritable traits are subject to evolutionary selection. Data regarding the heritability of primates' capacities to deceive with awareness and detect deception (or cooperation) are thin, to put it mildly. Basic brain structure might be genetically hardwired, but much of what our brains can do is determined by environment–organism interactions and other forms of learning. The line between nature and nurture here is quite blurred. Human and other higher primate communities now are socially quite complicated, but we have little data about what the communities were like when we and they were developing our capacities for social interpretation. What types of cognitive skills were required when we hunted and gathered on the African savannah during the Pleistocene (or whenever our skills in interpretation and communication allegedly arose)? Looking at what we do now does not provide the answer.

One reason for caution has to do with the fact that the total number of genes in human DNA is currently estimated at around 30,000. At least 50% of these genes are concerned with brain development. Nevertheless, basic math belies any one gene-one neuron connection. We have billions of neurons in our head. There is no way even 15,000 genes could code for them, much less for their synaptic connections, exactly. In only very simple creatures, such as the nemotode *Caenorhabditis* (which has 302 neurons with about 7,000 neuronal connections), do we find direct genetic programming for brain structure. This picture is even more bleak for those who wish to find genetic programs for our higher cognitive functions, which are located primarily in cortex, for it appears that most of the genetic specification for our brain concerns the more primitive structures. Our genes do not seem to worry as much about how to wire our cortex as they do making sure our sensory transducers are constructed properly (which of course may be the point, since this allows flexible learning in response to a changing environment). In short, arguments for innateness must be drawn very carefully, for it is difficult to separate environmental factors from genetic ones in the brain, especially when dealing with very complicated and high-level traits that may well have developed over long periods of time and quite possibly primarily under forces of social selection.

To reinforce this last point, there are several examples from primates that some of their intelligent behavior falls prey to the social-learning suspicion. Indian macaques, driven to the sea by deforestation, developed the ability to find clams and crack them open on rocks to get at the nutritious meat. This activity, which is certainly intelligent, is not, however, an adaptation in itself; in fact, at first only the younger monkeys cracked clams, while older ones did not (or could not) learn how (as in the more famous example of Japanese macaques' potato washing). But after a generation or two, all young monkeys were learning the behavior. As with most biological adaptations, this socially learned adaptive behavior became fixed in the population but not because the monkeys had been selected to crack clams, much less that they have a gene for clam-cracking; rather, in neo-Lamarkian fashion, the trait was acquired and then passed down (though not, of course, genetically). Furthermore, primatologists now speak of chimpanzee cultures, which involve certain population-specific social practices, such as cracking nuts or grooming with leaves (Wrangham, McGrew, de Waal & Heltne, 1994).

Now, if such intelligent behaviors are socially learned in primates, despite the fact that they may be subserved by some cognitive ability that is an adaptation, we must be especially wary in imagining that human deceptive practices or theory of mind abilities are adaptations rather than socially learned skills. Just as literacy surely relies on cognitive adaptations but is just as surely not an adaptation itself, and just as macaques' clam-cracking is adaptive but not an adaptation itself, human intelligence in the form of representing other minds and deceiving intentionally might very well be adaptive but not an adaptation.

It may seem incredible that our ability to discern and distinguish among our own mental states (seeing beliefs and desires for what they are) and imputing mental states to others was not always there. But both knowledge of our own minds and of other minds was perhaps a discovery or invention, or even required a theory—a piece of folk psychology—to come into being. Mental states, at least in others, are unobservable. It is possible that discernment of one's own mental states was originally inchoate, requiring conceptual structures, possibly sophisticated linguistic categories, to be tried, tested, and to fall into place. Only then did humans understand and classify their own mental states as we now do. Imputation of action-guiding mental states to others might then have been a further theoretical development, one that has been so predictively successful that it is now handed down rapidly and effortlessly at our mothers' knees. If so, mind reading, despite being adaptive, is not an adaptation. At present, no arguments have been given to show that this social-learning account of our mind-reading capacities is less plausible that the adaptationist alternative. The burden here is clearly on the adaptationists about mind reading, for they have told a story that vastly oversteps what is required of a remotely adequate adaptationist account.

FACE READING, AGAIN

We don't intend to be unduly skeptical about the possibilities for adaptationist accounts of some traits that subserve social intelligence. Indeed, we believe face recognition and face-reading represents an adaptation that is crucial to social intelligence and that may, along with general inductive abilities, subserve the development of the types of deception and mind reading in which humans engage. In *The Expression of the Emotions in Man and Animals*, Darwin (1872) offers a substantial account of the evolution of facial expressions and of our ability to read the faces of conspecifics that satisfies most, if not all, the criteria Brandon sets for a complete adaptation explanation. The account is least satisfactory, but not totally unconvincing, in providing the component of a complete adaptation explanation that establishes that the relevant facial expressions appear below the level of the social primates—the component that is necessary to secure confidence that the trait is inherited rather than learned. But let's grant that the evidence for the characteristic facial expressions in lower primates suffices to establish heritability.

Darwin proposed that certain facial expressions indicate six core emotions: fear, anger, surprise, disgust, happiness, and sadness. The appropriate movements of the facial musculature are expressed and recognized by individuals across cultures, suggesting they are universal within our species. Ekman, Levinson, and Freison (1985) have confirmed Darwin's hypothesis. There are six universal facial expressions with characteristic movements of the facial musculature that correlate with specific physiological responses, such as skin conductance and temperature. Furthermore, in modern subjects the relevant facial expressions are experienced as subserved by the relevant underlying emotion.

Still, we can ask what did our *Homo sapiens* ancestors detect in their fellows' faces? Most certainly they detected that certain movements of the facial musculature expressed certain behavioral tendencies in conspecifics, for example, the tendency to be on the verge of doing harm or the willingness to mate. Did they detect the underlying emotions as the emotions they are? Did they impute these emotions to others? We don't know for sure. Indeed, we don't know anything about how early *Homo sapiens* experienced their own mental states, let alone what, if any, mental states they imputed to others. No doubt early *Homo sapiens* experienced something when they displayed "anger," or "fear," or "surprise." Whether that something was what we now discern and classify as anger, fear, or surprise is a different and much more contentious matter. Caution, even skepticism, on this matter is compatible with the view that the six basic facial expressions in fact express the six basic emotions and that both the expression and recognition for them were selected for. The caution is that we cannot just assume Cartesian transparency of our minds to ourselves. Indeed, it is commonplace of contemporary mind science to assume that a good deal of mental life is opaque to its owner. The underlying emotions may have always been there but not seen for what they were. We should not just assume that the first-personal case of classifying mental states is or was dramatically different from the situation of coming only gradually to discern and classify certain regularities in the external world.

Darwin himself says that it is not obvious that children read faces as youngsters, adolescents, and adults do. Evidence suggests that they don't. Children see faces as faces and are very interested in them. However, we know that the neuronal mechanisms that subserve basic face recognition, seeing a face as a face, are mostly subcortically wired. More advanced face-reading abilities may develop later according to genetically specified instructions or they may be developed inductively. We don't yet know because we don't yet know the genes or neural pathways that subserve these higher forms of face reading.

Therefore, it seems safe to assume that our human ancestors could read faces and respond appropriately. The ability to do so appears to be an adaptation. It is less clear that seeing the faces of conspecifics as expressing emotions and intentions as well as certain behavioral tendencies is a form of social intelligence that is genetically specified, and it is unclear that doing so adds anything from the perspective of fitness enhancement. Seeing our own emotions and those of others for the emotions they are is adaptive if knowing what is true is adaptive. But again it is less clear that seeing minds more truthfully and completely is an adaptation.

CONCLUSION

We are afraid that we have not advanced the discussion much beyond the debate Darwin entered into with Alfred Russell Wallace, the codiscoverer of evolution by natural selection. Wallace, a strict adaptationist, held that natural selection could account for most practical life-sustaining traits but not for humans' well-developed cognitive abilities—certainly, not for anything resembling the ability to produce music or develop science. Darwin, on the other hand, believed that these higher capacities are by-products of cognitive traits that were useful to our ancestors (see discussion in Gould, 1980). We side with Darwin—but not enthusiastically, given the dearth of data. Perhaps, though, in this time of great expectations for the genetic identification and engineering of all types of interesting traits, it is enough to remind others that, despite wishful thinking to the contrary, we still do not know exactly which mental traits are adaptations. We hope we have at least offered some instructive signposts on what to look for and what to look out for in any attempt to offer adaptation explanations for a trait as elusive as intelligence.

REFERENCES

Barkow, J., Cosmides, L., & Tooby, J. (Eds.). (1992). *The adapted mind: Evolutionary psychology and the generation of culture*. New York: Oxford University Press.

Baron-Cohen, S., Tager-Flusberg, H., & Cohen, D. J. (Eds.). (1993). *Understanding other minds: Perspectives from autism*. Oxford: Oxford University Press.

Bogdan, R. J. (1997). *Interpreting minds: The evolution of a practice*. Cambridge, MA: The MIT Press.

Brandon, R. N. (1990). *Adaptation and environment*. Princeton, NJ: Princeton University Press.

Byrne, R. W. (1995). *The thinking ape*. Oxford: Oxford University Press.

Byrne, R. W., & Whiten, A. (1988). *Machiavellian intelligence: Social expertise and the evolution of intellect in monkeys, apes, and humans*. Oxford: Oxford University Press.

Darwin, C. (1872). *The expression of emotions in man and animals*. Introduction, afterword, and commentaries by P. Ekman (1998). New York: Oxford University Press.

de Waal, F. (1996). *Good natured: The origins of right and wrong in humans and other animals*. Cambridge, MA: Harvard University Press.

de Waal, F., & Luttrell, L. (1988). Mechanisms of social reciprocity in three primate species: Symmetrical relationship characteristics or cognition? *Ethology and Sociobiology, 9,* 101–118.

Ekman, P., Levinson, R. W., & Freison, W. V. (1985). Autonomic nervous system activity distinguishes among emotions. *Science, 221,* 1208–1210.

Flanagan, O. (2000). *Dreaming souls: Sleep, dreams, and the evolution of the conscious mind.* New York: Oxford University Press.

Gardner, H. (1983). *Frames of mind.* New York: Basic Books.

Gillan, D. J., Premack, D., & Woodruff, G. 1981. Reasoning in the chimpanzee: I. Analogical reasoning. *Journal of Experimental Psychology: Animal Behavioral Processes, 7,* 1–17.

Goleman, D. (1995). *Emotional intelligence.* New York: Bantam Books.

Gould, S. J. (1980). *The panda's thumb: More reflections on natural history.* New York: Norton.

Gould, S. J. (1991). Exaptation: A crucial tool for an evolutionary psychology. *Journal of Social Issues, 47*(3), 43–65.

Gould, S. J., & Lewontin, R. C. (1978). The spandrels of San Marco and the Panglossian paradigm: A critique of the adaptationist programme. *Proceedings of the Royal Society of London, 205,* 581–598.

Linden, E. (1999). *The parrot's lament: And other true tales of animal intrigue, intelligence, and ingenuity.* New York: Dutton.

Mesterton-Gibbons, M., & Dugatkin, L. (1992). Cooperation among unrelated individuals: Evolutionary factors. *The Quarterly Review of Biology, 67,* 267–281.

Olton, D. S. (1978). Characteristics of spatial memory. In S. H. Hulse, J. Fowler, & W. K. Honig (Eds.), *Cognitive processes in animal behavior.* Hillsdale, NJ: Lawrence Erlbaum Associates.

Olton, D. S. (1979). Mazes, maps, and memory. *American Psychology, 34,* 588–596.

Olton, D. S., & Samualson, R. J. (1976). Remembrance of things past: Spatial memory in rats. *Journal of Experimental Psychology: Animal Behavioral Processes, 2,* 97–116.

Siegel, J. (1999). Narcolepsy: A key role for hypocretins (orexins). *Cell, 98*(4), 409–412.

Sternberg, R. J. (1990). *Metaphors of mind.* Cambridge: Cambridge University Press.

Straub, R. O., Seidenberg, M. S., Terrace, H. S., & Bever, T. G. (1979). Serial learning in the pigeon. *Journal of the Experimental Analysis of Behavior, 32,* 137–148.

Taylor, C., & McGuire, M. (1988). Reciprocal altruism: 15 years later. *Ethology and Sociobiology, 9,* 67–72.

Terrace, H. S. (1984). Simultaneous chaining: The problem it poses for traditional chaining theory. In R. J. Hernstein & A. Wager (Eds.), *Quantitative analysis of behavior.* Cambridge, MA: Ballinger.

Thompson, R. F. (1993). *The brain: A neuroscience primer.* New York: W. H. Freeman.

Trivers, R. (1971). The evolution of reciprocal altruism. *Quarterly Review of Biology, 46,* 35–57.

Tsien, J. (2000). Building a brainier mouse. *Scientific American,* 62–68.

Whiten, A., & Byrne, R. W. (1988). Tactical deception in primates. *Behavioral and Brain Sciences, 11,* 233–273.

Wilkinson, G. (1988). Reciprocal altruism in bats and other mammals. *Ethology and Sociobiology, 9,* 85–100.

Winberg, J., & Porter, R. H. (1998). Olfaction and human neonatal behavior: Clinical implications. *Acta Paediatrica, 87,* 6–10.

Woodruff, G., & Premack, D. (1981). Primitive mathematical concepts in the chimpanzee: Proportionality and numerosity. *Nature, 293,* 568–570.

Wrangham, R. W., McGrew, W. C., de Waal, F. B. M., Heltone, P. (Eds.). (1994). *Chimpanzee cultures.* Cambridge, MA: Harvard University Press.

10

Environmental Complexity and the Evolution of Cognition

Peter Godfrey-Smith
Stanford University

STARTING SIMPLE

One problem faced in discussions of the evolution of intelligence is the need to get a precise fix on what is to be explained. Terms like *intelligence*, *cognition*, and *mind* do not have simple and agreed on meanings, and the differences between conceptions of intelligence have consequences for evolutionary explanation. I hope the chapters in this volume enable us to make progress on this problem. The present contribution is mostly focused on these basic and foundational issues, although the last section of the chapter looks at some specific models and programs of empirical work.

Some people have a very demanding picture of what is required for intelligence, thinking that it always involves such sophisticated skills as planning, language use, and perhaps even some type of consciousness. To these people, intelligence is to be contrasted with instinct. Perhaps in this rich sense of the term, intelligence is even to be contrasted with the simpler types of learning, such as learning through reinforcement (operant conditioning). From this first point of view, the problem of explaining the evolution of intelligence is explaining why instinct and other simple behavioral capacities were not enough, why evolutionary processes took a few organisms so far beyond these basic behavioral skills.

Another approach uses terms such as *intelligence* and *cognition* in much less demanding senses. In this second approach, intelligence is not restricted to a few exceptional cases in the biological world—humans and perhaps some primates. Rather, intelligence exists to some degree in a huge range of living systems. Humans have much more of it than cockroaches, but cockroaches do have some of it.

According to this second view, all the mechanisms that enable organisms to coordinate their behavior with conditions in the world involve some degree of intelligence. Therefore, there is no opposition between intelligence and what is often referred to as instinct. An instinctive behavior can involve perception, and a good deal of processing and feedback to ensure the right match between behavior and circumstances. According to this second view, that is a low-level variety of intelligence.

Maybe it is difficult to motivate the second, less demanding approach with the term *intelligence*, which has such definite commonsense usages. Perhaps it is better to present this view with the aid of a less everyday term, such as cognition. Therefore, this chapter mostly discusses the evolution of cognition rather than the evolution of intelligence. The term *mind* is another broad one, but it has its own capacity to mislead because for many people, it is closely linked with consciousness and a sense of self.

Given this, we can describe the second approach by saying that a great range of living things have some cognitive capacities. In many cases, these capacities are extremely limited. The capacities we habitually refer to as intelligent in humans, such as the capacities for planning and conscious reflection, comprise one type of cognition. But when a fish negotiates its way around a reef, or a rat finds its way back to a food source, the internal processes responsible for these behaviors are varieties of cognition as well.

Does it matter which of these two general approaches to the evolution of cognition we take? Certainly it does not much matter what we decide to refer to with the terms "intelligent" or "cognitive." Either way, the problems remain of explaining how nervous systems evolved and of explaining how humans became so much smarter, in many respects, than other organisms. However, I think it often does make a difference how we view and describe the continuities between human and nonhuman psychological capacities. A great deal depends on how much significance we place on the distinction between animals that use language and those that do not, for example. Views about nonhuman cognition often have ethical consequences, and consequences for a range of issues in the philosophy of mind.

In any case, my own approach is along the lines of the second option previously described. I approach the problem with a broad and very undemanding concept of cognition. My aim is to set out with a broad concept of cognition and ask: Can we formulate a generalization about why these types of capacities will tend to evolve? Because I use cognition to refer to such a broad class of capacities, cognition is not a single evolutionary discovery, restricted to a single lineage of organisms. Cognition of various kinds has been discovered and rediscovered by evolution many times, just as eyes and wings have been discovered independently several times. And just as we find with eyes, cognitive machinery is very diverse. There are plenty of ways to process information and control behavior; a central nervous system is one way but not the only way. An important feature of this view, which is discussed in more detail below, is that cognition shades off into other kinds of biological capacities and processes. In some cases it is hard to distinguish cognition from other control systems in the body and hard to distinguish behavior from such things as growth, development, and the regulation of metabolism.

Cognition is diverse, but it might be possible to find a common type of evolutionary story that applies in all or most of these diverse cases. With such a general framework in hand, we can then ask more specific questions about why certain types of cognition evolved. When is learning favored over less flexible strategies of dealing with the world? And if one is to learn, when is learning through individual trial and error better than learning by imitating a parent? What brings about the transition to a planning intelligence? When is what primatologists refer to as "theory of mind" (taking other individual organisms to have a mind) favored? And what is responsible for the explosion of mental capacities found in the evolution of humans?

It might be that all these explanations are so diverse that it is pointless to try to link them under a general principle. I do not deny that possibility. But my own approach is to outline and cautiously defend one possible generalization about the adaptive value of cognition. The generalization is intended to be a fairly obvious one, something that has been expressed in partial or imperfect ways dozens of times before, dating back to the 19th century. My aim here is more to make a vague existing idea into a precise one than to present an novel idea. I do think it could be of considerable help to discussions about the evolution of cognition if this underlying idea, and its possible rivals, were made explicit and precise in people's minds.

THE ENVIRONMENTAL COMPLEXITY THESIS

My proposal for a general first principle about the evolution of cognition is as follows: The function of cognition is to enable the agent to deal with environmental complexity.

Each of the key terms in the environmental complexity thesis (ECT) requires clarification. The term *function* is understood here in a strong sense. To ascribe a function in this sense is to offer an evolutionary hypothesis. The function of a trait or structure is the effect or capacity it has that has been responsible for its success under a regime of natural selection. When we say that the function, in this strong sense, of the thorns on a plant is to deter herbivores from eating the plant, we are not just saying that the thorns help the plant by deterring herbivores. We are saying that thorns were selected for in evolutionary processes because they tended to have the effect of deterring herbivores. The ECT makes a similar claim about cognition.

The ECT is a broader and more abstract claim than the one about the thorns, but very abstract functional claims can certainly be made. Eyes have evolved many times, and they make use of various different types of mechanisms. But a general claim can be made about their evolutionary function: The function of eyes is to respond in discriminative ways to light and hence to enable the organism to make use of information about the world that is carried in light (Gibson, 1966; Dretske, 1981). We can also formulate an even more general thesis about the function of perceptual mechanisms: They all respond, with some degree of sensitivity or discrimination, to some physical or chemical variables that impinge causally on the organism and in such a way as to enable the organism to make use of information about the world that is carried by these variables.

Some might say that when we formulate a broad generalization like this, we are saying something so obvious or empty as to make it not worth the effort of saying. I disagree. First, it is important to be able to embed specific functional claims made about biological structures within a more general picture of what the organism as a whole is doing. Second, it is actually quite hard to get these generalizations right, and plenty of puzzling questions can get raised along the way. For example, in the claims about perception I previously made, I used the concept of information. Although many people, including scientists, talk about information in a casual and unreflective way, it is a subtle and difficult concept. The philosopher Fred Dretske (1981) developed a detailed theory of where information is found in the physical world and of how everyday talk about information is related to the technical discussions of information theory in engineering. Information, for Dretske, is found where there is contingency and correlation. Any variable in the world that has a range of possible states is a source of information. When the state of a source of information is correlated with the state of another variable as a consequence of physical laws, the second variable carries information about the source. For Dretske, information is a resource that organisms use to make their way through the world; cognitive systems are information-consuming, or information-exploiting, systems.

Without careful, explicit discussions like Dretske's, it would be unclear whether or not it is really justifiable to use the concept of information when making generalizations about the function of eyes and other perceptual systems.

Whenever I use the term *information*, I have Dretske's sense in mind. Later, I discuss the concept of *environmental complexity* in some detail; this is another concept that it can be easily discussed without having a clear idea of what is being said.

So far I have said that the ECT is an attempt to give a general functional explanation of cognition. Functional explanations have received much attention in the philosophical literature, especially over the past 20 years or so (for a collection of classic and recent articles, see Allen, Bekoff, & Lauder, 1998). In this chapter, I do not discuss the many issues that have arisen in these debates, as the present topic is not a functional explanation in general but evolutionary hypotheses about cognition. All that is important for present purposes is the idea that functional explanations are attempts to describe, in shorthand, the processes of mutation and natural selection that were responsible for the origination and maintenance of biological structures. Functional explanations are attempts to isolate the effects or dispositions of a structure that were responsible for the natural selection of that structure. Therefore, functional claims are teleological only in this specific Darwinian sense.

I previously stated that I would be using a broad and undemanding sense of the term *cognition*. But how broad? What exactly is cognition? What is the set of organisms in which it is found?

I understand cognition as a collection of capacities that, in combination, allow organisms to achieve certain kinds of coordination between their actions and the world. This collection typically includes the capacities for perception, internal representation of the world, memory, learning, decision making, and the production of behavior. This set of capacities, according to the ECT, has the function of making possible patterns of behavior that enable organisms to effectively deal with complex patterns and conditions in their environments.

So although the ECT is expressed as a connection between cognition and environmental complexity, it really embeds two separate claims. One is the claim that the immediate role of cognition is to control behavior. The other is the claim that the point of this control of behavior is to deal with environmental complexity.

Think of cognition here not as a single type of process but as a biological tool kit used to direct behavior. There is no single list of tools found across all the organisms with cognitive capacities; different organisms have different collections of tools, according to their circumstances and history. So when I listed "perception, internal representation of the world, memory, learning (etc.)" above, it should not be thought that this has to be a description of a set of recognizable and distinct modules common to all cognitive systems. Rather, I am referring to a set of capacities that are realized in very different ways in different organisms, a set of capacities that shade into each other and shade off into other, noncognitive parts of the biological machinery. Also, the capacity for internal representation of the world is one about which there is enormous disagreement within philosophy and cognitive science (Stich & Warfield, 1994). Here again, some people understand this ability in a very demanding way, perhaps requiring language, while others view a very wide range of mechanisms for registering external events as representational in some sense. Here I assume a very loose and undemanding view of representation, but the issues surrounding that concept are too complex to go into here.

In the list of basic cognitive capacities given above, some are more fundamental than others. Perception is very fundamental; learning is somewhat less so. It is true that all macroscopic animals are thought to be able to learn, in at least a minimal sense. Bees have been shown to have quite impressive ways of learning the location of food sources, and fruit flies have been conditioned to exhibit avoidance behaviors in some of the same types of ways found in more celebrated learners, such as rats and pigeons. The neural basis for the most minimal kinds of learning is often studied using sea slugs. Still, learning is not in principle essential to cognition. A behavioral pattern that is completely insensitive to any refinement through learning, but that does involve the coordination of actions with perceived environmental conditions, does display a minimal type of cognition.

If learning is not essential, then where does cognition stop? Do plants have it? What about bacteria? By any normal standard, plants and bacteria do not have minds and do not exhibit cognition. However, my suggestion is that cognition shades off into other kinds of biological processes. There is not much point in trying to draw an absolute line. Plants and bacteria do exhibit some capacities for flexible response to environmental conditions, using environmental cues to control development and metabolism. These are low-level cases of the same types of capacities that, in more elaborate cases, do constitute cognition.

Many bacteria can adjust in adaptive ways to circumstances that are changing around them. Dretske (1986/1994) discussed aquatic bacteria that use little internal magnets to track the distinction between north and south, enabling them to move toward water with their required chemical properties. Bacteria also make use of external cues to adjust their metabolic activity. A famous case is the *lac operon* system in *Escherichia* bacteria. These bacteria can respond to a change in local food type through processes in which the availability of a nutrient affects the regulation of genes that code for enzymes able to digest that nutrient.

Plants are able to direct a range of their activities with the aid of cues from the external world. Within activities here, I include some cases that fall naturally under the headings of growth or individual development and others that might be distinguished from development and considered genuine behavior. Silvertown and Gordon (1989) argue at length that plants can behave, but they use an extremely broad conception of behavior. I suggest a narrower construal; one rough way to distinguish plant behavior from plant development is to say that behavioral changes must be reasonably rapid and also reversible. Given this, there will be a large range of cases in which plants adaptively control individual development with environmental cues and a smaller range of cases in which they control behavior. Genuine plant behaviors include the behaviors of Venus fly traps, and a large range of reversible responses to local light conditions.

Some of the ways in which plants use environmental cues are quite sophisticated. For example, many plants can determine not just that they are being shaded but that they are being shaded by other plants. This is done by detecting the wavelength properties of reflected light. The plants respond to shading by growing longer shoots (Silvertown & Lovett Doust, 1993). Lest I leave out the least glamorous biological kingdom, some soil fungi have a reflex that enables them to trap and digest tiny wandering worms.

Although it makes sense to distinguish control of plant behavior from control of plant development, for many theoretical purposes these can be seen as similar capacities. From the point of view of theoretical modeling, control of developmental processes and control of behavior have much in common (see section 4 below). And the temptation to use intentional and cognitivist terms when describing control of plant development in more informal ways can be strong. David Attenborough begins his book *The Private Life of Plants* as follows: "Plants can see. They can count and communicate with one another" (1995, p. 7). Most of the phenomena Attenborough is referring to involve control of growth and development, such as tactile exploration by a young vine, that is looking for a tree to climb.

I said that plants use much of their "smarts" for controlling growth and development, rather than behavior. In fact this phenomenon is not restricted to plants but is found in vertebrate animals as well. In certain fish, capacities for perception and information processing are used in directly regulating central aspects of development. These fish determine whether or not they will develop as male or female via perception of their relative size within the population (Francis & Barlow, 1993). Therefore, when I said earlier that the ECT links cognition first to behavior and then to environmental complexity, this was a slight oversimplification. Even in animals, sometimes cognition controls things other than behavior.

I have spent some time discussing capacities for flexible response, which do not constitute genuine cognition on any normal standard. My aim in discussing these cases is to suggest that cognition shades off into other kinds of biological processes; even though plants do not exhibit cognition and people do, there is no single scale between them and us with a threshold marking a transition to genuine cognition. Rather, all or practically all living organisms have some capacities for responding to environmental changes and conditions. Sometimes environmental cues are used to control metabolic processes or development, and sometimes they are used to consciously choose where to plant crops. In ordinary talk and in theoretical discussion, we habitually pick out only some of these capacities as intelligent or cognitive, and the decision to do so can be guided by a mixture of criteria. Complexity and flexibility play a role but so does the time scale at which responses occur. There is nothing wrong with that; my point is just that there are some fundamental similarities between real cognition and much simpler capacities for control of biological processes, and there is no reason to seek a sharp cutoff between the two classes.

As some terminology might be useful here, I will say that plants and bacteria have a number of *proto-cognitive* capacities. These are capacities for controlling individual growth, development, metabolism, and behavior by means of adaptive response to environmental information. The term *development* refers here only to processes within an individual lifetime; evolutionary change is not classified as proto-cognitive. Complex multicellular organisms like ourselves also contain subpersonal systems with some of the proto-cognitive capacities of simpler whole organisms. The vertebrate endocrine and immune systems are examples. This paper does not discuss the very difficult questions raised by the attribution to proto-cognitive capacities to higher level systems, such as ant colonies.

In stressing that cognition shades off into other proto-cognitive biological processes, I am asserting a version of what is sometimes called a continuity assumption about cognition. The simplest biological capacities that we might consider proto-cognitive are cases of flexibility in behavior or development (among others) controlled by a fixed response to a physically simple environmental cue, but where the nature of the response is not determined directly by the physical properties of the cue. (There has to be some "arbitrariness" in how the cue affects the system, to use a term due to Levins, 1968.) As we add different types of flexibility of response, and different kinds of inner processing of the output of perceptual mechanisms, we reach consecutively clearer cases of cognition. However, there is no single path that takes us from the simplest cases to the most elaborate. There are various ways of adding sophistication to the mechanisms of behavioral control, ways which will be useful to different organisms according to their circumstances. The ability to expand or contract the range of stimuli coupled to a given response is one important sophistication (Sterelny, 1995). The ability to learn through reinforcement is another, yet another is the ability to construct a cognitive map of spatial structure in the environment (a further discussion of this case follows). It is an error to try to describe a single hierarchy of cognitive skills, from simplest to most complex. Here, as elsewhere, there are many distinct kinds of complexity.

Compare two imaginary organisms that both have good spatial memory. One is more sophisticated than the other because it can remember more features of the environment and can use its knowledge to find novel routes to where it wants to go. However, this first organism can only acquire this spatial information by first-hand experience, by laboriously traveling and remembering the terrain. The second organism has a more limited capacity to remember features and to manipulate its internal model of the world, but it can acquire its knowledge in a richer variety of ways. It can infer spatial structure from the behavior of other organisms. In some respects the first organism is smarter, but in other respects, the second is smarter.

As we add sophistication to the tool kit of behavior-guiding capacities, we eventually reach clear, unmistakable cases of cognition; and not all of these clear cases involve humans. Some birds, such as Clark's nutcrackers in the southwest United States, hide stores of food when supplies are good and retrieve the stores in times of scarcity. To do this requires a sophisticated combination of perceptual abilities and spatial memory. In the sense in which I am using the term cognition, there is nothing marginal about such cognitive capacities.

Therefore, I claim that we reach uncontroversial cases of cognition before we reach language use, and I have left out all mention of the qualitative, first-person side of mental life. My overall position is that we do have reasonably good evidence to posit rich qualitative states in nonhuman animals, but that is a separate point that does not matter to the point of this discussion.

To use a very broad sense of cognition, as I do here, does not require postulation of fundamental similarity in the cognitive processes in all these diverse cases. Indeed, I have been stressing the opposite—the diversity of ways in which cognitive and proto-cognitive capacities are realized. Many people have given general overarching theories of how all cognitive processes work. Examples include the general theories of learning that dominated psychology in the middle decades of this century. If one has an overarching theory of this kind, then one will want to have a broad term such as cognition to capture what one is generalizing about. (Although many of the behavioral psychologists who defended general theories of learning would not have liked the term cognition.) I am skeptical about those overarching theories of cognitive processes and mechanisms, and I use a broad sense of cognition for what might be called more ecological reasons. There is a certain kind of job that the collection of processes I call cognitive performs. For various reasons, organisms acquire capacities for behavior and machinery to control this behavior. The behavioral machinery acquired is diverse, and so are the mechanisms used to control this behavior. Our sophisticated human mental abilities are one instance of this evolutionary phenomenon, but the abilities of bees and jaguars are as well. Understanding the evolution of cognition is understanding this whole domain of evolution's products.

ON COMPLEXITY

The ECT claims that the function of cognition is to enable organisms to deal with environmental complexity. What exactly is environmental complexity? There is much explaining needed on this point (see also Godfrey-Smith, 1996).

I suggest that the most useful concept of complexity is a simple one. Complexity is heterogeneity. Complexity is variety, diversity, doing many different things, or having the capacity to occupy many different states.

There are many different kinds of heterogeneity and hence many kinds of complexity. It is not just unnecessary, but positively mistaken, to try to devise a single scale to order all environments from the least to the most complex; rather, any environment will be heterogeneous in some respects and homogeneous in others. Environments can be heterogeneous in space and in time, and spatial and temporal heterogeneity exists at many different scales. In that respect, environment with a large number of different possible states that come and go over time is a complex environment, and so is an environment that is a patchwork of different conditions across space. The heterogeneity property is not the same in these two cases, but in both cases heterogeneity can be opposed to homogeneity. A complex environment is in different states at different times, rather than the same state all the time; a complex environment is different in different places, rather than the same all over. Whether a particular type of complexity is relevant to an organism will depend on what the organism is like—on the organism's size, physiology, needs, and habits. The heterogeneity properties of environments are objective, organism-independent properties, but among the countless ways in which an environment is structured and patterned, only some will be relevant to any given organism. (See Levins, 1968, for a classic discussion of some of these issues.)

In the ECT, I said that cognition enables agents to "deal" with environmental complexity. That terminology suggests that environmental complexity is seen as posing problems for organisms. Often this is so, but I do not want to put too much weight on the concept of a problem (Lewontin, 1983/1985). In some cases, environmental complexity provides what would normally be called an *opportunity* rather than a problem. A population might be located in a fairly benign set of circumstances, but one where tracking and adapting to environmental complexity makes it possible for some individuals to gain a reproductive advantage over others. Natural selection works in a comparative way; the absolute level of hardship generally is not important in understanding evolutionary processes within a population. Therefore, while I often write of the "problems" posed by environmental complexity in this paper, occasionally I will use the term "opportunities" as well. The distinction between the terms is mostly an everyday one, which should not be taken too seriously in this context.

If we think of complexity just as heterogeneity, this concept of complexity can be applied to organisms as well as to environments. An organism is complex to the extent that it is heterogeneous. Again, there are different kinds of heterogeneity; an organism can be heterogeneous in many different respects. (For different concepts of organismic complexity, see McShea, 1991.)

Cognitive capacities themselves are complex, so the ECT can be seen as claiming that one kind of organic complexity has been produced by evolution to enable organisms to deal with environmental complexity. Dealing with complex problems by means of perception and action can be seen as a special case of a more general phenomenon: dealing with environmental complexity by means of flexibility.

This way of looking at the ECT is illustrated by the proto-cognitive capacities that were discussed in the previous section of this paper. When a plant has the ability to adaptively alter its development to suit its environment, this is a case of complexity in the plant's developmental capacities that enables the plant to adapt to heterogeneity in its environment. Similarly, why do E. coli bacteria have their *lac operon* system of gene regulation? The preferred food of E. coli bacteria is glucose, but sometimes glucose is not available while other sugars are. The variability in the availability of different sugars is one type of environmental complexity faced by bacteria. Metabolic machinery is expensive, and E. coli have apparently been selected to economize in their production of enzymes. Therefore, the enzyme needed to digest lactose is not produced in the absence of lactose; instead, the production of the enzyme is controlled by an environmental cue. Thus, the cue used is the presence of lactose itself (and also the amount of glucose available to the cell; see Lodish et al., 1995). The system of gene regulation used by the bacteria in this situation constitutes one kind of complexity in these organisms, and this complex mechanism has a functional explanation, of the strong type discussed earlier. The function of the *lac operon* system is to enable E. coli bacteria to deal effectively with one type of environmental complexity—variation in the availability of different sugars.

As stated earlier, I do not claim that bacteria exhibit cognition; this is at most a case of proto-cognition. However, the ECT claims that the explanations for more complex and genuinely cognitive capacities tend to have a similar general shape as this explanation for a property of bacteria. The point of acquiring complex systems for behavioral control is to enable the organism to deal with variation in what the environment confronts the organism with and variation in the opportunities the environment offers.

Environmental complexity figures in the evolutionary processes that give rise to cognition. But where does environmental complexity itself come from? And what should we make of cases when environmental complexity is itself the product of organisms and their activities?

Environmental complexity itself has many sources. For the purposes in this discussion, I will make a loose distinction between two main categories. One source is the class of physical processes that are more or less independent of the activities of the organisms under consideration. Seasonal cycles provide an obvious example. And many resources that are relevant to an organism's well-being will be scattered through space in a way that is largely independent of the organism's own actions and properties.

When some type of organism acquires, through evolutionary processes, a way of tracking and dealing with environmental complexity of this first kind, the explanatory pattern described by the ECT has a straightforward causal directionality, but there are other cases in which the situation is more complicated. These are cases where the environmental complexity that organisms must deal with is either a causal product of, or is constituted by, the activities of other organisms within the same population. Then we have a situation that can exhibit feedback, or a coupling of organism and environment. (Lewontin, 1983/1985, Odling-Smee, 1988).

The most graphic examples are probably those that involve competitive interactions between animals. If the only way for one to obtain and hold a resource is by winning contests with other individuals in the same population, then these other organisms constitute a key part of one's environment. Their behavioral complexity constitutes part of the environmental complexity one must deal with, so the behavioral capacities of organisms similar to oneself are the source of a crucial kind of complexity in one's own environment.

In behavioral ecology, contests of this kind are modeled with game theory (Krebs & Davies, 1987). Most mathematical game theory models only remain simple enough to be comprehensible when many idealizations are made. Surrounding a few well-understood cases explicitly modeled with game theory, there is now a great deal of informal verbal "modeling" (in scare quotes) and computer simulation of these types of interactions. In fact, some have claimed that feedback processes of this kind are the key to understanding the evolutionary transition to genuine human intelligence. Those suggestions will be discussed in the section that follows.

My present point is that these phenomena are not incompatible with the ETC. The ECT need not be understood in a way in which the processes generating environmental complexity are casually autonomous, or independent of the activities of the evolving population in question. The ECT is compatible with the view that an important aspect of environmental complexity for many organisms is complexity that is made up of, or caused by, the activities of other organisms of the same species. In those cases, the ECT describes one part of a larger causal cycle—the part in which environmental complexity puts selective pressure on organisms' cognitive capacities. The other part of the cycle is the part in which the behaviors of organisms influence or determine the relevant patterns of environmental complexity.

So some environmental complexity for a given organism is made up of the activities of other organisms in that population. What about organisms from other species, which constitute sources of food, or sources of danger, for the organisms with which we are concerned? Again, my two-way distinction here is rough and ready. To the extent that the relevant activities of other species are causally influenced by the properties and activities of the population under consideration, we have a case of the second coupled type. Predator–prey interactions are a classic example. In general descriptions of ecological relationships, people often stress that every species is connected to virtually ever other, through direct or indirect causal chains. Clearly, however, this is a matter of degree. It is an error to overgeneralize about the richness of interspecific connections, just as it is an error to treat organisms as if all they ever have to deal with is an independent, causally autonomous, physical environment.

I have been contrasting relatively simple cases in which organisms are responding to environmental complexity that is causally independent of them and more complicated cases in which the environmental complexity depends on the organisms in significant ways. But even in the simpler class of cases, it should not be thought that I am suggesting that the evolutionary processes are simple and predictable. Much environmental complexity is not relevant to any given organism, and the factors that contribute to some aspect of complexity posing a problem are diverse and subtle. Suppose one moves through the world like a monkey, swinging from tree branches. Then the relevance of diversity in the size and strength of these branches depends very much on one's size. If one is small, most branches will hold and if they do not, a fall is unlikely to lead to serious harm. If one is larger, paths through the forest must be chosen with care and pose a significant information-processing problem because of the causal role of one's own weight (Povinelli & Cant, 1995). Some branches will break, leading to a dangerous fall, while others will bend in ways that affect one's next possible moves. Heterogeneity in the properties of tree branches is thus relevant in different ways, and in different degrees, to differently sized organisms.

The mere presence of environmental complexity that is relevant for a given type of organism does not automatically generate cognition, or even natural selection for it. The consequences of relevant environmental complexity also depend on many other features of the organism and its ecology. The fact that the ECT is expressed as a simple generalization should not be taken to downplay the role for architectural constraints in explaining why evolution takes the course it takes in a particular case. (These constraints are famously discussed in Gould & Lewontin, 1979.) For some organisms, getting smart is not really an evolutionary option, a consequence of their basic biological layout, their characteristic developmental sequence, or their overall ecology. Even for those that could, in principle, start to respond to environmental variation by tracking and behaviorally adapting to it, the appropriate genetic variation has to arise, and there will be costs associated with the machinery required to take a smart approach.

It is also well understood that some kinds of environmental complexity can be effectively dealt with by buffering it or blocking it out. One can respond to a threat not only by being smart but also by becoming impervious to it, via a strong shell or via sheer size. Some organisms, including many insects, deal with certain kinds of environmental complexity with an r-selected strategy for reproduction, in which there is massive reproduction in good times and little activity in bad times. To take this strategy it is necessary to be able to produce huge numbers of quickly maturing offspring when times are good. All this makes for a lack of cognitive machinery in r-selected organisms.

Therefore, whether evolution takes a lineage of organisms down a path toward increased cognitive capacity is contingent on a great range of factors, many of them having to do with the raw materials that evolution has to work with in that particular case. However, this fact does not make the ECT false or naïve. The ECT, when it applies to some particular case, is one part of a more complicated and detailed explanation.

THE ECT AS A COMPONENT IN MANY EVOLUTIONARY SCENARIOS

This paper has discussed the ECT in extremely general terms. This final section discusses some specific models and programs of empirical work. I discuss four examples, each focused on understanding a specific type of cognition (or proto-cognition). I suggest that the ECT is one component in many diverse scenarios that have been discussed in connection with the evolution of cognition.

Example One: Phenotypic Plasticity

Several times in this paper I stated that cognition, understood in my broad way, shades off into other biological processes, especially those that use signals, from the environment or elsewhere, to control adaptive responses. One important class of cases in the category I have been calling proto-cognitive is the phenomenon of phenotypic plasticity, especially in plants.

In the paradigm cases, phenotypic plasticity is a phenomenon in which a single plant genotype can produce a variety of forms (phenotypes) or can take a variety of developmental paths, where the choice is determined by an environmental cue transduced by the plant (Bradshaw, 1965; Schlichting & Pigliucci, 1998; Sultan, 1987). A plant might have a wet-environment and a dry-environment phenotype, for example, or might alter its form according to altitude and accompanying climatic conditions, as in the classic experiments of Clausen, Keck, and Hiesey (1948). In these cases, the plant has some mechanism for transducing an environmental cue and of controlling development as a function of the state of the cue. The cue, the plant phenotype, and the environmental variables that are being adapted to might be discrete or continuous. (When the organism's response is a discrete choice this is sometimes called *polyphenism*, but I will not make that terminological distinction here.)

No nervous system is involved in these cases, and in general it is growth and development, rather than behavior, that is being controlled. However, this type of phenomenon is a useful zero order case for discussions of models of adaptive response to environmental conditions. There are formal similarities between these capacities and cases of real cognition. Indeed, in the 1990s two mathematically identical evolutionary models were published independently (Moran, 1992; Sober, 1994). One was presented as a model of the advantages of learning (Sober), while the other was presented as a model of the advantages of plastic control of development (Moran).

How do the models and theoretical discussions look? Assume that an organism confronts an environment that has a range of alternative possible states. The organism has a range of possible developmental options. The alternative environmental states have consequences for the organism's chances of surviving and reproducing, and the best developmental option for one environmental state is not the best option for another. The organism receives imperfect information about the actual state of the environment, as a consequence of correlations between environmental conditions that matter to it and environmental conditions that directly affect its periphery. There are several ways to respond to the problem. One way is to be able to buffer out the environmental variation—perhaps by being big, or strong, or restricting exposure in some way. Another way is to adapt to the most common or the most critically important environmental state. Yet another way is to use a flexible strategy—to use environmental information to determine the organism's phenotype in accordance with how the environment is perceived.

For example, Drew Harvell (1986) investigates defenses against predators produced by colonial marine invertebrate animals called bryozoans, or sea moss. The bryozoans Harvell studies are able to detect the presence of predatory sea slugs, making use of a water-borne chemical cue. When sea slugs are around, the bryozoans produce spines. The spines have been shown not only to effectively reduce predation but also to incur a significant cost in terms of growth, so they are detrimental when sea slugs are not around.

This is a rudimentary form of perception. The bryozoans show sensitivity to an environmental cue that is not practically important but that carries information about a more important state of the world, the presence of predators. The organisms use a cue to produce an adaptive response to a more important distal environmental state.

In cases like these, a complete explanation for the organism evolving a smart or proto-cognitive capacity includes a description of the problem posed by environmental complexity—the fact that predators are sometimes, but not always, present. However, the explanation includes much more as well. We also need to know the reasons for a proto-cognitive response being favored over buffering, adaptation to the most common condition, or some other dumb strategy.

When will the proto-cognitive strategy be favored? There is no simple answer, but many models developed by biologists and others can be pieced together to give a partial answer (Godfrey-Smith, 1996). Some parts of the story are intuitive. To use a proto-cognitive strategy, the organism needs a suitable signal from the environment. If there is no way of tracking the relevant states of the environment, it is better to produce a single "cover-all" phenotype or to adapt to the single most common or important environmental state. Parts of information theory and signal detection theory can be used to describe exactly what types of properties an environmental cue must have in order for it to be worth using. When does one want to choose a flexible strategy over an inflexible strategy? Only when one's environmental cue is good enough and one doesn't make too many of the wrong kinds of errors. Even if one can track the world with some reliability, if one type of wrong decision is sufficiently disastrous, it may be best never to behave in a way that risks this error. Principles like those are close to commonsense. But these models also have a number of more subtle features. For example, it can matter a great deal how payoffs from individual encounters or trials are related to each other in their effects on overall fitness—whether payoffs are summed or multiplied (Levins, 1968; Seger & Brockman, 1987). The principles discussed by these models of plasticity cast light on both proto-cognition and genuine cognition as well. The models describe the first step towards cognition—opting for a flexible response to a heterogeneous environment.

Example Two: The Evolution of Associative Learning

The second example I discuss is a computer simulation of the evolution of associative learning, explored by Todd and Miller (1991). This simulation explores the evolution of the architectural properties of simple networks of neurons, using what is known as the genetic algorithm. The aim is to see when evolution will select for organisms that exhibit one of the simplest kinds of learning—classical conditioning.

The neural networks can usefully be imagined as embodied in simple marine animals that are born in the open sea but that settle to an immobile life feeding on passing food particles. Once an animal has settled, its only problem is to decide whether or not to feed, when presented with each item of possible food. The environment contains both food and inedible or poisonous particles, in equal proportions. When food is eaten, the organism gains an energetic benefit, and when poison is eaten, the organism pays a cost, though the error is not fatal.

Particles of possible food have two types of properties that the organisms can perceive—color and smell. Food smells sweet and poison smells sour, but in this turbulent environment, smells can mislead. The probability of a sweet smell, given the presence of food, is 0.75. The probability of a sour smell, given poison, is also 0.75.

The color of food is not affected by turbulence, but color is unpredictable in a different respect. In half of the population's environment food is red and poison is green, but in the other half, the colors are reversed. Within each of these two microenvironments, color is 100% reliable.

Each generation contains a large number of individuals of different types, which settle at random in the two different microenvironments. At the end of a fixed period, they reproduce (sexually) according to their accumulated fitness, with the possibility of mutation and recombination of genes. The new generation then floats about and settles in the environment at random and the cycle begins again.

The neural networks placed in this scenario are constrained to have only three units or nodes. These nodes are like idealized nerve cells. Despite these limited resources, there are many possibilities for the networks' architectures, and these architectures evolve in the model by natural selection across generations. Units can function as input devices of various kinds (red detectors, green detectors, sweet detectors, or sour detectors). There is just one type of output unit (eating), and a hidden unit, which mediates between a detector and a motor unit, is also a possibility. The range of units an individual has, and the combinations of unit connections, are determined by its genetic makeup.

Connections between units can be hardwired with either an excitatory or inhibitory one-way connection, or they can be plastic and altered by the individual's experience. If the genotype specifies a plastic connection, then the connection is shaped over time by what is known as a Hebbian learning rule. If those two units tend to fire at the same time in the individual's experience, they acquire a positive connection between them—one unit comes to have a (one-way) excitatory connection to the other. If they do not tend to fire together, the connection becomes negative or inhibitory. The question the model is intended to address is: When and in what ways will individuals with the ability to learn evolve in the population? The question is interesting because Hebbian learning is discussed at length by neuroscientists, and they hunt for Hebbian learning in the synapses of the brain. But from the evolutionary point of view, it is often not obvious what use Hebbian learning has. If two neurons tend to fire together, what is the point of also making one excite the other?

At the start of a run of the Todd and Miller simulation, the population consists of randomly configured individuals, most of whom do not fare well. For example, some will not have a motor unit and will never eat, or will have a motor unit connected to an input unit that has the wrong setting—it might tell the organism to always eat when the present food particle smells sour. Another type of miswiring might be called *the academic*. An individual can have two input units and a motor unit but only learnable connections between all three units, connections which are initially set at zero. Suppose such a creature lands in a patch where food is red; then it will learn the statistical association between redness and a sweet smell—the red-color input unit will tend to be on at the same time as the sweet-smell unit. However, nothing is inducing the individual to eat. The motor unit will never be turned on, and its knowledge of the world will not do the individual any good, as far as nutrition is concerned.

Two kinds of wiring do work well for the organism though. One has a fixed positive connection between a sweet-smell sensor and a motor unit, with nothing else that influences behavior. This organism will generally eat when there is food present—in the present case, it will make the right decision 75% of the time. After a short period, these individuals tend to proliferate in the population.

The best possible wiring is a variant on this one, which has a fixed connection between a sweetness sensor and a motor unit and also a learnable connection between a color sensor and the motor unit. From the start this individual will tend to eat when there is food because the smell sensor is controlling the motor unit. In addition, there will be a correlation between eating and some particular state of the color sensor. If the microenvironment is a red-food one, then when the organism eats it will also tend to be seeing red. This correlation establishes a connection between the color sensor and the motor unit, and (given the right initial settings) this connection will eventually be strong enough to control the motor unit by itself. Then the eating behavior will be controlled by a 100% reliable cue for the remainder of the individual's life. Typical runs of the simulation begin with the fairly rapid evolution of the simple, hardwired, smell-guided networks, and some time afterward learners appear and take over.

This simulation illustrates the advantages associated with two kinds of behavioral complexity. Consider first the contest between individuals that always eat every particle that drifts by and individuals that use smell as a cue. If everything in the environment were food, there would be little point in controlling behavior with perception, especially with an only partially reliable environmental cue. However, the environment used by Todd and Miller is one where food and poison drift by with equal frequencies. This is one type of environmental complexity, and it has the consequence that a permanently eating architecture will have low fitness when compared to an individual that uses smell as a cue. A different type of environmental complexity, and a different reliability relationship between a cue and the world, explains the evolution of learning. The total environment in which these organisms live is spatially heterogeneous—in half the environment food is red and in the other half food is green. If food were red in the whole environment, it would not be worth taking the time to learn that food is red, and a network with a red detector hardwired to the output unit would be optimal. But Todd and Miller use an environment that is heterogeneous in this respect as well; and although the color of food is not predictable in advance, the past experience of an individual is a good guide to the future. That is what is needed for learning to be more useful than an inflexible behavioral program.

Example Three: Spatial Memory and Cognitive Maps

For a mobile animal, one very important kind of environmental heterogeneity is heterogeneity in the distribution of resources, dangers, and other factors in space. Spatial structure plays a very different role for a plant, of course, or for an animal like a clam, which does not move around the world. But once an organism is on the move, as most terrestrial animals must sometimes be, spatial structure in the environment is of prime importance.

Some of this environmental heterogeneity can be dealt with by various forms of buffering. But evolutionary responses to the problem of dealing with space have produced some impressive and complicated forms of cognition, even in small and otherwise behaviorally simple animals. The mechanisms associated with bee dances, which direct workers from the hive to sources of food, are one famous example, but it has turned out that bees as individuals also show good spatial skills. They can learn to reliably associate a source of food with either single landmarks or with geometrical structure in a set of landmarks. In recent years, much attention has been directed to spatial memory in food-storing birds, such as the Clark's nutcracker in the southwestern United States and marsh tits in England. Clark's nutcrackers hide thousands of pine seeds as a food source for the winter. It appears that these birds have specialized spatial memory abilities that do not extrapolate (as far as has been determined) to superiority over other birds in nonspatial memory tasks (see Roberts, 1998, for the bee and bird examples in this paragraph).

In 1948, E. C. Tolman suggested that both animals and humans make their way through space by using *cognitive maps*, or rich internal representations of spatial structure in the environment. After initial controversy and some decades of neglect during the heyday of strict forms of behaviorism, the concept of a cognitive map is again being used by ethologists and comparative psychologists (Tolman, 1948; Thinus-Blanc, 1988; Roberts, 1998). The concept of a cognitive map is controversial in a number of respects. First, there is a good deal of vagueness and ambiguity in how it is applied by different researchers (Bennett, 1996). Some use the term to refer specifically to postulated internal structures that work in psychological processing in ways reminiscent of ordinary, external maps. In this narrow sense, the hypothesis that an animal has a cognitive map requires, at a minimum, a capacity to devise novel detours and shortcuts in response to obstruction of more familiar paths. Sometimes the term is used more broadly to refer to almost any kind of spatial memory. Tolman, for example, distinguished strip maps and comprehensive maps within the more general category of cognitive maps. Strip maps represent only a path to a goal; they are dependent on the starting point of the animal. Comprehensive maps are richer representations of the overall spatial structure in some domain, so they can be used despite variation in starting points, new obstacles, and so on. It can be argued, however, that the sort of behavior associated with strip maps is easily explained without talking of inner maps at all; the animal is just executing a sequence of behaviors in response to a set of cues or landmarks. Some sophistication in memory is clearly involved, but there is no need to postulate an inner maplike structure.

However, there are experimental results that do justify a richer interpretation of some animals' inner processing of spatial information. A simple and striking case is found in an experiment by Tolman and Honzik (1930). Rats were trained in a maze that has three different paths to a single supply of food. Path 1 is shorter than Path 2, and Path 2 is shorter than Path 3. The rats were easily able to learn to prefer the best available path. After a few days of training, Path 1 was almost always chosen first. If Path 1 was blocked (at an early point), the rats would go back and take Path 2. If Path 2 was also blocked, they would settle for path 3. So far, this only shows a fairly routine, but very useful, type of reinforced learning. The impressive behavior resulted when Path 1 was blocked in a novel way for the first time. Path 1 has its final section in common with Path 2, but Path 3 reaches the food independently of this common section. Therefore, when this final part of Path 1 is blocked, that has the effect of making Path 2 useless as well. What will the rats do when Path 1 is blocked in this novel way? Their history of conditioning has taught them that when Path 1 is blocked, Path 2 is the next choice. But if the rats are smart enough to realize the consequences of this novel way of blocking Path 1, they should choose Path 3 directly and not waste time on Path 2. In Tolman and Honzik's experiment, a large majority of rats, upon encountering the novel obstruction on the later part of Path 1 for the first time, returned to the junction point of the three paths and immediately chose Path 3. They did not follow their failure on Path 1 with an attempt at Path 2; they had somehow been able to represent the new obstacle as rendering Path 2 useless as well.

Tolman and Honzik interpreted this as showing "insight" on the part of the rats, following the Gestalt psychologist Köhler, who had found similar results with chimps. Tolman did not, for some reason, use this experiment in the famous 1948 discussion, which introduced the concept of a cognitive map. Instead, he used results which, to my mind, were much less convincing than his 1930 insight experiment. (Thinus-Blanc, 1988, erroneously reports Tolman 1948 as actually discussing the insight experiment in support of the cognitive map concept, an interesting case of wishful thinking, or of post hoc improvement of Tolman's paper!) Perhaps Tolman did not think of the insight experiment as showing specifically spatial cognitive skills but a more general capacity to draw conclusions and reason beyond the immediate lessons of conditioning. However the cognitive map concept is used, this 1930 experiment does appear to show a capacity to construct and manipulate some sort of internal model of spatial structure in the environment. In qualification of this, I should note that Tolman and Honzik found it quite tricky to devise a maze in which most of their rats would consistently show this spatial insight. For example, insight was consistently shown only when the maze was made of elevated tracks, not tunnels.

Another kind of experiment designed to investigate innovative behavior based on representation of spatial structure studies the use of short cuts. Both dogs and chimps can be shown hidden pieces of food in an environment, with the order of their exposure to the food corresponding to an inefficient path from food item to food item. Once released, the animals in both cases are able to find the food items and move from item to item, using a path that is new and more direct and efficient than the one they were trained on. (In effect, the chimps do a reasonable job at what mathematicians refer to as a traveling salesman problem.) Again, the behavior produced does not correspond to any motor routine or action pattern for which the animal was trained, and these experiments also control for such possibilities as olfactory detection of the food (Menzel, 1997; Roberts, 1998).

All of these experiments are associated with some controversy. For example, it can be argued that to the extent that animals are simply moving from one memorized landmark (or point specified by its relation to a set of landmarks) to another, there is justification for attributing memory to the animal but not a cognitive map (Bennett, 1996). Menzel (1997) found deviations from "traveling salesman" optimality when macaques were tested on whether they chose the optimal path from item to item, or simply went toward the closest piece of food at each decision point. But it is noteworthy that the best of this work, such as the Tolman and Honzik insight experiment, does involve behavior that appears to justify the postulation of internal representation of the world and fairly complex use of the representations in guiding behavior, without the animal having a capacity for public language. There is a tradition in philosophy of denying that any animal that lacks language can properly be said to think or represent. In recent years, Davidson (1975/1984) has been the most influential defender of this view. It was held in a different form by Dewey (1929/1958) and is often associated with Wittgenstein (1953) and his followers. Such views struggle to make sense of the skills in animal path choice discussed above. Whether or not these animals are able to represent the world in the richest, most philosophically loaded sense of represent, they do seem to be doing some kind of representation or mapping of the spatial structure of their environment (see also Allen & Bekoff, 1997). Problems and opportunities associated with spatial structures in environments have apparently generated a range of sophisticated cognitive skills.

Example Four: Social Intelligence Models

Explaining the evolution of such capacities as learning (example two) and the ability to represent spatial structure in an environment (example three) has usually been thought not to be difficult. However, it is a different matter to explain the highly developed and distinctive cognitive capacities of humans and nonhuman primates. Over 20 years ago, Nicholas Humphrey suggested that primates seem to have too much brain power to be explained by the demands of such activities as foraging for food. He suggested that the problems primates use this intelligence to deal with stem from the social complexity of their environments (Humphrey, 1976/1988). In particular, much primate life is concerned with the formation and maintenance of alliances, the policing of dominance hierarchies, and a variety of other social tasks that involve a mixture of competition and cooperation. Humphrey's suggestion, which had been partially anticipated by others, was that high primate intelligence evolved in response to the problem of dealing with this kind of complexity. Because each individual primate comprises part of the environment for the others in a population, we have the ingredients for a process of feedback, in which each increase in intelligence produced by evolution adds to the complexity of the social environment that individuals face.

This idea has come to be known as the Machiavellian intelligence hypothesis (Byrne & Whiten, 1988; Whiten & Byrne, 1997). I use the term *social intelligence* rather than *Machiavellian intelligence*. As Whiten and Byrne state, the term Machiavellian should not be taken to suggest that all the behaviors involved in the hypothesis are manipulative and deceitful. They mean to include "cunning cooperation," which contributes to individual reproductive success (Whiten & Byrne, 1997, pp. 12–13). Whiten and Byrne do mean to exclude, however, any suggestion of natural selection operating at the level of groups rather than individuals—they mean to exclude the idea that intelligent cooperation could evolve for the good of the group. As I do think the term "Machiavellian intelligence" continues to mislead, suggesting the darker side of social behavior, and I also do not want to rule out some role for group selection in these processes. I prefer to use the term *social intelligence hypothesis*. Like Gigerenzer (1997), I reserve Machiavellian as a narrower term, specifically for behaviors involving exploitation rather than cooperation.

The social intelligence hypothesis is compatible with the ECT; it is a specific instance of the ECT that involves a special kind of environment. In the previous section, I argued that the ECT need not be understood in a way that requires the environment in question to be independent of the population that is evolving. In any social animal, a key part of an individual's environment is made up of the other members of the social group, with all their behavioral capacities. The same is true to a lesser extent with many nonsocial animals. In cases like these, the ECT describes one particular explanatory arrow within a larger explanatory structure, a structure that links cognitive capacities and environmental complexity in a coupled way. At any given time, the individuals in a social population face environmental complexity in the form of the behavioral patterns of the other local members of the population. This environmental complexity may or may not give more intelligent individuals an advantage over less intelligent individuals by some specific measure of intelligence relevant to the situation. If intelligence is favored, and if this kind of intelligence is inherited, then over time intelligence will increase in the population. If the intelligent individuals themselves display more complex patterns of behavior than others in the population, then this increase in intelligence will in turn entail an increase in the complexity of the social environment faced by later individuals. This process may or may not have a runaway, positive-feedback character. One should not assume that a runaway process is the only outcome. For example, other constraints and costs might start to assume a larger role once the individuals reach a certain level of intelligence.

The social intelligence hypothesis has been developed in a number of different specific versions. Stronger versions claim that social complexity has been the key factor in producing the high levels of primate intelligence; weaker versions see this as one explanatory factor that might work in conjunction with others. For example, some suggest a role for special problems associated with foraging for the ripe fruits favored by primates—it might be that primates require especially sophisticated cognitive maps of their nonsocial environments. (Whiten & Byrne, 1997, contains discussions of a range of alternatives to the social intelligence hypothesis.) Different versions of the hypothesis also stress different aspects of social living—direct competition between males for mates, dealing with dominance hierarchies, cooperative foraging, and so on.

As Gigerenzer (1997) notes, the social intelligence hypothesis is sometimes associated with the suggestion that the overall degrees of complexity in social and nonsocial environments (or social and nonsocial aspects of an environment) can be compared and that social environments are more complex. As I previously stated, I am a skeptic about the project of giving overall measures of complexity across environments; any environment is complex in some respects and simple in others. Gigerenzer is similarly skeptical about these complexity measures. But where Gigerenzer appears to think that this problem makes it pointless to generalize about the role of complexity in the evolution of cognition, I think the environmental complexity thesis is a useful general principle despite the absence of a unitary scale of environmental complexity.

As I understand them, most but not all of the specific hypotheses discussed under the general category of social intelligence can be seen as applications of the ETC. The versions that do fall under the ECT are those that stress the role of cognition in dealing with the behavioral complexity of other individuals within a social group. An example of a hypothesis in this general area that does not fall under the ECT is one version of the protean behavior hypothesis, discussed by Geoffrey Miller (1997). Miller suggests that animals like primates have been selected to be able to produce genuinely unpredictable behavior. Unpredictable behavior has fairly obvious advantages when an animal is escaping from predators and more subtle advantages in situations involving conflict and bluffing, as discussed in game theory. In those cases, producing unpredictable behavior itself requires no special cognitive sophistication. However, Miller also suggests that capacities for novel, creative behavior will help individuals attract mates, especially in situations of female choice, and these behavioral capacities are facilitated by a large brain. There are several ways in which this scenario might work, but consider one case. Suppose there has been selection for behavioral novelty in males, and suppose these novel mating displays succeed by taking advantage of a general feature of perceptual and cognitive mechanisms—the fact that novelty attracts attention. Then any evolved increase in cognitive sophistication due to this process cannot be seen as an application of the ETC. A complex social environment might be created by male behaviors in this case, but cognition is not being selected as a way of dealing with complexity. On the other hand, if females are being strongly selected for the capacity to see through all this behavioral noise and make adaptive choices, there will be selection, compatible with the ECT, for cognitive sophistication in females.

All these sex-specific hypotheses about the advantages of cognition in primates have a problem stemming from the basic similarity between male and female brains in the most intelligent primates (as Richard Francis stressed to me). If selection only favors elaborate cognition in one sex, then the other sex will have much of its brain treated by the theory as a mere by-product. Big brains are too expensive to be treated like male nipples; big brains as by-products would be analogous to peacock tails on peahens. If both sexes are being selected to be smart, but in very different ways, then the problem posed by the lack of obvious sexual dimorphism is more subtle and hard to assess. In any case, I introduce these speculations about unpredictable behavior not to endorse them but to illustrate the fact that while the ECT is very broad, it does not trivially encompass any possible explanation for the evolution of cognition. The ECT only covers cases where environmental complexity, either social or nonsocial, creates a problem, or an opportunity, for some type of organism, and the problem leads to natural selection favoring individuals with an ability to use cognition to coordinate behavior with the state of the environment.

In earlier discussions of social intelligence, there was sometimes the appearance of a sharp either-or characteristic to the debates about social and nonsocial complexity; either primates became smart for social reasons, or they became smart for reasons having to do with nonsocial aspects of their ecology. But as Byrne (1997) argues, there is plenty of room for mixed explanations in which a number of factors have a role. Byrne himself posits three distinct evolutionary transitions in the evolution of intelligence in monkeys, apes, and humans. In this scenario, the evolutionary branch containing monkeys and apes (haplorhines) became smarter than its relatives because of selection for social intelligence. But the great apes (chimps, bonobos, humans, gorillas, orangutans) branched off from this group and became smarter because of selection for technical intelligence, which involves planning and sophisticated tool use in activities such as foraging. And then the branch that led to modern humans was perhaps again the subject of selection for social intelligence, in part because of larger group size. This scenario is very speculative, as Byrne stresses, but it provides a good example of a mixed story about the evolution of human cognition. It would be a mistake to only pursue pure social intelligence hypotheses, out of an overly strong attachment to explanatory simplicity.

In closing, I provide a more detailed summary of what the ECT claims.

Environmental Complexity Thesis (more detailed version)

The basic pattern found in the evolution of cognition is a pattern in which individual organisms derive an advantage from cognitive capacities in their attempts to deal with problems and opportunities posed by environmental complexity of various kinds. Cognitive capacities confer this advantage by enabling organisms to coordinate their behavior with the state of the environment. Cognition itself should be thought of as a diverse tool kit of capacities for behavioral control, including capacities for perception, internal representation of the world, memory, learning, and decision making. These capacities vary across different types of organisms and are not sharply distinguished from other biological capacities, some of which have a proto-cognitive character. The environment referred to in the

ECT includes the social environment, and there are some reasons to believe that problems posed by social complexity have been very important in the evolution of primate and human intelligence. Many specific evolutionary scenarios that have been discussed as possible explanations of particular cognitive capacities are instances of the ECT or have the ECT as a part.

ACKNOWLEDGMENTS

Thanks to Richard Francis, Lori Gruen, and Kim Sterelny for discussions and correspondence on these issues.

REFERENCES

Allen, C., Bekoff, M., & Lauder, G. (Eds.). (1998). *Nature's purposes: Analyses of function and design in biology.* Cambridge, MA: MIT Press.
Allen, C., & Bekoff, M. (1997). *Species of mind.* Cambridge, MA: MIT Press.
Attenborough, D. (1995). *The private life of plants.* Princeton, NJ: Princeton University Press.
Bennett, A. T. D. (1996). Do animals have cognitive maps? *Journal of Experimental Biology, 199,* 219–224.
Bonner, J. (1988). *The evolution of complexity.* Princeton, NJ: Princeton University Press.
Bradshaw, A. D. (1965). Evolutionary significance of phenotypic plasticity in plants. *Advances in Genetics, 13,* 115–55.
Byrne, R. W. (1997). "The Technical Intelligence Hypothesis: An Additional Evolutionary Stimulus to Intelligence," in Whiten and Byrne (1997) pp. 289–311.
Byrne, R. W., & Whiten, A. (Eds.). (1988). *Machiavellian intelligence: Social expertise and the evolution of intellect in monkeys, apes and humans.* Oxford, UK: Clarendon Press.
Clausen, J., Keck, D., & Hiesey, W. M. (1948). *Experimental studies on the nature of plant species III. environmental responses of climatic races of Achillea* (Carnegie Institution of Washington Publication 581). Washington DC.
Davidson, D. (1984). Thought and talk, In *Essays on truth and interpretation* (pp. 155–170). Oxford: Oxford University Press. (Original work published 1975)
Dewey, J. (1958). *Experience and nature* (Rev. ed.). New York: Dover. (Original work published 1929)
Dretske, F. (1981). *Knowledge and the flow of information.* Cambridge, MA: MIT Press.
Dretske, F. (1994). Misrepresentation. In Stich & Warfield (Eds.), Mental representation: A reader (pp. 157–73). Oxford, UK: Blackwell. (Original work published 1986)
Francis, R., & Barlow, G. W. (1993). Social control of primary sex determination in the Midas cichlid. *Proceedings of the National Academy of Sciences, USA, 90,* 10673–10675.
Gibson, J. J. (1966). *The senses considered as perceptual systems.* Boston: Houghton Mifflin.
Gigerenzer, G. (1997). The modularity of social intelligence, In Whiten & Byrne (Eds.), *Machiavellian intelligence II: Extension and evaluations* (pp. 264–288). Cambridge, UK: Cambridge University Press.
Godfrey-Smith, P. (1996). *Complexity and the function of mind in nature.* Cambridge: Cambridge University Press.
Gould, S. J., & Lewontin, R. C. (1979). The spandrels of San Marco and the panglossian paradigm: A critique of the adaptationist program. *Proceedings of the Royal Society, London, 205,* 581–598.
Harvell, D. (1986). The ecology and evolution of inducible defenses in a marine bryozoan: Cues, costs, and consequences. *American Naturalist, 128,* 810–823.
Humphrey, N. (1988). *The social function of intellect.* In Byrne & Whiten. (Original work published 1976)

Krebs J., & Davies, N. (1987). *An introduction to behavioural ecology* (2nd ed.). Oxford, England: Blackwell.

Levins, R. (1968). *Evolution in changing environments*. Princeton, NJ: Princeton University Press.

Lewontin, R. C. (1985). The organism as the subject and object of evolution, In R. Levins & R. C. Lewontin (Eds.), *The dialectical biologist*. Cambridge, MA: Harvard University Press. (Original work published 1983)

Lodish, H., Baltimore, D., Berk, A., Zipursky, S. L. Matsudaira, P., & Darnell, J. (1995). *Molecular cell biology* (3rd ed.). New York: Freeman.

McShea, D. (1991). Complexity and evolution: What everybody knows. *Biology and Philosophy, 6*, 303–24.

Menzel, C. R. (1997). Primates' Knowledge of their Natural Habitat. In Whiten & Byrne (Eds.), *Machiavellian intelligence II: Extensions and evaluations* (pp. 207–239). Cambridge, UK: Cambridge University Press.

Miller, G. (1997). *Protean primates: The evolution of adaptive unpredictability in competition and courtship*. In Whiten & Byrne (pp. 312–340).

Moran, N. (1992). The evolutionary maintenance of alternative phenotypes. *American Naturalist, 139*, 971–989.

Odling-Smee, F. J. (1988). Niche-constructing phenotypes. In H. C. Plotkin (Ed.), *The role of behavior in evolution* (pp. 73–132). Cambridge, MA: MIT Press.

Povinelli, D. J., & Cant, J. G. (1995). Arboreal climbing and the evolution of self-conception. *Quarterly Review of Biology, 70*, 393–421.

Roberts, W. A. (1998). *Principles of animal cognition*. Boston: McGraw-Hill.

Schlichting, C., & Pigliucci, M. (1998). *Phenotypic evolution: A reaction norm perspective*. Sunderland, MA: Sinauer.

Seger, J., & Brockman, J. (1987). What is bet-hedging? *Oxford Surveys in Evolutionary Biology, 4*, 181–211.

Silvertown, J., & Gordon, D. (1989). A framework for plant behavior. *Annual Review of Ecology and Systematics, 20*, 349–366.

Silvertown, J., & Lovett Doust, J. (1993). *Introduction to plant population biology*. Oxford, England: Blackwell.

Sober, E. (1994). The adaptive advantage of learning versus a priori prejudice. In *From a biological point of view* (pp. 50–70). Cambridge: Cambridge University Press.

Sterelny, K. (1995). Basic minds. *Philosophical perspectives, 9*, 251–270.

Stich, S. P., & Warfield, T. A. (Eds.). (1994). *Mental representation: A reader*. Oxford, England: Blackwell.

Sultan, S. (1987). Evolutionary implications of phenotypic plasticity in plants, In M. Hecht, B. Wallace, & G. T. Prance (Eds.), *Evolutionary Biology, Vol. 21* (pp. 127–78). New York: Plenum.

Thinus-Blanc, C. (1988) Animal spatial cognition. In L. Weiskrantz (Ed.), *Thought without language* (pp. 371–395). Oxford: Clarendon Press.

Todd, P. M., & Miller, G. F. (1991). Exploring adaptive agency II: Simulating the evolution of associative learning. In J. A. Meyer & S. W. Wilson (Eds.), *From Animals to Animats: Proceedings of the First International Conference on the Simulation of Adaptive Behavior* (pp. 306–1315). Cambridge MA: MIT Press.

Tolman, E. C. (1948). Cognitive maps in rats and men. *Psychological Review, 55*, 189–208.

Tolman, E. C., & Honzik, T. H. (1930). 'Insight' in rats. *University of California Publications in Psychology, 4*, 257–275.

Whiten, A., & Byrne, R. W. (Eds.). (1997). *Machiavellian intelligence II: Extensions and evaluations*. Cambridge: Cambridge University Press.

Wittgenstein, L. (1953). *Philosophical investigations*. G. Anscombe (Trans.). New York: Macmillan.

11

On Theory in Comparative Psychology

Harry J. Jerison
Professor Emeritus
University of California at Los Angeles

The fundamental theory of comparative psychology is the Darwinian theory of evolution by natural selection. Shortly after Darwin published *The Origin of Species* in 1859 (see Darwin, 1985), his "bulldog," Thomas Huxley, anticipated this conclusion in a frequently reprinted lecture to workingmen delivered in 1860:

> I have endeavoured to show that no absolute structural line of demarcation, wider than that between the animals which immediately succeed us in the scale, can be drawn between the animal world and ourselves; and I my add the expression of my belief that the attempt to draw a psychical distinction is equally futile, and that even the highest faculties of feeling and intellect begin to germinate in lower forms of life. (1899, p. 152)

Huxley's belief about the evolution of feelings and mind has been vindicated by a century and a half of research in ethology and comparative psychology. In this essay, I present my own understanding of the issues. I include data supporting my views, primarily by referring to two recent chapters published elsewhere (Jerison, 2000, 2001), to several older reviews (Jerison, 1982, 1991), and to my book of a quarter of a century ago (Jerison, 1973). I make no effort to offer comprehensive summaries or adequate critiques of the views of others who have analyzed the evolution of behavior or presented theories of comparative psychology, although I

Note added in proof: Systematic Biologists presently designate as "amniote" what here is referred to as "reptile" and "mammal-like reptile." I retain the older usage to emphasize the major increase in neural processing capacity at the reptile-mammal transition.

of course cite the work that is most relevant for my perspective. My purpose is to relate my work on the evolution of brain size to our goal of understanding comparative psychology.

THE EVOLUTIONARY PROCESS

Three decades ago, in a review of theoretical issues, Hodos and Campbell (1969) alerted us to the danger of unsophisticated acceptance of an Aristotelian scale of nature as the model for what happened in evolution. The problem may be reflected in Huxley's phrase, "begin to germinate," which suggests a direction and inevitable advance in evolution from lower to higher forms. The phrase is unfortunate. The correct present view is that genetically determined traits that can be identified in living species all have evolutionary histories and were derived from related traits in earlier species. When one can identify an evolutionary phylogeny, it can be true that later species are at a higher grade with respect to some traits than earlier species, but it is a tricky question that requires much more discussion than is appropriate for this essay (Gould, 1976).

The higher faculties in the human species were surely derived from related, perhaps lower but at least different, traits in ancestor species. Evolutionary novelties are understood as relatively small genetic modifications of earlier traits, which are nevertheless manifested phenotypically as dramatically different traits. In Jerison (2000), I present the following hypothetical example of a small genetic modification of a trait and the way it would produce a dramatic phenotypic effect, an effect that could distinguish humans from apes:

> A possible genetic blueprint of a species might include code for the following instruction to regulate growth in a primordial nerve cell: "perform 32 cell divisions and then stop." If that instruction were followed and no cells died, 4,294,967,296 nerve cells would be produced. Imagine now a major (but small) mutation, which changed "32" to "34." This small change would yield 17,179,869,184 nerve cells. Were these fated to be neocortical neurons the mutation would be about right to distinguish the number of neurons in the brain of a chimpanzee from that in a human (Pakkenberg & Gundersen, 1997). In this example, the code may seem overly simple, but it is that kind of code that can be written, and it is a code that would have a very great morphometric effect. Instructions that are significantly more complex may be beyond the capacity of genes to encode information.

As with almost all organismic traits, behavioral or morphological, phenotypes are produced by an interaction of the genotypes with the environments in which the genetic instructions are carried out. The genotypes are always definable in principle by the structure of certain molecules, chains of nucleotides, which are the classical genes. These form the genetic code. They are the blueprint, as it were, for generating the phenotypes: organs and organisms. The evolutionary rules governing genotypic variation and change within a species emphasize random mutations rather than natural selection. Their evolution can usually be ascribed to genetic drift. Selection operates on the phenotypes, however, and serves to change the frequencies of the corresponding genotypes across generations of a species to increase the likelihood of reproductive success. Natural selection is thus directional; its direction is determined by environmental effects, and it can be thought of as a mechanism that enables genetic systems to track a changing environment.

In a nutshell, that is how evolution works. There is nothing special about the traits that concern comparative psychologists, nothing to require special versions of evolutionary theory to understand the place of those traits in the history of life. Evolutionary theory remains the basic theory for comparative psychology, most easily appreciated for genetically determined traits. There is a matter of emphasis, however, in that the genotypes of few behavioral traits are well understood, and their phenotypic expression is determined to a significant extent by postnatal developmental factors. For many of the traits of special interest to comparative psychologists, it is probably usually the case that the genotypes are themselves complex and do not normally involve single genes.

THE SPECIAL PROBLEM OF COMPARATIVE PSYCHOLOGY

From its beginnings as an experimentally oriented scientific discipline, comparative psychology has been devoted to the analysis of learning in different animal species (e.g., Lubbock, 1888; Thorndike, 1898). It emphasized traits that were obviously environmentally determined. How could such traits be studied as having evolved? The answer was to create a construct, learning ability, which could presumably be genetically determined and which might have evolved in different ways and to different extents in different species. There could have been higher and lower grades of learning ability.

The first problem for theory in comparative psychology arises from the strange discoveries about learning ability. Much of Macphail's (1982) marvelous review of comparative vertebrate intelligence is concerned with the research literature on this topic. His conclusion, simply put, is that the fundamentals of learning are similar in all vertebrate species in which they have been studied. Researchers on the fundamentals of learning, whether or not they sympathize with Macphail's conclusions, appear to accept it pragmatically in their choice of species. The fundamentals of conditioning have been analyzed most intriguingly in sea slugs (Byrne, 1987) and fruit flies (Tully, Preat, Boynton, & Del Vecchio, 1994), extending Macphail's judgment to invertebrates. Because of this apparent uniformity across species, the neurochemical correlates of the operation of the fundamentals are being studied in these less "complex" animals. Their nervous systems are smaller and have fewer elements, and the fundamentals of learning appear to be the same in all metazoans.

If one is concerned with other dimensions of behavior, such as social behavior or animal communication, one reaches a similar conclusion. Most metazoan animals are social, and the fundamentals of simple sociality may be evident even in the analysis of microorganisms. We have known this for more than half a century (Allee, 1931). Almost all animals are known to communicate at least some information either to conspecifics or to other species in the form of sexual displays, warning calls, threat gestures, and so forth. One of the great discoveries about the ethology and comparative psychology of animal communication, the dance of the bees (von Frisch, 1950), was recognized by the award of a Nobel prize, and common principles derived from an evolutionary framework became the foundation of sociobiology (Wilson, 1975) and its offspring, modern evolutionary psychology (Buss, Haselton, Shackelford, Bleske, & Wakefield, 1998). One can catalog behavioral dimensions for sociality and for communication, but can one develop an evolutionary scheme in which a comparative analysis is helpful? It is hard to suggest a positive answer.

During the past decade a dominant effort among evolutionists has been to determine phylogenetic relationships, or cladistics (Patterson, 1987). This is performed by analyzing a traits-by-species data matrix: a listing of the presence or absence of traits in a variety of species, which may include quantitative values of traits when these are available. The relationships among the species with respect to the traits are then subjected to various computational schemes to determine a most likely phylogeny to relate the species. Any set of behavioral, morphological, and molecular traits can be used in the trait matrix, as can any sample of species. Behavioral traits that have been used for such analysis usually involve relatively small differences among species with respect to fixed action patterns (Brooks & MacLennan, 1991). I am not aware of any behavioral traits involving higher mental processes as having been used in this way. Macphail's conclusion about the difficulty of differentiating species with respect to intelligence appears to be correct enough to make such traits difficult to use for cladistics.

Although it involves no fundamental challenge to evolutionary analysis, the common understanding of the importance of environmental factors for human behavior can lead to skepticism about invoking a theory so reliant on genetics for understanding the mind. We know intuitively, for example, that aspects of language must be genetically determined because it is a universal human trait, and we recognize the validity of efforts to understand the evolution of the language sense. On the other hand, our intuition is equally strong and obviously valid about the importance of the environment because the actual language that one uses depends on where one was reared. Any theory of comparative psychology must be concerned with the multiple causal systems that control behavior in different species and should address the problem of how systems involving both genetic and environmental controls evolve. The approach that I adopt, which treats facts about brains as elements of a theory of mind, does not avoid the problem. It meets the challenge because both structure and function of a mature brain, at least in birds and mammals, is determined by an elaborate interaction between genetic systems and operations of the developing brain. The brain is a perfect organ to analyze as a structure shaped by the interaction between nature and nurture. An outstanding example is the way the visual system develops in mammals. The number of cortical neurons in this system are probably determined by genetic instructions, but their survival and the way they respond to stimulation are both determined to a major extent by the visual information that is received during critical periods of an animal's development (Hubel, 1988). The formal evolutionary issues relevant for comparative psychology are, to a significant extent, the same as these issues for comparative neurology, and the nature–nurture issue is not ignored if our models for psychology are neurological.

BRAIN EVOLUTION AS AN APPROACH TO BEHAVIORAL EVOLUTION

My work on brain evolution provides an alternative to a purely behavioral theoretical analysis of the evolution of mind. I undertook it without intending to develop a theory, but it works as theory by tying mind to a feature of the brain that is especially suitable for an evolutionary analysis. The connection is based on the idea that brain size can serve as a neural surrogate for behavioral variables, a kind of statistic for the analysis of mind as its parameter. It is a bit of a stretch, but the basic ideas are a century old, modernized only by the development and application of better morphometrics, modern neuroscience, and more sophisticated mathematical and statistical analytic methods. It does not lead to a comprehensive theory in the grand tradition, but it makes many intuitions about comparative behavior understandable, and it leads to inferences that provide useful insights into what evolved when mind evolved.

I was led to the approach by Karl Lashley (1949), who discussed "persistent problems in the evolution of mind" in his presidential address to the American Society of Naturalists:

> The only neurological character for which a correlation with behavioral capacity in different animals is supported by significant evidence is the total mass of tissue, or rather, the index of cephalization, measured by the ratio of brain to [the 2/3-power of] body weight, which seems to represent the amount of brain tissue in excess of that required for transmitting impulses to and from the integrative centers. (p. 33)

I tried very hard to find out why this simple brain trait worked as Lashley described it, and it was in that connection that I recognized that brain size functioned as a kind of statistic for other brain traits as parameters. Its extension to mind traits is the hypothetical leap that makes it a theory of mind, and that its evolutionary history is easy to analyze makes it a useful approach to the evolution of mind. The success of this effort was due to a few simple facts about the brain and its work, which could have been demonstrated early in the history of the neurosciences, though their significance is still often unrecognized (cf., e.g., Gazzaniga, 1995, who represents a consensus about how complex brains are, a consensus that refuses to recognize that some important things about brains are surprisingly simple.)

Brain size is a natural statistic that estimates the total neural information-processing capacity of an animal as well as other important quantitative aspects of structure and function in living brains (Jerison, 1991). This conclusion is based on mammalian data, but it can be extended to all vertebrates, because all vertebrates are, in a way, bundles of cells. The way their bodies work is a kind of summation of the work of their cells. Most living cells are approximately the same size (within an order of magnitude), and they are packed efficiently in organs. The size of cells is limited by physical constraints on the membranes that bound them, and efficient packing density is a normal optimizing effect in living systems. As a result, when an organ is assembled, its size appears to be determined by the same controlling mechanism or genetic program that puts together other organs of the body, as well as the whole animal. There is more to this story, of course, and it is well told by a number of authors (e.g., Aiello & Wheeler, 1995; Schmidt-Nielsen, 1984).

To illustrate more specifically how brain size works as a natural statistic, consider Fig. 11.1, which is a graph that combines data from Brodmann (1913), Elias and Schwartz (1971), Ridgway (1981), and Ridgway and Brownson (1984) on the relationship between total cortical surface and brain size. The 50 species are from the orders Artiodactyla, Carnivora, Cetacea, Edentata, Insectivora, Marsupialia, Monotremata, Perissodactyla, Primates, Proboscidea, and Rodentia. It is clear that if one knows the size of the brain in a mammal one can estimate the area of the brain's cortical surface, across species, with remarkable accuracy. That kind of estimation is what good statistics are supposed to provide.

The surface-volume relationship used to illustrate the efficiency of brain size as a statistic is worth a few more remarks. Its most important implication is for the relationship of brain size to neural information processing capacity. It also shows, perhaps surprisingly, that the human brain is less convoluted than expected for a mammal in our brain-size range.

The relationship to processing capacity follows from a kind of syllogism about how neural information is organized in the cerebral cortex. The unit of in-

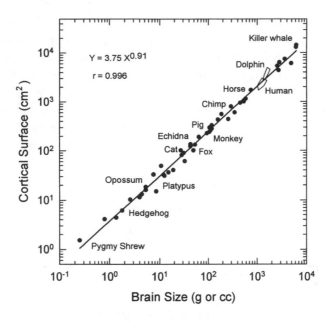

FIG. 11.1. The relationship between cortical surface and gross brain size in 50 species of mammals. Each point represents a species. In addition, two labeled minimum convex polygons indicate within-species variability in humans (N = 23) and dolphins (*Tursiops truncatus*, N = 13). Several species are labeled by name to indicate the diversity of the sample. *Note.* From "Evolution of Intelligence," by H. J. Jerison, 2000, in R. J. Sternberg (Ed.), *Handbook of Human Intelligences*. Copyright © Cambridge University Press. Reprinted with permission.

formation may be defined at various levels, such as the synapse or the neuron. At another level, the cortical column is identified as a higher order unit. The number of cortical columns in a mammal's brain should be directly related to the information processing capacity of that brain, and because cortical columns are fairly uniform in diameter (Szentagothai, 1978), their number must be proportional to the cortical surface area. Figure 11.1 shows that total brain size estimates the surface area, and hence it estimates the neural information processing capacity of a brain. Other data sets are available that lead to the same conclusion if we consider the single neuron or the synapse as the unit of information (Jerison, 1991, 2000, 2001).

One is led to the conclusion on convolutedness by the position of the small human data polygon in Fig. 11.1, which lies significantly below the regression line. That the slope of the regression line is 0.91 rather than 2/3 means that, between-species, mammalian brains differ in shape when they are different in size. (The log surface-volume regression slope for bodies of the same shape that differ in volume is always exactly 2/3.) The difference in shape, which takes the form of a change in surface area beyond that required for a change in volume, is obviously produced by the folding of the cortical surface into convolutions. The orderliness of the effect evidenced by the high correlation coefficient indicates that within the mammals essentially all (about 99%) of the variance between-species in cortical surface area (the equivalent of convolutedness) is accounted for by brain size. A species exactly on the regression line has the expected amount of folding, but a species, such as the human species, that lies below the regression line has less than the expected amount of folding. It is less convoluted than expected (see Jerison, 1991, for additional discussion).

STRUCTURE OF THE THEORY

My brain-based analysis of the evolution of mind, which is a theory for comparative psychology, begins with the assumption that behavioral information and neural information are equivalent, that they are related to one another quantitatively and in a simple way. Behavioral information has been defined in the cognitive sciences by formal information theory (Shannon & Weaver, 1949). It is a function of the number of yes–no changes of state in a channel through which it is transmitted. The behavioral definition works for many cognitive phenomena, as documented in the annual publications of the *Attention and Performance* symposia beginning three decades ago (Sanders, 1967). Neural information is similarly defined as digital information, the all-or-none action potentials that can be recorded with suitable equipment from single nerve cells. Although there is also important neural analog information (changes in electrical potential at the membrane and neurotransmitter functions, for example), the idea of all-or-none units of information transmission in the nervous system has been a useful organizing principle in neurophysiology for all of the twentieth century.

The point is that as theory one can consider the neural and behavioral flow of information as parallel events, and whatever one can learn about one of these can be applied to one's understanding of the other. To use statements about neural events as equivalents for behavioral events is analogous to the classical scientific method of representing physical events by mathematical operations. Physical theories take advantage of the simplifications provided by the logical structure of the mathematical operations. The nervous system is not as elegant a logical analog as a mathematical system, but it is more easily understood than behavioral or mental systems that operate in parallel with it. A set of statements about the nervous system may then stand in for the comparable statements about behavior or the mind. Brain size, the gross weight or volume of a whole brain, has been my usual neural measure, and my analysis has exploited the simplicity of that measure.

In my analysis of the evolution of the brain, I have used many facts about the relations among different animal species with respect to gross brain size, which I have treated as a statistic that estimates other facts about the brain (Jerison, 1973, 1991, 1997). The central assertion of the analysis is that brain size estimates total information-processing capacity, following the argument presented in the previous section in which this assertion was explained for neural information. It can then be invoked as a theoretical statement for behavioral information. It implies a definition of *intelligence* as follows:

> Definition: Intelligence is the behavioral consequence of the total neural-information processing capacity in representative adults of a species, adjusted for the capacity to control routine bodily functions.

With relatively few assumptions, which are easy to justify, the definition leads to an operational definition of intelligence as a measurable trait that evolved in animals. It is, first of all, a species trait, measured as an average value for adult animals. The data in Fig. 11.1 enable us to measure total processing capacity by gross brain size. The adjustment for routine bodily functions required by the definition is determined from the regression of log brain size on log body size and is called a brain-body *allometric* function. Intelligence in a species is then the residual from the regression. Because the data are logarithmic, the residual is the quotient of measured brain weight divided by the expected brain weight as determined by the regression. That residual is called *encephalization*, and because it is a quotient, it is an encephalization quotient, or *EQ*. There are, as you can imagine, many refined statements about how to do the regression analysis and which species must be sampled. These are also criticisms of the use of so simple a method, but the basic definition remains intact, given agreements about the refinements. The most valid criticism, with which I strongly agree, is of the oversimplifications, which ignore important details about the organization of brains. (For more on the statistical and mathematical methods, see Harvey & Pagel, 1991, and for more on the application to brain evolution see Jerison, 1991, and Martin, 1990.)

The oversimplification is, of course, in the suggestion of the discredited "mass action" as a model for brain function. We have learned too well the lessons of the intricate organization of localized system within the brain to accept mass action as a correct model. However, that it works, as I show, as a model for the brain's evolution and the evolution of mind implies a certain fundamental truth about mass action, which is worth examining. It can be justified partly as a way to acknowledge that the major neural control systems involved in higher mental processes are spread throughout many parts of the brain (Goldman-Rakic, 1988). But mass action as related to encephalization has a more interesting implication for comparative psychology. At a gross level, we know that brains reach their adult size in different species for different reasons. A given level of encephalization is an outcome of convergent evolution, reached by different evolutionary paths. Bats and mice have brains of similar size, yet the bat's neocortex is largely specialized for audition (Grinnell, 1995), whereas a mouse's is a normal mammalian brain with all of the sensory and motor areas represented approximately correctly (Braitenberg & Schüz, 1998). Procyonids provide another example of comparable encephalization that reflects different specializations. The coati mundi's sensorimotor cortex has an expanded snout region reflecting the role of its rhinarium in exploring its environment, whereas the raccoon's has comparably expanded representation of its forepaws because of its role as a handler of fish and other objects in a primatelike way (Johnson, 1990; Welker, 1990).

I have called such specialized expansion the principle of *proper mass*, that the amount of neural tissue encumbered by a process is related to the importance of the process in the life of an animal. However, since encephalization is a kind of summing across such specializations, if we consider encephalization as a measure of animal intelligence, we accept the important idea that this intelligence is a plural phenomenon, that there are different kinds of intelligences that have evolved in different species. The definition, therefore, requires that we accept a limitation on the possibility of developing a unitary comparative psychology. I believe that the limitation is unavoidable as a fact of evolution, and I believe it correct to acknowledge it in a theory of comparative psychology.

If we accept the definition, its most powerful applications may be to inferences from fossil data as direct evidence on the evolution of mind. One can measure brain size in fossil birds and mammals and estimate body size in the same species. This has been done in many vertebrate species (Edinger, 1975; Hopson 1979; Jerison, 1973; Radinsky, 1978). It has been an especially notable approach to analyzing the fossil evidence in the human lineage (Falk, 1992; Conroy et al., 1998).

A "fossil brain" in a mammal or bird is actually a cast molded by the cranial cavity, and in most species these are shaped like freshly dissected brains with dura intact, and their size is about the same as that of a brain. Body size is estimated from skeletal remains and is probably no less adequate than measurements on a living animal. In any case, one can include data on fossils in the analysis of encephalization, which is important for one's ability to develop evolutionary scenarios to explain the changes that can be identified.

INFERENCE ABOUT THE EVOLUTION OF MIND

I summarize all presently available vertebrate brain-body data in Fig. 11.2. The data are from over 2,000 species. In many graphs, the picture appears simpler because one graphs only groups relevant to one's theme, and these groups may be nonoverlapping. In viewing the comprehensive graph of Fig. 11.2, one should keep in mind that the total number of known vertebrate species is close to 50,000. There are perhaps 25,000 bony fish (Osteichthyes) species, more than 9,000 birds (Aves), nearly 5,000 mammals (Mammalia), more than 6,000 reptiles (Reptilia), more than 4,000 amphibians (Amphibia), about 700 species of cartilaginous fish (Chondrichthyes), comprising the sharks, rays, and skates, and about 70 species of jawless fish (Agnatha), the lampreys and hagfish. The sample in Fig. 11.2 is fairly representative except that there are, perhaps understandably because this is an essay by a mammal for other mammals, mammalocentric—too many mammal species compared with the others. I have also added electric fish, separately from other bony fish, as an additional complication, although its simplicities should be evident.

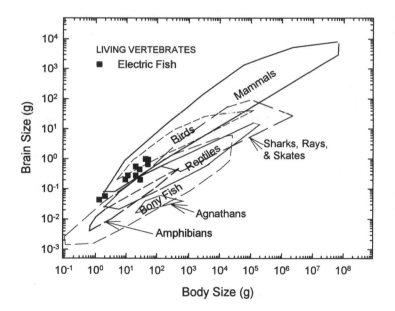

FIG. 11.2.   Brain-body relations in 2,018 living vertebrate species enclosed in minimum convex polygons. The samples are 647 mammals; 180 birds; 1,027 bony fish; 41 amphibians; 59 reptiles; 59 cartilaginous fish (sharks, rays, and skates); and 5 agnathans, or jawless fish. Electric fish are Mormyriformes. (Unpublished data courtesy of Professor Andy Bass of Cornell University. Most of the other bony fish data are unpublished except as in this graph, data courtesy of Professor Roland Bauchot of the University of Paris VII.) Note that birds and mammals overlap one another as higher vertebrates, and reptiles amphibians and fish overlap one another as lower vertebrates. Electric fish, however, are in the higher vertebrate range of encephalization, and chondrichthyans (sharks, rays, and skates) overlap the lower and higher vertebrate ranges.

There are many unusual inferences about animal mind and its evolution that can be developed from this simple approach. One unusual inference is on present relationships among living vertebrates. A first general inference: Mammals and birds are similar in intelligence as defined here; the relatively small number of species of sharks and their relatives also include many species in the mammalian range of encephalization, and comparative psychologists might well consider that a challenge for their perspective. From the fossil record, the first evolutionary experiment with intelligence was in a shark species that lived over 250 million years ago. (This fossil shark is not identified as a point in Fig. 11.2.) We are no longer surprised by the overlapping distributions of mammals and birds, in view of the performance of Pepperberg's (1994) gray parrot and the way pigeons, rats, and people function in Skinner boxes (Skinner, 1957).

The graph of the present situation in living vertebrates in Fig. 11.2 is based on all presently available data. The data of each group are represented by convex polygons drawn to contain all of the individual data. This procedure is illustrated in Fig. 11.3, below, for the living reptile polygon. To the extent that the polygons are distinct, one distinguishes the groups from one another, and from Fig. 11.2 we can see the extent to which one is justified in discussing lower versus higher vertebrates. The sharks and electric fish confound the picture, but the distinction is generally easy to maintain.

We should be impressed by the data on cartilaginous fish. One of the benefits of my approach is that it points one to comparisons that might not otherwise be considered. One does not know how to measure or define animal intelligence behaviorally, but from their encephalization, it is clear that sharks and their relatives deserve much closer scrutiny by comparative psychologists than they have received. There are additional comparisons that should be made. The approach would single out parrots as birds to study because they are among the most encephalized of living birds, justifying Pepperberg's effort. The corvids form the only other living avian group that is in their range, and the common crow is surely worth a close look. Among the cartilaginous fish, the most encephalized appears to be the manta ray (*Manta birostris*), and we know almost nothing about the normal behavior of this gentle giant, but other shark species are also unusually encephalized (Northcutt, 1989). My approach does not attempt to explain the details of the behavior of a species, but it is clearly useful in helping us choose the species to study. In evaluating behaviors in more detail, my approach raises issues about the amount of information-processing capacity that they require.

Of the other living species, the electric fish (Mormyriformes) are also unusual in relative brain size. There is a good clue to the source of their encephalization from comparative neuroanatomy. The electric organs, used by different species of these fish in sensing a variety of things, such as conspecifics, the flow

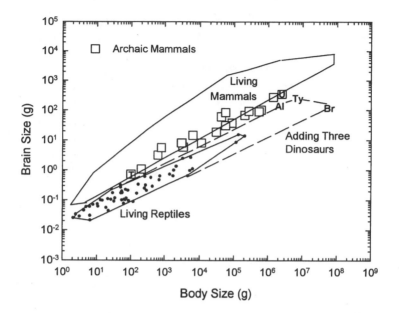

FIG. 11.3. Brain-body relations in mammals and reptiles, each class enclosed in a minimum convex polygon. Labeled archaic mammals are the Mesozoic *Triconodon mordax* (T) and the early Cenozoic *Uintatherium anceps* (U). Labeled dinosaurs are Allosaurus (Al), *Tyrannosaurus* (Ty), and *Brachiosaurus* (Br). Data points on living reptiles illustrate the construction of a minimum convex polygon of minimum area to contain all the points within a polygon with no interior angles greater than 180 degrees. Adding the dinosaurs merely extended the reptilian polygon to be more like that of mammals, when the body size range was extended.

of water, and so forth, project to an enlarged cerebellum, which could be mistaken for cerebrum (Butler & Hodos, 1996). It is a challenge to ethologists and comparative psychologists to measure and analyze the utility of the neural extra processing performed by that system. The analogy might be to the enlarged inferior colliculi in bats specialized for echolocation because these structures are especially implicated in auditory analysis. We could, in principle, relate their size to the amount of information they handle. The forebrain in these bats is not unusually enlarged, but it is specialized for auditory analysis with enlarged auditory projection areas compared with other sensory areas (Grinnell, 1995).

A second and unusual inference from such data can be made by adding evidence from fossils, as shown in Fig. 11.3: Dinosaurs did not become extinct because of their stupidity. Their intelligence, defined by their encephalization, was appropriate for reptiles of their body size, and there were some species of dinosaurs that were relatively large brained, perhaps in the size range of living birds (Jerison,

2000, 2001; Hopson, 1979). This inference is also interesting in the light of recent conclusions about the relationship of dinosaurs to reptiles and birds.

Most paleontologists are convinced from their study of the fossil record that birds should be treated as a surviving group of dinosaurs, specialized by feathers and flight and relatively small body size for unusual niches, but this is not well supported by the evidence of encephalization. Most dinosaur species, as I previously mentioned, were in the reptilian range, and the few that were in the avian range (ornithomimids, or ostrich-dinosaurs) are known from less than 100 million years ago, much later in history than the earliest birds. I illustrate fossil data on encephalization in Fig. 11.3, which is also relevant to mammalian encephalization, but I do not indicate information on fossil birds. Only a few are known, and all specimens lie within the polygon of living birds in Fig. 11.2. They lie near the lower edge of the polygon but are above the reptile polygon. We know nothing about encephalization in the small dinosaurs most closely related to birds, such as Compsognathus (Ostrom, 1976), a fossil that was a possible contemporary of the earliest bird, and we need the information to clarify the relationships with respect to brain evolution. These were events of more than 150 million years ago, the age of the earliest bird, Archaeopteryx, which was as encephalized as the smallest brained of living birds, pigeons and gallinaceous birds.

There had to be a transition between a reptilian and avian grade of encephalization, and one needs a fossil record of that period between 150 and 200 million years ago when the transition probably occurred. Within the birds, the enlargement of forebrain characterizing all living birds, the Wulst, which is probably homologous to mammalian primary visual cortex, was not present in Archaeopteryx, although it appears in birds known from the late Cretaceous, approximately 75 million years ago. Brain enlargement that evolved when Wulst evolved presumably had behavioral significance, related to this increase in information processing capacity, but we have no idea what advantages accrued. We may have a sense of their effect by examining the reptile-mammal transition about which there is somewhat more information.

The transition periods are especially interesting for suggesting the specialized neurobehavioral adaptations that might have been met by the evolution of new forms. I tried to analyze the available information about the beginnings of encephalization in mammals compared with their immediate ancestors among reptiles, the mammal-like reptiles (Therapsida). It was possible to develop a scenario that could explain the origins of major mammalian neural, and perhaps behavioral, adaptations, and I review that scenario in a later section. From an evolutionist's perspective, the scenario has features that can be identified in a comparable scenario explaining the evolution of language in the earliest human ancestors, which I also present. First, a few more inferences and a general conclusion about the evolution of behavior and mind as it can be inferred from the analysis of encephalization.

A third inference from the analysis of gross data, evident in Fig. 11.4 and based on comparative neuroanatomy, is genuinely surprising. Contrary to recently published claims (Deacon, 1997), the human species does not have unusually enlarged prefrontal neocortex. Although it is large, human prefrontal neocortex is exactly as large as expected in a brain as enlarged (encephalized) as the human brain. Since behavioral functions of prefrontal neocortex are now well understood (Krasnegor, Lyon, & Goldman-Rakic, 1997), the behavioral implications of this result are especially interesting. Despite the small size of the sample, the graph in Fig. 11.4, based on Uylings and Van Eden (1990), is impressive because the relationship reflected in the almost perfect correlation is so strong. The interpretation is straightforward. If a mammalian brain evolves to human size, it must have prefrontal neocortex that is the size of human prefrontal neocortex because of the way prefrontal cortex is connected to the rest of the brain. There is a kind of symmetry, like the fact that the walls of one side of a rectangular building have to be as

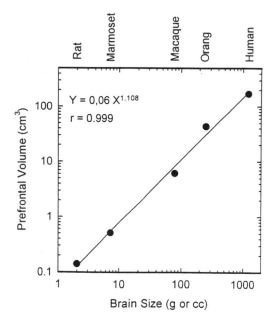

FIG. 11.4. Volume of prefrontal neocortex as a function of brain size. *Note.* Data adapted from "Qualitative and quantitative comparison of the preferred cortex in rat and in primates, including humans," by H. B. M. Uylings and C. G. Van Eden, 1990.

tall as the walls of the other side. The size of prefrontal neocortex reflects the way the brain works in the control of information. If the information is distributed throughout many regions (Goldman-Rakic, 1988), the size of each region must be determined by how extensively it is connected with other regions. Prefrontal neocortex is often described as an executive organ for brain functions: It controls the functions of many other parts of the brain. The size of this controller system has to be related to the size of the systems that it controls. Because of its extensive network of controls to other parts of the brain, enlargement almost anywhere in the brain for any reason would be reflected in an appropriate corresponding enlargement of prefrontal cortex. The human brain is, in fact, a normal primate brain in all respects except gross size. Given its gross size, however, the sizes of its parts must be appropriately enlarged and this includes the human prefrontal neocortex. The brain hangs together and works as a unified system in which the sizes of the parts are appropriate to one another and to the size of the whole brain (Jerison, 1997).

From the quantitative analysis of fossil evidence there are other important inferences, some of which have been common knowledge for many years but unsupported by actual evidence. For example, it is usually assumed that neocortex expanded during mammalian evolution, but only when I analyzed the data quantitatively was I able to support that assumption. I was able to show that the conventional wisdom was correct by analyzing fossil endocranial casts. In mammalian endocasts, neocortex can be identified as cortex dorsal to the rhinal fissure, and this fissure is often recognizable in an endocast. Until I performed the quantitative analysis, the situation was in doubt, and very experienced and competent students of this kind of fossil evidence had rejected the idea that such changes had been demonstrated (Radinsky, 1978). The measurements that I could make were primitive, based on two-dimensional lateral views of a large sample of endocasts, but their adequacy for the problem was supported by the fact that in this same sample of species the olfactory bulbs did not change in relative size (Jerison, 1990). The relative size of the neocortical area in two-dimensional projection clearly was greater in later progressive species than in earlier more primitive species during the 60 million years of mammalian evolution that I was able to examine. I exploited this particular result when I developed a scenario for the evolution of human language, which I present later in this chapter.

EVOLUTIONARY EVENTS

The geological and fossil records are now quite well-known, and one can present reasonably definite accounts of significant times of change in vertebrate evolution during the past 500 million years. The eras are the Paleozoic (550 to 250 million years ago), the Mesozoic (250 to 65 million years ago), and the Cenozoic (65 million years ago to the present). These are subdivided into periods (e.g., Jurassic, Tertiary) and epochs (e.g., Eocene, Pliocene), which I will date if I mention specific events. If the words are unfamiliar, one can always go to a dictionary.

The earliest vertebrates were jawless fish of about 450 million years ago, and the first land vertebrates were amphibians, which appeared between 350 to 400 million years ago. Reptiles appeared about 50 million years later. Because fossil endocasts are available for analysis, and because brains evolved as appropriately engineered organs for their work of controlling the body, one can correlate the evolution of the brain with other events in the history of life. Although there were important changes in the organization of the brain during the Paleozoic era, there is no evidence of measurable encephalization, except in the fossil shark (about 300 million years old) mentioned earlier. Most species were lower vertebrates, comparable to their relatives that are alive today. Intelligence as I have defined it did not change significantly during the entire evolutionary history of the lower vertebrates (Jerison, 1973). However, the variety of behaviors in living species of lower vertebrates, which are also at this grade of encephalization, illustrates the behavioral diversity that can be supported by an unexpanded nervous system. ("Lower" and "higher" can properly refer to status with respect to encaphalization, which would label only birds and mammals as unambiguously higher vertebrates.)

The earliest birds appeared in the late Jurassic period, about 150 million years ago evolving from dinosaurian roots, and the earliest mammals in the late Triassic period, about 225 million years ago evolving from the rather different therapsid (mammal-like) reptiles. Birds and mammals were encephalized relative to their closest relatives among the reptiles, with brains 2 to 4 times the size of reptiles of comparable body size.

There were major environmental changes at transition times during this history. The most extensive occurred at the end of the Paleozoic era, at the transition from the Permian to the Triassic period, about 250 million years ago. The most popularly recognized extinction, which may have resulted in the final extinction of dinosaurs, occurred about 65 million years ago and was probably caused by a comet or asteroid striking a region near the Yucatan peninsula of Mexico. The latter is called the K-T event (from the German, *Kreidezeit-Tertiärzeit*) that ended the Cretaceous period of the Mesozoic era and initiated the Tertiary period of the Cenozoic era. Less dramatic extinctions occurred at other transition times. An important one is known to have occurred about 35 million years ago, at the transition from the Eocene to Oligocene epochs of the Cenozoic era, during the adaptive radiation of progressive mammal species, which I discuss later in this chapter.

Vertebrate tetrapod encephalization began in the earliest mammalian species, which are known from about 225 million year ago. Endocasts have not yet been prepared from those fossils, but from the appearance of the skull one recognizes expansion of the cranial cavity appropriate to the grade of encephalization of the least encephalized of living mammals. The oldest known mammalian endocast is about 150 million years old, from the species *Triconodon mordax*, a member of a group unrelated to any living mammal, but it is as encephalized as living hedgehogs and opossums. The earliest placental mammals probably appeared about 100 million years ago, and their endocasts are known from at least 75 million years ago (Jerison, 1990, 2000; Kielan-Jaworowska, 1986). All Mesozoic mammals were small, generally the size of mice or rats, and the largest was the size of a house cat. They were all encephalized to about the same extent, 2 to 4 times that of reptiles. This level of encephalization was stable for all of the Mesozoic and for the first 10 million years of the Cenozoic, an interval of about 170 million years, illustrating the conservatism of brain evolution.

For completeness, I outline the evidence on major mammalian encephalization during the Tertiary period of the Cenozoic era. There is insufficient space to discuss this record in detail or to suggest scenarios to explain it. That was a major goal of my book on the subject, which I published a quarter of a century ago (Jerison, 1973). Mesozoic and early Cenozoic mammals were at a kind of steady state of the evolution of encephalization with brains averaging about one third the size of average living species. The grade persists today among all insectivores and many marsupials and is best represented by the Virginia opossum (*Didelphis marsupialis*).

I graphed most of the available data on that grade of evolution in Fig. 11.3. I also show some data on dinosaurs and illustrate with the data on living reptiles the way such data are analyzed nonparametrically with convex polygons. The long period of stability in encephalization suggests that the mammals had discovered rather stable niches, and that after the end of the Mesozoic, following the great extinction of larger land animals such as dinosaurs, they radiated into new niches with relatively little requirement for enhanced capacities at processing information.

Primates are among the most ancient of living orders of mammals, with suggestions that they may have appeared during the Cretaceous period at the end of the Mesozoic, as many as 70 million years ago. They are relatively common fossils of the Eocene epoch (extending between 55 to 35 million years ago). Primates appear always to have been more encephalized than their contemporaries, and this was true of the many lemurlike species that had appeared during the Eocene. Their contemporaries averaged *EQ* of approximately 0.3 or 0.4, whereas the Eocene primates ranged between 0.5 and 0.8 on this measure of encephalization. Primate brains of the time also had distinctly modern shapes, surprisingly similar to those of living lemurs. However, all of the living orders of mammals had appeared by that time, at least 35 million years ago, and some advance in encephalization can be recognized in these species. During the late Eocene there is evidence of the earliest of the anthropoid primates, but encephalization in these animals was still in the range of their lemuroid contemporaries, about $EQ = 0.5$.

There was increasing diversification in mammalian adaptation during the Eocene epoch, and although they had not reached a primate grade, other progressive orders of mammals had appeared and their species were somewhat more encephalized than the archaic orders, which is evident even on casual inspection of their endocasts (Jerison, 1990; Radinsky, 1978). (The descriptions *archaic* and *progressive* refer merely to whether an order has become extinct.) The brain evolved conservatively, and the pattern of change is best described as punctuated equilibria for most vertebrate lineages, with long periods of stasis in relative brain size. The rapid recent evolution of encephalization in the human lineage, beginning in the Pliocene epoch about 4 million years ago, was unusual.

The transition from the Eocene to the Oligocene epoch 35 million years ago signaled a significant effect on the appearance of the mammalian brain as well as on its relative size. Geologically the time is known as the Grand Coupure, a period of significant mountain building and related activity. Perhaps this explains the enlarged and more modern-looking brains represented as fossil endocasts in many species. But the convolutions are identifiably arranged as in modern species, and the degree of encephalization appeared to reach the level of the living descendant species. The record is quite good for the orders Carnivora, Artiodactyla, and Perissodactyla, the living carnivores and ungulates. Major gyri and sulci are clearly identifiable, and labeling systems used for living brains are easy to apply to the fossils. Encephalization had approached or reached the level of average living mammals, defined as $EQ = 1.0$. There is only one well-studied primate species of that age, the 30 million year old *Rooneyia*, a tarsier-like form that had lived in Texas. Its skull and brain are both larger than but remarkably like that of living species, and its encephalization has been determined as at least $EQ = 1.5$. By the transition from the Oligocene to the Miocene epoch (about 20 million years ago), the level of encephalization in mammals was comparable to that of their living descendants, excepting only the major developments in the human lineage, which can be traced to the beginning of the Pliocene, with evidence on the brain available beginning almost 4 million years ago. I review that record briefly later in this chapter as part of a speculation on the evolution of language.

SELECTION FOR ENCEPHALIZATION:
REPTILES INTO MAMMALS

Brain tissue is metabolically among the most expensive of bodily tissues (Aiello & Wheeler, 1995). Evolution is often thought of as an optimizing process in which costs are balanced by benefits, and the question follows: What benefits were associated with the enlargement of the brain in these mammals to make its energetic cost worthwhile? The answer has to be speculative, of course, because we were not on the scene when the critical events occurred. The issue is to present a reasonable scenario. With a few calculations on living brains, I develop such a scenario on the basis of how reptiles and mammals presently use information about the environment to guide their movements. I follow the uniformitarian hypothesis, a version of parsimony that states that the laws of nature in the past were the same as in the present (Simpson, 1970).

During much of the Paleozoic era, the synapsids and therapsids, the mammal-like reptiles, were the dominant land vertebrates. Archosaurians, or "ruling reptiles" including dinosaurs, first appeared at the end of that era. The mammal-like reptiles became extinct at about the middle of the Mesozoic era, and the archosaurians had become extremely diversified by that time and throughout that era. The behavioral scenario to describe the changing environments tracked by natural selection begins by recognizing that most Paleozoic reptiles were diurnal and relied primarily on visual information to guide their movements. I suggest that the therapsids became extinct when the ruling reptiles displaced them in diurnal niches and that aberrant nocturnal "therapsids" which we know retrospectively as mammals, survived. The earliest mammals had evolved adaptations for nocturnal niches in which they did not face competition or predation from archosaurians.

Life in nocturnal niches depends on sensory modalities other than vision. In this discussion, I am concerned only with sensory-perceptual adaptations, although other adaptations, such as endothermy and the evolution of small body size, are also obviously important. For my scenario, I calculate the amount of neural machinery required for nonvisual senses to be computationally equivalent to the visual system. For convenience, I work with auditory information, as if the earliest mammals were batlike in relying on echolocation. We know that living bats construct a three-dimensional world from such auditory information and that their world is comparable to our visual world (Grinnell, 1995). Visual and auditory senses for distance information might both be spatial senses, but the neural machinery for vision and audition is packaged in different ways.

The neural control of visual information in amphibians and reptiles involves significant amounts of information processing that occurs in the neural retina of the eye (Lettvin, Maturana, McCulloch, & Pitts, 1959). Additional processing is performed at subcortical neural centers, such as the superior colliculi, and although some analysis may take place in their forebrains, these species have no cerebral cortex. Processing at the level of the colliculi appears understandable in the framework of signal detection theory as distinguishing neural signals from neural noise (Ewert, 1974; Roth, 1987).

From data on living species, one can estimate that there were several hundred thousand retinal ganglion cells in each eye of the reptilian forbears of the mammals. There may have been several million nerve cells in other layers of the neural retina (cf., Polyak, 1957; Roth, 1987) and comparably large numbers of photoreceptors. The computational problem is to determine the effect on the organization of the brain if one were to replace the reptilian diurnal, neural retinal system with other neural sensory systems. This had to be accomplished by early mammals if their movements after dark were to be coordinated with information about the environment.

If in the earliest mammals the auditory system were to evolve as a primary system for distance information, the sensory information and the location of the neural control networks would be quite different from that in the visual system. In living reptiles there are only between 50 and 1,000 sense cells (hair cells) in each cochlea, indicating that hearing has a relatively minor role in their lives (Wever, 1978). However, even in mammals such as bats, where we know that the auditory system is critically important, there are only about 35,000 sense cells (hair cells) in each cochlea. This number, so much smaller than the number of photoreceptors, is typical for all living mammals.

The neural analysis by any sensory system converts sensory data into information about the external environment, and the initial information received by the sense cells has to be analyzed by neural networks elsewhere in the system. This analysis itself could be similar in auditory and visual systems. We know how that analysis can take place in the neural control in Ewert's toads, a signal detection analysis of neural data in the colliculi that enables them to know how to catch a fly. The amount of analysis might be similar for an equivalent analysis with the auditory system, for example, in the way echolocating bats catch moths (Grinnell, 1995). This is more detail than we need to know about how the system might function, however. Our problems are only how large the system must be and where it would be packed.

These are packaging problems. It may take as many as 5 million neurons in each retina of a reptile, or 10 million neurons in all, to process information about the environment useful for the control of movement. We can assume (as a first approximation, of course) that this is the number of neurons that would be required to do the same job with auditory and other nonvisual modalities. In no nonvisual system is there a peripheral structure comparable to the neural retina as a place to pack the neurons of the network. For example, in the peripheral auditory apparatus there is space beneath the basilar membrane of the cochlea for the auditory bipolar cells but no more than the same number of bipolars as hair cells can be stored there.

The argument also follows, with somewhat more detail, from the hierarchical structure of the networks. Retinal photoreceptors in reptiles communicate directly with as many as one million first order retinal bipolar neurons, which then communicate with even more association neurons in the retina, and it is these that communicate with the ganglion cells, which are the cell bodies of the optic nerve. The retinal neurons for processing visual information are, thus, second, third, or fourth order neurons in a synaptic chain. The comparable hierarchy in the auditory system in all living vertebrates has a maximum of 70,000 first order bipolar neurons peripheral to the brain in the spiral ganglion. The second, third, and fourth order auditory neurons are all in the brain, proper. They are in the medulla, midbrain, and thalamus in lower vertebrates, and in mammals there is an additional level of neural processing in the neocortex. If the early mammals were to do with hearing (and other modalities) what their reptilian ancestors did with vision, they had to evolve networks to do the equivalent processing, presumably with a similar hierarchical structure. As we have seen, something of the order of 10 million neurons are in the retinal neural networks, and for the other modalities to do the job, this is the number that would have to be packed in the brain.

This is the same as the total number of cortical neurons in the half-gram mouse brain (Braitenberg & Schüz, 1998). If we were to provide neural machinery for the information processing performed in the neural retina of a reptile with the processing done by nonvisual neural machinery in the brain proper, we would have to add the equivalent of a mouse brain to the premammalian reptile brain. We have to add about 0.5 g of brain.

With these numbers, we can turn to quantitative data on fossils (Jerison, 1973). To model the reptilian ancestors of mammals, I take the unusually small (for early reptiles) lower Triassic (about 250 million years ago) therapsid, *Thrinaxodon*, which weighed about 500 g and had an 0.4 g brain. As the early mammal, I take the upper Jurassic (about 150 million years ago) *Triconodon*, which may have been a bit large for a mammal of the time. It weighed about 100 g and had an 0.7 g brain. Evolving from a *Thrinaxodon*-sized therapsid to a *Triconodon*-sized mammal required a half order of magnitude reduction in body size and an appropriately adjusted brain size. From a regression analysis of the data of Fig. 11.3, I can estimate the expected brain size in a 100 g reptile as 0.15 g. To transform the therapsid into *Triconodon*, we add the difference between 0.7 g and 0.15 g, or 0.55 grams of brain, a four or fivefold increase in brain size. The transformation added a mouse-sized brain, as it were, which is the right amount according to our calculations.

MAMMALIAN INTELLIGENCE

We now have a complete answer. The amount of encephalization that occurred when the earliest mammals evolved can be explained as a solution of a packaging problem of where to put the extra processing machinery for the sensory systems (10 million neurons) that had to replace or supplement vision. From comparative neuroanatomy, we infer that the extra machinery was packed into a new neural forebrain structure that evolved in mammals, the cerebral cortex. However, sometimes even a simple solution has complications, and one effect of this kind of packaging may be the major clue to the relationship of encephalization to intelligence.

Several different nonvisual systems would have contributed information for this scenario, in particular the auditory, olfactory, and tactile systems. In addition, the visual system could continue to provide information about the external environment for a nocturnal species, provided that it evolved to be sensitive to weak visual stimuli that are available in the evening or at night. The rod system of the retina, basically a mammalian specialization, is appropriate for these responses. Thus, there are four different neural systems to provide information about the external environment, and in living mammals they are packed into different regions in the cortex.

The complication for the operation of these systems occurs because the information from the different component systems would refer to a common set of events in the external environment. The neural response to the information from each modality would presumably be similar to that recorded from the superior colliculi of Ewert's (1974) toads. These consist of bursts of firing of nerve cells in a network, and there would be no way to identify the bursts as having originated in a common environmental event. The analysis of the information from several sensory systems would have to be integrated in some way, and more neural machinery would be required to effect the integration.

The integration presumably took the form of identifying common features in the information from each modality, such as a description of the source as an object in an external world. There would also have to be codes with regard to where the object was and when the object was sensed. In short, the integration would be by translating the neural patterns into a common code to represent events in the external world as objects placed in space and time. From a computational perspective, the brain's problem is a pattern-recognition problem rather than a simple signal-detection problem. In more classical terms, one might consider the problem as the creation of perceptual worlds or Umwelten (von Uexküll, 1934/1957), and this seems a good characterization of the work of a mammalian brain, in particular of the cerebral cortex. In effect the brain's work is to create a real world, or in less dramatic terms, to provide knowledge about the real world. This is very different from a brain as a reflex machine implied by Ewert's toads.

If I were to go beyond my definition presented earlier in this chapter, it would be to restrict intelligent processing to pattern recognition. I would attempt to distinguish this kind of integrative activity from the brain's work as a reflex machine, although one assumes that both integrative and reflex activities occur in all mammalian brains. The critical added processing is the creation of a real world by the brain, as it were, or in less dramatic terms, the processing supports the integrative activity that enables an animal to know the real world. This seems a fundamental feature of intelligence in any animal. One reason to resist going beyond the working definition, however, is the difficulty one would face in attempting an operational bottom-up approach within such a definition. At a fundamental level, one would have to specify purely neural distinctions between pattern recognition and signal detection. In direct analysis of neural activity it is impossible to make such a distinction. The computer analogy is to attempt to distinguish, in a blind test, between small samples of machine code for a pattern-recognition program from samples of code during a signal-detection program and to identify the programs. It is presumably possible, but it would be a formidable problem in cryptanalysis.

BRAIN AND PERCEPTION

Because I tied the evolution of intelligence to the evolution of encephalization, and because I analyze the major advance in encephalization that occurred when the mammals evolved as having involved a shift in perceptual modalities, I must comment on the brain's role in perception. It is conventional in neuropsychology to draw maps of the brain indicating localized sensory and motor areas, and in older maps one drew silent areas representing association cortex. That view has been recognized for several decades as unsustainable (Diamond, 1979). Association functions that relate the activities of sensory and motor systems to one another are intercalated among the sensory and motor areas, and those areas extend over almost the entire neocortex (Jones & Powell, 1970). There are no silent areas. Furthermore, we recognize that sensory analysis at the level of the neocortex usually involves multiple projections of superficially similar information. There are many duplicate maps of the body on the brain, including at least a dozen separate projections in the primate brain from different parts of the visual field (Zeki, 1993). If one had to describe neocortical functions in very few words it would be that they control perceptual and voluntary motor performance, and neocortex evolved in response to requirements to enhance such performance. The enhancement added the cognitive dimension.

Images of mind (Posner, 1994), determined by metabolic activity in the brain and recorded as PET and functional MRI scans of the living brain, show that foci of activity correlated with behavior and experience are spread throughout many parts of the brain. Although such images demonstrate localized activation by specialized human mental activities, the local regions are very extensive. There are about 15 million neurons under a square centimeter of cortex (Rockel, Hiorns, & Powell, 1980), and a typical human brain scan localizes activity in at least several square centimeters of cortex. Thus, a localization involves a very wide area and very large amounts of processing capacity. One should note, too, the extent to which there are multiple activation patterns, which suggest interaction among parts of the brain. There are usually several regions of maximum activity rather than a single focal region responsive to a mental activity. The extent to which functions are localized is partly a function of the way the measurements are performed. Localized functions are measurable as activity in single nerve cells, but these cells are presumably parts of extensive networks of neurons. All or almost all of these networks process information from the external environment. Most significantly, these networks, which can be characterized as supporting perceptual and cognitive processing, can account for essentially all of the cortical surface.

In the quantitative example of mammalian encephalization as the solution to a packaging problem, I explained the increase in brain size as related entirely to perceptual and cognitive processing. The additional tissue was assumed to be doing sensory analysis of the kind done in the neural retina of frogs (Lettvin, Maturana, McCulloch, & Pitts, 1959) and that it was also integrating that analysis as knowledge of a real world. It is interesting that when one analyzes the work of the brain in living monkeys and humans, one also correlates neural activation with handling information from the external world. We describe the behavioral aspects of the work as attending and responding to images, sounds, words, and ideas (Posner, 1994). Returning to the computer analogy, the point can be made that good pattern recognition is the most demanding work that computers can do and requires the most processing capacity. One can reach a similar conclusion about brains. To generate knowledge of the external world, to perceive that world and understand its structure and function, is the brain's most demanding work and is the basic reason for the brain's enlargement. I have tried to show how this was true early in mammalian evolution, and I believe that it remains true in living mammals, including humans.

HOMINID ENCEPHALIZATION 1: THE BEGINNINGS OF LANGUAGE

The evolution of a prehominid anthropoid into a hominid species occurred early in the Pliocene epoch, perhaps 4 or 5 million years ago. Present evidence is that humans share a prehominid ancestor with living chimpanzees. This provides some clues about our mental origins because we know a fair amount about the mental capacities of chimpanzees (Kummer & Goodall, 1985; Passingham, 1982; Premack & Woodruff, 1978). We know, for example, that we share with chimpanzees the conservation of mass as discussed by Piaget (Premack & Kennell, 1978); the ability to make, use, and train others to use primitive tools (Boesch & Boesch, 1983); and educability in the use of languagelike symbols (Savage-Rumbaugh et al., 1993). We also share the ability to learn to distinguish ourselves from others on the basis of fairly abstract information, such as that provided by a reflection in a mirror (Gallup, 1979), which indicates that, like us, chimpanzees have a knowledge of self.

These shared behavioral traits were presumably in the repertoire of our common ancestor, which means that we evolved from a species that had the mental capacities required by those traits. Some, but not all, of these capacities are shared with the other two great ape genera, the orangs and gorillas, as well as with chimpanzees, but no one has yet demonstrated that any other anthropoid primates (i.e., monkeys and gibbons), possess them. The evidence is not all in on just how much is shared, nor does everyone agree on how to interpret the behavioral data as evidence of cognitive capacities, but we and the great apes appear to be closer relatives with respect to those capacities than either of us are to other anthropoids.

Among the more spectacular recent discoveries on our shared capacities has been the educability of chimpanzees and other great apes in the use of language. I am as impressed as everyone else by the remarkable performance, but I believe that the extraordinary performance of chimpanzees in languagelike activities involves different cognitive capacities than the ones we humans developed. My reactionary view, contradicting that of my friends in the ape-language field, is that our use of language is uniquely human, and I hold it on the basis of the logic of an evolutionary analysis and scenario. It is a theme that has its roots in the kind of analysis presented earlier of the origin of mammalian encephalization.

HOMINID ENCEPHALIZATION 2:
SIZE OF THE NEUROLINGUISTIC SYSTEM

My analysis begins with the neurological status of language, namely, that it is controlled by an enormous neocortical system. As I argued earlier, very large neocortical systems evolved in mammals to control activity that should be described as perceptual and cognitive. I distinguish these from three other major psychological categories: learning, social behavior, and communication, which occur in all vertebrates and can be controlled by very small nervous systems. When their neural control is large, I think of perceptual-cognitive dimensions as having been added to, for example, social behavior or communication. From my perspective, human language is, therefore, a priori a perceptual-cognitive adaptation.

To identify selection pressures that were effective during the prehominid-hominid transition and that were met by a languagelike adaptation, I sought to identify problems of adaptation that required unusual perceptual-cognitive capacities. I recognized, of course, that those capacities would not necessarily have resembled language as we know it, although they had to evolve into such a language capacity. The role of language in human communication had to be secondary both in time and in importance according to this evolutionary analysis because pressures for improved communication would have led to a different kind of initial adaptation, which would not have required much expansion of the brain for its control. However, even in its beginnings, language may have been preadaptive for present human language and its place in communication, and it was, according to my scenario.

The first step in this evolutionary narrative is to suggest for the ancestral species an environmental niche characterized by adaptive requirements that would put unusual demands on the already large perceptual-cognitive brain system of a prehominid or early hominid primate. The environmental requirements, I propose, were in the climatic change in the Mediterranean basin, which reduced the size of the normal forest habitat for a chimpanzee-like primate species—the prehominid of my scenario. As I imagine them, some individuals of the prehominid populations were adapted to live in the desertlike or savanna region at the forest's edge and were able to shift to a more carnivorous diet than that typical for primate species (cf., Pilbeam, 1984). It was in the neurogenetics of those individuals that I would identify the precursors of language.

HOMINID ENCEPHALIZATION 3: SOCIAL PREDATION

The niche that was available was for a carnivorous predator, but the animals that invaded it successfully were social vocal primates similar to living chimpanzees, and not members of the order Carnivora. The model of a species adapted for such a niche is the well-studied timber wolf (Peters & Mech, 1975), a proper social carnivore, with a proper profile of morphological, neural, and behavioral adaptations for life in this niche. There are information-processing requirements for the adaptations that are fulfilled easily by wolves, which are average mammals in encephalization. Meeting those requirements would strain the neural-processing capacity of an anthropoid primate species, however, despite its being more than twice as encephalized as wolves, because anthropoid primates had lost the capacity to use certain critical information during the course of their evolution. My view is that the specialized information-processing requirements were met in our hominid ancestors by a new adaptation that eventually evolved into human language.

The special demand of this niche is that it involves the navigation of a very large territory and range by a socially integrated group of predators to harvest prey in sufficient numbers to support the predators. In living wolves, a typical territory is of the order of several hundred square kilometers. In contrast, a typical daily range of living gorillas and chimpanzees for normal foraging may be only a few hundred square meters (Pickford, 1988). A successful predator must "know" its territory, and this means that it must have a good cognitive map of it and remember the map's history and status. The sensory and neural equipment of wolves, in contrast to that of apes, provides the clue for the new anthropoid adaptation that was required and that appeared in our hominid ancestors.

For their adaptations as social predators, wolves have an elaborate scent-marking system coupled with normal olfactory bulbs, more than 50 times the size of the almost vestigial human olfactory bulbs but the expected size suggested by data on other land mammals (Jerison, 1991). Wolves are, therefore, properly recognized for their excellent olfactory sensation and perception. The brain systems receiving the olfactory information include the piriform lobes and schizocortex, and eventually hippocampus. We know very little about how olfactory information is used in cognition, partly, of course, because humans are peculiarly deficient in that sense modality. Our intuitions about how olfaction would work in normal mammals are bound to be inadequate. Olfactory information in living carnivores is known to be sufficient to enable individuals to identify other animals individually (Brown & Macdonald, 1985; Rasa, 1973; Roeder, 1983), and we probably should think of it as having a role comparable to that of vision in our lives. This means that it could be used to create maps formed with edges and borders and so forth, and populated by animals and other objects—at least we should imagine this as something that can be constructed from olfactory data.

The fate of these maps in controlling action would be comparable to that of a well-remembered map in our own lives. Mapping and memory about maps are among the functions that involve important hippocampal control (Horn, 1985; Squire, 1987), and the system for wolves presumably involves significant sensory analysis of scent marks, coupled with the establishment of appropriate cognitive maps. The system would have access to all of the mapping and memory functions in which hippocampal control occurs. We should imagine the perceptual world constructed by a wolf from olfactory information as based on input from olfactory bulbs coupled with appropriate analysis by hippocampus, paleocortical, and neocortical structures. The wolf's model of reality would be an experienced real world that corresponds more to the one humans build from visual information than to the one humans build (or fail to build) from odors.

There is a neurobiological problem for an anthropoid species adapting to a social predator's niche. An anthropoid primate has the right central neural machinery for the adaptation—appropriately large hippocampus and related structures—but because the system as a whole in all mammals is normally coupled peripherally to the olfactory bulbs, it would be unlikely to work as well when coupled with the almost vestigial olfactory bulbs of anthropoids. (The adaptational problem is like that of a species with vestigial eyes and retina, evolving under selection pressures to have access to the central visual system.) A solution to the adaptational problem could take advantage of the fact that the hippocampus, which may be thought of as a neural central processing unit in the brain's control of the required cognitive adaptation, is a polysensory structure that can be accessed by other senses. My idea is that the transition to the hominid grade was correlated with the evolution of other peripheral access to the cognitive system that controls a predator's mapping of its range. The other access, I propose, was primarily by the use of the auditory–vocal channel, which is highly developed in anthropoid primates.

It is an odd picture, but I think it works. Instead of urinating and sniffing (the scent marking and sensing that wolves do), we can imagine our ancestor as marking with sounds and sensing the sounds—talking to itself, as it were, but in primitive tongues. The picture is odd, but no odder than another use of an auditory–vocal channel that evolved in some cetaceans and in insect-eating bats, in which echoes from vocalizations are used in the elaborate sonar system that evolved in these species, and from which they construct and know the external world. The picture for our ancestors would be adequate for access to the cognitive systems for mapping and remembering important features of the external world (i.e., for knowing that world). The vocalizations could be with a very small vocabulary. A model for that might be the three-word vocabulary of vervets to signal the presence of eagles, leopards, or snakes (Cheney & Seyfarth, 1990). The hominid vocabulary would have to be larger to encode relevant environmental features, less rigid to be responsive to more diverse environmental features, and less frenetic, not a danger signal that commanded escape but a knowledge signal that helped construct a map of the world.

The suggestion is, in summary, that an auditory–vocal system was established for marking and knowing a territory or range, that this system sent information to appropriate old-brain and neocortical systems, and that the information was integrated with other knowledge of the external world. It would be a new perceptual-cognitive system. This new language sense would interact with the very elaborate, older mammalian perceptual-cognitive systems that are based on vision, touch, and other senses. The older systems enable chimpanzees to be so much like humans in so many ways, but humans probably know them only in a distorted way. Our own knowledge of the external world is elaborated by the language dimension—built not only from sensory mappings that we share with other anthropoids as well as most mammals, but by important inputs to the mapping that comes from our language sense as it has evolved in *Homo sapiens*.

This scenario offers a solution to an adaptational problem: how an anthropoid can succeed as a social predatory mammalian species without normal olfactory bulbs. It also has implications for other aspects of hominid evolution because it describes a new cognitive system that is obviously usable for communication with conspecifics. Communication with the auditory–vocal channel is common in primates as warning calls and other social messages that elicit a variety of behaviors. The communication by hominids using their range-marking system would be of a new kind, however, because the information transmitted by the auditory–vocal channel would be incorporated directly into the listener's knowledge of the external world rather than act as a releaser or elicitor of specialized behavior.

HOMINID ENCEPHALIZATION 4:
LANGUAGE, COGNITION, COMMUNICATION,
AND CONSCIOUSNESS

As I have pointed out before, animal communication is normally a system of commands to other animals that can be thought of as having coevolved with the system of responses to those commands. The vervet calls are good examples of what I mean. We can think of the calls as danger signals that elicit appropriate escape action as the normal response. The cognitive dimension of this interaction could be completely absent; it probably is absent in most danger signals in most species, although for other reasons we can assume that it is present in vervets (Cheney & Seyfarth, 1990). In any case, normal animal communication could be a purely reflex system without a cognitive dimension.

The feature of human language that my scenario would emphasize is that it began as a cognitive rather than communicational adaptation. That it evolved into the characteristic communication system of our species implies that our communication is not like that of other mammals. Once the adaptation of using auditory and vocal signs to label the geographic environment had appeared, its utility for communication is fairly obvious. What individual A knew could become part of what individual B knew if B merely listened while A vocalized. The only other species in which something close to this is believed to occur are echo-locating bats, which can intercept one another's calls and their echoes and, in that sense, experience one another's worlds. I have speculated that this sort of thing could have developed in dolphins as well, and that the additional neural machinery in the dolphin's brain might process such information into something more nearly like human language (Jerison, 1986).

I should state this conclusion about language more dramatically. Because language contributes to our knowledge of reality in the same general way as information received by the conventional senses, such as the eye and ear, when we communicate with language we communicate information that contributes to our reality. The listener or reader receiving the message incorporates it into his or her reality and then knows the same world that we know as we communicate. Communication with language is, thus, a sharing of awareness or consciousness. We literally read minds when we read a realistic text and enter the minds of the characters as if we were living their fictional lives. This very common experience is really very odd, and it is one of the stranger features of the human mind.

This view of language leads to an unusual view of the nature of human consciousness in an evolutionary framework. There are two aspects of consciousness. The first, and biologically most important, is in connection with one's knowledge of the external world and should be thought of as the problem of awareness, or representation, or imagery. Why do we know a pictorial world with solid objects and so on? This is biologically more important because the evidence is overwhelming that all birds and mammals are conscious in this sense, and this may also be true for other vertebrates. Herrnstein (1985) has shown that pigeons can identify faces that people miss, presumably from pictorial cues. Griffin (1976) has argued persuasively for a universality for this kind of consciousness, or awareness. From my perspective, this means that in most vertebrates, certainly in birds and mammals, the work of the brain includes the construction of a possible real world from sense data, and that possible world is the reality that the animal knows. The function of this construction is to make sense of an otherwise overwhelming mass of neural data that refers to the external world.

The other kind of consciousness involves an awareness of self that is unusual. It is not only the self as an object, which is really the same as any other object of which one may be aware or conscious in the first sense. It is the knowledge that the self is different from other objects in that it generates knowledge and knows that it knows. Why would such a self be created by a brain? A functional explanation is that this kind of self is necessary if one is to have human language as a dual adaptation for both perceptual-cognitive uses and for communication. Our knowledge of the external world is too important to be compromised by confusion about where it came from. If we can know another's external world simply by hearing, or reading, some statements, it is important that we be able to distinguish this known world from the reality that we know when our information comes through the usual sensory channels (i.e., when we see and hear and touch things). We can also know an external world by remembering it, and if our memories are verbalized that information, too, can enter into our awareness of the moment as information about the external world. The point is that language is so potent a medium for knowledge that it may be essential that knowledge carried by that medium be distinguished from other knowledge. By being self-conscious, we can distinguish images generated by the spoken or written word from images generated at the sensory and motor surfaces of the body in interaction with nonverbal external information. We can distinguish image from reality. It is another oddity about the mind that we don't always succeed in making the distinction, as any schizophrenic and many mystics and dreamers can tell us.

FINAL REMARKS

In view of my emphasis on the importance of encephalization for understanding the phenomena studied by comparative psychologists and as a foundation for theory, let me conclude, first, with some words of caution from the honeybee's world. In insects, the analogues to the vertebrate brain appear to be head ganglia called mushroom bodies. These "brains" are largest in roaches, bees, and wasps but contain no more than about 400,000 neurons (Erber, Homberg, & Gronenberg, 1987). Mice, which are among the smallest of vertebrates, have half-gram brains (about 1/50 of an ounce) with about 10 million neocortical nerve cells, and 30 million additional brain cells, mainly in the cerebellum. The data on the mouse are from Braitenberg and Schüz (1998), who also note that there are about 80 billion synapses in the mouse neocortex. The vertebrate numbers are very large. Those of insects are small. Yet behaviorally, in the analysis of learned behavior, honeybees cannot be distinguished from mice, rats, or other vertebrates on the tasks Macphail (1982) reviewed. Although he is not especially sympathetic toward Macphail's conclusions, Bitterman (1988) performed the required experimental analysis of the behavior of honeybees. Animals evidently do not live by brains alone, even for their higher mental processes. The result is perplexing and exposes an obvious gap in our understanding of intelligence. But in this essay on comparative psychology, I defined intelligence in terms of encephalization, which is measurable only in vertebrates, and I hope I am forgiven for simply excluding the clearly different set of adaptations and control that evolved in insects from this analysis. There is no fossil evidence at all on the evolution of brain size in insects. I agree with Bitterman's judgment that the result is due to convergent evolution and would assume, further, that the neural mechanisms underlying the behavior are likely to be quite different in invertebrates and vertebrates.

The narratives to illustrate the value of my approach are conventional evolutionary scenarios, which seek features in the ecological niche entered by an evolving species that make a particular adaptation more successful than the related adaptation of the ancestor species. In the most general terms, having a brain is an adaptation for controlling a body, for moving about in the world (if the animal is motile, as are most living vertebrates), and for exercising other forms of control. How does a larger brain improve an animal's chances to survive and reproduce? Human intuition usually attributes the improvement to the ability to think deeper and better thoughts, but that really makes no sense in the larger scheme of things. The improvement has to be related to better control of action and reaction tied to some environmental change that made the previously evolved method of neural control less effective than it was in the previous normal environment. It can never be anticipatory of greater opportunities but must be a response to a present challenge. If it appears to be anticipatory, it must be understood as preadaptive, an evolutionary accident that made a valid and useful adaptation applicable to a different environmental challenge that had not affected its initial viability. My scenario on language emphasizes this view because I reject the possibility of the origin of language in a requirement for communication. Such a requirement would have led to very different adaptations, with less uncertainty about the meaning of the message and a smaller investment in neural machinery.

In every instance, encephalization is a solution involving packing more material into the control system, and there has to be a reason for putting more in. My two narratives had different reasons because different environmental changes were being coped with. For the earliest mammals it was not so much a changed environment as the availability of an unexploited nocturnal environment. In my tale of human origins, including the place of language, I assumed a chimpanzee or gorilla-like life that was challenged by an environmental change that reduced the available habitat. Although some predation is a normal part of anthropoid life in the living chimpanzee, it is not the major requirement that I described in my scenario. I should note that predation may not have been essential. A scavenger's life involving an extensive range would have essentially the same challenges for a chimpanzee-like primate.

My analysis also emphasizes that information-processing capacity is what is gained when there is encephalization. It emphasizes cognition rather than purely motor skills, such as throwing (cf., Calvin, 1983; Wilkins & Wakefield, 1995), or scenarios about the nutritional systems that enable encephalization by improved nutritional capacities (Falk, 1992; Martin, 1990). I do not reject approaches emphasizing such dimensions, but I believe that the driving environmental forces that actually supported encephalization as an adaptation were those that could be met only by additions to the total information-processing capacity of the brain.

I have just noted the great difficulties that would be faced if one attempted to extend the analysis to insects, but there is no difficulty in the case of birds. There is a fair consensus now that the bird's forebrain is homologous to that of mammals, although the structure homologous to mammalian cortex is not layered and has the superficial appearance of enlarged basal ganglia (Karten, 1991). That structure, nevertheless, could support the control of avian behavior, which, like that of mammals, could only be effected by enlarging the control system. The details will, of course, be different in birds and in mammals, just as they are different among species of mammals, but the strategy of the analysis is the same.

To conclude, let me restate an important limitation of my approach that I think limits any theory of comparative psychology. Tying mind and its evolution to the evolution of encephalization rather than to that of small systems in the brain implies a particular, and I believe correct, view of what evolved when higher mental capacities evolved. Were we to focus on regional specializations in the brain, even on very large regions such as the prefrontal neocortex, we might consider a notion of modular control in which the subsystems that can be identified could have evolved independently of one another. The evidence of the brain and of the way it hangs together suggests that independent evolution of either behavioral or morphological modules did not occur. There could always be dominant modalities that might have driven the process, but the evolution of a modality had to be accompanied by the evolution of the systems connected to its operation.

The evolution of such a system involves a genetic code, and we have no sense of how a genetic code might specify the control of complex mental performance. Codes can specify only simple things, such as the structure of molecules. I suggested the level of complexity that can be encoded in my example at the beginning of this chapter of how to generate the correct number of neocortical neurons in a hominoid. I have no idea how code could be written at a molecular level to specify localized functions of sensory-perceptual systems. Grand theories of comparative psychology should be evolutionary theories in which such codes are among the elements. My elements remain information-processing units, and my theorizing has been on how and why their number changed in vertebrates under natural selection.

Finally, an odd feature of the genetic code, as it must be written to account for nature–nurture interactions, is that it must, in some sense, include a representation of the environment. A code for neural growth might have the following form: grow branches in all directions but let only those branches survive that run into a particular biochemical environment. Another code might be written to lay down appropriate environments within which growth could occur. By mapping the layouts of the environment, the details of growth could be regulated without having to have the full map encoded in the genetic material. The extent to which a mature nervous system is described by the genetic material is nevertheless remarkable, as indicated by the general uniformities of structure and function. All humans have language, presumably because of code in our genetic material. All mammals have identifiable and comparable maps in their brains that label information as visual, auditory, and so forth. All vertebrates have brains divided into at least forebrain, midbrain, and hindbrain. These must be uniformities imposed by the genetic code in each group, and variations in the codes are what evolved. All primates have visual cortex, but if they are deprived of visual experience, it develops incorrectly, so the code to direct embryonic neurites growing in an embryonic brain to become elements of the visual cortex also depends on, or assumes, the experience in some way. We have no idea how this is done. That is the problem of encoding the environment to be tracked by natural selection, and this confession of ignorance may be a good note on which to end.

REFERENCES

Aiello, L. C., & Wheeler, P. (1995). The expensive-tissue hypothesis: The brain and the digestive system in human and primate evolution. *Current Anthropology, 36,* 199–221.

Allee, W. C. (1931). *Animal aggregations: A study in general sociology.* Chicago: University of Chicago Press.

Bitterman, M. E. (1988). Vertebrate-invertebrate comparisons. In H. J. Jerison, and I. L. Jerison (Eds.), *Intelligence and evolutionary biology* (pp. 251–276). Heidelberg: Springer-Verlag.

Boesch, C., & Boesch, H. (1983). Optimization of nut-cracking with natural hammers by wild chimpanzees. *Behaviour, 34,* 265–286.

Braitenberg, V., & Schüz, A. (1998). *Cortex: Statistics and geometry of neural connectivity* (2nd ed.). Heidelberg: Springer-Verlag.

Brodmann, K. (1913). Neue Forschungsergebnisse der Grosshirnrindenanatomie mit besonderer Berucksichtung anthropologischer Fragen. [New research results on cerebral neuranatolmy with reflections on anthropological issues.] *Verhandlungen des 85ste Versammlung Deutscher Naturforscher und Aerzte in Wien,* 200–240.

Brooks, D. R., & MacLennan, D. A. (1991). *Phylogeny, ecology, and behavior: A research program in comparative biology.* Chicago: University of Chicago Press.

Brown, R. E., & Macdonald, D. W. (Eds.). 1985. *Social odors in mammals,* Vol. 2. Oxford: Clarendon Press.

Buss, D. M., Haselton, M. G., Shackelford, T. K., Bleske, A. L., & Wakefield, J. C. (1998). Adaptations, exaptations, and spandrels. *American Psychologist, 53,* 533–548.

Butler, A. B., & Hodos, W. (1996). *Comparative vertebrate neuroanatomy.* New York: Wiley-Liss.

Byrne, J. H. (1987). Aplysia; Associative modification of individual neurons. In G. Adelman (Ed.), *Encyclopedia of neuroscience* (Vol. 1, pp. 65–67). Boston: Birkhaüser.

Calvin, W. H. (1983). *The throwing Madonna.* New York: McGraw-Hill.

Cheney, D. L., & Seyfarth, R. M. (1990). *How monkeys see the world.* Chicago: University of Chicago Press.

Conroy, G., Weber, G., Seidler, H., Tobias, P. V., Kane, A., & Brunsben, B. (1998). Endocranial capacity in an early hominid cranium from Sterkfontein, South Africa. *Science, 280,* 1730–1731.

Darwin, C. (1985). *The origin of species.* Middlesex, England: Penguin Classics. (Original work published 1859.)

Deacon, T. W. (1997). *The symbolic species: The co-evolution of language and the brain.* New York: Norton.

Diamond, I. T. (1979). The subdivisions of the neocortex: A proposal to revise the traditional view of sensory, motor, and association areas. *Progress in Psychobiology and Physiological Psychology, 8,* 1–43.

Edinger, T. (1975). Paleoneurology, 1804–1966. *Advances in Anatomy, Embryology, and Cell Biology, 49,* 12–258.

Elias, H., & Schwartz, D. (1971). Cerebro-cortical surface areas, volumes, lengths of gyri and their interdependence in mammals, including man. *Zeitschrift für Saugetierkunde, 36,* 147–163.

Erber, J., Homberg, U., & Gronenberg, W. (1987). Functional roles of the mushroom bodies in insects. In A. P. Gupta (Ed.), *Arthropod brain: Its evolution, development, structure, and functions* (pp. 485–511). New York: Wiley-Interscience.

Ewert, J. P. (1974). The neural basis of visually guided behavior. *Scientific American, 230,* 34–42.

Falk, D. (1992). *Braindance.* New York: Henry Holt.

Gallup, G. G., Jr. (1979). Self-awareness in primates. *American Scientist, 67,* 417–421.

Gazzaniga, M.S. (Ed.). (1995). *The cognitive neurosciences.* Cambridge, MA: MIT Press.

Goldman-Rakic, P. S. (1988). Topography of cognition: Parallel distributed networks in primate association cortex. *Annual Review of Neurosciences, 11,* 137–166.

Gould, S. J. (1976). Grades and clades revisited. In R. B. Masterton, W. Hodos, & H. J. Jerison (Eds.), *Evolution, brain and behavior: Persistent problems* (pp. 115–122). Hillsdale, NJ: Lawrence Erlbaum Associates.

Griffin, D. R. (1976). *The question of animal awareness.* New York: Rockefeller University Press.

Grinnell, A. D. (1995). Hearing in bats: An overview. In R. R. Fay & A. M. Popper (Eds.), *Hearing by bats* (pp. 1–36). Heidelberg, Germany: Springer-Verlag.

Harvey, P. H., & Pagel, M. D. (1991). *The comparative method in evolutionary biology.* Oxford: Oxford University Press.

Herrnstein, R. J. (1985). Riddles of natural categorization. *Philosophical Transactions of the Royal Society (London), B308,* 129–144.

Hodos, W., & Campbell, C. B. G. (1969). Scala naturae: Why there is no theory in comparative psychology. *Psychological Review, 76,* 337–350.

Hopson, J. A. (1979). Paleoneurology. In C. Gans, R. G. Northcutt, and P. Ulinski (Eds.), *Biology of the reptilia* (Vol. 9, pp. 39–146). London and New York, Academic Press.

Horn, G. (1985). *Memory, imprinting, and the brain.* Oxford: Clarendon Press.

Hubel, D. H. (1988). *Eye, brain, and vision.* New York: W. H. Freeman.

Huxley, T. H. (1899). *Man's place in nature (with other anthropological essays).* New York: D. Appleton. (Original work published 1863)

Jerison, H. J. (1973). *Evolution of the brain and intelligence.* New York: Academic Press.

Jerison, H. J. (1982). The evolution of biological intelligence. In R. J. Sternberg (Ed.), *Handbook of human intelligence* (pp. 723–791). London: Cambridge University Press.

Jerison, H. J. (1986). The perceptual worlds of dolphins. In R. J. Schusterman, J. Thomas, & F. G. Wood (Eds.), *Dolphin cognition and behavior: A comparative approach* (pp. 141–166). Hillsdale, NJ: Lawrence Erlbaum Associates.

Jerison, H. J. (1990). Fossil evidence on the evolution of the neocortex. In E. G. Jones, and A. Peters (Eds.). *Cerebral Cortex* (Vol. 8A, pp. 285–309). New York, Plenum.

Jerison, H. J. (1991). *Brain size and the evolution of mind: 59th James Arthur lecture on the evolution of the human brain.* New York: American Museum of Natural History.

Jerison, H. J. (1997). Evolution of prefrontal cortex. In N. Krasnegor, R. Lyon, & P. Goldman-Rakic (Eds.), *Development of the prefrontal cortex: Evolution, neurobiology, and behavior* (pp. 9–26). Baltimore, MD: Brookes.

Jerison, H. J. (2000). *Evolution of intelligence.* In R. J. Sternberg (Ed.), *Handbook of human intelligence* (2nd ed.). Cambridge: Cambridge University Press.

Jerison, H. J. (2001). The evolution of neural and behavioral complexity. In G. Roth & M. F. Wullimann (Eds.), *Brain evolution and cognition.* New York: Wiley.

Johnson, J. I. (1990). Comparative development of somatic sensory cortex. In E. G. Jones and A. Peters (Eds.), *Cerebral cortex* (Vol. 8B, pp. 335–449). New York: Plenum.

Jones, E. G., & Powell, T. P. S. (1970). An anatomical study of converging sensory pathways within the cerebral cortex of the monkey. *Brain, 93,* 793–820.

Karten, H. J. (1991). Homology and evolutionary origins of the "neocortex." *Brain, behavior and evolution, 38,* 264–272.

Kielan-Jaworowska, Z. (1986). Brain evolution in Mesozoic mammals. In J. A. Lillegraven (Ed.), [G. G. Simpson Memorial Volume]. *Contributions to Geology, University of Wyoming, Special Paper, 3,* 21–34.

Krasnegor, N., Lyon, R., & Goldman-Rakic, P. (Eds.). (1997). *Development of the prefrontal cortex: Evolution, neurobiology, and behavior.* Baltimore, MD: Brookes.

Kummer, H., & Goodall, J. (1985). Conditions of innovative behaviour in primates. *Philosophical Transactions of the Royal Society (London), B308,* 203–214.

Lashley, K. S. (1949). Persistent problems in the evolution of mind. *Quarterly Review of Biology, 24,* 28–42.

Lettvin, J. Y., Maturana, H. R., McCulloch, W. S., & Pitts, W. H. (1959). What the frog's eye tells the frog's brain. *Proceedings, Institute of Radio Engineers, 47,* 1940–1951.

Lubbock, J. (Lord Avebury). (1888). *On the senses, instincts, and intelligence of animals with special reference to insects.* London: Kegan Paul, Trench.

Macphail, E. M. (1982). *Brain and intelligence in vertebrates.* Oxford: Clarendon Press.

Martin, R. D. (1990). *Primate origins and evolution: A phylogenetic reconstruction.* London: Chapman & Hall.

Northcutt, R. G. (1989). Brain variation and phylogenetic trends in elasmobranch fishes. *Journal of Experimental Zoology* (Suppl. 2, 83–100).

Ostrom, J. H. (1976). *Archaeopteryx* and the origin of birds. *Biological Journal of the Linnean Society, 8,* 91–182.

Pakkenberg, B., & Gundersen, H. J. G. (1997). Neocortical neuron number in humans: Effect of sex and age. *Journal of Comparative Neurology, 385,* 312–320.

Passingham, R. E. (1982). *The human primate.* San Francisco: Freeman.

Patterson, C. (Ed.). (1987). *Molecules and morphology in evolution: Conflict or compromise?* Cambridge: Cambridge University Press.

Pepperberg, I. M. (1994). Vocal learning in African grey parrots: Effects of social interaction. *Auk, 111,* 300–313.

Peters, R. P., & Mech, L. D. (1975). Scent-marking in wolves. *American Scientist, 63,* 628–637.

Pickford, M. (1988). The evolution of intelligence: A palaeontological perspective. In H. J. Jerison, and I. L. Jerison (Eds.), *Intelligence and evolutionary biology* (pp. 175–198). Heidelberg: Springer-Verlag.

Pilbeam, D. (1984). The descent of the hominoids and the hominids. *Scientific American, 250,* 3, 84–96.

Polyak, S. (1957). *The Vertebrate Visual System,* (H. Küver, Ed.). Chicago: University of Chicago Press.

Posner, M. I. (1994). *Images of mind.* New York: Scientific American Library.

Premack, D., & Kennell, K. (1978). Conservation of liquid and solid quantity by the chimpanzee. *Science, 202,* 991–994.

Premack, D., & Woodruff, G. (1978). Does the chimpanzee have a theory of mind? *Behavioral and Brain Sciences, 4,* 515–526.

Radinsky, L. (1978). Evolution of brain size in carnivores and ungulates. *American Naturalist, 112,* 815–831.

Rasa, O. A. E. (1973). Marking behaviour and its social significance in the African dwarf mongoose, *Helogale undulata rufula. Zeitschrift für Tierpsychologie, 32,* 293–318.

Ridgway, S. H. (1981). Some brain morphometrics of the Bowhead whale. In T. F. Albert (Ed.), *Tissues, structural studies, and other investigations on the biology of endangered whales in the Beaufort Sea* (Final Report to the Bureau of Land Management, U. S. Dept. of Interior (Vol.2, pp. 837–844). College Park, Maryland: University of Maryland.

Ridgway, S. H., & Brownson, R. H. (1984). Relative brain sizes and cortical surfaces of odontocetes. *Acta Zoologica Fennica ,172,* 149–152.

Rockel, A. J., Hiorns, R. W., & Powell, T. P. S. (1980). The basic uniformity in structure of the neocortex. *Brain, 103, 221–244.*

Roeder, J. J. (1983). Memorisation des marques olfactives chez la Genette (*Genetta genetta L.*): durée de reconnaissance par les femelles de marques olfactives de males. [Memorization of olfactory marks in the genet (*genetta genetta L.*): The duration of female recognition of male olfactory marks.] *Zeitschrift für Tierpsychologie, 61,* 311–314.

Roth, G. (1987). *Visual behavior in salamanders.* Berlin: Springer-Verlag.

Sanders, A. F. (Ed.). (1967). *Attention and performance.* Amsterdam: North-Holland.

Savage-Rumbaugh, E. S., Murphy, J., Sevcik, R. A., Brakke, K. E., Williams, S. L., & Rumbaugh, D. M. (1993). Language comprehension in ape and child. *Monographs of the Society for Research in Child Development, 58*(3–4), 1–254.

Schmidt-Nielsen, K. (1984). *Scaling: Why is animal size so important.* Cambridge: Cambridge University Press.

Shannon, C. E., & Weaver, W. (1949). *The mathematical theory of communication.* Urbana, IL: University of Illinois Press.

Simpson, G. G. (1970). Uniformitarianism: An inquiry into principle, theory, and method in geohistory and biohistory. In M. K. Hecht, & W. C. Steere (Eds.), *Essays in evolution and genetics in honor of Theodosius Dobzhansky* (pp. 43–96). Amsterdam: North-Holland.

Skinner, B. F. (1957). The experimental analysis of behavior. *American Scientist, 45,* 343–371.

Squire, L. R. (1987). *Memory and the brain.* Oxford: Oxford University Press.

Szentagothai, J. (1978). The neuron network of the cerebral cortex: A functional interpretation. *Proceedings of the Royal Society (London), Series B, 201,* 219–248.

Thorndike, E. L. (1898). Animal intelligence: An experimental study of the associative processes in animals. *Psychological Monographs, 2,* (4, Whole No. 8).

Tully, T., Preat, T., Boynton, S. C., & Del Vecchio, M. (1994). Genetic dissection of consolidated memory in Drosophila. *Cell, 79,* 35–47.

Uylings, H. B. M., & Van Eden, C. G. (1990). Qualitative and quantitative comparison of the prefrontal cortex in rat and in primates, including humans. In H. B. M. Uylings, C. G. Van Eden, J. P. C. De Bruin, M. A. Corner, & M. G. P. Feenstra (Eds.), *Progress in Brain Research,* 85 (pp. 31–62). Amsterdam: Elsevier.

von Frisch, K. (1950). *Bees: Their chemical senses, vision, and language.* Ithaca, New York: Cornell University Press.

von Uexküll, J. (1957). *Streifzüge durch die Umwelten von Teiren und Menschen.* In C. H. Schiller (Ed.). *Instinctive behavior: The development of a modern concept* (pp. 5–80). New York: International Universities Press. (Original work published 1934) [A stroll through the worlds of animals and men.]

Welker, W. I. (1990). Why does cerebral cortex fissure and fold? A review of determinants of gyri and sulci. In E. G. Jones & A. Peters. *Cerebral cortex* (Vol. 8B, pp. 1–132). New York: Plenum Press.

Wever. E. G. (1978). *The reptile ear: Its structure and function.* Princeton, NJ: Princeton University Press.

Wilkins, W. K., & Wakefield, J. (1995). Brain evolution and neurolinguistic preconditions. *Behavioral and Brain Sciences, 18,* 161–226.

Wilson, E. O. (1975). *Sociobiology: The new synthesis.* Cambridge, MA: Harvard University Press.

Zeki, S. (1993). *A vision of the brain.* London: Blackwell.

12

Evolutionary Contagion
in Mental Software

Aaron Lynch
Independent Researcher

EVOLVING THOUGHT CONTAGIONS:
AN INTRODUCTION

The idea of cultural evolution resembling biological evolution has a long history. For example, William James (1880) published an essay drawing parallels between cultural evolution and biological evolution. More recently, Cloak (1973, 1975) has formally examined the general evolution of *elementary self-replicating instructions* as phenomena of both neural memory and the molecular memory of nucleic acids. His analysis uses a very broad definition of the word "instruction" that includes all neural structures that regularly respond to a characteristic cue with a characteristic behavior. By analogy to the way many computer instructions may constitute computer software, many neurally stored instructions (in Cloak's broad sense) may constitute *mental software*.[1] In a term that is perhaps more self-explanatory, as well as more general in some ways and more specific in other ways, I have used the term *thought contagion* to refer to

---

[1]Cloak (1975) uses the term *programming of the nervous system*. Balkin (1998) uses the related term *cultural software* in his book *Cultural Software: A Theory of Ideology*, one of many titles in the literature on evolution and transmission of culture. As with the term *mental software* used in the introduction to this chapter, such terms are metaphors that may help make the subject more accessible to nonspecialists, but that are not necessary for the analysis. Some forms of self-propagating mental software might be viewed as mental software viruses, but one cannot presume either harm or benefit.

289

self-propagating ideas. Inasmuch as any idea can play at least a passive role in self-propagation by merely existing in someone's brain, a more formal definition may be based on whether the idea has actually resulted in self-propagation. In its formal, broad sense, the term *thought contagion* therefore denotes the following: a memory item, or portion of an individual's neurally stored information, whose causation depended critically upon prior instantiation of the same memory item in one or more other individuals.[2] The study of thought contagions has numerous implications, some of which pertain to the evolution of intelligence. Specifically, it pertains to the evolution of the collective intelligence of populations and the individual intelligence of humans.

The theoretical paradigm of ideas programming for their own propagation is called thought contagion theory or, strictly speaking, the thought contagion hypothesis. It encompasses distinct hypotheses about how propagation parameters correlate with the nature of what is believed, often in ways that do not depend on truth, utility, rationality, or even emotional appeal.

Thought contagion theory is a theory of the evolutionary epidemiology of ideas, in which ideas can propagate by various means. These include ideas causing hosts to have more children, impart their ideas to a higher fraction of children, engage in more peer to peer persuasion, retain their ideas longer, and even interfere with the spread of competing beliefs (Lynch, 1996). Evolution happens by differentials in the rates of such transmission modes.

While comparisons between biological and cultural evolution go back over a century, as do comparisons between cultural and biological contagion, specific comparisons of the evolutionary epidemiology of ideas to the evolutionary epidemiology of infectious organisms are necessarily much newer. The book *Evolution of Infectious Disease* (Ewald, 1994) describes the biological kind of evolutionary epidemiology as "an emerging discipline" (p. 7). True evolutionary epidemiology of ideas is also a late twentieth century development, even as precursors can be found in nineteenth century work. With both fields recently emerging, comparisons between them are therefore newly emerging as well. For example, both fields can discuss the forces driving evolution toward virulence or symbiosis of contagions: neither field assumes that all contagions are pathogenic, but neither assumes an inevitable path to symbiosis for all contagions. Although the

---

[2]The term *memory item* as used here may differ from Cloak's term *instruction* in some ways. For example, memory items can include ongoing internal material processes that respond in characteristic ways to characteristic cues even if processes per se are not ordinarily regarded as structures. Certain high-level collective processes may be viewed as containing memory items, as can small matter-energy processes such as neurons, synapses, cells, or the self-sustaining voltage and flow patterns of charge carriers in the static RAM flip-flops of an electronic computer. Multiple neural memory items may be viewed as mental software, though again, this metaphor is not critical. The term *thought contagion* is also intended to carry a neutral connotation, as even laughter, joy, and so forth can be called contagious in common parlance. For further discussion of terminology and variants thereof see Lynch, (1996, 1998, 2000, 2001).

evolutionary epidemiology of ideas can be developed without reliance on metaphors to the biological counterpart (Lynch, 2001), analogy and metaphor may play useful roles when explaining the theory in nonmathematical terms.

The evolutionary epidemiology of ideas (also called *thought contagion theory* for simplicity) focuses mainly on certain phenomena of population psychology that are not simply scaled-up versions of individual psychology. It does so without attempting to replace existing social sciences. It also does not deny that there are cases where population psychological phenomena can be substantially understood as a scaling-up of individual thought. Because many thought contagions have nontruth-contingent or nonutility-contingent modes of transmission, they can have distinct effects on the evolution of intelligence in both a population as a whole and its individual members.

Expressed in symbolic and mathematical terms (Lynch, 2001), the evolutionary epidemiology of memory items, such as ideas and beliefs, allows for numerous kinds of propagation events that can each have their own event rate parameters.[3] The symbolic representation of such events allows for a drier analysis in which metaphors to mental software, computer viruses, biological contagions, diploid genes, plasmids, prions, and so forth are absent. Examples of transmission events would be $A + \sim A \rightarrow 2A$ (host of memory item A plus nonhost of memory item A yields two hosts of A), $2A \rightarrow 2A + \sim A \rightarrow 3A$ (two hosts of A have a baby nonhost of A who is subsequently inculcated with A by the parents), $A \rightarrow \sim A$ (host of A drops out), and so forth.[4] Combinations of memory items can be represented as well, with an asterisk (*) indicating simultaneous instantiation in a single host. This leads to many more kinds of events and possible propagation parameters, with few limits other than the level of modeling complexity acceptable to the researcher. By not relying on metaphors (or appeals to unproven isomorphisms), the mathematical analysis avoids trouble with certain cultural features such as the range of delays between the birth and inculcation of a child.

The quantitative methods allow for a fairly rigorous and falsifiable method of presenting contagion hypotheses that may prove useful when surveys are done to measure propagation parameters. In a less quantitative discussion, it is convenient to distill those various parameters into three main factors of propagation: transmissivity, receptivity, and longevity of a belief or idea. Transmissivity refers to how much retransmitting behavior the belief enjoys in its existing hosts. Receptivity refers to how receptive the nonhosts are to the belief. Longevity refers to how long a host of the belief remains a host before dropping out

---

[3]Other methods of mathematically analyzing cultural evolution have been developed, such as those of Boyd and Richerson (1985) and Cavalli-Sforza and Feldman (1981), to name a few.

[4]The term *host of* A in this context simply means the person who holds memory item A.

or dying. Beliefs need nonzero levels of all three factors to propagate widely. Generally, ideas with the highest levels of these three propagation factors out-propagate alternatives with lower propagation factors, leading to the evolution by natural selection of ideas. Those ideas that play a particularly active role in elevating their propagation factors are often the special ones for which thought contagion theory offers distinct utility.

EVOLUTIONARY THOUGHT CONTAGION AND THE DIFFERENCES BETWEEN INDIVIDUAL INTELLIGENCE AND POPULATION INTELLIGENCE

The evolutionary epidemiology of ideas raises some distinctions between intelligence as an individual phenomenon and intelligence as a population phenomenon. On the population level, the differential replication, formation, and recombination of ideas often becomes a method of collectively thinking and making decisions. Those ideas that cause the greatest retransmission rates from their hosts tend to out-populate the alternatives over time. In doing so, they can also become the most frequent participants in the recombination of existing ideas and the formation of new ideas. Such thought contagions include ideas spreading by inducing evangelism, abundant child raising, dropout prevention, and interference with the spread of competing beliefs. On the population level, these effects are clearly not all scaled-up versions of the individual's internal neural operations. This would hold even if neural operations within the individual brain prove to involve replication phenomena in their own right, such as those proposed by Calvin (1996). On the other hand, if the Pythagorean theorem or Copernican astronomy spread by population mechanisms that strongly depend on valid reasoning in key individuals, then thought contagion analysis might not offer any surprises. The decisions made by the population on these matters would closely resemble the decisions of well-informed individuals. On many topics, however, wildly erroneous beliefs may cause more transmissions per host per year than fairly accurate beliefs, giving rise to types of mistakes that only a population can achieve. Here, propagation parameters elevated for nontruth-contingent reasons may override the effects of individual intelligence to produce widely held beliefs that differ dramatically from those that might come from a talented individual working with enough time and resources to answer the question at hand.

Consider the rather popular belief that one needs to find a romantic partner of a compatible astrological sign. One hypothesis for this idea's propagation is that it is simply attractive to think that one can choose a partner by relatively simple formulas. If a large population sector reaches this conclusion in unison, then the population mind, at least of this sector, would function much as a scaled-up version of the individual mind. Yet the idea apparently also causes singles who have it to raise the subject of astrological-sign compatibility with new potential partners, in order to determine compatibility. This leads to a second type of hypothesis: that the idea spreads itself into more minds by exploiting human mating to cause communication behavior. It may implicitly tell some hosts to send several copies of this idea to potential partners before accepting anyone for further dating. In that respect, this particular thought contagion resembles a chain letter without the paper. It also resembles the way a computer virus programs for its own retransmission in a computer network. Although it does not erase its host's memory, it can make it harder to find a partner deemed compatible by arbitrarily narrowing the field. Therefore, like a sexually transmitted microorganism, astrological mating ideas might use human mating for their own reproduction in a way that reduces biological reproduction. If so, that mode of transmission would tend to rule out predominantly genetic hypotheses of astrological mating ideas. The idea may spread in the population without the benefit of any innate tendency toward it. It may even spread by mechanisms that override general tendencies toward biologically adaptive modes of thought.

The belief in astrological compatibility need not be rigid to propagate parasitically. Some, for example, may have enough interest to ask a date's star sign without necessarily dropping someone just because of astrological incompatibility. Still, even in these cases, the idea may spread as a sexually transmitted belief. A common outcome of exchanging signs is a determination of putative incompatibility, with the incompatibility inference rate depending on the specific strains of astrological-mating schemes. Many dating pairs who play this game are therefore given a suggestion that they are incompatible. If people are generally more superstitious than they like to admit, then this suggestion may play a part in causing them to discontinue dating someone. For example, one or the other, or both, may give up in the face of challenges that inevitably arise. They may conclude consciously or unconsciously that their problems result from inherent incompatibility rather than resolvable differences, increasing the chances of a breakup. If an astrological-mating thought contagion thereby succeeds in causing the relationship to break up, then it can cause its host to go back to dating other people and again raising the subject of astrology with new people. If the idea fails to cause the relationship to break up, then its host will go through a long, possibly permanent episode of horizontal noncontagiousness in which he or she no longer brings the subject up to potential mates. Therefore, if the frequency of susceptible nonhosts is high enough, the idea will serve its own propagation more effectively by contributing to the breakup of relationships. A similar mechanism may help explain the evolutionary epidemiology of the AIDS virus in humans: Part of its transmission may result from terrifying hosts out of their relationships and back into dating as singles (Lynch, 1996). The evolutionary interests of the belief may thus severely clash with those of its host's genes: The belief benefits by favoring a chronically single life, while the host's genes may benefit reproductively from a long-term relationship.

An evolutionary conflict between the astrological belief and the genes of its host may also change with changing prevalence of the idea and those suscepti-ble to it. If, for example, susceptible nonhosts of the belief become quite rare, then variants of the belief might win by reducing breakups and favoring more parent to child idea transmission. Such variants might, for example, find most couples compatible rather than incompatible. A continued supply of young people reaching dating age without learning astrological dating beliefs from their parents might stop this from happening, though. That would happen espe-cially if adherents who stay together and have children usually drop the astro-logical-dating idea by the time their own children grow up.

Intermittent reinforcement may also play a role in raising the communica-tion rate of astrological compatibility ideas. When people exchange astrological signs, they will be rewarded with a discovery of compatibility on an intermittent random schedule. This may lead to high rates of the communication behavior. Significantly, the ideas themselves determine the average reinforcement sched-ule for their own expression. Far from always evolving toward a better or higher population intelligence, the process may actually impair people's abilities to think rationally and to satisfy their personal goals.

Astrological ideas may also exhibit thought contagion principles outside the singles population. There too, the process may not be driven by rationality or personal utility so much as the ideas' effectiveness in self-propagation. People who believe in astrology may often try to give their friends and family the sup-posed benefit of the belief system by sharing astrological advice and forecasts, thus exposing others to astrological thought contagions. Once received, the ideas benefit from the proponent's good intentions: When trying to give helpful advice to friends and family, the astrological messenger usually occupies a posi-tion of trust to the listener. As family and friends, listeners can also form a cap-tive audience, especially to a putatively helpful message. Even those listeners who do not know the adherent well can still find that the helpful structure of as-trological messages engenders trust.

Despite all of this, most listeners still do not convert from just a single expo-sure. Yet astrological beliefs may enjoy a mechanism of provoking multiple artic-ulations of themselves, and hence multiple exposures for the nonhost. With each day's change of horoscopes, the adherent may find new and sincere rea-sons for sharing astrology with others. Those not adopting the ideas on first ex-posure may thus get numerous additional exposures.

Although the underlying suggestion to become an astrological believer can remain constant from one exposure to the next, the specific forecasts keep changing. That makes subsequent persuasion attempts sound just different enough to prevent blanket rejections from many listeners. Any skepticism raised by one horoscope need not apply to a subsequent forecast because the specific content differs. By not thinking, "I've heard this all before," listeners may refrain from shutting out astrological messages for a longer time than they would for a more monotonous message. By their very structure, astrological belief systems may thus keep the conversion attempts flowing and the ears listening. The time-honored impact of repeating a message many times may thus give astrological thought contagions a special propagation advantage.

Other popular beliefs running counter to modern science may also spread through cultural selection mechanisms. As with astrological ideas, beliefs in extrasensory perception (ESP) and psychic powers may owe much of their prevalence to evolutionary epidemiological effects. For example, if someone has a dream that just happens to match subsequent real life experience, the coincidence may be more salient and memorable than the usual disconnection between dreams and reality. Many people may thus preferentially remember dreams that seem true. The coincidence of dream and reality may also lead one to spend more time thinking about it. But thinking about it more can lead in turn to talking about it more—if it is not too private. A dream contemplated for 10 minutes of the following day might in principle be discussed 10 times more often than a dream recalled for just 1 minute of the following day. News of coincidences may thus be differentially retransmitted.

Once someone thinks that they have the special powers of ESP, they may also have more motives to tell others about it. Being regarded as having special powers can, after all, be seen as having social advantages. This may further amplify the recursive transmission of ESP beliefs. Some people also spread messages about psychic powers specifically to make money by offering psychic services, books, and so forth. They could often be unbelievers, parasitizing the popular misbelief. Yet they also act symbiotically with it, because they help to spread the idea in order to profit from its prevalence. The real believers may be the customers, whose role in belief propagation becomes that of helping to pay for advertisements that spread belief in psychic powers. Only a small fraction of those hearing an ad for a psychic hotline, for example, need be persuaded that psychic powers exist and are available from the hotline in order to continue the advertisement's broadcast to still other listeners.

As new people become exposed to the concept, they may start looking more intensely for coincidences between their dreams or thoughts and subsequent events. Merely looking for such coincidences can increase the likelihood of finding them. Therefore, as existing believers enunciate the ESP concept to new listeners and help spread it through advertisements, new listeners may start to engage in the coincidence-seeking that can make believers of them too. The new listeners may also simply convert to the belief in ESP even without experiencing anything that seems like an ESP discovery in themselves.

A belief in ESP might also be more vivid and gripping than more ordinary ideas about limited mental powers. Thus, some of those who do not think of themselves as psychic but who still believe in ESP may spend more time thinking about mental powers than they would spend if they held more boring ideas about the mind. This might also lead to more thinking about special mental powers and, in turn, more retransmission of the beliefs in them.

Notice that all of this belief propagation can proceed without ESP or psychic powers having any basis in reality. The belief in ESP may thus be an erroneous belief that is more likely to arise and spread in a population than in a solitary individual contemplating his or her mental abilities. As with the belief in astrological compatibility, the idea illustrates the difference between population intelligence and individual intelligence. When ideas have sufficiently strong self-propagation mechanisms that are not truth contingent, the population may exhibit a lower level of intelligence than its individual members.

As erroneous thought contagions spread in the population, they also gain added chances of developing more contagious variations. Those that spread to the most individuals have the most chances of acquiring still more contagious additions or variations. Meanwhile, the most contagious ideas have the greatest number of chances of combining with other highly contagious ideas as well, giving them more chances of developing a symbiotic cotransmission advantage. Thus, the formation of new and contagious combinations of ideas tends to disproportionately build on those ideas that were most contagious in the past. As a result, highly elaborate but unfounded belief systems can arise, such as those involving astrology and parapsychology. Other simple to elaborate thought contagions exert a strongly irrational influence on stock markets (Lynch, 2000; in press) and numerous other areas of life (Lynch, 1996). The population mind, distinct from the individual mind, may thus go awry with a vengeance for some kinds of topics.

One might suppose that the more serious ideas being produced by today's academic scientists are totally above thought contagion effects such as those that might propagate psychic claims and astrology. Yet even scientific ideas can spread by surprisingly nontruth-contingent mechanisms, especially when they become popularized. Consider the evolutionary psychology hypothesis that female mating preferences for wealth, status, and power evolved genetically (e.g., Buss, 1994). One alternative explanation is the differential spread of ideas: that parents and other relatives preferentially tell daughters to marry money, marry power, and variants thereof to prevent them from bringing back unexpected child-raising expenses to the extended family (Lynch, 1996). Additionally, women who have learned to marry socioeconomically may, especially in past centuries, have left and inculcated more surviving offspring than women who found poor men equally acceptable. Meanwhile, men who sought mates based on female earning prospects may often have gone mateless, due to the largely cultural economic roles of women. Such men would pass their mores down to fewer offspring. Such differential idea propagation would apply in numerous societies around the world, possibly explaining the observation by Buss et al. (1990) that women in many cultures value a mate's prospective earning potential more than men do. Purely genetic evolution in the Stone Age might have favored preferences based on male body features, because physical features would have played a greater role in a man's ability to reproduce and provide— back before real-estate, money, and farming. Indeed, undeniably cultural practices, such as arranged marriage, female genital mutilation, and special restraints on women's freedom might be seen as evolving partly in support of cultural imperatives to mate socioeconomically by repressing innate female sexual desire. Finally, parental efforts to influence daughters' socioeconomic mating priorities might be widely witnessed by nonscientists, whereas genetic factors for such preferences have apparently not been identified, even in the laboratory. While not constituting a formal study, such wide differences in personal observation might be expected to give high intellectual receptivity to the idea that socioeconomic mating preferences are culturally instilled.

Despite the possible propagation advantages for alternative hypotheses, the idea that female wealth preference is mainly or purely innate may enjoy even more contagion advantage. For example, men of higher than average income or social status could have a special receptivity to the idea that female socioeconomic mate preferences are innate. A rich man whose wife is less than half his age, for example, may feel better thinking that his wife's attraction to him is every bit as biological as his attraction to her. He may also have amorous motives for retransmitting this idea to his wife and his acquaintances, hoping again that everyone will see the relationship as true love. Many peers could then have similar retransmission motives, setting up a recursive transmission process. Wealthier men also get more attention, influence, and imitation—both directly and through mass media. That can further propagate whatever ideas spread among them. Meanwhile, wealthy single men can have their own amorous motives for telling women that the desire for a wealthy man is innately universal: They may consciously or unconsciously see transmitting the idea a way to boost their own mating appeal. Both married and single men of high socioeconomic status may also have great receptivity to the idea as a rationalization for having extramarital affairs or multiple relationships with women. They may then feel sexual motives for spreading the evolutionary psychology hypothesis to women to help persuade women that having sex with these men would be innately natural for the women. Retransmitting the biological hypothesis can thus serve, consciously or unconsciously, as a sexually motivated way of persuading women to set aside monogamy mores, adultery taboos, and so forth. Heterosexual sex may motivate these communications, but other heterosexual males may also be exposed to the hypothesis if they are in close social proximity to the discussions. This would allow recursive heterosexually motivated transmission even among males.

Many women may show high receptivity to the idea as well, because it can be seen as scientifically rationalizing their planned or actual mate choices, especially with rich or powerful men. This would include, for example, rationalizing a decision to have sex with a high-status married man. It could also justify choosing husbands socioeconomically, leading to a belief to mate-choice correlation in females. That could produce a belief to wealth correlation in females too, because more of these women might marry into wealth than would women who do not see themselves as biologically driven to prefer partner wealth. If wealthy females are disproportionately imitated as well, the correlation might add to the transmission advantages of wealthy males being disproportionately imitated. Additionally, the females with whom high-status males choose to discuss the innate socioeconomic mating hypothesis might disproportionately be women the men find attractive. These desired females could ipso facto receive more attention and consequently better idea transmission among both sexes—although stereotyping might give them lower idea transmission rates in the area of scientific ideas.

If the idea does in fact spread particularly well among the rich and powerful, then its hosts would presumably have greater means of supporting or controlling scientific research, publications, and institutions. This could give their ideas a transmission edge even in academic circles. Indeed, just having the idea become popular in the larger society can become a basis for writing and selling books about it. Moreover, males who have this idea may feel an increased sexual incentive to achieve wealth and project the appearances of wealth. If the innate partner-wealth preference idea does in fact lead to greater male strivings for wealth, then its propagation might lead to greater emphasis on wealth and consequent attainment of wealth in society at large, and in the host population of innate wealth preference believers in particular. That, too, could give more influence to the innate partner–wealth preference idea in scientific research funding and publication. Increased desire to make displays or hints of wealth may also have more surprising consequences, such as increasing stock market interest and stock market talk, fostering more stock market thought contagion.[5]

Beliefs in the innateness of other norms, mores, and religious tendencies previously seen as culturally transmitted may also exhibit distinct thought contagion

---

[5]The connection of increased societal materialism to increased interest in stocks is discussed by Shiller (2000), although not in relation to the spread of the innate partner-wealth hypothesis.

advantages. Some believers may consciously or unconsciously see innateness hypotheses for mores and beliefs as attractive rationalizations for those mores and beliefs. This can make them more receptive to the genetic hypotheses and more eager to retransmit the hypotheses to justify their cultures to others.

It becomes important to note that a tentative thought contagion analysis does not substitute for actually doing further scientific research. The genetic partner–wealth hypothesis, for example, could spread despite being false, or despite being true! Even if a belief owes much of its propagation to nontruth-contingent selection mechanisms, this does not automatically mean that the belief is false. In this particular case, rapid propagation of a mainly genetic wealth-preference hypothesis could happen whether or not the observed wealth preferences of women arise from genes, ideas, or a combination thereof. One role for thought contagion analysis might be in helping identify certain kinds of possible biases in scientific research or communications. Yet the main point is again that intelligence as a population phenomenon could work quite differently from intelligence as an individual phenomenon—even at the level of the scientific community.

With this discussion of the evolutionary epidemiology of an evolutionary psychology hypothesis, alert readers may notice that even thought contagion hypotheses can spread by nontruth-contingent thought contagion principles. This is true. There is indeed an evolutionary epidemiology of evolutionary epidemiology of beliefs. There is even an evolutionary epidemiology of that in turn, and so on, leading to what Hofstadter (1979) called a "strange loop" of self-referentiality. Still, even if ideas about the evolutionary epidemiology of beliefs spread rampantly, this is not necessarily bad; it could lead to more self-awareness by the population of how it reaches conclusions (or nonconclusions). Such self-awareness at the population level could make the process more intelligent—at least if Hofstadter's thesis holds true and extends to population self-awareness.

Therefore the thought contagion hypotheses about beliefs in innate partner–wealth preferences, psychic powers, astrology, and numerous other topics could very well spread as thought contagions in their own right. However, the entire theoretical paradigm of thought contagion theory must have at least a sliver of validity in order to spread by its own principles. It must even have a sliver of validity to go extinct by its own principles. In other words, the thought contagion paradigm cannot be totally false and still be an example of itself.

Even scientific and pseudoscientific ideas about intelligence may have their fates dramatically altered by the difference between individual intelligence and population intelligence. For example, much historical evidence indicates that German Nazism and anti-Semitism were indeed mass movements, rather than collections of terrible orders handed down from above (Goldhagen, 1996). In particular, beliefs in the intellectual and general superiority of a supposed Aryan race may have spread as mass thought contagions in prewar Germany.

One transmission advantage may have been that espousing Aryan-supremacist and overtly Nazi ideology could have been a roundabout way of announcing, "I am superior!" Many people who could count themselves as Aryan may have felt like expressing such a message; but, realizing that direct bragging often meets with skepticism and opprobrium, they may have considered enunciations of Nazi ideology as attractive methods of indirect self-praise. Expounding a theory that people with certain kinds of physical features, surnames, or other conspicuous cues are superior can be an indirect way of calling oneself superior—especially if the person doing the expounding happens to exhibit those desired cues. Many listeners who could count themselves as Aryan apparently exhibited receptivity based on the flattering nature of the message. Their adopting the ideology would allow them to privately flatter themselves as superior. Yet many new converts could also have completed the cycle by going on to view retransmission as an indirect way of voicing superiority claims. This would allow for a recursive process of transmission, adoption, and retransmission that could spread Nazism to large numbers of people. An era of widespread insecurities, such as the Great Depression and the Germans' defeat in World War I, could have intensified this cycle by making people more eager to adopt and retransmit superiority beliefs. Yet the ideology may have had numerous other propagation mechanisms as well.

Consider what it would have been like to eat lunch with several people during the early days of Nazism. Suppose too that a man at the table starts openly voicing Nazi ideology. Ideas of a supposedly superior race being cheated by such a supposedly inferior race as the Jews tend to make believers angry. The Nazi may thus sound quite angry and threatening in voicing his convictions. He believes his "race" to be victims of enormous crimes, and he expresses opinions that opponents to Nazism must be ruthlessly and violently defeated. You don't believe a word he says, but do you speak up? For most people, the answer is no. You just want to avoid a heated argument with an angry man who thinks his enemies should be killed, and who belongs to an armed movement that quickly established its violent reputation. In such a way, the Nazi may intimidate the non-Nazi into silence, and into granting more speaking time to the Nazi. This not only favors the spread of Nazi ideology, but it also blocks the spread of non-Nazi ideologies. Believing in his intellectual and overall superiority, the Nazi also tends to behave as if he has more authority over a situation than he does. Therefore, even when opponents are not intimidated into silence, the Nazi may appear as more of an authority figure. This may make people in the Nazi's audience more inclined to accept the ideology being expressed.

Once someone gave tentative acceptance to Nazism and joined the movement, the party's intimidating tactics may have tended to suppress ideological wavering and dropping out. To drop out could have been taken as a grave betrayal calling for a violent end. This could have added to the longevity of Nazi adherence.

The conspiracy tenets in Nazi ideology added to the level of Nazi anger, which strengthened its capacity to intimidate opponents into silence. That silence extended to a variety of settings, such as leaving Nazis unopposed in passing out leaflets or inviting people to political rallies. Conspiracy tenets could also have helped the Nazi dismiss contrary beliefs as products of the supposed conspiracy, and the people who held contrary beliefs as either co-conspirators or unwitting conspiracy victims. This may have added to the longevity of Nazism in its average host, while adding stigma to the silencing effects that Nazism had on non-Nazis. Conspiracy tenets would have made non-Nazis feel further deterred from expressing their own beliefs by the possibility of being regarded as coconspirators with Jews and other supposedly inferior groups. Easily created and hard for most people to disprove, the Nazi conspiracy tenets may thus have intensified the thought contagion.

But the Nazi thought contagion also told its hosts that the fate of the world depended on spreading the ideas. Moreover, the ideas implied that the Aryan Nazi, being superior intellectually and otherwise, was far more qualified than anyone else to spread his or her ideas. This may have helped rationalize crimes against anyone who stood in their way, including the murder of people who opposed them politically. And murdering nonhosts again tends to raise the relative prevalence of the Nazi belief system, at least in the short run. But less extreme competitive propagation acts, such as defaming or bodily attacking political opponents and disrupting their public presentations, also helped Nazism spread long before Nazis rose to power (Noakes & Pridham, 1983). A desire to confiscate wealth from Jews and others may have added to the financial dimension of motives for retransmitting Nazism and sabotaging other political movements.

Nazi ideology also contained intensely nationalistic ideas from the outset (Noakes & Pridham, 1983). This did, of course, give the movement an emotional appeal, a factor easily seen using noncontagion analysis. Yet a nationalistic emotional appeal may have been more evolutionarily adapted to some population sectors than others. The sector to which it was apparently most adapted was the large contingent of defeated World War I veterans. And while attracting the war's losers might normally seem disadvantageous in expanding the movement to society at large, these particular losers were the men most capable of violence and intimidation. Therefore, their presence in the movement may have greatly amplified the belief system's ability to propagate by intimidating nonhosts into silence. German Communism, in contrast, was apparently poorly adapted to spreading among nationalistic German veterans—and may thus have accrued less ability to spread by scaring unbelievers into silence.

During the early 1930s, a large unemployed population would have felt the wealth confiscation motive more acutely, adding to the infectiousness of Nazi anti-Semitism. However, the unemployed would also have had plenty of free time for spreading beliefs. For these reasons, the worldwide depression may have helped decide when the Nazi thought contagion could replicate much faster than the growth threshold of infection rate exceeding removal rate. Often cited as the factor that makes hateful, conspiratorial ideologies credible and emotionally attractive, economic hardship may also motivate adherents to retransmit. For example, a desire to announce, "I am not to blame for my poverty" can become an added motive for retransmitting ideologies that formally place the blame on others. Therefore, the economic insecurity that creates a desire to say something positive about oneself may be subverted by thought contagions like Nazism. However, while economic trouble apparently helps to decide when such thought contagions spread, the actual mechanism of spread may be much more complex than a simple principle that trouble causes Nazism. In this respect, Nazism might resemble an influenza virus: Although the onset of winter helps set the timing of outbreaks, the weather itself does not explain how the virus spreads.

Some ideological precursors that eventually combined into Nazism may have spread for similar reasons. Anti-Semitism has its origins in the cultural evolution of Christianity (Goldhagen, 1996). Yet the more extreme pre-Nazi forms of anti-Semitism and nationalism, because they inspired so much anger, may also have gained propagation advantages by intimidating nonadherents into silence. As with overt Nazism, these earlier forms of anti-Semitism may likewise have promoted feelings of superior belief-spreading qualification on the part of adherents. Once the specifically racist forms of anti-Semitism arose through erroneous nineteenth century biology, they may also have spread by spawning a new form of intimidation that was not possible for earlier anti-Semitism: Anyone who challenged the new racist anti-Semitism could be branded as possibly having Jewish blood, with all the inferiority implications for the racial anti-Semite. For those who did not consider themselves Jewish, it may therefore have been much easier to leave racial anti-Semitism unchallenged, giving it a higher longevity factor. Indeed, an insecure desire to prove to oneself and others that one's blood could not be called "tainted" may have unconsciously motivated racial anti-Semites to voice their opinions more intensely and more often, adding transmissivity advantages to racial anti-Semitism over other anti-Semitisms.

The wealth confiscation motive would also have intensified proselytism for racial anti-Semitism more than for other forms of anti-Semitism. The most racist forms viewed theft of Jews' possessions as taking or even taking back from the inherently and irredeemably undeserving, so hosts may have felt stronger motives to proselytize racist variants of anti-Semitism as a stronger rationalization for plundering Jewish wealth.

Ideologies of racial superiority before, during, and after World War II may also have motivated adherents to have more children. Holding such ideologies could easily have led believers to conclude that it was their duty to propagate their "race" for the betterment of nation and the world. Because the extra children would have been heavily exposed to the belief systems of their parents, such an effect could have helped spread pre-Nazi anti-Semitisms, as well as overt Nazism and other racist ideologies around the world.

As the proto-Nazi thought contagions of extreme nationalism and racial anti-Semitism spread to hundreds, thousands, and millions of people, the odds increased that one of those infected would have exceptional oratorical skills. And the beliefs themselves, by arousing such intense passions, tended to intensify the oratory that eventually flowed from Adolf Hitler.

Although extreme "master race" nationalism and racial anti-Semitism may have enjoyed all these propagation advantages, the ideologies also had an inherent tendency to incite their adherents into war once the host population was large enough to control an entire country. This immediately limited and set back the movement in countries forced into alliance against Germany. The intensity of passions arising from the Nazi belief set were apparently so great that Hitler could not resist going to war on multiple fronts, too. This fact ultimately slated him and his movement for military defeat. Therefore, the contagion forces that gave rise to the Führer and his movement happened, in this case, to bring on a drastic fall in host population as defeated and disillusioned adherents dropped out en masse.

Even generations after the fall of the Third Reich, Nazi thought contagions continue to spread at a lower level in Europe and the United States. Some of the same mechanisms apparently still play a part, such as beliefs in one's own intellectual superiority in promulgating political messages and the intimidation of some nonbelievers into silence. Yet there may be some new or modified mechanisms propagating neo-Nazi thought contagions in recent years.

Wearing the swastika may have helped spread prewar Nazism by provoking people to ask what it meant. The resultant answers to questions would then become an opportunity to retransmit Nazi ideology without being perceived as proselytizing. That could in turn lead others to wear the swastika. After the party became widely known, swastikas could convey Nazi affiliation without need for explanation. Yet the symbol fell into serious disrepute in the postwar period, and the party was banned in Germany. This may have created evolutionary contagion advantages for new symbols that have similar effect. The neo-fascist skinhead practice of shaving one's scalp might be one example. As with the earliest Nazi swastikas, a shaved scalp can certainly provoke people to ask questions. This too can lead to belief transmission that is not rejected as overt proselytizing. Like body piercing and other conspicuous fashions (Lynch, 1997), it may have also had an attention-grabbing transmission among neo-fascist movements.

More recently, a gruesome 1998 racist killing in Jasper, Texas focused wide attention on the influence of racist gangs in United States prisons, such as the Aryan Brotherhood (Jones, 1998). Part of the problem is that assault laws are not enforced very well among inmates. This allows gangs to spread by offering protection to potential recruits, much as street gangs apparently do in many neighborhoods. Concentrating a population of susceptible individuals in a confined space with abundant opportunity to communicate with each other may hasten the spread of thought contagions much as it hastens the spread of influenza. This may disproportionately spread neo-Nazism among the convict and ex-convict populations. Convicts may also have more insecurities motivating them to claim superiority, again favoring Nazi thought contagions. Finally, convicts and ex-convicts may give the same type of intimidation advantages to modern neo-Nazism as the World War I German veterans did for the German Nazi movement of the 1920s and 1930s.

Extreme progun and militia movements, which may have intimidation mechanisms of propagation on their own in the modern United States, may show an intensified intimidation effect when combined with hateful ideologies such as Nazism and racism. People may be less willing to voice personal disagreement with someone expressing a strongly progun doctrine, while those spreading such doctrines may often feel their life or safety depends on it.[6] The progun movement, the militia movements, and neo-Nazi movements may thus spread synergistically as large, combined ideological packages. Indeed, the original Nazi emphasis on armed violence and paramilitary activity may also support this combination of racism and private armed militarism.

Neo-Nazism may still propagate through the media as well. As extreme ideologies lead some of their adherents to commit sensational killings, the modern media often respond by giving air time to the ideas of the killers or their ideological associates. This ideological air time would come in addition to possible contagion effects of publicizing violent acts themselves. In 1999, for example, a member of the white supremacist World Church of the Creator went on a killing spree that was followed by numerous long interviews being given to Matthew Hale, the organization's leader. Only a small fraction of those listening to the interviews needed to be persuaded in order to cause net propagation for neo-Nazism. It is also possible that proportionately more people were converted away

---

[6]Some discussion of the spread of progun and militia movements is in Lynch (1996).

from such ideology by hearing it in association with murder, but it would take an organized study to find out.

Finally, the Internet accelerates all types of thought contagions in modern times, but may disproportionately accelerate Nazism and other extremist ideologies. A possible reason is not just that it is technically easier for one to acquire or publish extreme messages, but also that it is socially easier to retransmit them. Many people who would feel socially or economically deterred from voicing Nazi ideology around neighbors or coworkers can do so with relative anonymity and social impunity on the Internet. The higher per-host transmission rate can then lead to a self-sustaining movement and higher prevalence for the ideologies.

Racial ideologies certainly did not originate in Germany and then spread to the United States in the twentieth century. Rather, the neo-Nazi ideologies combine with racist belief systems that had propagated for centuries in the United States. Those U.S. racial ideologies largely focused on people of African descent, starting in the days of slavery.

With their own assertions of the mental inferiority of people of African descent, such U.S. racist ideologies may have shown still further distinct mechanisms of propagation at the population level. For example, those who thought Africans and African Americans were subhuman would presumably have felt justified in using them as slaves. Those who acquired conspicuous sums of essentially stolen wealth by holding slaves may then have attracted imitators of European descent looking for ways to get rich themselves. The methods of using slaves and the beliefs behind slavery would thus have enjoyed much the same transmission advantages of other lucrative practices. Increased wealth for the slave holder could also have brought more imitation simply by raising the social status of plantation owners. This may have helped their racist ideas spread even to people who were successful in completely different lines of business that could not incorporate slavery. In effect, slaves were paying, through their stolen labor, for the prominent retransmission of proslavery beliefs from high-status individuals. Slavery also paid for the kidnapping and transport of more slaves as well. Furthermore, slave holders of past centuries might have gained more reproduction from wealth stolen through slavery. By making the male slave holder richer, it may have made him more able to attract females with high reproductive potential and allowed him to afford more offspring.[7] This, in turn, could have caused more parent-to-child transmission of proslavery beliefs—including ideas about racial inferiority of blacks. As if this weren't enough, all types of

---

[7]Note that the effects of a man's wealth on the number of children he fathers may have been different in past centuries than in the twentieth century. Additionally, wealth increases can lead to more children even if there is negative wealth to fertility correlation—an effect explained toward the end of this chapter.

direct and indirect beneficiaries, such as those doing business with slave plantation owners, may have had financial reasons to advocate racist and proslavery
ideas. With a substantially slave-based society resulting, fierce racism may even
have helped intimidate some nonracists into silence on the subject, much as
Nazism did in the twentieth century. People may also have transmitted and
adopted racist thinking as ways of indirectly claiming superiority, again resembling Nazism. All these factors could have further amplified the transmission
advantages of racist thought contagions.

Thought contagions did not all run in favor of racism, however. As the
slave population swelled, more and more people became aware of the practice
and its cruelty. Advertisements for slaves being sold would certainly have
raised awareness as well, as would articles on the subject. Moreover, an aboli-
tionist movement had some transmission advantages of its own. Those who
believed in abolition felt a strong desire to spread their beliefs in order to help
rescue the slaves.

Ultimately a civil war ensued and slavery was ended, but racist beliefs continued. To this day, there are apparently U.S. citizens who adopt and express
racist ideas as a form of self-flattery and indirect bragging of putative superiority. Economic motives for adopting and spreading racist beliefs may also exist
in some sectors of society. Moreover, the economic and familial harm done by
slavery and its aftermath have fostered negative socioeconomic stereotyping
of African Americans. Many non-African Americans may then retransmit
those negative stereotypes as an indirect way of calling themselves superior.
They may also transmit general theories of the superiority of whites (a conspicuous color cue) as an indirect way of implying their own superiority, much
as may have happened with prewar German racism. Scapegoating others for
one's own problems can also be a reason for adopting and retransmitting racist
ideas in the modern United States, again exhibiting some possible similarities
to prewar Nazism—even if at a lower level. Finally, the most extreme and
overt racist ideologies of today may intimidate some nonbelievers into silence,
much as with prewar Nazism.

The evolutionary epidemiology of ideas about intelligence and race may thus
be another prime example of how population intelligence can differ in mechanics and conclusions from individual intelligence. Given the enormous consequences that racist notions of intellectual and general superiority have had on
the world, the phenomena of racism apparently also illustrate the importance of
taking evolutionary epidemiology into account when considering how population intelligence differs from individual intelligence. Of course, this volume is
titled *The Evolution of Intelligence* rather than *The Evolution of Unintelligence*, but
it is important to point out that evolution does not automatically and uniformly
seek out what we would call an upward trend.

THOUGHT CONTAGION EFFECTS IN THE EVOLUTION OF INDIVIDUAL INTELLIGENCE

Besides affecting how intelligently a population handles particular questions such as the validity of astrology, racism, and so forth, the evolutionary epidemiology of ideas may also affect the prevalence of ideas that have a fairly broad impact on the cognitive and social intelligence of the individual. The idea that spanking is good for children or effective as discipline may be an example. Straus and Paschall (1998, 1999) have done research indicating that the corporal punishment of children correlates negatively with their subsequent cognitive development. Straus, Sugarman, and Giles-Sims (1997) have also found that spanking tends to produce antisocial behavior in the long run (2 years later), even when parents use it to reduce antisocial behavior.

These negative results raise the question of how belief in spanking could have propagated so widely in past generations. If population intelligence mirrored the best of individual intelligence, one might expect that parents would simply discover what works best in the long run and then adopt that practice en masse. Centuries of accumulated wisdom might also be expected to yield nearly optimal child-raising methods. An alternative, evolutionary thought contagion hypothesis starts by assuming that in the short run, children reinforce spanking behavior of their parents through temporarily reduced antisocial behavior. If the children do in fact temporarily reduce antisocial behavior in response to parental spanking, or temporarily reduce antisocial behavior discernible to parents, and if this leads to increased spanking behavior by parents, then the children's antisocial behavior would act as a negative reinforcer for the parent's spanking behavior.[8] Such prompt behavioral reinforcement may thus lead parents to repeat their spanking behavior more often, which could more effectively help the children learn the idea of spanking. Such conditioning might even strengthen parents' belief in the effectiveness of spanking, leading more of them to eventually suggest its use on grandchildren and spread the idea that it is effective. It may also displace nonviolent methods of conflict resolution and cause later emotional disturbances that lead to violence (Straus & Yodanis, 1996). All of this can raise the chances that the spanked children will become spankers themselves when they grow up and have children of their own, consistent with actual observation (Murphy-Cowan & Stringer, 1999). Epidemiologically, what is important is that the thought contagion can propagate in part by increasing the fraction of offspring effectively inculcated—what I have labeled an *efficiency parental* transmission mechanism (Lynch, 1996).

---

[8]See Skinner (1953) for more discussion of negative and positive behavioral reinforcers.

In some cases, the negative long-term consequences of spanking might produce a vicious cycle: the more parents spank, the more antisocial and cognitively slowed behavior results over time. That, in turn, may lead to more frequent and intense corporal punishment and the learning of more severe corporal punishment ideas by children. For example, they may learn to think that the misbehaving child deserves severe physical punishment. When they grow up, they may have trouble considering the possibility that they suffered as children for nothing, leading to greater longevity of belief retention. Cognitively, the physically punitive parents may fail to see that their own behavior has contributed to their children's antisocial conduct and instead conclude that previous corporal punishments were just not severe enough. This could raise the severity of the corporal punishment ideas they express physically and retransmit verbally. In extreme cases, such a vicious cycle may lead to the serious bodily injury or death of a child. Nevertheless, if the injury and death rates are low enough, then efficiency parental transmission advantages may propel prospanking ideas to high prevalence.

The idea that one can use fear and punishment to maintain order over a large brood may also make parents willing to have more children. If they do, this would constitute a quantity parental effect. Those parents who have enough children to suffer serious parental stress may also spank more often in reaction to their stress. This would lead to a family-size to spanking correlation that can add further to the spanking idea's quantity parental replication. All of this may help the idea spread despite its ineffectiveness. Thus, an idea that tends to lower both the cognitive and social intelligence of individuals may spread by way of quantity and efficiency parental transmission.

The idea of corporal punishment evolved early enough to become incorporated into religious texts. The Biblical proverb that "He who spares the rod hates his son" (Proverbs 13:24, Revised Standard Version) is one example. Once the idea spread widely enough to become incorporated into vigorously spreading religious belief systems, it may have enjoyed further propagation advantages by spreading symbiotically with numerous religious ideas having strong propagation advantages of their own.[9] Ideological mutation and variation seem to have occurred to some extent over the past several thousand years. Popular proverbs now include "Spare the rod, spoil the child," often without knowledge of the Biblical connection.

The increased roles of nonparental and nonreligious sources of information may have helped reduce the U.S. adult approval of corporal punishment from 94% in 1968 to 68% in 1994, as documented by Straus and Mathur (1996).

---

[9]Numerous propagation advantages of religious ideas are discussed, for example, in Lynch (1996, 1997, 1998, 2001), and Stark (1996).

Books filled with expert child-raising advice have proliferated in recent decades, as have discussions of the subject on the radio, TV, and in other media. Meanwhile, the size of the baby-boom fostered peer-to-peer propagation of thought contagions by raising the population density of those born in the 1950s and early 1960s. Antispanking messages could thus spread rapidly not only by major media but also by accelerated word of mouth. Desires to help prevent violence and child abuse could have made those who held antispanking beliefs more motivated to propagate the antispanking beliefs to peers of child-raising age. A great deal of legislation for the prevention of child abuse has also passed since 1968, giving further centralized transmission to messages that limit or prevent corporal punishment. Health care workers, social workers, psychologists, teachers, and other professionals have also played an important role in disseminating research-based advice directly to parents in recent years. Still, both the earlier proliferation of corporal punishment ideas and their subsequent decline may have played a nongenetic part in the evolution of individual social and intellectual intelligence.

The evolutionary epidemiology of ideas may also nongenetically affect the evolution of individual intelligence through changes in early brain development. Research finds that stimulating early home environments have a positive effect on cognitive development (e.g., Bradley et al., 1989). Yet the ideas of the parents may exert strong influences on home environment in matters ranging from the choice of playthings to the way parents interact with and educate their young. Thus, the parentally transmitted ideas might evolve under selection pressures similar to those pertaining to genes.

As the sheer number of symbiotic ideas needed to compete in modern society rises, the level of stimulation given to young, developing brains may rise as well. This would include the vast number of horizontally spreading ideas that can at times spread much faster than parentally spreading ideas. Thus, even without evolution of more intelligence-promoting genes or intelligence-promoting child-raising ideas, the accelerating pace of cultural change may be contributing to upward trends in mental aptitudes by increasing mental stimulation. Just such an upward mental functioning trend has apparently been observed in the form of the Flynn effect. Named after James Flynn, the Flynn effect is a long-term upward trend in IQ test results of several points per decade. It adds up to very substantial increases over the span of generations (Flynn, 1984, 1987). It may, by the present cultural evolution hypothesis, have resulted from increased mental stimulation caused by a profusion of ideas and the attendant acceleration of cultural change. This would be consistent with data linking an early stimulating environment to cognitive development (e.g., Bradley et al., 1989). Urbanization and modern communication may accelerate the contagion of ideas involved: urbanization by placing people in closer contact with each other, and modern communications by making it easier and faster to communicate quickly and widely. A stimulating effect from proliferating ideas need not be the only force behind the Flynn effect to warrant consideration as a possible contributing factor. Reduced corporal punishment of children, changes in educational practices, increased parental attention, child labor laws, child abuse laws, greater affluence, more leisure time for parents, and so forth might all have played roles as well. Some of these other factors may involve thought contagions in their own right.

The self-propagation of ideas can also drive the evolution of genes and beliefs that favor lower levels of intelligence, however. The ancient discovery that vaginal sex causes childbirth led to numerous ways of voluntarily controlling reproduction. Yet this led to parental propagation advantages for religions with moral codes that tend to channel sex drives into reproductive acts (Lynch, 1996; Stark, 1996). In modern times, this may create a new kind of problem: Those whose genes or infant-care ideas lead to modest intelligence may drop such religions and moral codes at lower rates than those whose genes or infant-care ideas lead to high intelligence. At the same time, knowledge about birth control and the reasons for using it may be more readily acquired by those who demonstrate vigorous cognitive functioning. The result is potentially more reproduction for genetic and cultural factors that favor moderate rather than high intelligence. Trends in cognitive performance, such as those suggested by the Flynn effect, might thus be composed of factors working for and against increased intelligence. The net result over the past century seems to be a positive cognitive performance trend, at least as measured by IQ tests. One might argue, however, that the Flynn effect could have been an even more strongly positive trend if a hypothesized correlation between intellectual functioning and acceptance of birth control did not exist.

Possibly countering this effect, however, are the beliefs with strong peer-to-peer contagion patterns that may selectively lower the reproduction rates of their hosts. The idea of astrological mate choice may be just such a thought contagion, and it may reduce the number of acceptable partners and duration of relationships, thus potentially reducing fertility. If such thought contagions enjoy greater receptivity in people of modest rather than high intellectual functioning, then their spread would tend to promote an upward evolution in intellectual functioning over the generations. If strong enough to act appreciably in just a few generations, such phylogenetic selection effects might even have contributed to the Flynn effect.

Still other thought contagions may exert positive or negative phylogenetic effects on the evolution of individual intelligence. Racist ideologies such as Nazism and white supremacy doctrines, for example, might exert a negative phylogenetic effect on the evolution of individual intelligence. As discussed earlier, these belief systems may lead adherents to have more children. If such thought contagions also encounter greater receptivity or longevity in people of modest rather than high intellectual functioning, then their spread could cause a downward evolution of intellectual functioning over the generations—a high irony given the claims of superiority and the eugenic tenets. For example, people lacking genetic or cultural factors that promote critical thinking skills may be more susceptible to Nazi persuasion or they may drop the beliefs less often, ultimately resulting in their having more children to propagate a supposedly superior race. The effect might be greater in the postwar era, when considerable public evidence has accumulated against the prospects for a glorious Third Reich. Thought contagions of racist ideology might thus tend to diminish the average cognitive functioning of individuals over the generations, or to stop cognitive functioning from rising as much as it might have due to the Flynn effect and other factors. However, the relative importance of the several proposed phylogenetic effects of thought contagions on the evolution of individual intelligence cannot be determined without empirical study.[10]

In the future, technologies such as intelligence-enhancing drugs, genetically modified human zygotes, and brains enhanced with artificial intelligence could turn the evolution of intelligence into a more heavily cultural phenomenon. An eagerness to gain competitive advantages would make quite a few people receptive to the idea of pharmaceutically and genetically improved intelligence. There would also be a special appeal to intelligence enhanced by implanting devices into the brain or replacing the brain with something nonbiological; many would see it as fulfillment of the quest for immortality.

Nevertheless, taboos against using such technologies might also proliferate. Hosts of the taboos could have more children due to greater retention of restrictive doctrines that call for large families, for example. The technologies might also delay reproduction for some users by leading them to spend more time in college and graduate school, resulting in smaller family sizes. Additionally, the technologies might lead people to more faithfully retain ideologies calling for vigorous evangelism. That would favor the evolution and spread of ideologies explicitly banning intelligence-enhancement technology. Countering this effect would be the possibility that those who use such technologies would be more eloquent and effective at expressing their opinions to others. They might also maintain better recollection of their opinions into old age as they resist con-

---

[10]The phylogenetic effects might not match the ontogenetic effects for such belief systems as astrological dating, Nazism, and so forth. One could argue, for example, that an ideology that emphasizes intellectual superiority might ontogenetically increase cognitive abilities even if it phylogenetically decreases cognitive abilities. Conversely, one could argue that an ideology calling for rigid adherence to a simplistic worldview would have negative ontogenetic effects along with negative phylogenetic effects. In either case, emphasis on intellectual achievement certainly does not require a racist ideology.

ditions such as Alzheimer's disease. Depending on the technology involved, they might also live longer. Such improvements in survival, recall, and communication could help their beliefs about artificial mental enhancement spread by increasing the ideas' transmissivity, receptivity, and longevity factors. Greater abilities could also give users of such technologies more success and higher social status, leading to more peer-to-peer imitation per person. Alternately, greater intellectual abilities may deprive people of some pleasant illusions that motivate them to strive for success. Still, even illusions and moods can be technologically manipulated, and to some extent already are pharmaceutically; so perhaps we should still expect believers in artificial mental enhancement to exhibit higher status and consequent imitation.

Counter to what was said previously, the idea of artificial mental enhancement might even spread parentally. For example, it might help believers attract mates with high reproductive potential, by making the believer richer, wittier, more powerful, and so forth. If higher income is part of this attraction boost, the mental enhancement might help believers earn money to support children as well. These effects could lead to added child-inculcation for proenhancement ideas. This would not require a positive correlation between wealth and fertility rates, either. In a mixture of socioeconomic and ideological evolution, those whose beliefs lead to small family sizes tend to subdivide their wealth less often over the generations. This allows their small-family mores to disproportionately accumulate at higher socioeconomic strata. In other words, parentally transmitted mores that cause large family size may thereby also reduce the average host wealth by subdivision, leading to a negative wealth to family size correlation. (Remember the adage that correlation does not imply causation.) Additionally, strong beliefs in college education can reduce family sizes by delaying parenthood, while simultaneously causing higher per capita income for those who hold strong procollege ideas. Overall, multiple ideas leading to small families can cause wealth concentration, rather than wealth concentration directly causing smaller family size. Hence, there is no inherent inconsistency between a negative wealth to family size correlation and the hypothesis that increasing the earning power of a randomly (or nonrandomly) chosen subpopulation can lead to more children for that subpopulation. In particular, there is no inconsistency with the possibility that the host population of ideas favoring artificial brain-enhancement could grow by way of quantity parental transmission. Some might even use artificial mental enhancement to reduce reproductive delays traditionally associated with college through faster learning and quicker graduation. Still, we do not yet know what effect artificial mental enhancement could have on reproduction rates. Moreover, even if artificial mental enhancement slightly lowers reproduction rates, it may offset this by leading to a higher fraction of children imitating their parents. This could happen simply because of the parents having more money, power, and social status, or because of parents being more clever at passing their beliefs down to children.

Thus, some factors could help spread the belief in artificial mental enhancement, whereas other factors could help spread taboos against using such technology. An interesting population dynamic process could thus arise, giving intelligence as a population phenomenon considerable new influence on intelligence as an individual phenomenon.

REFERENCES

Balkin, J. M. (1998). *Cultural software: A theory of ideology.* New Haven CT: Yale University Press.

Boyd, R., & Richerson, P. (1985). *Culture and the evolutionary process.* Chicago: University of Chicago Press.

Bradley, R. H., Caldwell, B. M., Rock, S. L., Barnard, K. E., Gray, C., Hammond, M. A., Mitchell, S., Siegel, L., Ramey, C. T., Gottfried, A. W., & Johnson, D. L. (1989). Home environment and cognitive development in the first 3 years of life: A collaborative study involving six sites and three ethnic groups in North America. *Developmental Psychology, 25* (2), 217–235.

Buss, D. M. (1994). *The evolution of desire: Strategies of human mating.* New York: Basic Books.

Buss, D. M., Abbott, M., Angleitner, A., Asherian, A., Biaggio, A., Blanco-VillaSeñor, A., Bruchon-Schweitzer, M., Ch'u, Hai-yuan, Czapinski, J., DeRaad, B., Ekehammar, B., Fioravanti, M., Georgas, J., Gjerde, P., Guttman, R., Hazan, F., Iwawaki, S., Janakiramaiah, N., Khosroshani, F., Kreitler, S., K. Lachenicht, L., Lee, M., Liik, K., Little, B., Lohamy, N., Makim, S., Mika, S., Moadel-Shahid, M., Moane, G., Montero, M., Mundy-Castle, A.C., Little, B., Niit, T., Nsenduluka, E., Peltzer, K., Peinkowski, R., Pirttila-Backman, A., Ponce De Leon, J., Rousseau, J., Runco, M. A., Safir, M. P., Samuels, C., Sanitioso, R., Schweitzer, B., Serpell, R., Smid, N., Spencer, C., Tadinac, M., Todorova, E. N., Troland, K., Van den Brande, L., Van Heck, G., Van Langenhove, L., & Yang, Kuo-Shu. (1990). International preferences in selecting mates: A study of 37 Cultures. *Journal of Cross-Cultural Psychology, 21* (1), 5–47.

Calvin, W. H. (1996). *The cerebral code: Thinking a thought in the mosaics of mind.* Cambridge, MA: The MIT Press.

Cavalli-Sforza, L., & Feldman, M. (1981). *Cultural transmission and evolution: A quantitative approach.* Princeton, NJ: Princeton University Press.

Cloak, F. T. (1973). *Elementary self-replicating instructions and their works: Toward a radical reconstruction of general anthropology through a general theory of natural selection.* Paper Presented to the Ninth International Congress of Anthropological and Ethnographical Sciences, Chicago. Reproduced online at http://www.thoughtcontagion.com/cloak1973.htm.

Cloak, F. T. (1975). Is a cultural ethology possible? *Human Ecology, 3*(3), 161–182.

Ewald, P. (1994). *Evolution of infectious disease.* Oxford: Oxford University Press.

Flynn, J. R. (1984). The mean IQ of Americans: Massive gains 1932–1978. *Psychological Bulletin, 95*(1), 29–51.

Flynn, J. R. (1987). Massive IQ gains in 14 nations: What IQ tests really measure. *Psychological Bulletin, 101*(2), 171–191.

Goldhagen, D. J. (1996). *Hitler's willing executioners: Ordinary Germans and the Holocaust.* New York: Knopf.

Hofstadter, D. R. (1979). *Gödel, Escher, Bach: An eternal golden braid.* New York: Basic Books.

James, W. (1880). Great men, great thoughts, and the environment. *The Atlantic Monthly, 46*(276), 441–459.

Jones, C. (1998, June 18). Prisons can cultivate hatred. *USA Today*, p. 7A.

Lynch, A. (1996). *Thought contagion: How belief spreads through society*. New York: Basic Books.

Lynch, A. (1997). Gedankeninfektion Wie Überzeugungen Menschen Finden *gdi-impuls*, 15(3), pp. 42–54. (English original also published as "Thought Contagion and Mass Belief". Available online at http://www.thoughtcontagion.com/tcamb.htm.)

Lynch, A. (1998). Units, events, and dynamics in memetic evolution. *Journal of Memetics - Evolutionary Models of Information Transmission, 2* [Online]. Available: *http://www.cpm.mmu.ac.uk/jom-emit/1998/vol2/lynch_a.html*

Lynch, A. (2000). Thought contagions in the stock market. *Journal of Psychology and Financial Markets, 1*(1), 10–23.

Lynch, A. (2001). *Units, events, and dynamics in the evolutionary epidemiology of ideas* [Online]. Available: http://www.thoughtcontagion.com/UED.htm.

Lynch, A. (in press). Thought contagion in the stock markets: A general framework and focus on the Internet bubble. *Derivatives Use, Trading and Regulation*.

Murphy-Cowan, T., & Stringer, M. (1999). Physical punishment and the parenting cycle: A survey of northern Irish Parents. *Journal of Community and Applied Social Psychology, 9*(1), 61–71.

Noakes, J., & Pridham, G. (Eds.). (1983). *Nazism: 1919–1945*. Exeter, England: University of Exeter Press.

Shiller, R. (2000). *Irrational Exuberance*. Princeton, NJ: Princeton University Press.

Skinner, B. F. (1953). *Science and human behavior*. New York: Macmillan.

Stark, R. (1996). *The rise of Christianity: A sociologist reconsiders history*. Princeton, NJ: Princeton University Press.

Straus, M. A., & Mathur, A. K. (1996). Social change and trends in approval of corporal punishment by parents from 1968 to 1994. In D. Frehsee, W. Horn, and K. Bussman (Eds.), *Violence Against Children* (pp. 91–105). Berlin and New York: Walter de Gruyter.

Straus, M. A., & Paschall, M. J. (1998). *Corporal punishment by mothers and child's cognitive development: A longitudinal study*. Paper of the Family Research Laboratory, University of New Hampshire [Online]. Available: http://www.unh.edu/frl/cp51japa.htm.

Straus, M. A., & Paschall, M. J. (1999). *Corporal punishment by mothers and children's cognitive development: A longitudinal study two age cohorts*. Paper presented at the 6th International Family Violence Research Conference, Durham, NH: University of New Hampshire Family Research Laboratory.

Straus, M. A, Sugarman, D. B., & Giles-Sims, J. (1997). Spanking by parents and subsequent anti-social behavior of children. *Archives of Pediatrics & Adolescent Medicine, 151*(8), 761–767.

Straus, M. A., & Yodanis, C. L. (1996). Corporal punishment in adolescence and physical assaults on spouses in later life: What accounts for the link? *Journal of Marriage and the Family, 58*(4), 825–841.

13

Evolution of Avian Intelligence, With an Emphasis on Grey Parrots (Psittacus erithacus)

Irene M. Pepperberg
University of Arizona
The Media Lab, MIT

Determining what constitutes avian intelligence, much less what selection pressures might have shaped the cognitive architecture that underlies intelligent behavior, is a daunting task. Even after two decades of examining the cognitive and communicative abilities of Grey parrots (*Psittacus erithacus*) and of following colleagues' studies of the capacities of other avian species, I have more questions than answers. Given these many questions, however, five interrelated ones, three general and two specific to birds, appear particularly relevant to discussions of nonhuman intelligence: First, what actually *is* intelligence? Second, can we judge nonhuman capacities using human tasks and definitions? Third, how do we fairly test creatures with different sensory systems from ours? Fourth, how does a nonmammalian brain process information? Fifth, to what extent do avian cognitive capacities match those of mammals? Ongoing studies provide only preliminary answers to the first four questions, but considerable data exist to respond to the fifth. To summarize the state of our knowledge, I examine con-

315

cepts of intelligence and different types or specializations of intelligence, and I review the history of avian cognitive research and studies that indicate advanced cognition, with an emphasis on Grey parrots. I then present some ideas concerning the evolution of intelligence in parrots and possibly other birds.

HOW CAN WE STUDY AVIAN INTELLIGENCE?

The term *intelligence* garners as many definitions as researchers in the field (see Sternberg & Kaufman, 1998), probably because intelligence is not a unitary entity, but is rather "a bag of devices and processes, endowments and aptitudes, that together produce behavior we see as 'intelligent'" (Byrne, 1995, p. 38). In this discussion, however, I characterize intelligence via two abilities. The first is simply the capacity to use experience to solve current problems: A bird faced with green and red fruits, for example, has *learned* and *recalls* that red indicates ripe and tasty and green indicates unripe and bitter, and thus chooses red. The second is a more complicated ability to choose, from among many sets of information acquired in many domains, the set appropriate to the current problem; in the example above, the ability to recognize conditions for which selection of green fruit might be wise (e.g., when red indicates spoilage). An organism limited to the first ability has learned some important associations but lacks flexibility to transfer and adapt information, which is a hallmark of intelligence.

Two problems arise, however, with even this broad definition. First, tasks used to evaluate nonhumans are always interpreted from the standpoint of human sensory systems and perceptions of intelligence. Second, we find that specific avian abilities vary greatly across species. How important are these problems?

Human biases underlie all evaluations of nonhumans, but we can address such problems by designing tasks relevant to an animal's ecology and physiology. We study songbirds' cognitive processing, for example, not by how they resolve match-to-sample problems on colored lights but by how they categorize, repeat, discriminate, and order songs in a territorial encounter (e.g., Kroodsma & Byers, 1998; Todt & Hultsch, 1996). For the importance of such design, consider a reverse analogy: A bird testing humans within an avian context might assess how well song choice by men attracts mates and repels intruders; with perhaps few exceptions, a bird would conclude that humans are incompetent (Pepperberg, 1999). One might even argue that, with respect to the naturalist intelligence proposed by Gardner (1999), nonhumans likely outshine their human brethren. Thus, extreme care must be taken in experimental design.

Avian abilities do differ across species, and no one species illustrates the range of avian intelligence. Birds with large vocal repertoires learn auditory discriminations faster than birds with small repertoires (e.g., Cynx, 1995); caching birds are superior to noncachers in spatial but not nonspatial tasks (Olson,

Kamil, Balda, & Nims, 1995). Knowledge that cachers often do not have large vocal repertoires and versatile songsters generally do not cache precludes exact cross-species comparisons of similar types of intelligence and intraspecies studies of different types of intelligence, and may limit research on the extent to which information transfers across domains. These problems might be resolved by positing that such differences correspond to various specialized forms of intelligence across human subjects (e.g., Gardner, 1983, 1999; Kamil, 1988; Sternberg, 1985) and, as for humans (Sternberg, 1997), that different abilities are mediated by the same basic, underlying processing capacities. Caching and song storage involve different brain areas, but no one has unequivocally determined if different mechanisms encode changes representing learning and memory within these different structures. Even so, whether or not specialized avian abilities reflect specific or general mechanisms, studies that demonstrate both the range of avian capacities and possible outcomes of evolutionary pressures suggest that research on avian cognition is a worthy endeavor.

THE STUDY OF AVIAN COGNITION

Prior to the 1970s, most researchers examined few avian species other than pigeons (but see below), studies concentrated primarily on topics such as delayed match-to-sample (e.g., Berryman, Cumming, & Nevin, 1963; Blough, 1959; Maki & Leuin, 1972; Roberts, 1972; Smith, 1967), and avian abilities were shown to be inferior to those of mammals (e.g., Premack, 1978). The 1970s cognitive revolution in animal behavior, however, proposed that levels and types of intelligence in nonhumans formed a continuum with those of humans, suggested the application of human cognitive approaches to nonhumans, and inspired researchers to study a wide range of behavior across species (see Hulse, Fowler, & Honig, 1978). As a consequence, data challenging mammalian primacy emerged from field and laboratory studies that used nontraditional species and investigated topics once reserved for work with mammals and even primates (Hulse, Page, & Braaten, 1990; Olson, Kamil, & Balda, 1993; Pepperberg, 1990b, 1994).

In no small measure, neurobiology heightened interest in avian cognition. Researchers in the 1960s and 1970s suggested that mammalian correlations of brain structure (i.e., absolute brain size and particularly relative cortical size; Jerison, 1973; Lenneberg, 1973) and intelligence might not hold for birds. Even in the early 1900s, Kalischer (1901), using rather primitive techniques, found that striatal rather than cortical areas might be involved in avian intelligence. His research was overlooked for several decades, but later elegant experiments drew more convincing parallels between avian learning and memory and these striatal areas (e.g., Cobb, 1960; see also Karten, 1969; Nottebohm, 1980;

Striedter, 1994). On studies of reversal learning (Gossette & Gossette, 1967; Gossette, Gossette, & Riddell, 1966; Matyniak, Wheeler, & Stettner, 1971), set learning (Dücker, 1976; Kamil & Hunter, 1970; Stettner & Matyniak, 1968), oddity problems (Pastore, 1955), number-related problems (Braun, 1952; Koehler, 1943, 1950, 1953; Lögler, 1959; Pastore, 1961; Rensch & Dücker, 1973) and insight detour problems (Dücker & Rensch, 1977; Krushinskii, 1960; Zorina, 1982), birds with the greatest striatal development (e.g., crows, parrots, and mynahs; Portmann, 1950; Portmann & Stingelin, 1961) performed more accurately than birds with lesser development (e.g., pigeons and domestic fowl) and were often superior to some monkeys (e.g., Hodos, 1982; Stettner & Matyniak, 1968; Zorina, 1982). Grey parrots, for example, performed at high levels on problems involving simple labeling and intermodal associations (Koehler, 1950, 1953; Lögler, 1959; Mowrer, 1950, 1954; Thorpe, 1964, 1974), and could respond as accurately on new problems as on related training problems (i.e., on transfer tests; Koehler, 1943; Lögler, 1959). This ability to transfer information between problems is generally considered evidence for advanced cognitive capacities (e.g., Premack, 1978; Rozin, 1976). Moreover, lesions in striatal areas appeared to interfere with learning (Stettner, 1967, 1974). Such findings suggested that birds do not need an extensive cerebral cortex to perform complex cognitive tasks and that the extent of avian intelligence, based primarily on studies on pigeons, might be markedly underrated. Recent studies examining additional brain areas (e.g., Bingman, Riters, Strasser, & Gagliardo, 1998; Clayton & Lee, 1998; DeVoogd, Krebs, Healy, & Purvis, 1993) have increased our knowledge of various avian competencies.

STUDIES OF AVIAN ABILITIES

Categorization

Categorization is the ability to sort the world into definable bins. Birds clearly categorize: They sort items into shelter or not-shelter, food or not-food, predator or not-predator, mate or not-mate, conspecifics or allospecifics. Sorting has also been tested formally. Pigeons (*Columba livia*), for example, distinguish slides showing trees or people from slides that do not (Herrnstein, Loveland, & Cable, 1976), but they do not readily transfer this capacity to artificial stimuli like autos (Herrnstein, 1984; however, see Bhatt, Wasserman, Reynolds, & Knauss, 1988). Great tits (*Parus major*; Shy, McGregor, & Krebs, 1986), song sparrows (*Melospiza melodia*; Stoddard, Beecher, & Willis, 1988), and budgerigars (*Melopsittacus undulatus*; Dooling, Brown, Klump, & Okanoya, 1992) categorize conspecific and allospecific song types. However, are birds limited to dividing their world into target categories versus everything else (Shy et al.,

1986) or to simple forms of the naming game (associating a label, be it a word or other symbol, with a specific category; Bhatt et al., 1988; Brown, 1973)? Can they respond not only to specific properties or patterns of stimuli but also to classes or categories to which these properties or patterns belong (Premack, 1978; Savage-Rumbaugh, Rumbaugh, Smith, & Lawson, 1980; Thomas, 1980)? Can, for example, birds go beyond noting what is or is not green to recognizing the relationship between a green pen and a bit of grass? Noting greenness is stimulus generalization; recognizing the category *color* is categorical class formation (Zentall, 1996). How these abilities differ must be clarified to understand the significance of categorization.

Although defining these two abilities is simple, separating them is not (Pepperberg, 1996, 1999). Stimulus generalization "implies memorizing a specific reference stimulus or set of stimuli followed by responses to new stimuli based on a failure to discriminate between the reference stimuli and the new stimuli" (Thomas & Lorden, 1993, p. 132; Zentall, 1996). Categorical class formation, in contrast, is the ability "to respond similarly to discriminated stimuli" (Zentall et al., 1986, p. 153). The distinction between stimulus generalization and categorical class formation is clear for some classes, such as arbitrary ones formed by an experimenter—e.g., squiggles versus straight lines. Subjects may not discriminate squiggles but classify them appropriately. For other classes, the distinction is less clear, particularly if we ask nonhumans about the class. An animal might not, for example, use human criteria to sort slides into the class *bird*. Responses might be based on presence or absence of beaks; slides omitting the beak might be sorted incorrectly. New bird slides (e.g., penguin), differing considerably for humans from reference pictures, might be indistinguishable to or not be distinguished by an animal sorter. Even for a forced identity or nonidentity choice, decisions could be based on, for example, beak size. Specifically, nonhumans might not have a humanlike category *bird*. The extent to which nonhumans form categorical classes is as yet unknown (Pepperberg, 1996, 1999; Zentall, 1996).

One approach to solving this problem uses symbolic labels (Pepperberg, 1983, 1996, 1998) and requires a subject not only to create classes based on concrete attributes (e.g., red) but also to form multiple, hierarchical classes. A subject learns, for example, to form separate classes of color and shape labels: Arbitrary, abstract sound patterns ("red," "4-corner"), or hand or pictorial signals representing physical attributes (e.g., redness, squareness) are grouped into higher order abstract classes whose labels are also arbitrary patterns (i.e., "color," "shape"). The ability to form these classes is not elementary, even for humans: Children who learn that one set of objects is labeled "red" and another "blue" may still not have concepts of redness or blueness that are generalized to novel items (Rice, 1980) or subsumed into "color". Acquiring the category "color" and color labels, for example, means a subject distinguishes color from other categories such as size or shape; isolates certain colors as focal points and others as their variants; understands that each color label is part of a class of labels linked under the category label "color"; and produces each label appropriately (de Villiers & de Villiers, 1978). Can a bird respond in such a manner?

One avian species, the Grey parrot, apparently does (Pepperberg, 1983). The subject, Alex, not only labels many objects, hues, and shapes but also understands that "blue", for example, is one instance of the category labeled "color", and that for any item with both color and shape, specific instances of these attributes (e.g., blue, 3-corner) represent different categories. Thus, he classifies items having one of seven colors and five shapes with respect to either category based on a vocal query of "What color?" or "What shape?" (Pepperberg, 1983). This task tests if he comprehends categorical concepts, not just sorting items into categories. Because Alex must categorize the same item with respect to shape at one time and color at another, the task involves flexibility in changing the basis for classification. Such capacity for reclassification indicates an abstract aptitude similar to that of chimpanzees (Hayes & Nissen, 1952/1971).

In two more complicated tasks, Alex is given collections of seven unique combinations of items. In the first task, he is queried "What color is object-X?"; "What shape is object-Y?"; "What object is color-A?"; or "What object is shape-B?" (Pepperberg, 1990a). In the second task, he provides information about the specific instance of one category of an item uniquely defined by the combination of two other categories, for example, "What object is color-A and shape-B?" Other items exemplify one, but not both, defining categories. The task requires him to understand all elements in the query and categorize conjunctively (Pepperberg, 1992). On both tasks, his accuracy matches that of marine mammals (e.g., Schusterman & Gisiner, 1988).

Same–Different

In the 1970s, comprehension of same–different was singled out as requiring complex relational abilities not typically attributable to nonprimates, and specifically not to birds (Mackintosh, Wilson, & Boakes, 1985; Premack, 1978, 1983). Comprehending same–different is more complex than learning to respond to match-to-sample or oddity-from-sample. For Premack (1983), the former not only requires use of arbitrary symbols to represent same–different relationships between sets of items but also the ability to denote which attribute is same or different. The latter, in contrast, requires a subject to show only a savings in the number of trials needed to respond to B and B as a match after learning to respond to A and A as a match (and likewise for trials on C and D after learning to respond to A and B as nonmatching). Match-to-sample and nonmatch-to-sample responses might even be based on old–new or familiar–unfamiliar contrasts (Premack, 1983), i.e., on the relative number of times A versus different Bs are seen. A subject that understands same–different, however, not only knows that two nonidentical blue items are related in the same way as are two nonidentical green objects—in terms of color—but also knows that the two blue items are related in a different way than are two nonidentical square items and, moreover, can transfer this knowledge to any attribute and to difference (see Pepperberg, 1999; Premack, 1978).

For birds, natural behavior patterns of individual recognition, vocal dueling, and song matching (e.g., Beecher & Stoddard, 1990; Falls, 1985; Godard, 1991; Godard & Wiley, 1995; Kroodsma, 1979; Naguib & Todt, 1998; Stoddard, 1996; Stoddard, Beecher, Horning, & Campbell, 1991) require same–difference-based discrimination, implying that such discrimination is an adaptive trait. In the laboratory, however, budgerigars' apparent discrimination of similarities and differences in canaries' calls may be based instead on learning the unique characteristics of individual calls (Park & Dooling, 1985). Similar results were found in song discrimination studies on cliff and barn swallows (*Hirundo pyrrhonota*, *Hirundo rustica*; P. Stoddard & M. Beecher, personal communication, 1986) and great tits (Shy et al., 1986). Song sparrows appeared to make fine acoustic distinctions among conspecific song syllables in a habituation–dishabituation experiment (Nelson, 1987; Stoddard et al., 1988), but data must be interpreted carefully with respect to same–different because these birds can memorize large numbers of song types (e.g., Stoddard, Beecher, Loesche, & Campbell, 1992) and thus may have responded based on familiarity. Studies showing how different sound features differentially affect conspecific song recognition and discrimination of conspecific from allospecific song demonstrate just how difficult it is to design experiments to show that birds understand same–different the way Premack would require. For example, field sparrows (*Spizella pusilla*) differentially weigh information in various song features and thus results could depend on the feature an experimenter chooses to study (Nelson, 1988). In addition, experimental design may not demonstrate a subject's perception of same–different. Starlings (*Sturnus vulgaris*), for example, classify novel series of ascending or descending tones as same–different from ascending or descending reference series, but, unless pressed, only for sequences within the range of training frequencies (Hulse et al., 1990). Nevertheless, none of these studies required labeling the same–different relation or transfer to novel situations (e.g., calls or songs of different species), nor did any of these tasks demonstrate (to humans) that a bird truly understands what attributes are same or different (Pepperberg, 1987a).

Other same–different demonstrations have also been inconclusive (e.g., Hulse, 1993). Pigeons seem to learn to respond to the matching sample, to learn little about the nonmatching alternative, and thus to acquire a concept of same but not different (see Edwards, Jagielo, & Zentall, 1983; Premack, 1978; Zentall, Edwards, Moore, & Hogan, 1981; Zentall, Hogan, & Edwards, 1984). Related alternative mechanisms could not be ruled out in other studies (Holmes, 1979; Lombardi, Fachinelli, & Delius, 1984; Urcuioli & Nevin, 1975); pigeons seemed, for example, to have an unlearned predisposition to choose the odd stimulus from a set (Wilson, Mackintosh, & Boakes, 1985) and did not learn the same–different concept. Other data show what seem to be some level of same–different comprehension in pigeons (e.g., Cook, Cavoto, & Cavoto, 1995; Santiago & Wright, 1984; Wasserman, Hugart, & Kirkpatrick-Steger, 1995; Wright, Santiago, & Sands, 1984; Wright, Santiago, Urcuioli, & Sands, 1984; Young, Wasserman, & Dalrymple, 1997), but not within Premack's (1983) criteria: In some studies, birds may have responded to homogeneity versus nonhomogeneity, the presence or absence of a target (i.e., a dissimilar spot in a field of similar patterns), or to familiar (from multiple presentations) versus nonfamiliar items. In no case did the data did show that a bird could use symbols for "same" and "different" in a manner comparable to that of language-trained chimpanzees, humans, or even appropriately trained monkeys.

The parrot Alex, however, has learned abstract concepts of same–different and to respond to the absence of information about these concepts if nothing is same or different. Thus, when shown two identical items or items that vary with respect to some or all attributes of color, shape, and material, he utters the appropriate category label, thereby indicating which attribute is same or different for any combination (Pepperberg, 1987a). If nothing is the same or different, he replies "none" (Pepperberg, 1988). He responds accurately to novel items, colors, shapes, and materials, including those he cannot label and to the specific queries, not from rote training or the physical attributes of the objects: Accuracy was still above chance when, for example, he was queried "What's same?" for a red and a blue wooden square. If he were ignoring the query and responding based on prior training, he would have determined and produced the label of the one anomalous attribute (in this case, "color"). Instead, he gave one of the two appropriate answers ("shape" or "mah-mah" [matter]). Test conditions were not identical to, but were at least as rigorous as, those used in Premack's (1976, 1983) chimpanzee study. In addition, Alex transfers his concept of same–different and absence to untrained situations. He responded appropriately the first time he was shown two objects of equal size after learning to answer "What color (matter) is bigger (smaller)?" for any two items (Pepperberg & Brezinsky, 1991). He first asked "What's same?", then he said, "none."

Spatial Memory

Spatial memory is an area in which some birds excel. Many studies of avian memory are independent of spatial attributes (e.g., coding, Grant, 1993;

Zentall, Sherbourne, & Steirn, 1993; excitatory or inhibitory learning, Hearst & Sutton, 1993; serial learning, Terrace, 1993; primacy effects, Wright, 1994), but the most striking memory feats are shown by caching birds, such as Clark's nutcrackers (*Nucifraga columbiana*), that remember locations of thousands of stored seeds for up to 9 months (Balda & Kamil, 1992). Laboratory tests (Kamil & Balda, 1990) have shown that accuracy declines as recovery proceeds and that the decline is a consequence of differential memory for different cache sites. Better remembered sites are recovered first, but memory is not based on inherent physical characteristics of the site, nor do cache order, site preferences, or stereotypic movement patterns affect recovery accuracy (Balda & Kamil, 1989; Kamil & Balda, 1985). Thus, the cache recovery task is not analogous to list learning in birds and mammals. Birds keep track of sites they have already emptied and those that remain full, though not with perfect accuracy (Balda, Kamil, & Grim, 1986; Kamil & Balda, 1990). The mechanism of such behavior has not yet been determined, but data suggest selective forgetting of emptied sites (Kamil, Balda, Olson, & Good, 1993). These birds may be adaptively specialized for spatial memory and learning; they are superior to other species on spatial tasks but not on general learning tasks such as color nonmatching to sample (Kamil, Olson, & Balda, 1992). Interestingly, caching birds have relatively larger hippocampal areas (the brain area associated with memory and spatial behavior) than do birds less dependent on spatial memory (e.g., Basil, Kamil, Balda, & Fite, 1996; Krebs, 1990; Sherry, Jacobs, & Gaulin, 1992); for closely related species, the correlation likely relates to demands of their ecological niche and to how the birds acquire, encode, and use, as well as remember, spatial information (Bednekoff, Balda, Kamil, & Hile, 1997). Some birds remember not only where they cache but also when and what they cached (Clayton & Dickinson, 1998).

Numerical Capacities

Numerical studies in animals are difficult (Pepperberg, 1999). Even for humans, researchers disagree on the content and ordering of stages of numerical ability (e.g., Davis & Pérusse, 1988; Frydman, 1995; Fuson, 1988, 1995; Gallistel, 1988; Gelman & Gallistel, 1986; Siegler, 1991; Starkey & Cooper, 1995) and the role of language in numerical tasks. Do language and number skills depend on development of the same underlying cognitive capacities (Dehaene, 1992; Lenneberg, 1971), or does labeling merely separate the less and more advanced numerical skills (e.g., Gallistel & Gelman, 1992)? In some humans, brain damage impairs numerical abilities leaving memory, language, and reasoning intact, and vice versa (Butterworth, 1995); other data discount "a single brain area where numerical knowledge would be concentrated" (Dehaene & Cohen, 1995, p. 115). This dichotomy may be resolved by positing that basic number sense (of quantities and their relations) is encoded in the intraparietal cortex, with correlates across species, and that other number skills require coordination among many brain areas (possibly absent in nonhumans; Dehaene, Dehaene-Lambertz, & Cohen, 1998). Such proposals, however, render animal studies even more daunting.

Nevertheless, birds demonstrate numerical abilities. Canaries can select a three-item set from simultaneous displays of other quantities, or the second, third, or fourth item in a group (Pastore, 1961); budgerigars (Koehler, 1943, 1950), pigeons (Arndt, 1939), and jackdaws (*Corvus monedula*; Schiemann, 1939) can learn to eat a specific number of items. Such birds are said to have, for example, a "threeness" concept. Pigeons recognize more versus less (i.e., relative numerosity; Alsop & Honig, 1991; Emmerton, 1998; Fetterman, 1993; Honig, 1991; Rilling, 1967; Roberts & Mitchell, 1994; NB, some papers also examine this concept with respect to timing). Grey parrots, jackdaws, and ravens (*Corvus corax*) can match simultaneous quantities up to 8, pigeons up to 5 or 6, and chickens up to 2 or 3. Some corvids and parrots can also open boxes randomly containing 0, 1, or 2 baits until they obtain a fixed number that depend on nonnumerical cues (e.g., black lids denote 2 and red lids 4; Braun, 1952; Koehler, 1943, 1950; Lögler, 1959). Thus, both the number of boxes to be opened to obtain the exact number of baits, and number of baits sought, could vary on each trial. Wild birds are sensitive to quantifiable sequential auditory patterns. For example, crows (*Corvus brachyrhynchos*) may use temporal patterns of caw numbers for individual recognition (Thompson, 1968, 1969); some species respond differentially to distinct sets of repetitions of neighbors' vocalizations (carduelid finches and hybrids, Güttinger, 1979; wood peewees, *Contopus virens*, Smith, 1988; blackbirds, *Turdus merula*, Wolfgramm & Todt, 1982). The Grey parrot Alex uses English number labels to quantify physical sets of £ 6; items need not be familiar, identical, or have a specific pattern, brightness, or mass. He also quantifies subsets in heterogeneous groups (e.g., keys in sets of corks and keys; Pepperberg, 1987b).

However, recognizing and even labeling quantity uses number as a descriptor or categorical marker (Gallistel, 1993), which differs from counting (see Fuson, 1988; von Glasersfeld, 1993), where a subject produces a standard sequence of number tags; applies a unique number tag to each item to be counted; remembers what has been counted; and knows that the last number tag used tells how many items are there. Subitizing, an enumeration process, also differs from counting and may use preattentive mechanisms in a fast, effortless, perceptual apprehension £ 4 (e.g., Aoki, 1977; Atkinson, Campbell, & Francis, 1976; Kaufman, Lord, Reese, & Volkmann, 1949; Klahr, 1973; Stevens, 1951; Taves, 1941). Not surprisingly, researchers argue as to the relative complexity of subitizing and counting and validity of using £ 4 to denote subitizing (e.g., Davis

& Pérusse, 1988; Gallistel & Gelman, 1991; Starkey & Cooper, 1995). No avian subjects, however, count in the sense described for humans (Fuson, 1988); in all cases, birds may be using a perceptual strategy.

In an attempt to distinguish counting from subitizing, the parrot Alex was given collections of four groups of items varying in two colors and two object categories (e.g., blue and red keys and cars) and was asked to quantify items uniquely defined by the combination of one color and one object category (e.g., "How many blue key?"; Pepperberg, 1994). His accuracy (83.3%) replicates that of humans in a comparable study by Trick and Pylyshyn (1989, 1993), who argue that humans cannot subitize if a task involves labeling the quantity of a subset of items distinguished from other subsets by a conjunction of qualifiers. Because procedures that control for alternative explanations of behavior in one species may not provide controls in others, comparable performance cannot ensure comparable mechanisms across species. Even so, Alex's data suggest that a nonhuman, nonprimate, nonmammal has a level of competence that, in a chimpanzee, would be taken to indicate a human level of intelligence.

Communication

Communication is a window into many avian cognitive and learning capacities. Use of specific vocal patterns for individual recognition has been discussed. Some species' ability to acquire and process hundreds of songs (e.g., mockingbirds, *Mimus polyglottos*, Howard, 1974; marsh wrens, *Cistothorus palustris*, Verner, 1975; brown thrashers, *Toxostoma rufum*, Kroodsma & Parker, 1977) is not only evidence for extensive learning and memory but may also provide data on serial pattern recognition. Nightingales (*Luscinia megarhynchos*), for example, learn strings of over 60 different songs by chunking strings sung by their tutors into packages of three to seven songs; when singing, they maintain serial order of the packages but not necessarily that of songs within each package (Hultsch & Todt, 1989). Further studies show that the storage and production process does not simply involve paired associations between song types (Hultsch & Todt, 1992). Marsh wrens appear to learn not only the order of their own several hundred songs but also those of their competitors, and they may attempt to jam these neighbors by anticipating the next song in the neighbors' series during counter-singing (Kroodsma, 1979). Many of the categorization and numerical studies previously discussed in this chapter are based partly on avian vocal capacities. Preliminary studies of sentinel behavior (alerting of a group to danger by one sentinel member) suggest that some psittacids (maroon-fronted parrots, *Rhynchopsittica terrisi*, Lawson & Lanning, 1980; white-fronted Amazons, *Amazona albifrons*, Levinson, 1980; short-billed white-tailed black cockatoos, *Calyptorhynchus funereus latirostris*, Saunders, 1983; indigo macaws,

Anodorhynchus leari, Yamashita, 1987; Puerto Rican parrots, *Amazona vittata*, Snyder, Wiley, & Kepler, 1987), corvids (crows, Maccarone, 1987; Florida scrub jays, *Aphelocoma coerulescens coerulescens*, McGowan & Woolfenden, 1989) and even chickens (*Gallus gallus*, Evans, Evans, & Marler, 1993) may possess abilities similar to those of vervet monkeys (*Cercopithecus aethiops*) in using vocal calls to categorize different predators (e.g., Seyfarth, Cheney, & Marler, 1980). Grey parrots use English speech sounds to label and categorize items, quantify arrays, and respond to queries concerning similarity and difference and relative and conjunctive concepts (Pepperberg, 1990a, 1992, 1994; Pepperberg & Brezinsky, 1991); for example, for any two items, Alex can be asked "What's same?" or "What's different?"; "How many?"; or "What color (matter) is bigger (smaller)?" To respond appropriately, he must not only understand the individual concepts involved but also determine which concept is being targeted and from what domain an answer need originate, apropos my original definition of intelligence. His abilities suggest striking parallels between birds and primates.

EVOLUTION OF AVIAN INTELLIGENCE

Do, however, avian and primate abilities share similar origins? The cognitive and social behaviors of primates have been studied extensively (e.g., Byrne, 1995; de Waal, 1989; Tomasello & Call, 1997), and numerous theses exist for the origins of their capacities. Humphrey (1976), for example, proposes that intelligence (and presumably the need for cognitive processing) is a correlate of a complicated social system and a long life—that is, that intelligence is the outcome of a selection process favoring animals that remember and act upon knowledge of detailed social relations among group members. More generally, Rozin (1976) defines intelligence as flexibility in transferring skills acquired in one domain to another. Might these two patterns also drive parrot cognition and vocal behavior?

Long-lived birds that have complex social systems, not unlike those of some primates, could use abilities honed for social gains to direct other forms of information processing and vocal learning. Add some further needs for categorical classes (e.g., to distinguish neutral stimuli from predators, poisonous from edible plants), abilities both to recognize and remember environmental regularities and adapt to unpredictable environmental changes over extensive lifetimes, and a communication system usable in dense foliage—capacities of parrots are then not so surprising. Indeed, Marler (1996) proposes some similar parallels between birds and primates, though not specifically for parrots. I suggest, however, a scenario with one additional contingency.

I propose intelligence as an evolutionary correlate not only of memory and flexibility but also of the ability to choose what to ignore as well as what to process. Of critical importance is that the choice be active and not the result of, for example, a sensory filter, because an organism must be able to re-evaluate the relative worth of information as situations change. I also contend that such choice, although a critical component of many aspects of behavior, is most clearly observed in communication.

My proposal is derived from studies by Smith (1997), who argues that communication is best understood as being "forged in the linking of different individuals" (p. 31) and that if we know both the information a recipient receives from a signal and its response to that information, we have data leading to an understanding of the recipient's processing abilities. Of critical importance is Smith's argument that both content and contextual information—the source and circumstances surrounding the emitting of a signal—are part and parcel of what a recipient must process. And that the result is a weighting of input before a reaction is emitted; this weighting tells not only that processing has occurred but also provides details of how an information hierarchy is formed.

How does Smith's work clarify why communication enables us to see intelligence as a means of actively choosing what to ignore as well as what to process? The answer is that birds tell us, by what they do and do not vocally reproduce, the outcome of such choice. Wild Grey parrots have the capacity to reproduce environmental noises (e.g., sounds of a nearby stream) as well as conspecific and allospecific vocalizations—but reproduce only the latter two (e.g., Cruickshank, Gautier, & Chappuis, 1993; May, 1995). As I noted in earlier publications (Pepperberg, 1998, 1999), reproducing the former would be maladaptive (e.g., rustling of leaves may have many implications, from the approach of a predator to the blowing of wind; the context and use of such a learned vocalization, unlike that of another bird, would be unclear). Some evolutionary pressure likely selected against such behavior—that is, directed a hierarchy of what was important to learn.

Such selection also likely occurred in nonhuman primates—an animal unable to form an information hierarchy would be unable to act—but evaluating the results of such selection for animals that do not learn their vocalizations is far more complicated. Other metrics must be used. When, for example, a vervet monkey ignores a leopard kill strategically placed by an experimenter, the argument is that the monkey does not recognize the kill as evidence for the predator's likely presence—that is, the monkey lacks a certain form of intelligence (Cheney & Seyfarth, 1990). An alternative explanation is that the monkey uses the kill to infer that the leopard is satiated and unlikely to hunt again soon; the monkey thus ignores the information as an indicator to increase its vigilance. Choosing between these, and possibly other, alternatives is not a simple matter for researchers using such an experimental design to study vervets or any other animal.

I thus propose that, with respect to vocal learning, parrots provide a clearer observational case for what they treat as viable or nonviable input. Obviously, parrots process a large variety of input. Nevertheless, even if they locate a

stream by its sound, they rank the sound at a low level with respect to its reproduction, and we can use this lack of reproduction as evidence for hierarchical
learning and cognitive processing. Parrots thus demonstrate a biologically relevant cognitive ability that is relatively easily measured in nature (Balda, Kamil,
& Bednekoff, 1997). I will not belabor this point; such observational and
correlational material does not lend itself to rigorous hypothesis testing. In addition, evolutionary pressures may affect different cognitive abilities differently in
different species in different habitats, and intelligence is not unitary (Byrne,
1995). The data merely suggest that the combination of intelligence and advanced communication skills may have arisen not only in primate or even mammalian lines but also in birds, and that it directs not only learning but also what
is appropriate to learn.

SUMMARY

In sum, Sternberg and Kaufman's (1998) conclusions about human intelligence
appear applicable to nonhumans; we need only substitute *species* for *culture*:
Species designate as "intelligent" the cognitive, social, and behavioral attributes
that they value as adaptive to the requirements of living.... To the extent that
there is overlap in these attributes across *species*, there will be overlap in the *species'* conceptions of intelligence. Although conceptions of intelligence may vary
across *species*, the underlying cognitive attributes probably do not.... As a result
there is probably a common core of cognitive skills that underlies intelligence in
all *species*, with the cognitive skills having different manifestations across the
species. (p. 497)

ACKNOWLEDGMENTS

This material is based upon work supported by the National Science Foundation under Grant No. 9603803 and contributors to The Alex Foundation. I
thank Diana May, Spencer Lynn, and Dr. Pamela Banta for many relevant discussions and Dr. Donald Kroodsma for comments on the manuscript.

REFERENCES

Alsop, B., & Honig, W. K. (1991). Sequential stimuli and relative numerosity discriminations
    in pigeons. *Journal of Experimental Psychology: Animal Behavior Processes, 17,* 386–395.
Aoki, T. (1977). On the counting process of patterned dots. *Tohoku Psychologica Folia, 36,*
    15–22.
Arndt, W. (1939). Abschließende Versuche zür Frage des "Zähl"—Vermogens der
    Haustaube [Concluding research on the question of "number" ability in the domestic pi-
    geon]. *Zeitschrift für Tierpsychologie, 3,* 88–142.
Atkinson, J., Campbell, F. W., &. Francis, M. R. (1976). The magic number 4±0: A new look
    at visual numerosity judgments. *Perception, 5,* 327–334.

Balda, R. P., & Kamil, A. C. (1989). A comparative study of cache recovery by three corvid species. *Animal Behaviour, 38,* 486–495.

Balda, R. P., & Kamil, A. C. (1992). Long-term spatial memory in Clark's nutcracker, *Nucifraga columbiana. Animal Behaviour, 44,* 761–769.

Balda, R. P., Kamil, A. C., & Bednekoff, P. A. (1997). Predicting cognitive capacity from natural history. In V. Nolan, Jr. & E. D. Ketterson (Eds.), *Current ornithology* (Vol. 13, pp. 33–66). New York: Plenum.

Balda, R. P., Kamil, A. C., & Grim, K. (1986). Revisits to emptied cache sites by Clark's nutcrackers (*Nucifraga columbiana*). *Animal Behaviour, 34,* 1289–1298.

Basil, J. A., Kamil, A. C., Balda, R. P., & Fite, K. V. (1996). Differences in hippocampal volume among food storing corvids. *Brain, Behavior, and Evolution, 47,* 156–164.

Bednekoff, P. A., Balda, R. P., Kamil, A. C., & Hile, A. G. (1997). Long-term spatial memory in four seed-caching corvid species. *Animal Behaviour, 53,* 335–341.

Beecher, M. D., & Stoddard, P. K. (1990). The role of bird song and calls in individual recognition: Contrasting field and laboratory perspectives. In W. C. Stebbins & M. A. Kerkley (Eds.), *Comparative perception* (Vol. 2, pp. 375–408). New York: Wiley.

Berryman, R., Cumming, W. W., & Nevin, J. A. (1963). Acquisition of delayed matching in the pigeon. *Journal of the Experimental Analysis of Behavior, 6,* 101–107.

Bhatt, R. S., Wasserman, E. A., Reynolds, W. F., Jr., & Knauss, K. S. (1988). Conceptual behavior in pigeons: Categorization of both familiar and novel examples from four classes of natural and artificial stimuli. *Journal of Experimental Psychology: Animal Behavior Processes, 14,* 219–234.

Bingman, V., Riters, L. V., Strasser, R., & Gagliardo, A. (1998). Neuroethology of avian navigation. In R. P. Balda, I. M. Pepperberg, & A. C. Kamil (Eds.), *Animal cognition in nature* (pp. 201–226). London: Academic.

Blough, D. S. (1959). Delayed matching in the pigeon. *Journal of the Experimental Analysis of Behavior, 2,* 151–160.

Braun, H. (1952). Uber das Unterscheidungsvermögen unbenannter Anzahlen bei Papageien [Concerning the ability of parrots to distinguish unnamed numbers]. *Zeitschrift für Tierpsychologie, 9,* 40–91.

Brown, R. (1973). *A first language: The early stages.* Cambridge, MA: Harvard University Press.

Butterworth, B. (1995). Editorial. *Mathematical Cognition, 1,* 1–2.

Byrne, R. (1995). *The thinking ape: Evolutionary origins of intelligence.* Oxford: Oxford University Press.

Cheney, D. L., & Seyfarth, R. M. (1990). *How monkeys see the world: Inside the mind of another species.* Chicago: University of Chicago Press.

Clayton, N. S., & Dickinson, A. (1998). Episodic-like memory during cache recovery by scrub jays. *Nature, 395,* 272–274.

Clayton, N. S., & Lee, D. W. (1998). Memory and the hippocampus in food-storing birds. In R. P. Balda, I. M. Pepperberg, & A. C. Kamil (Eds.), *Animal cognition in nature* (pp. 305–336). London: Academic.

Cobb, S. (1960). Observations on the comparative anatomy of the avian brain. In D. I. Ingle & S. O. Waife (Eds.), *Perspectives in biology and medicine* (Vol. 3, pp. 383–408). Chicago: University of Chicago Press.

Cook, R. G., Cavoto, K. K., & Cavoto, B. R. (1995). Same-different texture discrimination and concept learning by pigeons. *Journal of Experimental Psychology: Animal Behavior Processes, 21,* 253–260.

Cruickshank, A. J., Gautier, J.-P., & Chappuis, C. (1993). Vocal mimicry in wild African Grey Parrots, *Psittacus erithacus. Ibis, 135,* 293–299.

Cynx, J. (1995). Similarities in absolute and relative pitch perception in songbirds (starling and zebra finch) and a nonsongbird (pigeon). *Journal of Comparative Psychology, 109,* 261–267.

Davis, H., & Pérusse, R. (1988). Numerical competence in animals: Definitional issues, current evidence, and a new research agenda. *Behavioral and Brain Sciences, 11,* 561–579.

Dehaene, S. (1992). Varieties of numerical abilities. *Cognition, 44,* 1–42.

Dehaene, S., & Cohen, L. (1995). Toward an anatomical and functional model of number processing. *Mathematical Cognition, 1,* 83–120.

Dehaene, S., Dehaene-Lambertz, G., & Cohen, L. (1998). Abstract representation of numbers in the animal and human brain. *Trends in Neurosciences, 21,* 355–361.

de Villiers, J. G., & de Villiers, P. A. (1978). *Language acquisition.* Cambridge, MA: Harvard University Press.

DeVoogd, T. J., Krebs, J. R., Healy, S. D., & Purvis, A. (1993). Relations between song repertoire size and the volume of brain nuclei related to song: Comparative evolutionary analyses amongst oscine birds. *Proceedings of the Royal Society of London, B254,* 75–82.

de Waal, F. B. M. (1989). *Peacemaking among the primates.* Cambridge, MA: Harvard University Press.

Dooling, R. J., Brown, S. D., Klump, G. M., & Okanoya, K. (1992). Auditory perception of conspecific and heterospecific vocalizations in birds: Evidence for special processes. *Journal of Comparative Psychology, 106,* 20–28.

Dücker, G. (1976). Erlernen von drei verschiedenen Positionen durch Vogel [Learning of three distinct positions by birds]. *Zeitschrift für Tierpsychologie, 42,* 301–314.

Dücker, G., & Rensch, B. (1977). The solution of patterned string problems by birds. *Behaviour, 62,* 164–173.

Edwards, C. A., Jagielo, J. A., & Zentall, T. R. (1983). Same/different symbol use by pigeons. *Animal Learning & Behavior, 11,* 349–355.

Emmerton, J. (1998). Numerosity differences and effects of stimulus density on pigeons' discrimination performance. *Animal Learning & Behavior, 26,* 243–256.

Evans, C. S., Evans, L., & Marler, P. (1993). On the meaning of alarm calls: Functional reference in an avian vocal system. *Animal Behaviour, 46,* 23–38.

Falls, J. B. (1985). Song matching in Western meadowlarks. *Canadian Journal of Zoology, 63,* 2520–2524.

Fetterman, J. G. (1993). Numerosity discrimination: Both time and number matter. *Journal of Experimental Psychology: Animal Behavior Processes, 19,* 149–164.

Frydman, O. (1995). The concept of number and the acquisition of counting concepts: The "when", the "how", and the "what" of it. *Cahiers de Psychologie Cognitive, 14,* 653–684.

Fuson, K. C. (1988). *Children's counting and concepts of numbers.* New York: Springer–Verlag.

Fuson, K. C. (1995). Aspects and uses of counting: An AUC framework for considering research on counting to update the Gelman/Gallistel counting principles. *Cahiers de Psychologie Cognitive, 14,* 724–731.

Gallistel, C. R. (1988). Counting versus subitizing versus the sense of number. *Behavioral and Brain Sciences, 11,* 585–586.

Gallistel, C. R. (1993). A conceptual framework for the study of numerical estimation and arithmetic reasoning in animals. In S. T. Boysen & E. J. Capaldi (Eds.), *The development of numerical competence* (pp. 211–223). Hillsdale, NJ: Lawrence Erlbaum Associates.

Gallistel, C. R., & Gelman, R. (1991). Subitizing: The pre-verbal counting process. In W. E. Kessen, A. Ortony, & F. I. M. Craik (Eds.), *Thoughts, memories, and emotions: Essays in honor of George Mandler* (pp. 65–81). Hillsdale, NJ: Lawrence Erlbaum Associates.

Gallistel, C. R., & Gelman, R. (1992). Preverbal and verbal counting and computation. *Cognition, 44,* 43–74.

Gardner, H. (1983). *Frames of mind: The theory of multiple intelligences.* New York: Basic Books.

Gardner, H. (1999). Are there additional intelligences? The case for naturalist, spiritualist, and existential intelligences. In J. Kane (Ed.), *Education, information, and transformation* (pp. 111–131). Upper Saddle River, NJ: Merrill/Prentice Hall.

Gelman, R., & Gallistel, C. R. (1986). *The child's understanding of number* (2nd ed.). Cambridge, MA: Harvard University Press.

Godard, R. (1991). Long-term memory of individual neighbours in a migratory songbird. *Nature, 350,* 228–229.

Godard, R., & Wiley, R. H. (1995). Individual recognition of song repertoires in two wood warblers. *Behavioral Ecology & Sociobiology, 37,* 119–123.

Gossette, R. L., & Gossette, M. F. (1967). Examination of the reversal index (RI) across fifteen different mammalian and avian species. *Perception and Motor Skills, 27,* 987–990.

Gossette, R. L., Gossette, M. F., & Riddell, W. (1966). Comparisons of successive discrimination reversal performances among closely and remotely related avian species. *Animal Behaviour, 14,* 560–564.

Grant, D. S. (1993). Coding processes in pigeons. In T. R. Zentall (Ed.), *Animal cognition: A tribute to Donald A. Riley* (pp. 193–216). Hillsdale, NJ: Lawrence Erlbaum Associates.

Güttinger, H. R. (1979). The integration of learnt and genetically programmed behaviour: A study of hierarchical organization in songs of canaries, greenfinches, and their hybrids. *Zeitschrift für Tierpsychologie, 49,* 285–303.

Hayes, K. J., & Nissen, C. H. (1971). Higher mental functions of a home-raised chimpanzee. In A. Schrier & F. Stollnitz (Eds.), *Behavior of nonhuman primates* (Vol. 4, pp. 57–115). New York: Academic. (Original work published 1956)

Hearst, E., & Sutton, S. (1993). Generalization gradients of excitation and inhibition: Long-term memory for dimensional control and curious inversions during repeated tests with reinforcement. In T. R. Zentall (Ed.), *Animal cognition: A tribute to Donald A. Riley* (pp. 63–86). Hillsdale, NJ: Lawrence Erlbaum Associates.

Herrnstein, R. J. (1984). Objects, categories, and discriminative stimuli. In H. L. Roitblat, T. G. Bever, & H. S. Terrace (Eds.), *Animal cognition* (pp. 233–261). Hillsdale, NJ: Lawrence Erlbaum Associates.

Herrnstein, R. J., Loveland, D. H., & Cable, C. (1976). Natural concepts in pigeons. *Journal of Experimental Psychology: Animal Behavior Processes, 2,* 285–301.

Hodos, W. (1982). Some perspectives on the evolution of intelligence and the brain. In D. R. Griffin (Ed.), *Animal mind—human mind* (pp. 33–56). Berlin, Germany: Springer-Verlag.

Holmes, P. W. (1979). Transfer of matching performance in pigeons. *Journal of the Experimental Analysis of Behavior, 31,* 103–114.

Honig, W. K. (1991). Discrimination by pigeons of mixture and uniformity in arrays of stimulus elements. *Journal of Experimental Psychology: Animal Behavior Processes, 17,* 68–80.

Howard, R. D. (1974). The influence of sexual selection and interspecific communication on Mockingbird song (*Mimus polyglottos*). *Evolution, 28,* 428–438.

Hulse, S. H. (1993). Absolutes and relations in acoustic perception by songbirds. In T. R. Zentall (Ed.), *Animal cognition: A tribute to Donald A. Riley* (pp. 335–353). Hillsdale, NJ: Lawrence Erlbaum Associates.

Hulse, S. H., Fowler, H. S., & Honig, W. K. (Eds.). (1978). *Cognitive processes in animal behavior.* Hillsdale, NJ: Lawrence Erlbaum Associates.

Hulse, S. H., Page, S. C., & Braaten, R. F. (1990). Frequency range size and the frequency range constraint in auditory perception by European starlings (*Sturnus vulgaris*). *Animal Learning & Behavior, 18,* 238–245.

Hultsch, H., & Todt, D. (1989). Song acquisition and acquisition constraints in the Nightingale, *Luscinia megarhynchos. Naturwissenschaften, 16,* 83–85.

Hultsch, H., & Todt, D. (1992). The serial order effect in the song acquisition of birds: relevance of exposure frequency to song models. *Animal Behaviour, 44,* 590–592.

Humphrey, N. K. (1976). The social function of intellect. In P. P. G. Bateson & R. A. Hinde (Eds.), *Growing points in ethology* (pp. 303–317). Cambridge: Cambridge University Press.

Jerison, H. J. (1973). *Evolution of the brain and intelligence.* New York: Academic.

Kalischer, O. (1901). Weitere Hittheilung zur Grosshirn localization bei den Vögeln. [Further communication on the cerebrum localization (or localization of the cerebrum) of birds.] *Sitzungsbericht der Koniglich Preussisehen Akademic der Wissenschaften zu Berlin, 1,* 428.

Kamil, A. C. (1988). A synthetic approach to the study of animal intelligence. In D. Leger (Ed.), *Nebraska symposium on motivation: Comparative perspectives in modern psychology* (Vol. 7, pp. 257–308). Lincoln, NE: University of Nebraska Press.

Kamil, A. C., & Balda, R. P. (1985). Cache recovery and spatial memory in Clark's nutcrackers (*Nucifraga columbiana*). *Journal of Experimental Psychology: Animal Behavior Processes*, 11, 95–111.

Kamil, A. C., & Balda, R. P. (1990). Differential memory for cache sites in Clark's nutcrackers (*Nucifraga columbiana*). *Journal of Experimental Psychology: Animal Behavior Processes*, 16, 162–168.

Kamil, A. C., Balda, R. P., Olson, D. J., & Good, S. (1993). Returns to emptied cache sites by Clark's nutcrackers, *Nucifraga columbiana*: a puzzle revisited. *Animal Behaviour*, 45, 241–252.

Kamil, A. C., & Hunter, M. W., III. (1970). Performance on object discrimination learning set by the Greater Hill mynah, *Gracula religiosa*. *Journal of Comparative and Physiological Psychology*, 73, 68–73.

Kamil, A. C., Olson, D. J., & Balda, R. P. (1992, November). *Performance of seed-caching corvids during color non-matching*. Paper presented at the annual meeting of the Psychonomic Society, St. Louis, MO.

Karten, H. J. (1969). The organization of the avian telencephalon and some speculations on the phylogeny of the amniote telencephalon. *Annals of the NY Academy of Sciences*, 167, 164–179.

Kaufman, E. L., Lord, M. W., Reese, T. W., & Volkmann, J. (1949). The discrimination of visual number. *American Journal of Psychology*, 62, 498–525.

Klahr, D. (1973). Quantification processes. In W. G. Chase (Ed.), *Visual information processing* (pp. 3–34). New York: Academic.

Koehler, O. (1943). 'Zähl'-Versuche an einem Kolkraben und Vergleichsversuche an Menschen ['Number' ability in a raven and comparative research with people]. *Zeitschrift für Tierpsychologie*, 5, 575–712.

Koehler, O. (1950). The ability of birds to 'count'. *Bulletin of the Animal Behavior Society*, 9, 41–45.

Koehler, O. (1953). Thinking without words. *Proceedings of the XIVth International Congress of Zoology*, 75–88.

Krebs, J. R. (1990). Food storing birds: Adaptive specialization in brain and behaviour? *Philosophical Transactions of the Royal Society*, B329, 55–62.

Kroodsma, D. E. (1979). Vocal dueling among male marsh wrens: Evidence for ritualized expressions of dominance/subordinance hierarchies. *Auk*, 96, 506–515.

Kroodsma, D. E., & Byers, B. E. (1998). Songbird song repertoires: An ethological approach to studying cognition. In R. P. Balda, I. M. Pepperberg, & A. C. Kamil (Eds.), *Animal cognition in nature* (pp. 305–336). London: Academic.

Kroodsma, D. E., & Parker, L. D. (1977). Vocal virtuosity in the Brown Thrasher. *Auk*, 94, 783–785.

Krushinskii, L. V. (1960). *Animal behavior: Its normal and abnormal development* (Basil Haigh, trans.) New York: Consultants Bureau.

Lawson, R. W., & Lanning, D. V. (1980). Nesting and status of the Maroon-fronted parrot (*Rhynchopsitta terrisi*). In R. F. Pasquier (Ed.), *Conservation of New World parrots* (ICBP Technical Publication No. 1, pp. 385–392). Washington, DC: Smithsonian Institution Press.

Lenneberg, E. H. (1971). Of language, knowledge, apes, and brains. *Journal of Psycholinguistic Research*, 1, 1–29.

Lenneberg, E. H. (1973). Biological aspects of language. In G. A. Miller (Ed.), *Communication, language, and meaning* (pp. 49–60). New York: Basic Books.

Levinson, S. T. (1980). The social behavior of the White-fronted Amazon (*Amazona albifrons*). In R. F. Pasquier (Ed.), *Conservation of New World parrots* (ICBP Technical Publication No. 1, pp 403–417). Washington, DC: Smithsonian Institution Press.

Lögler, P. (1959). Versuche zur Frage des 'Zähl'-Vermögens an einem Graupapagei und Vergleichsversuche an Menschen [Studies on the question of 'number' sense in a Grey parrot and comparative studies on humans]. *Zeitschrift für Tierpsychologie*, 16, 179–217.

Lombardi, C. M., Fachinelli, C. C., & Delius, J. D. (1984). Oddity of visual patterns conceptualized by pigeons. *Animal Learning & Behavior, 12*, 1–6.

Maccarone, A. D. (1987). Sentinel behaviour in American crows. *Bird Behaviour, 7*, 93–95.

Mackintosh, N. J., Wilson, B., & Boakes, R. A. (1985). Differences in mechanism of intelligence among vertebrates. *Philosophical Transactions of the Royal Society, B308*, 53–65.

Maki, W. W., & Leuin, T. C. (1972). Information-processing by pigeons. *Science, 176*, 535–536.

Marler, P. (1996). Social cognition: Are primates smarter than birds? In V. Nolan, Jr. & E. D. Ketterson (Eds.), *Current ornithology* (Vol. 13, pp. 1–32). New York: Plenum.

Matyniak, K. A., Wheller, G. L., & Stettner, L. J. (1971). Reversal learning in the crow, *Corvus americanus*. *Communications in Behavioral Biology, 6*, 177–185.

May, D. L. (1995). [Grey parrots in the Central African Republic.] Unpublished raw data.

McGowan, K. J., & Woolfenden, G. E. (1989). A sentinel system in the Florida scrub jay. *Animal Behaviour, 37*, 1000–1006.

Mowrer, O. H. (1950). *Learning theory and personality dynamics*. New York: Ronald.

Mowrer, O. H. (1954). A psychologist looks at language. *American Psychologist, 9*, 660–694.

Naguib, M., &. Todt, D. (1998). Recognition of neighbors' song in a species with large and complex song repertoires: The Thrush Nightingale. *Journal of Avian Biology, 29*, 155–160.

Nelson, D. A. (1987). Song syllable discrimination by song sparrows (*Melospiza melodia*). *Journal of Comparative Psychology, 101*, 25–32.

Nelson, D. A. (1988). Feature weighting in species song recognition by the field sparrow (*Spizella pusilla*). *Behaviour, 106*, 158–182.

Nottebohm, F. (1980). Brain pathways for vocal learning in birds: A review of the first ten years. *Progress in Psychobiology and Physiological Psychology, 9*, 85–124.

Olson, D. J., Kamil, A. C., & Balda, R. P. (1993). Effects of response strategy and retention interval on performance of Clark's nutcrackers in a radial maze analogue. *Journal of Experimental Psychology: Animal Behavior Processes, 19*, 138–148.

Olson, D. J., Kamil, A. C., Balda, R. P., & Nims, P. J. (1995). Performance of four seed caching corvid species in operant tests of nonspatial and spatial memory. *Journal of Comparative Psychology, 109*, 173–181.

Park, T. J., & Dooling, R. J. (1985). Perception of species-specific contact calls by budgerigars (*Melopsittacus undulatus*). *Journal of Comparative Psychology, 99*, 391–402.

Pastore, N. (1955). Discrimination and delayed response learning in the canary. *Psychological Reports, 1*, 307–315.

Pastore, N. (1961). Number sense and "counting" ability in the canary. *Zeitschrift für Tierpsychologie, 18*, 561–573.

Pepperberg, I. M. (1983). Cognition in the African Grey parrot: Preliminary evidence for auditory/vocal comprehension of the class concept. *Animal Learning & Behavior, 11*, 179–185.

Pepperberg, I. M. (1987a). Acquisition of the same/different concept by an African Grey parrot (*Psittacus erithacus*): Learning with respect to color, shape, and material. *Animal Learning & Behavior, 15*, 423–432.

Pepperberg, I. M. (1987b). Evidence for conceptual quantitative abilities in the African Grey parrot: Labeling of cardinal sets. *Ethology, 75*, 37–61.

Pepperberg, I. M. (1988). Comprehension of "absence" by an African Grey parrot: Learning with respect to questions of same/different. *Journal of the Experimental Analysis of Behavior, 50*, 553–564.

Pepperberg, I. M. (1990a). Cognition in an African Grey parrot (*Psittacus erithacus*): Further evidence for comprehension of categories and labels. *Journal of Comparative Psychology, 104*, 41–52.

Pepperberg, I. M. (1990b). Some cognitive capacities of an African Grey parrot (*Psittacus erithacus*). In P. J. B. Slater, J. S. Rosenblatt, & C. Beer (Eds.), *Advances in the study of behavior* (Vol. 19, pp. 357–409). New York: Academic.

Pepperberg, I. M. (1992). Proficient performance of a conjunctive, recursive task by an African Grey parrot (Psittacus erithacus). Journal of Comparative Psychology, 106, 295–305.

Pepperberg, I. M. (1994). Evidence for numerical competence in a Grey parrot (Psittacus erithacus). Journal of Comparative Psychology, 108, 36–44.

Pepperberg, I. M. (1996). Categorical class formation by an African Grey parrot (Psittacus erithacus). In T. R. Zentall & P. R. Smeets (Eds.), Stimulus class formation in humans and animals (pp. 71–90). Amsterdam: Elsevier.

Pepperberg, I. M. (1998). The African Grey parrot: How cognitive processing might affect allospecific vocal learning. In R. P. Balda, I. M. Pepperberg, & A. C. Kamil (Eds.), Animal cognition in nature (pp. 381–409). London: Academic Press.

Pepperberg, I. M. (1999). The Alex studies: Cognitive and communicative abilities of Grey parrots. Cambridge, MA: Harvard University Press.

Pepperberg, I. M., & Brezinsky, M. V. (1991). Acquisition of a relative class concept by an African Grey parrot (Psittacus erithacus): Discriminations based on relative size. Journal of Comparative Psychology, 105, 286–294.

Portmann, A. (1950). Système nerveux. In P. P. Grassé (Ed.), Traité de Zoologie (Vol. 15, pp. 185–203). Paris, France: Masson.

Portmann, A., & Stingelin, W. (1961). The central nervous system. In A. J. Marshall (Ed.), Biology and comparative physiology of birds (Vol. 2, pp. 1–36). New York: Academic.

Premack, D. (1976). Intelligence in ape and man. Hillsdale, NJ: Lawrence Erlbaum Associates.

Premack, D. (1978). On the abstractness of human concepts: Why it would be difficult to talk to a pigeon. In S. H. Hulse, H. Fowler, & W. K. Honig (Eds.), Cognitive processes in animal behavior (pp. 421–451). Hillsdale, NJ: Lawrence Erlbaum Associates.

Premack, D. (1983). The codes of man and beasts. Behavioral and Brain Sciences, 6, 125–176.

Rensch, B., & Dücker, G. (1973). Discrimination of patterns indicating four and five degrees of reward by birds. Behavioural Biology, 9, 279–288.

Rice, M. L. (1980). Cognition to language: Categories, word meanings, and training. Baltimore, MD: University Park Press.

Rilling, M. (1967). Number of responses as a stimulus in fixed interval and fixed ratio schedules. Journal of Comparative and Physiological Psychology, 63, 60–65.

Roberts, W. A. (1972). Short-term memory in the pigeon: Effects of repetition and spacing. Journal of Experimental Psychology, 94, 74–83.

Roberts, W. A., & Mitchell, S. (1994). Can a pigeon simultaneously process temporal and numerical information? Journal of Experimental Psychology: Animal Behavior Processes, 20, 66–78.

Rozin, P. (1976). The evolution of intelligence and access to the cognitive unconscious. In J. M. Sprague & A. N. Epstein (Eds.), Progress in psychobiology and physiological psychology (Vol. 6, pp. 245–280). New York: Academic.

Santiago, H. C., & Wright, A. A. (1984). Pigeon memory: Same/different concept learning, serial probe recognition acquisition, and probe delay effects on the serial-position function. Journal of Experimental Psychology: Animal Behavior Processes, 10, 498–512.

Saunders, D. A. (1983). Vocal repertoire and individual vocal recognition in the short-billed white-tailed Black cockatoo, Calyptorhynchus funereus latirostris. Carnaby. Australian Wildlife Research, 10, 527–536.

Savage-Rumbaugh, E. S., Rumbaugh, D. M., Smith, S. T., & Lawson. J. (1980). Reference: The linguistic essential. Science, 210, 922–925.

Schiemann, K. (1939). Vom Erlernen unbennannter Anzahlen bei Dohlen [Learning about unnamed numbers in jackdaws]. Zeitschrift für Tierpsychologie, 3, 292–347.

Schusterman, R. J., & Gisiner, R. (1988). Artificial language comprehension in dolphins and sea lions: The essential cognitive skills. Psychological Record, 38, 311–348.

Seyfarth, R. M., Cheney, D. L., & Marler, P. (1980). Vervet monkey alarm calls: Semantic communication in a free-ranging primate. Animal Behaviour, 28, 1070–1094.

Sherry, D. F., Jacobs, L. F., & Gaulin, S. J. C. (1992). Spatial memory and adaptive specialization of the hippocampus. *Trends in Neurosciences, 15,* 298–303.

Shy, E., McGregor, P. K., & Krebs, J. (1986). Discrimination of song types by male great tits. *Behavioural Processes, 13,* 1–12.

Siegler, R. S. (1991). In young children's counting, procedures precede principles. *Educational Psychology Review, 3,* 127–135.

Smith, L. (1967). Delayed discrimination and delayed matching in pigeons. *Journal of the Experimental Analysis of Behavior, 10,* 529–533.

Smith, W. J. (1988). Patterned daytime singing of the eastern wood-pewee, *Contopus virens. Animal Behaviour, 36,* 1111–1123.

Smith, W. J. (1997). The behavior of communicating, after twenty years. In D. H. Owings, M. D. Beecher, & N. S. Thompson (Eds.), *Perspectives in ethology* (Vol. 12, pp. 7–53). New York: Plenum.

Snyder, N. F., Wiley, J. W., & Kepler., C. B. (1987). *The parrots of Luquillo: Natural history and conservation of the Puerto Rican Parrot.* Los Angeles, CA: Western Foundation for Vertebrate Zoology.

Starkey, P., & Cooper, R. G. (1995). The development of subitizing in young children. *British Journal of Developmental Psychology, 13,* 399–420.

Sternberg, R. J. (1985). *Beyond IQ: A triarchic theory of human intelligence.* New York: Cambridge University Press.

Sternberg, R. J. (1997). The concept of intelligence and its role in lifelong learning and success. *American Psychologist, 52,* 1030–1037.

Sternberg, R. J., & Kaufman, J. C. (1998). Human abilities. *Annual Review of Psychology, 49,* 479–502.

Stettner, L. J. (1967). Brain lesions in birds: Effects on discrimination acquisition and reversal. *Science, 155,* 1689–1692.

Stettner, L. J. (1974). Avian discrimination and reversal learning. In J. Goodman & M. W. Schein (Eds.), *Birds: Brain and behavior* (pp. 165–220). New York: Academic.

Stettner, L. J., & Matyniak, K. (1968). The brain of birds. *Scientific American, 218,* 64–76.

Stevens, S. S. (1951). Mathematics, measurement, and psychophysics. In S. S. Stevens (Ed.), *Handbook of experimental psychology* (pp. 1–49). New York: Wiley.

Stoddard, P. K. (1996). Vocal recognition of neighbors by territorial passerines. In D. E. Kroodsma & E. H. Miller (Eds.), *Ecology and evolution of acoustic communication in birds* (pp. 356–374). Ithaca, NY: Cornell University Press.

Stoddard, P. K., Beecher, M. D., Horning, C. L., & Campbell, S. E. (1991). Recognition of individual neighbors by song in the song sparrow, a bird with song repertoires. *Behavioral Ecology & Sociobiology, 29,* 211–215.

Stoddard, P. K., Beecher, M. D., Loesche, P., & Campbell, S. E. (1992). Memory does not constrain individual recognition in a bird with song repertoires. *Behaviour, 122,* 274–287.

Stoddard, P. K., Beecher, M. D., & Willis, M. S. (1988). Responses of territorial male song sparrows to song types and variations. *Behavioral Ecology & Sociobiology, 22,* 125–130.

Striedter, G. (1994). The vocal control pathways in budgerigars differ from those in songbirds. *Journal of Comparative Neurology, 343,* 35–56.

Taves, E. H. (1941). Two mechanisms for the perception of visual numerousness. *Archives of Psychology, 37,* 1–47.

Terrace, H. S. (1993). The phylogeny and ontogeny of serial memory: List learning by pigeons and monkeys. *Psychological Science, 4,* 162–168.

Thomas, R. K. (1980). Evolution of intelligence: An approach to its assessment. *Brain, Behavior, and Evolution, 17,* 454–472.

Thomas, R. K., & Lorden, R. B. (1993). Numerical competence in animals: A conservative view. In S. T. Boysen & E. J. Capaldi (Eds.), *The development of numerical competence* (pp. 127–147). Hillsdale, NJ: Lawrence Erlbaum Associates.

Thompson, N. S. (1968). Counting and communication in crows. *Communications in Behavioral Biology, 2*, 223–225.

Thompson, N. S. (1969). Individual identification and temporal patterning in the cawing of common crows. *Communications in Behavioral Biology, 4*, 29–33.

Thorpe, W. H. (1964). *Learning and instinct in animals* (2nd ed.). Cambridge, MA: Harvard University Press.

Thorpe, W. H. (1974). *Animal and human nature*. New York: Doubleday.

Todt, D., & Hultsch, H. (1996). Acquisition and performance of repertoires: ways of coping with diversity and versatility. In D. E. Kroodsma & E. H. Miller (Eds.), *Ecology and evolution of communication* (pp. 79–96). Ithaca, NY: Cornell University Press.

Tomasello, M. & Call, J. (1997). *Primate cognition*. Oxford: Oxford University Press.

Trick, L., & Pylyshyn, Z. (1989). Subitizing and the FNST spatial index model. University of Ontario, COGMEM #44. [Based on paper presented at the 30th Psychonomic Society Meeting, Atlanta, GA.]

Trick, L., & Pylyshyn, Z. (1993). What enumeration studies can show us about spatial attention: Evidence for limited capacity preattentive processing. *Journal of Experimental Psychology: Human Perception & Performance, 19*, 331–351.

Urcuioli, P. J., & Nevin, J. A. (1975). Transfer of hue matching in pigeons. *Journal of the Experimental Analysis of Behavior, 24*, 149–215.

Verner, J. (1975). Complex song repertoire of male Long-billed Marsh Wrens in Eastern Washington. *Living Bird, 14*, 263–300.

von Glasersfeld, E. (1993). Reflections on number and counting. In S. T. Boysen & E. J. Capaldi (Eds.), *The development of numerical competence* (pp. 225–243). Hillsdale, NJ: Lawrence Erlbaum Associates.

Wasserman, E. A., Hugart, J. A., & Kirkpatrick-Steger, K. (1995). Pigeons show same-different conceptualization after training with complex visual stimuli. *Journal of Experimental Psychology: Animal Behavior Processes, 21*, 248–252.

Wilson, B., Mackintosh, N. J., & Boakes, R. A. (1985). Matching and oddity learning in the pigeon: Transfer effects and the absence of relational learning. *Quarterly Journal of Experimental Psychology, 37B*, 295–311.

Wolfgramm, J., & Todt, D. (1982). Pattern and time specificity in vocal responses of blackbirds *Turdus merula L. Behaviour, 81*, 264–286.

Wright, A. A. (1994). Primacy effects in animal memory and human nonverbal memory. *Animal Learning & Behavior, 22*, 219–223.

Wright, A. A., Santiago, H. C., & Sands, S. F. (1984). Monkey memory: Same/different concept learning, serial probe acquisition, and probe delay effects. *Journal of Experimental Psychology: Animal Behavior Processes, 10*, 513–529.

Wright, A. A., Santiago, H. C., Urcuioli, P. J., & Sands, S. F. (1984). Monkey and pigeon acquisition of same/different concept using pictoral stimuli. In M. L. Commons, R. J. Herrnstein, & A. R. Wagner (Eds.), *Quantitative analysis of behavior* (Vol. 4, pp. 295–317). Cambridge, MA: Balliner.

Yamashita, C. (1987). Field observations and comments on the Indigo macaw (*Anodorhynchus leari*), a highly endangered species from northeastern Brazil. *Wilson Bulletin, 99*, 280–282.

Young, M. E., Wasserman, E. A., & Dalrymple, R. M. (1997). Memory-based same-different conceptualization by pigeons. *Psychonomic Bulletin & Review, 4*, 552–558.

Zentall, T. R. (1996). An analysis of stimulus class formation in animals. In T. R. Zentall & P. R. Smeets (Eds.), *Stimulus class formation in humans and animals* (pp. 15–34). Amsterdam: Elsevier.

Zentall, T. R., Edwards, C. A., Moore, B. S., & Hogan, D. E. (1981). Identity: The basis for both matching and oddity learning in pigeons. *Journal of Experimental Psychology: Animal Behavior Processes, 7*, 70–86.

Zentall, T. R., Hogan, D. E., & Edwards, C. A. (1984). Cognitive factors in conditional learning by pigeons. In H. L. Roitblat, T. G. Bever, & H. S. Terrace (Eds.), *Animal cognition* (pp. 389–405). Hillsdale, NJ: Lawrence Erlbaum Associates.

Zentall, T. R., Jackson-Smith, P., Jagielo, J. A., & Nallan, G. B. (1986). Categorical shape and color naming by pigeons. *Journal of Experimental Psychology: Animal Behavior Processes, 12,* 153–159.

Zentall, T. R., Sherbourne, L. M., & Steirn, J. N. (1993). Common coding and stimulus class formation in pigeons. In T. R. Zentall (Ed.), *Animal cognition: A tribute to Donald A. Riley* (pp. 217–236). Hillsdale, NJ: Lawrence Erlbaum Associates.

Zorina, Z. A. (1982). Reasoning ability and adaptivity of behavior in birds. In V. J. A. Novak & J. Mlikovsky (Eds.), *Evolution and environment* (pp. 907–912). Prague, Czechoslovakia: Cesko-Slovenska Akademic Věd. (Czechoslovak Academy of Science)

14

Intelligence as Predisposed Skeptical Induction Engines

Henry Plotkin
University College London

The theory of evolution is widely accepted as the central theorem of biology. It explains the origins of all living forms and many, though not all, of the attributes possessed by organisms. This must include human intelligence and culture. Intelligence is defined here very broadly as the ability of individual organisms to acquire information about the world that results in adaptive behavior. This chapter presents the view that there are different forms of intelligence, each of which is predisposed for the acquisition and processing of different kinds of information and the carrying out of different skilled actions. It is also argued that all forms of intelligence can be understood as being driven by the same processes that drive biological evolution. Because human culture is an extension of human intelligence, culture too can be understood in the light of what has become known as universal Darwinism. The value of this approach, which can be traced back at least to the nineteenth century, is that it locates individual intelligence within the larger context of biological evolution on the one hand and human culture on the other. However, there is also no doubt but that this is a viewpoint that makes some contentious claims that many psychologists would challenge. It also taps into a great and ancient philosophical controversy about whether or not knowledge is innate, which can be traced back to classical Greek philosophers such as Plato and Aristotle.

The argument is developed in this chapter within the following sequence. First, the chapter briefly discusses neo-Darwinism. Neo-Darwinism is by no means the only form of evolutionary theory in the contemporary literature. It is, though, the form most widely accepted at present and hence the form within which psychological issues should be framed. It will be characterized by an emphasis on a particular set of processes, the operation of which in sexually reproducing organisms conforms to what I refer to as a skeptical induction. The skepticism has its origins in the existence of pervasive change and uncertainty, the rates of occurrence of which spans a wide range of frequencies. Second, the question is posed as to why intelligence ever evolved at all. That is, why is it that hardwired, instinctive, behaviors, which is what the great majority of animals get by on, had to be supplemented by intelligently controlled behaviors. This is not a question that is often asked. I suggest that the answer lies in both the pervasiveness of change and the life-history strategies of some species. In order to deal with change and the spread of time that it covers, the main evolutionary program in some species has evolved and attached to itself a series of subsidiary evolutionary processes, one of which is intelligence. Third, given that some lineages of species have indeed evolved intelligence, the question is asked whether or not that intelligence is the same across all intelligent species or indeed the same within any one species, such as Homo sapiens . The evidence and arguments as to whether or not intelligence is some general and species-wide trait, or specific to particular kinds of information and action or to particular species, is summarized. I conclude that intelligence is always constrained and domain specific but not necessarily species specific. Fourth, even if intelligence is always constrained and domain specific, the question is then considered as to whether or not the central processes of these multiple intelligences might not nonetheless be general. This is what has been claimed by evolutionary epistemologists to be implicit in the evolutionary derivation of the origins of intelligence. While not conclusive (and not very much is conclusive in psychology) an argument is made that all forms of intelligence can be considered as conforming to the same basic processes as those that drive biological evolution. Finally, this fourth claim is extended to culture in general and to science in particular. The conclusion reached is that intelligence can be understood within the context of a hierarchy of skeptical induction engines, each tuned to a particular frequency of rates of change. Science, that most skeptical of all induction engines, is the ultimate uncertainty detector, able to reach the limits of observable and imaginable change.

EVOLUTION AS A SKEPTICAL INDUCTION ENGINE

Darwinian evolution is the outcome of the operation of three principles that describe the workings of three processes (Lewontin, 1970). The first is the principle of variation, the second is that of differential fitness, and the third is the heritability of fitness. In biological evolution as commonly understood, variation is the result of genetic mechanisms and developmental processes giving rise to variant phenotypes (the whole organism as an expression of genetic information shaped by individual development); differential fitness is the consequence of natural selection filters acting on those phenotypes to result in differences in individual survival and reproduction; and heritability occurs by way of the genetic transmission of information. However, there is generality to these principles and processes because their embodiment in mechanisms may vary widely. In the case of cultural evolution, for example, transmission might be linguistic, the variants might take the form of culture-specific beliefs, and the selection filters might be the efficacy of certain practices (Plotkin, 1997). Darwin originally used the theory to explain speciation. However, the idea of a more encompassing Darwinism applying to many more instances of biological states or systems being transformed in time goes back almost 140 years (see Cziko, 1995; Plotkin, 1994, for recent reviews). Individual development, learning and thought, and the operation of the immune system have all been considered in this way. Darwin himself was not averse to considering changes in language, both within individuals and language communities, in terms of the theory he developed to account for changes in species over time. This school of thought is sometimes referred to as universal Darwinism.

The operation of these principles or processes, whatever mechanisms they are embodied in, takes the logical form of induction, generalizing into the future what was acquired and what worked in the past. In the case of biological evolution, successful phenotypes feed their genes, which code for the adaptations bestowing high fitness values, back into the gene pool and their genes are thus conserved and available to future organisms. This is the pragmatic, conservative component of the evolutionary process. The generation of novel variants by mutation, the independent segregation of chromosomes at meiosis, and a number of other known chance-based events constitute a radical, inventive component of the process. This radical component injects novel, unpredictable variants into the system. This is necessary because evolution occurs within a sea of endless change. In effect, nature "'gambles' that the future will be the same as the past. At the same time it hedges its bets with aleatoric (chance) jumps, just in case it is not." (Plotkin & Odling-Smee, 1979, p. 14), hence the phrase "skeptical induction."

CHANGE, UNCERTAINTY, AND THE EVOLUTION OF INTELLIGENCE

If the world were single valued, then evolution would have proceeded to the production of perfectly fit organisms and then halted. The world, however, is not single valued. It is a dynamic and constantly changing place. Such change has its origins in both nonbiotic as well as biotic sources. Fluctuations in solar wind or continental drift are examples of the former, and migrations of populations or the evolution of other species are examples of the latter. Change is pervasive; it is the driving force of evolution. Indeed, the shift away from a static world view of post-Renaissance science, which was widely held up to the end of the nineteenth century, to one where the dynamics of flux and change are what have to be understood, which is the essence of twentieth century science, is one of the great contributions Darwin made to the history of human ideas and thought.

In its canonical form neo-Darwinism sets evolution within the context of the relatively slow and gradual changes wrought over geological time, and it explains the origin of species, their distribution in time and space, and the existence of adaptations. In his classic account, G. C. Williams (1966) admonished those who had recourse to group selection in their thinking and focused the attention of a generation of biologists on the gene as the unit of selection. Even though selection may operate at many levels, what are conserved and propagated, he argued, are genes. The reason for this emphasis is that Williams was seeking a powerful and elegantly simple explanation for adaptations, which conventionally are thought of as arising and being maintained over periods of tens or hundreds of thousands of years, or more. Adaptations are not the characteristics of one or a few organisms. They are stable, heritable characteristics of whole breeding populations and, eventually, species, becoming widespread and sustained over long periods of time. According to Williams, genes alone have the longevity to serve as the information sources for the conservation of adaptive features over such long periods of time. By comparison with individual genes, genotypes (the unique, except for monozygotic twins, collection of genes that characterize whole individual organisms) and phenotypes are transient and ephemeral entities that simply do not have the requisite constancy for maintaining adaptations in geological time.

It should be stressed that reference to what has been conventional in evolutionary thought is important. Increasing understanding about the great age of the earth and the fossil record have been powerful influences in the evolution of evolutionary biology over the last 200 years, hence the conceptual focus on longevity of conserved variants. Change, however, does not always occur slowly. While Darwin and others recognized sudden catastrophic, but not necessarily repeatable, change (for example, following from earthquake), it was the enduring consequences of such change, its irreversible nature, that was written about. Thus, such seemingly fast change could be subsumed under the old habits of thought of change as long-lasting. But what of reversible rapid change like fluctuations in temperature or shifts in the spatial location of food or water resources? Reversible and rapid change is defined as that which occurs at rates faster than the generational time of a species. Generational time in sexually reproducing species is the period between conception of an organism and when that organism becomes reproductively active and feeds its genes back into the gene pool. In a small rodent, this is a period of a few months; in humans, it is approximately 12 to 14 years in length. The latter figure represents about 40%, perhaps more, of the life span of individual members of the genus *Homo* during much the greater part of the evolution of our species. This is a significant proportion of life span and may encompass many forms of change, some of which are crucial to individual survival and reproduction. How can such change be adapted to?

The way in which the induction processes of evolution deal with change is crucially dependent on the relationship between rates of change and generational time, and because the latter is a species characteristic, that relationship is always species specific. The only form of change that can be detected and adjusted to solely by the main evolutionary program is change that occurs at a rate slower than generational time and which endures for periods greater than that species' generational time. One example is long-term weather changes. In such a case the main evolutionary program invents adaptations with the radical component of the skeptical induction process and conserves them with the pragmatic component of the process.

What, then, of change that occurs faster than generational time? These take different forms. One, like an earthquake, is sudden, and organisms may or may not survive such change depending on chance circumstances. In other words, evolution cannot cope with the wholly unpredictable. Another form is periodic and repeated change. An example of this are fluctuations in temperature when the occurrence of such fluctuations extend over intervals greater than generational time. (There is both a random daily and more orderly seasonal variation in temperature for organisms whose life span exceeds a year.) Hence, this form of change occurs across generation after generation. This is predictable unpredictability, and such predictable unpredictability can be adjusted to by the evolution of adaptations such as shivering, sweating, or even complex migratory behaviors. These adaptations require particular kinds of sensory inputs, comparator devices, and outputs to effectors. However, no information storage beyond that present in genes is necessary for the development of such adaptations in individual animals.

There is, though, another form of rapid change, of predictable unpredictability, that can and must also be adapted to, but to which special conditions attach. This is rapid change that has the characteristic of inducing conditions that are stable for significant periods of time, but nonetheless which do alter at rates faster than generational time. For relatively long-lived animals, the location of resources like food or shelter, or the features of social interactions such as the composition of alliances, are examples of these (which are the bread and butter of the behavioral and social sciences). The likelihood of change in social relationships within a social group characterized by the existence of alliances is so high that it extends beyond generational time as a constant in the life history of any social species, as is the likelihood of change in the spatial position of a resource. Like temperature fluctuation, therefore, the main evolutionary program must put in place devices for adapting to the general class of events that will change. This component of rapid change is predictable. Like all adaptations, the information for the construction of such adaptations resides in the genes. However, specific information relating to where a resource is in space or who exactly is a social ally cannot be stored in genes. This is the unpredictable component. However, it cannot be efficiently responded to like temperature fluctuations by physiological adaptations such as shivering, which has no learning or memory function attached. In the case of events like the position of a resource or the identity of a social ally, information is crucial to fitness. It involves changes that are faster than generational time but which may, and often do, endure for significant periods of an organism's life. This information has to be acquired and stored by each individual organism equipped by its genes with the capacity to gain and act on such information but not furnished by genes with the detail of the information itself. Such a capacity is what I am generically calling intelligence. The brain, with its accompanying psychological mechanisms of learning, memory, and thought, is the site of adaptations to rapid and reversible physical and social changes in the world, which nonetheless do endure for significant durations. Such events or conditions I refer to as short-term stabilities (Plotkin, 1994). (It is worth noting that the vertebrate immune system has a parallel role to play in adapting to rapid changes of state within the body. The consensus among immunologists since the 1950s is that the transformation in time that the immune system undergoes as it adapts to and deals with changes to the internal state of our bodies conforms as a set of processes to what I am referring to as a skeptical induction.)

A more specific definition of intelligence, then, is the capacity actually or potentially to respond to short-term stabilities with adaptive behaviors that are dependent on psychological mechanisms such as learning and memory. Such a definition places intelligence within the framework of a hierarchy of skeptical induction engines whose role is the generation of adaptations to change in the world. It does not preclude intelligence being considered as dependent on other psychological mechanisms. Indeed, apart from learning and memory, it in no way dictates what psychological processes and mechanisms are a part of intelligence, nor does it exclude there being individual differences between individuals in the functioning of these mechanisms.

CONSTRAINTS ON INTELLIGENCE

The argument so far is that the evolutionary origin of intelligence lies in the need to provide adaptive behaviors to change, change which nonetheless revolves around features of the world that may endure for significant periods of an animal's lifetime. Does this mean that intelligence is some single characteristic of intelligent animals? Before attempting to answer this question, it is worth considering what the known phylogenetic distribution of intelligent animals is and what form intelligence generally takes. The definition of intelligence given in this chapter includes learning (i.e., the ability adaptively to alter behavior as a consequence of experience). Intelligence in nonhuman animals, with some notable exceptions, has usually been demonstrated by the ability to learn. It is certainly the case that learning is the most common form of intelligence. Given estimates of around 10 million or more extant species of animals, and the very limited number of species the individuals of which have so far been tested for a capacity to learn, it is simply not possible to estimate what proportion of animal species are intelligent. What is known is that learning is a common property of many vertebrate species, especially mammals and birds. It may well be a defining characteristic of the subphylum. It is present also in certain species of the phylum Arthropoda (especially certain species of insects, though probably representing only a tiny fraction of the total number of species of insect) and possibly in the phylum Mollusca (which includes squids and octopods) as well, though here the evidence is contradictory. Given species differences in sensory and motor abilities, cross-species comparisons of learning are difficult to make and conclusions should be drawn with caution. What is clear is that associative learning in the form of classical conditioning and trial-and-error learning (the latter is sometimes referred to as operant conditioning) is certainly common to many diverse species of learner, including honey bees and humans (Bitterman, 1988; Dickinson & Shanks, 1995, respectively), and may be universally present in all intelligent species. Therefore, two points are clear from this most brief of surveys: Intelligence is probably a relatively rare trait, albeit common within the vertebrate subphylum. It is also probable that associative learning is the most common form of intelligence and may well be universal to intelligent species.

Running through learning theory across all of the twentieth century has been the central question of whether or not learning, in all animals that can learn, is the result of some single general process. The most widely offered candidate for a general learning process has been some form of associative learning device. In recent decades, the view that there are in fact different forms of learning both within and between different species, in addition to the widely accepted generality of associative learning, has become more common. However, the issue remains unresolved, and an understanding of this problem is not helped by there being virtually nothing known with any certainty about the anatomy and physiology of learning. Thus, recourse to the physical basis of intelligence in terms of changes to nervous system structure as a means of determining cross-species identities and differences in learning mechanisms is not yet possible and may not be available for quite some years to come.

What is clear, however, is the existence of functional differences in learning both between and within species—differences which ultimately must be based on differences in nervous system mechanisms of some kind. Consider the example of a classic study of spatial-learning ability differences in two species of vole that are members of the same genus (Gaulin & Fitzgerald, 1989). Drawing upon fundamental and well-supported theories of natural and sexual selection, Gaulin and Fitzgerald predicted sex differences in spatial-learning ability in the polygonous species, the meadow vole, but no such differences in the monogomous congeneric species, the prairie vole. The reasoning, briefly, was that both males and females of the monogomous prairie vole species are, as confirmed by field studies, relatively sedentary and hence have no need to be able to navigate accurately in space. The female meadow voles are also sedentary and might be expected not to have a strongly developed navigational ability. Male meadow voles, on the other hand, range widely, competing with other male meadow voles as they search for mates, which should result in strong selection for spatial-learning ability, hence the prediction of within-species sex differences in spatial learning, a prediction confirmed by experimental laboratory studies using a sequence of maze tests. This is a study that combines strong theory-based prediction, field observation, and laboratory experimentation. Because the demonstrated differences were within a species but between sexes, these are unlikely to be caused by major differences in sensory or motor characteristics. What Gaulin and Fitzgerald reported are functional differences, with causes that might derive from differences in attentional mechanisms, or perhaps even in hormonally induced differences in microstructural features in the neural networks within which the basic learning mechanisms reside. The precise causes of the differences are not known, but what is clear is the existence of a functional difference that is predictable from, and hence explicable within the context of, evolutionary theory.

Numerous other studies in nonhumans demonstrate the fit of learning in ways appropriate to the life-history strategy and ecological demands of species. For example, nectar-feeding birds visit many flowers, each of which yields a small amount of rapidly depleted food. Efficient foraging requires that the birds do not visit flowers randomly but that they remember where they have foraged in the recent past and hence avoid such flowers. A win-shift strategy, appropriate to efficient foraging in hummingbirds, has been shown in laboratory studies to be more easily acquired than a win-stay strategy (Cole, Hainsworth, Kamil, Mercier, &

Wolf, 1982; Kamil, 1978). Other examples include taste-aversion learning, which is a form of classical conditioning that results in an association between a taste (or smell) and nausea. Such learning occurs much more readily when the conditional stimuli are tastes or odors in species like rats, where the identity of food is normally established by smell or taste. However, in species such as quail, where animals identify food visually, the conditioning occurs more readily with visual conditional stimuli (Garcia & Koelling, 1966; Wilcoxon, 1971).

Many reviews of such constraints on learning are now available (e.g., Bolles & Beecher, 1988; Davey, 1989). Human intelligence is similarly constrained. Few psychologists now believe that language acquisition in children is the consequence of associative learning mechanisms (Pinker, 1994), that numerical learning and competence in children is a consequence of some general learning mechanism (Wynn, 1998), or that the learning of motor skills, such as riding a bicycle, employ the same mechanisms as those involved in attributing intentional mental states to others (Baron-Cohen, 1995). Some form of modularity of cognitive mechanisms within specific functional domains is widely accepted both by cognitive developmentalists (Hirschfeld & Gelman, 1994) and by neuropsychologists studying the effects of brain damage (Shallice, 1989).

Many years ago, Spearman (1927) suggested that intelligence comprises two broad components. The first he labeled g, for general intelligence. This is a characteristic of brain and mind that determines performance in all cognitive, intellectual functions. The second, s, for specific intelligence, comprised a more localized factor in intellectual function. Within the context of general intelligence theory, the account given here is weighted toward Spearman's s. In contemporary terms, this chapter is close to Gardner's (1983) conception of multiple, separate intelligences. This does not preclude the likelihood of a factor or factors like g, in the form of some feature of brain physiology, information processing, or efficiency of executive function that is common to all intelligent processes (Deary & Stough, 1996; Sternberg, 1985 for examples); both are a product of evolution. By definition, g does not vary within an individual, and there is no way of measuring it in related species of primate. On the other hand, s lends itself easily to evolutionary analysis because differences within and between species map onto the conception of adaptations to specific features of the world. This accounts for the emphasis paid in the evolutionary literature to specific cognitive skills.

In summary, there is increasing evidence from the study of both nonhumans and humans that intelligence is constrained and domain specific. While the origin of all intelligence lies in the need to provide adaptations to short-term stabilities, the latter take many different forms. Given this environmental variation of what conditions comprise a short-term stability, the empirical findings are not surprising. Only generically, then, is intelligence some single phenomenon. Its manifestation both within and between species will vary with the nature of the short-term stabilities present in the environments of species. It is the need for adaptation to these that have provided the selection pressures which mold the evolution of specific intelligences.

Such findings and views should occasion no surprise. No evolutionist would disagree with the general argument that intelligence is an adaptation to short-term stabilities, which it surely is. Nor could there be an argument that short-term stabilities will vary within and across species because the world is not single valued in either space or time. It follows that intelligence will have evolved into different forms, both within and between species. It is perfectly possible that there was initially some single unitary form of intelligence hundreds of millions of years ago. It is also possible that intelligence has evolved repeatedly and independently in different taxonomic lineages. Evidence as to which is correct will be very hard to discover, but neither scenario negates what the empirical studies now indicate. Intelligence does differ both between and within species. Yet for much of this century, most learning theorists, especially animal learning theorists, had an entirely different approach. Most were adherents to what was known as the general process view of learning and intelligence, which held that learning was the same in all species, with the possible exception of language learning in humans. Yet there were some major general process theorists, like Piaget and Skinner, who argued in different ways against even this exception. A corollary of the general process view is that of the tabula rasa first advanced by the empiricist philosopher John Locke in the seventeenth century. Locke (see Hidditch, 1975) argued that, contrary to the rationalist position of philosophers like Plato, no innate knowledge exists. We, and presumably all other intelligent creatures, enter the world as a blank slate upon which experience writes—we gain knowledge only through our senses. Now the problem with the general process or blank slate approach is that if all intelligence, all learning, is accomplished by some single general process, then we, or any other learner, can learn anything that comes to us through our senses, and being able to learn anything, we can potentially learn everything.

As we have already seen, the evidence tells us something different. We learn different things in different ways using different developmental sequences and different parts of our brains. However, there is another reason why the notion of a tabula rasa should be rejected. Given a small number of sensory channels and the ability to move in space, the number of possible things that could be learned is astronomically large. Even limited to learning by proximity, both spatial and temporal, the number of possible connections that could be learned is massive—in Edelman's (1987) phrase, the world is an unlabeled place, and this is an absolutely central problem. Being able to learn anything and hence learning everything would result in intelligence being an exceedingly slow and cumbersome process. Again notwithstanding the evidence that tells us that human and animal cognition is a relatively rapidly acting if somewhat imperfect set of devices, the logic of the evolution of intelligence tells us that this cannot be so. Intelligence, after all, evolved to deal with relatively rapid rates of change in the world. A clumsily slow process, slow because it just learned everything it could and only by chance learned what is important to the learner, would not be an effective adaptation to a world that changes fast, and hence which requires the ability to deal with the really salient parts of the world. Artificial intelligence investigators have had to deal with the same issue, which they labeled the combinatorial explosion, or frame problems. The only way to deal with this problem is to introduce constraints on intelligence that point it to specific places in the virtually unlimited search space that an unguided intelligence has to crawl all the way through. A related point has been made by Chomsky (1980, for example) and Fodor (1983) in the form of the poverty of the stimulus argument. This invokes the notion that cognitive modules contain information that allow them to transcend a degraded and impoverished environment. Their point is that the poverty of input to cognitive systems cannot explain the richness of the output. The classic example is linguistic input to infants not being able to explain their language competence. In both cases—the poverty of the immediate input and the size of the search space—what is invoked is constraint on cognitive function that originates in genetic information.

It must be stressed that within the psychological community at large this is an unresolved and contentious matter, one of the most contentious in psychology. It nonetheless is a view, common to evolutionists and shown by both evidence and argument, that cognition has to be shown what to learn about—it must come into the world with the slate already much written upon. What writes on the slate in the first instance is genetic information, which presumably (though I keep stressing we do not yet know anything of the actual neural mechanisms) is achieved by channeling attention and weighting neural networks such that they are better able to learn certain things than others. How has this information gathered in the gene pool of a breeding population or species? The answer is by the selection processes being constant across generations for learning only a limited number of things in some specific way. In this way, intelligence becomes skewed to deal effectively with just those short-term stabilities that bear on individual fitness. This is why much of intelligence is innate. We have to come into the world knowing what it is we must be intelligent about. We are pointed to the important regions of the search space. If we were not, we would not survive the vicissitudes of a shifting social and physical world.

INTELLIGENCE AS A SET OF SKEPTICAL INDUCTION ENGINES

In my view, both theory and evidence point to intelligence as functionally plural, to its being a set of predisposed intelligences dealing with different features of the world. However, even if intelligence is always constrained to be functionally domain specific, might it be that despite their manifest differences all intelligences are the products of identical processes? This question, as already indicated, has long been considered by psychologists investigating the processes and mechanisms common to all forms of intelligence. Here the question is asked specifically whether or not all forms of intelligence are induction engines. This is not a simple question, and currently there are no certain answers. At best, the notion that intelligence in all its forms conforms to a skeptical induction engine should be seen as a hypothesis to be tested both theoretically and empirically. There are, however, a number of pointers that suggest that there is partial support from evidence, as well as some arguments, to back up the hypothesis. First, there has been a long-standing acceptance by learning theorists that at least some forms of intelligence can be understood as the products of a skeptical induction engine, though they never used this particular phrase. Trial-and-error learning, also referred to as instrumental learning and operant conditioning, whereby humans and nonhumans alike learn what responses lead to what consequences, and specifically how to achieve rewards (reinforcement) and avoid punishment, has long been seen as conforming to the logic of induction, with explicit parallels being drawn to evolution (Baldwin, 1909; Pringle, 1951; Skinner, 1981; Staddon & Simmelhag, 1971). Similar analyses about the random generation of hypotheses (Krechevsky, 1932) and linguistic behaviors (MacWhinney, 1987) and their selection, fixation, and maintenance within individuals are examples of claims of intelligence being driven by inductive processes. In short, at least some forms of intelligence quite simply are skeptical induction engines.

· Creativity (James, 1880) and problem-solving thought (Piaget, 1971; Popper, 1972; Simon, 1969) have also been considered as analogous in process to, if not actually identical with, evolution, a school of thought known as evolutionary epistemology (Campbell, 1974). In this discussion, though, the similarity is looser and more descriptive. Yet it brings with it a second, powerful argument for viewing all forms of intelligence as skeptical induction machines. No form of intelligence is a priori in the strong philosophical sense of the phrase. No intelligence, in other words, stands outside of all experience and has always existed in the form in which it now manifests itself. Mathematics and logical calculus are most often singled out as having such an existence independent of biology, but these forms of intelligence are, in one important respect, no different from any other. All intelligence must be seen as biological in general and as extensions of evolution specifically. What may appear to be a priori, that which predisposes intelligence as described in the previous section of this chapter, is a consequence of a posteriori acquisition by the processes of evolution, the consequences of which become bound into DNA, which in turn then causes our nervous systems and cognitive modules to manifest the predisposed, constrained functioning that characterizes all cognitive function. All forms of intelligence begin in the processes of evolution and are a product of them and the environments in which they were operating. This, in turn, means that in principle all forms of intelligence can be reduced, at least partially, to the processes of evolution that formed them. I stress *at least partially* because we do not have the environments in which evolution occurred available to us and because intelligence in every individual case is also a product of the environment of development. Nonetheless, a partial mapping of intelligence onto evolution must be possible, even if we cannot achieve it now. Thus, even if not all forms of intelligence are literally skeptical induction machines, all forms of intelligence can be mapped onto the skeptical inductive logic of the processes of evolution, and the conditions of the world in which those processes operated, and still operate. Because intelligence of every kind evolved to deal with features of the world that needed to be conserved, intelligence is going to seem to map onto those features of the world at least to some extent. This will give the appearance of intelligence as a priori, especially certain forms of intelligence, such as mathematical reasoning, which we prize so highly. However, it is no more than an appearance of being a priori. All intelligence is a posteriori. Others have made similar suggestions (e.g., Cooper, 1987, 1989). I think this should be referred to as the strong evolutionary epistemological principle: Evolution determines all forms of intelligence; hence none are a priori and all forms of intelligence can be partially reduced to evolutionary processes.

A third point to note is that some forms of intelligence manifestly conform to the logic of deduction, not induction. However, just as associative learning can be considered a special case of inductive logic with highly restricted variance generation, so can deduction be considered an extension of inductive logic. This is certainly the case for classical conditioning where the constraints on new variant generation are so tight that it is the original association that is almost always regenerated. In other words, there are forms of intelligence where the skepticism is reduced to a minimum either in terms of what associations are acquired or how reasoning proceeds. Indeed, the probability of variance generation might be considered an important dimension along which to classify intelligence. Some forms of intelligence are more skeptical than others.

In deductive reasoning of all forms, a logical consequence relationship must always be present between two sets of propositions. One set is the premises and the other is the conclusion. Whether or not the logical consequence relationship takes syntactic or semantic form, the truth value of the propositions comprise a range of probabilities. If those probabilities are consistently high, then evolution for the tight coupling of deductive reasoning would have been selected for on the basis of inductive reasoning around propositions of such high truth value. For example, if one of the premises is the inductively arrived at proposition that "I am most at danger in the presence of predators," and the other is the proposition that "predators are on the prowl at night," then the conclusion that "night is a dangerous time" has high fitness value. What is being suggested is that the reasoning structures that characterize deduction owe their evolutionary origins to inductive intelligence operating in a world where some things are more certain than others. When one is dealing with high probabilities, there are two ways of arriving at a state of knowledge about the world. The one is through inductive computation of probabilities of an event by way of laborious and possibly dangerous experience. The other is to cut across that experience by deductively integrating other experiences to arrive more rapidly and safely at a conclusion by way of the logical consequence relationship.

The fourth and final point in the argument is that the processes that describe the transformation of living systems in time, which we call biological evolution, are exactly the same processes that drive the transformation of the immune system in time (Janewan, 1993; Jerne, 1967). It is also the case that neurobiologists studying the development of the nervous system consider the processes by which cellular and neuronal network differentiation occurs to be the same as those that drive evolution (Calvin, 1996; Changeux & Danchin, 1976; Edelman, 1987). There is a strong school of thought that considers cultural change to be driven by the same processes as evolution. If evolution, nervous system development, the immune system, and culture are all driven by the same processes that all conform to a skeptical induction, then why should intelligence in all its forms be an exception and not be governed by the same universal processes of variant generation, selection, propagation, and conservation? Of course, the nature of the variants, the selection filters, the method of conservation, and, as just indicated, the degree of skepticism, will vary and be embodied in entirely different mechanisms. The logic to which all these processes conform, though, may well be the same.

Two general points complete this section. The first is that while evolution occurs by way of the operation of certain processes, and many of the complex traits that it has led to also comprise those processes, one cannot make the assumption that all the products of evolution will do so. Specifically, some forms of intelligence may indeed be exceptions to the seemingly general rule. I have stressed the possibility of linkage with a skeptical induction at every point because it strengthens the linkage of individual intelligence to evolution on the one hand and culture on the other. It must be conceded, though (and this is my second point), that this is a viewpoint which would not gain universal acceptance by psychologists.

CULTURE AND CULTURAL CHANGE

As argued at the beginning of this chapter, culture is an extension of human intelligence. The ability to enter into and be a part of culture is a consequence of specific cognitive abilities and not a single, human-specific trait. It is more appropriate, therefore, to describe culture as a human-specific supertrait. However, exactly which features of human intelligence are essential for culture is an empirical issue that has received almost no attention. Despite a century of realization by such social science luminaries as Freud (1913), Mead (1928), and Levi-Strauss (1966) that culture and psychology are inextricably interleaved within each other, and despite a recent upsurge in modeling cultural change that requires some minimal theoretical commitment to mechanisms such as information transmission, there have been virtually no studies of the psychological mechanisms that are responsible for our being creatures of culture. This is an extraordinary omission by a science of mind, the most prominent feature of which is the creation of culture.

There are several possible empirical paths to be taken. For example, the attribution of intentional mental states in others, so-called theory of mind, has been hypothesized to be one of these essential cognitive abilities because of the role and prominence of social constructions in human culture (Plotkin, 1996, 1997). There is an increasing understanding of the development of theory of mind in infancy and early childhood, and so developmental studies of enculturation in children will allow some judgement to be made of the hypothesis, as would studies of individuals with impaired theory of mind modules.

Another and rather different path stems from the modeling of culture in recent years by theorists who make the strong assumption that cultural change is a form of evolutionary change driven by the same processes that drive biological evolution. In other words, that culture, too, is a form of skeptical induction engine. Such modeling had its beginnings in the writing of Murdock (1956) and was rapidly developed into a series of papers (Campbell, 1965; Cloak, 1975; Durham, 1976) and books (Boyd & Richerson, 1985; Cavalli-Sforza & Feldman, 1981; Dawkins, 1976; Lumsden & Wilson, 1981; Pulliam & Dunford, 1980), with some of the book authors also contributing many journal papers on the matter. Laland, Kumm, and Feldman (1995) provide a recent overview of what have come to be known as coevolutionary theories.

Such models and theories make two core assumptions. One is that cultural change is indirectly linked with biological evolution. This assumption will not be pursued further in this chapter. The other, as already stated, is that cultural change is evolutionary in form. This means that culture comprises components or units, with roles in cultural change analogous to that of genes in biological evolution. These replicators, memes to use Dawkins' (1976) term, appear in variant forms. Some of this variation is the result of random changes analogous to gene mutations, while other variants arise because of the ways that memes interact with one another, including their origins in multiple parents, a distinct disanalogy with the restricted genetic parenting of biological evolution. Whatever the origins of the variation, selection filters then act to conserve only a restricted subset of variant memes, which are copied and transmitted to members of the social group. Through this differential selection and transmission of variant memes, the frequencies of different memes in the culture's meme pool alters in time. In other words, there is a descent with modification in cultures in much the same way as biological evolution occurs through descent with modification. The mechanisms, of course, are entirely different, which does lead to some significant disanalogies. Nonetheless, the basic processes are identical, and they are characterized by the same logic of skeptical induction.

There is, though, much theoretical and empirical work to be done before one can reasonably claim that a science of culture has been developed along these lines. One does not have a science until one can manipulate and measure something empirically. We cannot do that yet with the notion of memes as replicators because we do not know what memes are, or even whether they comprise a single kind of entity (Plotkin, 1996). For some, memes are motor acts (e.g., actions that make up the construction of a stone axe). For others, they are ideas, values, knowledge, or hypotheses. A case could be made for them being larger scale entities, such as social constructions. Complicating the issue is the enormous difference in longevity of different features of cultures. Metaphysical beliefs, such as those in deities, have lasted for millennia, whereas fashion in clothes changes year by year in some cultures. Similar problems attach to identifying the entities upon which the selection filters act. In biological evolution, the genes are the replicators, and it is the phenotype, the expression in bodily form of the information carried in the genome and expressed during development, upon which selection acts. The phenotype is the interactor (Hull, 1980) or vehicle (Dawkins, 1976). What, then, is the cultural analogue of the phenotype? For example, if one observes the making of an arrowhead and then proceeds to fashion one for oneself, is the interactor the behavior of imitation or the artifact that is the end product of the imitation?

These are some of the important and difficult questions that will have to be resolved if a science of culture is to be achieved. One way of proceeding is to use particular subcultures as exemplars and test-beds to help in developing an understanding of culture at large. The study of changes in science and specific scientific communities has seen striking examples of this approach (e.g. Hull, 1988; Popper, 1972; Toulmin, 1967). Among the advantages of using the study of scientific communities as a means of better understanding the evolution of culture is the unusually high degree of recorded documentation of the entities that are evolving. Such records take the form of journals, books, notebooks, and conference proceedings. There is also the relative ease in identifying the component processes of evolution. Ideas, hypotheses, and theories are the replicators, and observation, preferably within an experimental setting, supplies one of the selection filters. These selection filters are deliberately set to act upon circumscribed phenomena in the world, which are the objectives of scientific knowledge. Hence, it is these real-world phenomena that constitute the analogues of the phenotype in science.

One of the most interesting outcomes of studying science in this way is the understanding of how science is at once both highly conservative and extremely skeptical as an engine for generating knowledge about the world. The insistence upon empirical validation and the replication of results defines science as a particular method of gaining knowledge. Empiricism is a very conservative methodology that sets relatively precise selection filters for hypotheses and theories. They are not, however, the only selection filters. Peer review in the publication process of science is a further selection device, as is the hurdle of acceptance by the journal readers who require a minimum degree of fit between reported results and the data and theories already accepted within a particular discipline. This is evidenced by the high percentage of scientific papers that are never cited after publication. On the other hand, science is also profligate in the extraordinary degree of variation that it generates. Commonplace within universities and other scientific institutions are conversations between colleagues in seminars and other forms of small meetings. These are all settings where transient variants are produced in large numbers. Less transient variants are recorded in the conference proceedings, which abound, and new journals are constantly appearing, along with the old, that carry the observations and varying ideas of scientists. These are the products of the intellectual search space of science being ground through the empirical and theoretical mills of practitioner scientists. Electronic publishing on the Internet is going to increase significantly the generation of variation in science but will likely reduce the rigor of the selection filters. The outcome for the scientific process will be interesting to observe.

It is worth repeating that science as an example of culture is the result of the operation of the evolved intelligence modules of each and every scientist. The product of science might seem remote from the world and abstract in the extreme, but understanding the evolution of science requires an understanding of the same psychological mechanisms as are needed for understanding preliterate cultures. Science is born of the same need to deal with change in an uncertain world and to reduce that change such that it can be adapted to. Modern physics can now explain and explore the very limits of change and uncertainty, yet this is an achievement that is bound by an unbroken thread that begins with the transformation of populations of organisms in time, which has resulted, in turn, in the evolution of intelligence by which individual organisms can adapt to immediately changing circumstances, and which links, finally, with the highly specific intelligence of one species of social ape to result in culture in general and science in particular.

A HIERARCHY OF SKEPTICAL INDUCTION ENGINES

A hierarchy is a partial ordering of entities. The hierarchy that is described in this chapter is a control hierarchy, with the ordering principle being the frequency of change to which adaptations can occur. Intelligence has evolved because of the need to deal with rates of change higher than can be dealt with by the main evolutionary program. Because of the need for rapid and effective function, intelligence is not a single, autonomous device that operates as a tabula rasa. The selection pressures that have led to the evolution of intelligence have resulted in a set of separate, semiautonomous cognitive modules, each of which is embedded within the main evolutionary program and hence constrained to be intelligent about different features of the world. The immune system is a parallel organ system to the nervous system, operating within a different sphere of change and uncertainty. Culture is another level in this embedded hierarchy. It is my prediction that as a science of culture evolves, clear links will be established between culture and the more fundamental levels of the hierarchy (i.e., individual intelligence and biological evolution). This will lead us to understand that all the cultures of Homo sapiens are constrained in the same ways and bear deep commonalities of structure.

Knowledge is gained by each level of this hierarchy, though force of habit makes most wince at the use of the word knowledge when applied to the main evolutionary program—information might be preferred. Such knowledge constitutes an adaptive fit between organic structure and features of the world that are important to the survival and reproduction of individual organisms. The processes by which such knowledge is gained conform to the logic of skeptical induction. This is an elegant and powerful conceptualization within which to ground our understanding of intelligence.

REFERENCES

Baldwin, J. M. (1909). *Darwin and the humanities*. Baltimore, MD: Review Publishing.
Baron-Cohen, S. (1995). *Mindblindness: An essay on autism and theory of mind*. Cambridge, MA: MIT Press.

Bitterman, G. (1988). Vertebrate-invertebrate comparisons. In H. J. Jerison & I. Jerison (Eds.), *Intelligence and evolutionary biology* (pp. 251–276). Berlin, Germany: Springer-Verlag.

Bolles, R. C., & Beecher, M. D. (Eds.). (1988). *Evolution and Learning*. Hillsdale, NJ: Lawrence Erlbaum Associates.

Boyd, R., & Richerson, P. J. (1985). *Culture and the evolutionary process*. Chicago: Chicago University Press.

Calvin, W. H. (1996). *The cerebral code*. Cambridge, MA: MIT Press.

Campbell, D. T. (1965). Variation and selective retention in sociocultural evolution. In H. R. Barringer, G. I. Blanksten, & R. W. Mach (Eds.), *Social change in developing areas: A reinterpretation of evolutionary theory* (pp. 19–45). Cambridge, MA: Shenkman.

Campbell, D. T. (1974). Evolutionary epistemology. In P. A. Schilpp (Ed.), *The philosophy of Karl Popper* (pp. 413–463). La Salle, IL: Open Court.

Cavalli-Sforza, L. L., & Feldman, M. W. (1981). *Cultural transmission and evolution: A quantitative approach*. Princeton, NJ: Princeton University Press.

Changeux, J-P., & Danchin, A. (1976). Selective stabilization of developing synapses as a mechanism for the specification of neuronal networks. *Nature, 264*, 705–711.

Chomsky, N. (1980). *Rules and representations*. New York: Columbia University Press.

Cloak, F. T. (1975). Is a cultural ethology possible? *Human Ecology, 3*, 161–182.

Cole, S., Hainsworth, F. R., Kamil, A. C., Mercier, T., & Wolf, L. L. (1982). Spatial learning as an adaptation in hummingbirds. *Science, 217*, 655–657.

Cooper, W. S. (1987). Decision theory as a branch of evolutionary theory: A biological derivation of the Savage axioms. *Psychological Review, 94*, 395–411.

Cooper, W. S. (1989). How evolutionary biology challenges the classical theory of rational choice. *Biology and Philosophy, 4*, 457–481.

Cziko, G. (1995). *Without miracles: Universal selection theory and the second Darwinian revolution*. Cambridge, MA: MIT Press.

Davey, G. (1989). *Ecological learning theory*. London: Routledge.

Dawkins, R. (1976). *The selfish gene*. Oxford: Oxford University Press.

Deary, I., & Stough, L. (1996). Intelligence and inspection time: Achievements, prospects and problems. *American Psychologist, 51*, 599–608.

Dickinson, A., & Shanks, D. (1995). Instrumental action and causal representation. In D. Sperber, D. Premack, & A. J. Premack (Eds.), *Causal cognition* (pp. 5–25). Oxford: Clarendon Press.

Durham, W. H. (1976). The adapted significance of cultural behaviour. *Human Ecology, 4*, 89–121.

Edelman, G. M. (1987). *Neural Darwinism: The theory of neuronal group selection*. New York: Basic Books.

Fodor, J. A. (1983). *The modularity of mind*. Cambridge MA.: MIT Press.

Freud, S. (1913). *Totem and taboo*. New York: Norton.

Garcia, J., & Koelling, R. A. (1966). Relation of cue to consequence in avoidance learning. *Psychonomic Science, 4*, 123–124.

Gardner, H. (1983). *Frames of mind: The theory of multiple intelligences*. New York: Basic Books.

Gaulin, S. J. C., & Fitzgerald, R. W. (1989). Sexual selection for spatial-learning ability. *Animal Behaviour, 37*, 322–331.

Hirschfeld, L. A., & Gelman, S. A. (Eds.). (1994). *Mapping the mind: Domain specificity in cognition and culture*. Cambridge: Cambridge University Press.

Hull, D. L. (1980). Individuality and selection. *Annual Review of Ecology and Systematics, 11*, 311–332.

Hull, D. L. (1988). *Science as a process: An evolutionary account of the social and conceptual development of science*. Chicago: University of Chicago Press.

James, W. (1880). Great men, great thoughts, and the environment. *Atlantic Monthly, 46*, 441–459.

Janewan, C. A. (1993). How the immune system recognizes invaders. *Scientific American, 269*, 73–79.

Jerne, N. K. (1967). Antibodies and learning: Selection vs. instruction. In G. C. Quarton, T. Melnechuk, & F. O. Schmitt (Eds.), *The neurosciences: A study program* (pp. 200–205). New York: Rockefeller University Press.

Kamil, A. C. (1978). Systematic foraging by a nectar-feeding bird, the Amakihi (*Loxops virens*). *Journal of Comparative and Physiological Psychology, 92*, 388–396.

Krechevsky, I. (1932). "Hypotheses" in rats. *Psychological Review, 39*, 516–532.

Laland, K. L., Kumm, J., & Feldman, M. W. (1995). Gene-culture co-evolutionary theory: A test case. *Current Anthropology, 36*, 131–156.

Levi-Strauss, C. (1966). *The savage mind*. Chicago: Chicago University Press.

Lewontin, R. C. (1970). The units of selection. *Annual Review of Ecology and Systematics, 1*, 1–18.

Lumsden, C., & Wilson, E. O. (1981). *Genes, mind and culture*. Cambridge, MA: Harvard University Press.

MacWhinney, B. (1987). The competition model. In B. MacWhinney (Ed.), *Mechanisms of Language Development* (pp. 249–308). Hillsdale, NJ: Lawrence Erlbaum Associates.

Mead, M. (1928). *Coming of age in Samoa*. New York: Mentor.

Murdock, G. P. (1956). How culture changes. In H. L. Shapiro (Ed.), *Man, culture and society* (pp. 247–260). Oxford: Oxford University Press.

Nidditch, P. H. (1975). On Locke's an essay concerning human understanding. Oxford, UK: Clarendon Press.

Piaget, J. (1971). *Biology and knowledge*. Edinburgh, England: Edinburgh University Press.

Pinker, S. (1994). *The language instinct*. London: Allen Lane.

Plotkin, H. C. (1994). *The nature of knowledge*. London: Allen Lane.

Plotkin, H. C. (1996). Some psychological mechanisms of culture. *Philosophica, 57*, 91–106.

Plotkin, H. C. (1997). *Evolution in mind*. London: Allen Lane.

Plotkin, H. C., & Odling-Smee, F. J. (1979). Learning change and evaluation: An inquiry into the technology of learning. *Advances in the Study of Behavior, 10*, 1–41.

Popper, K. R. (1972). *Objective knowledge*. Oxford: Oxford University Press.

Pringle, J. W. S. (1951). On the parallel between learning and evolution. *Behaviour, 3*, 174–215.

Pulliam, H. R., & Dunford, C. (1980). *Programmed to learn: An essay on the evolution of culture*. New York: Columbia University Press.

Shallice, T. (1989). *From neuropsychology to mental structure*. Cambridge: Cambridge University Press.

Simon, H. A. (1969). *The sciences of the artificial*. Cambridge, MA: MIT Press.

Skinner, B.F. (1981). Selection by consequences. *Science, 213*, 501–504.

Spearman, C. (1927). *The abilities of man*. New York: Macmillan.

Staddon, J. E. R., & Simmelhag, V. L. (1971). The superstition experiment: A re-examination of its implications for the principle of adaptive behavior. *Psychological Review, 78*, 3–43.

Sternberg, R. J. (1985). *Beyond IQ: A triarchic theory of human intelligence*. New York: Cambridge University Press.

Toulmin, S. (1967). The evolutionary development of natural science. *American Scientist, 55*, 456–471.

Wilcoxon, H. C. (1971). Illness-induced aversions in rat and quail: Relative salience of visual and gustatory cues. *Science, 171*, 826–828.

Williams, G. C. (1966). *Adaptation and natural selection*. Princeton: Princeton University Press.

Wynn, K. (1998). The psychological foundations of number: Numerical competence in human infants. *Trends in Cognitive Science, 2*, 296–303.

15

※

Get Smart

Paul Bloom
Yale University

There are two ways to study the evolution of intelligence. One can start with the fact of human uniqueness. Humans occupy, as John Tooby and Irven DeVore (1987) put it, the "cognitive niche." We deal with our environment, both physical and social, in a radically different way than other animals; we possess mental powers that have given rise to science, technology, art, government, and culture. These powers are either absent in other creatures, or exist only in considerably diminished forms.

From the perspective, a successful theory of the evolution of intelligence will require, among other things, that we characterize the nature of these unique capacities. Current proposals focus on the role of generative reasoning (Corballis, chap. 7, this volume), the representation of abstract propositions (Cosmides & Tooby, chap. 8, this volume), enhanced cultural learning (Lynch, chap. 12, this volume), and a large brain relative to the size of our bodies (Jerison, chap. 11, this volume). Several scholars also emphasize social, or Machiavellian, intelligence (Bradshaw, chap. 4, this volume; Byrne, chap. 5, this volume; Bjorklund, & Kipp, chap. 3, this volume; see also Humphrey, 1976; Trivers, 1971). Of course, it might be many factors are needed to explain human intelligence (e.g., Pinker, 1997). Having pinned down what intelligence is, one can go on to speculate as to the course of its evolution, and in particular, to address the question of why it has evolved only once in the history of the planet.

There is another approach, however. One can instead look at certain types of cognitive capacities that are shared across species, dropping the emphasis on human uniqueness. This fits with Sternberg's (chap. 1, this volume) observation that all theorists assume that, in some broad sense, intelligence involves adaptation to the environment. Intelligence from this perspective relates to perception and learning, and hence includes capacities that are shared across organisms—not just primates but also birds (Pepperberg, chap. 13, this volume), and perhaps even plants and bacteria (Godfrey-Smith, chap. 10, this volume). Once again, the goal here is to properly characterize the nature of this intelligence and to explain the conditions under which it will evolve. Under this broader conception of intelligence, one can look across species and, hence, there is much more to be said about the evolutionary conditions that give rise to its emergence. Some suggest, for example, that intelligence emerges as a consequence of the need to cope with short-term changes in the environment that could not be anticipated by natural selection (Plotkin, chap. 14, this volume) or of the need to deal with different forms of environmental complexity (Godfrey-Smith, chap. 10, this volume).

It would be silly to view these two approaches as if they are in conflict. Nothing much rests on how we choose to use the word *intelligent*, and the two approaches are best seen as addressing two related questions in the evolution of mind—how did uniquely human cognitive capacities evolve, and how did the cognitive capacities that different animals share evolve? None of the authors are confused about this; some even explicitly take the step to contrast these notions of intelligence, for example, by drawing the contrast between intelligence and cognition (Godfrey-Smith, chap. 10, this volume) or, somewhat more contentiously, between dedicated intelligence and improvisational intelligence (Cosmides & Tooby, chap. 8, this volume). In other words, everyone recognizes that the mental lives of humans are, in certain important regards, unique, and everyone recognizes that nonhumans engage in activities that are in some sense intelligent. The problem that one wants to address can be viewed as a matter of personal taste.

This isn't to say that there is general agreement among the contributors. Perhaps the biggest debate is over the relationship between the two approaches. Can one explain human intelligence as an enhanced version of what other animals, or at least other primates, possess? (In this case, a theory of animal intelligence would need only minor tweaking to turn into a theory of human intelligence.) Or does a proper theory of human intelligence require that we posit the emergence of something that no other animal possesses? To put it somewhat crudely, if you took a chimpanzee and enhanced what it already has—turned the dials on its mental capacities to higher settings—would the result be a human? There are other debates as well. To what extent is the evolution of intelligence the direct result of natural selection, as opposed to other nonadaptationist evolutionary processes (Flanagan, Hardcastle, & Nahmias, chap. 9; Grossman & Kaufman, chap. 2, this volume)? Is the intelligence possessed by humans and animals the product of a domain-general capacity, or is it better characterized as a cluster of domain-specific modules? Precisely how different are humans from other primates anyway?

In what follows, none of these questions will be answered. Instead, I will suggest a specific methodology, a way to study the evolution of human intelligence, that a few of the chapters discuss only in passing. I will suggest that the best way to construct a theory of the nature and evolution of human intelligence is to study the development of human intelligence in the child.

WHY DEVELOPMENT?

There is considerable precedent for this proposal. The reason Jean Piaget initiated the modern study of development was to understand the emergence of knowledge in the species; he accordingly described his research as "genetic epistemology." Sigmund Freud (1916) was deeply enthusiastic about this approach, proclaiming that "every individual somehow recapitulates in an abbreviated form the entire development of the human race" (p. 199). However, recapitulationist theories have been soundly refuted (see Gould, 1977). Why would one want to revive such a bad idea? On a personal note, my own research is mostly developmental, so my proposal might remind you of the saying that for someone who only has a hammer, every problem looks like a nail.

It turns out, however, that there are three reasons to look at development, none of which rest on any blanket assumption that ontogeny recapitulates phylogeny.

The first reason to look at development is that any account of the evolution of human intelligence requires a theory of what human intelligence is, and such a theory will be based in large part on developmental research. For example, one split in current theories of evolution concerns whether human intelligence is best characterized as a set of specialized modules or whether there exists, as an alternative to modules or in addition to them, one or more domain-general capacities. Any complete theory of the evolution of intelligence requires a resolution of this debate, and developmental research is perhaps the main source of empirical data here. (It is revealing here that Cosmides & Tooby (chap. 8, this volume), who defend the Swiss-army knife model of the mind, and Corballis (chap. 7, this volume), who attacks it, both cite developmental studies in support of their views.)

This is a pretty obvious point. In fact, in principle, every field within the social and biological sciences is relevant to the study of human cognitive evolution because data from every field is relevant to the study of the minds of modern humans. However, in practice, developmental psychology has always played a central role in the study of cognitive evolution.

The second reason to look at development is that theories of the evolution of intelligence make claims about the capacities that fall together and those that are distinct, as well as about the causal connections between different capacities. Suppose one was to say, as Corballis (chap. 7, this volume) does, that language, enhanced social cognition, and thinking about the past and future (mental time travel) are all the result of a single evolved capacity for generativity. If so, then one might expect these capacities to emerge together in the child. It would be an embarrassment for this view, for example, if theory of mind emerged at a much different age than mental time travel. More generally, any claim that A, B, and C are the manifestations of a single factor should predict, other things being equal, that A, B, and C emerge together in the developing child. To take a different kind of example, suppose someone was to maintain that uniquely human intelligence emerges as a result of some unitary factor, for example, the acquisition of complex syntax or the attainment of some specific brain structure. This makes the strongly developmental claim that there should be a qualitative shift in human intelligence at the point that this factor is present in children (e.g., once they acquire complex syntax or develop the relevant brain structure). More generally, any claim that Z is the primary component that makes people special should predict that, other things being equal, uniquely human cognitive traits should appear in the developing child only once Z comes into being.

Every paper in this collection that addresses the origin of human intelligence makes claims about the relationships, causal and otherwise, between different cognitive capacities, and all of these claims are testable using developmental research. In fact, I would make the stronger claim that this is the best way to test them.

Consider some alternatives. Work with nonhumans is plainly relevant here; if one argues that Z is necessary and sufficient for human intelligence, then it follows that nonhumans should lack Z. But studies of nonhumans cannot bear directly on theories about the relationship between certain uniquely human abilities, for obvious reasons. Another method that involves nonhumans is to test a theory of evolution of intelligence by seeing if one can turn a nonhuman into an animal with human intelligence. Most notably, if one thinks that the only difference between humans and other primates has to do with how humans are raised, then one can test the theory by raising a chimpanzee as if it were a human and seeing what happens. However, such experiments have both practical and conceptual problems (is it possible to raise a chimp like a human?) and they cannot be done for many predictions (if one thinks brain size is the key to human intelligence, then one is out of luck because there is no way to give nonhumans more brain size).

Alternatively, one might study pathologies in adults, but again it is hard to use this data to test predictions about evolution. Suppose one believes that intelligence was the product of a single factor Z, and one found that adults who, through trauma or stroke, lost Z but, nonetheless, were otherwise very smart. Would this refute one's theory? Not necessarily; there is a difference between the claim that Z is necessary for intelligence to *emerge* (the evolutionary claim) and the stronger claim that the presence of Z is necessary for intelligence to *occur*.

We can consider language. It is often argued that many of the unique properties of human mental life exist as the result of exposure to a natural language (e.g., Dennett, 1996; Whorf, 1956). For example, I have the concepts that I do and reason as I do in large part because I have learned English. There is much to say about this view (see Bloom, 2000), but one can't refute it by pointing out that there exist aphasic adults who are otherwise cognitively unimpaired. The fans of the language theory would legitimately reply that once language plays the role of structuring thought, it is no longer needed—once a house is built, it doesn't matter what you do with the blueprints. More generally, the dependencies that exist within the adult brain need not correspond to those that exist in either development or evolution. On the other hand, the study of development does serve as an excellent source of insight; the language theory discussed previously can be directly tested by looking at the mental lives of children who grow without language, either because of severe social deprivation or some congenital disorder (Bloom, 2000; see also Grossman & Kaufman, chap. 2, this volume, for discussion of how the study of genetic disorders can shape evolutionary theories.)

There is a third reason to look at development. Perhaps ontology really does recapitulate phylogeny in this domain. The process of cognitive evolution is the transition from a creature without human intelligence to an intelligent human being; the process of cognitive development is the same. Human intelligence, in the sense I define it in this chapter, evolved only once in the history of the planet. This raises the possibility that the process that gives rise to an intelligent species is the same process that gives rise to an intelligent individual. Maybe there is only way to construct a fully functional human mind; maybe there's only one way to get smart.

Even if this strong claim isn't correct, there are other reasons to expect strong parallels between development and evolution. All the complex cognitive capacities that we know of include parts that exhibit causal and logical dependencies. These dependencies must be honored in both evolution and development. If you need A to have B, and B to have C, then you know that A has to emerge not later than B, and B has to emerge not later than C. There is, for example, a logic to human language. Humans can't learn and use words without some ability to produce and perceive speech or sign; humans cannot make simple sentences and phrases without words; and humans cannot make complex sentences (such as embedded questions) without simple sentences and phrases. It is not surprising, then, that children start with the ability to produce and understand sounds or signs, then they learn words, then they combine words into phrases and short sentences, and then they produce longer and more complicated sentences. Evolution must have worked the same way: first came sounds (or signs), then words, then simple syntax, and then complex syntax. There is no other way to do it. If other aspects of human mental life have the same type of structure that we find in natural language, then we should find the same type of parallels between development and evolution.

There is a further point to make. When it comes to artifacts, one doesn't expect to find a parallel between evolution and development. If one were interested in the emergence of chairs through the course of human history, then one would learn nothing by watching someone build a modern chair. However, animals are different from artifacts in an important regard. Animals have to be viable at every stage, both in evolution and in development. What this means for humans is that, as our brains evolved in the last 5 to 6 million years, from a shared ancestor of our primates to the present, our brains always had to work; they always had to exhibit some cognitive capacity. By the same token, the brain of the human, as it develops, has to always be in good working order. Whatever happened to make the human mind special can't be—to change the example—like improving a computer by shutting it down and replacing the hard drive. Such a constraint holds for both evolution and development.

A CASE STUDY:
LANGUAGE AND SOCIAL INTELLIGENCE

As a case study, consider the question of the relationship between two aspects of human intelligence—our enhanced social cognition (or theory of mind) and, once again, human language. There are several perspectives here. Some scholars view social intelligence as a catalyst for the emergence of language; others see it the other way around, with language as the precursor to social intelligence; some see language and social intelligence as independent; and others have argued that they are deeply interdependent (for discussion, see Byrne (chap. 5, this volume), & Calvin (chap. 6, this volume), Jerison (chap. 11, this volume), also Calvin & Bickerton, 1999; Carruthers, 1996; Dennett, 1996). Of course, much depends on the particular aspects of language and social intelligence that one is interested in; there are different things to be said about phonology, for example, than for words and for syntax.

In fact, the evidence from development strongly suggests that the first view is right, that a rich social intelligence evolved prior to the emergence of language. Here's why: Studies of how young children learn simple object names show that this process is largely based on their ability to discern the referential intentions of other people. That is, when a 1- or 2-year-old child learns a word such as *dog*, he or she does so by figuring out (i.e., using cues such as direction of gaze and discourse context) that the person using the word means it to refer to a specific entity in the environment. Contrary to what is often assumed, then, simple object names are not learned through general associative mechanisms (for discussion and review, see Bloom, 2000).

This account is supported by several developmental experiments, and it nicely explains two otherwise mysterious facts. First, children with severe autism do not learn words, even though they are sometimes otherwise of high intelligence. This is what one would expect, given the fact that autism involves a severe deficit in reasoning about the minds of other people (Grossman & Kaufman, chap. 2, this volume). Second, nonhuman primates are terrible at learning words, even under conditions of extensive training. (Even under the most enthusiastic estimates, their vocabulary size never exceeds that of a normal 2-and-a-half-year old human, and the way in which they learn and use words is radically different from how a child does it.) Chimps are smart animals, and this limitation is quite surprising—except when one realizes that they show no spontaneous signs of understanding referential communication (see also Tomasello, 1998). This deficit in theory of mind that is shared by children with severe autism and nonhuman primates is what keeps them from learning words, and hence from learning language.

This argument suggests a causal dependency (i.e., one needs some degree of social intelligence to learn words). This leads to a conclusion about the evolution of the human mind: Members of our species could only learn words once they possessed this social intelligence because social intelligence evolved prior to the emergence of language.

I don't want to overstate this point; it is an argument, not a proof. It is conceivable, for example, that our primate ancestors were able to learn words some other way, without using social intelligence, then language evolved, and then social intelligence evolved, and this changed the character of how modern humans learn words. Such alternatives are possible; they're just very unlikely. (One would need to explain, for example, what this other way of word learning is, and why contemporary humans and primates, who are otherwise quite smart, are unable to use it.) There is much more to be said about the aspects of social intelligence that are needed for word learning and which are not; the point of this example is to show how developmental research can directly bear on the evolution of intelligence.

PROBLEMS AND MYSTERIES

Noam Chomsky (1980) draws the distinction between problems (questions that can be approached scientifically with some hope of success) and mysteries (questions that lie beyond the reach of our minds; see also McGinn, 1993). Animal intelligence, and the aspects of this intelligence that are shared by humans, possess a set of problems. We do not yet understand how creatures construct spatial maps, enumerate objects, or recognize faces, but we are making progress on these questions. The same holds for the study of potentially more modular processes such as language and, to a lesser extent, social intelligence. We can develop computational and neural models of these processes, and we can posit testable accounts of the conditions under which they arise; this research is part of an ongoing scientific research program of considerable promise.

However, there is the worrisome possibility that certain uniquely human aspects of intelligence pose a mystery in Chomsky's sense. Consider the more open-ended and creative human capacities that Descartes worried about—the ability to appreciate a joke, to invent a new machine, or to plan a topic of conversation. We don't know how people do these things, and we cannot explain these abilities in computational or neural terms. (There is of course a psychology of such capacities, but the empirical work here addresses questions at a different level. For example, work on the psychology of creativity asks how many types of creativity there are, the qualities that especially creative people posses, the social contexts that encourage creativity, and so on.) It was this type of intelligence that led Wallace to throw up his hands and abandon the theory of natural selection as applied to the human mind (see Cronin, 1991). Modern-day critics of evolutionary psychology have worried about exactly this issue, and it does seem as if the success stories of evolutionary theory have been in other areas.

It would be nice if research from cognitive development could help, but this area has the same problem. We are starting to learn something about the development of capacities such as vision, mathematical cognition, and language, but we know next to nothing about the emergence of the creative powers that are so strikingly human. Perhaps things will change and there will be some conceptual advance that will turn this mystery into a set of problems. Or perhaps we will be forever stuck with what Pinker (1997) calls "the ultimate tease," in which the most important central and salient aspects of our mental life will be forever beyond our understanding. Even if this worse case is true, however, there are clearly enough problems that remain to keep us busy for a very long time.

REFERENCES

Bloom, P. (2000). *How children learn the meanings of words*. Cambridge, MA: MIT Press.
Calvin, W. H. & Bickerton, D. (1999). *Lingua ex machina*. Cambridge, MA: MIT Press.
Carruthers, P. (1996). *Language, thought, and consciousness*. Cambridge: Cambridge University Press.
Chomsky, N. (1980). *Rules and representations*. New York: Columbia University Press.
Cronin, H. (1991). *The ant and the peacock*. Cambridge, UK: Cambridge University Press.
Dennett, D. C. (1996). *Kinds of minds*. New York: Basic Books.
Fodor, J. A. (1983). *The modularity of mind*. Cambridge, MA: MIT Press.
Freud, S. (1916). *Introductory lectures in psychoanalysis*. London: George Allen & Unwin.

Gould, S. J. (1977). *Ontogeny and phylogeny*. Cambridge, MA: Harvard University Press.

Humphrey, N. K. (1976). The social function of the intellect. In P. P. G. Bateson & R. A. Hinde (Eds.), *Growing points in ethology* (pp. 303–317). New York: Cambridge University Press.

McGinn, C. (1993). *Problems in philosophy: The limits of inquiry*. Cambridge, MA: Blackwell.

Pinker, S. (1997). *How the mind works*. New York: Norton.

Tomasello, M. (1998). Uniquely primate, uniquely human. *Developmental Science, 1*, 1–16.

Tooby, J., & Devore, I. (1987). The reconstruction of hominid evolution through strategic modeling. In W. G. Kinzey (Ed.), *The evolution of human behavior: Primate models*. Albany, NY: SUNY Press.

Trivers, R. (1971). The evolution of reciprocal altruism. *Quarterly Review of Biology, 46*, 35–57.

Whorf, B. L. (1956). *Language, thought, and reality*. Cambridge, MA: MIT Press.

Author Index

M

Maccarone, A. D., 326, *333*
MacDonald, B., 128, *143*
Macdonald, D. W., 278, *285*
Mackintosh, N. J., 83, *94*, 320, 322, *333*, *336*
MacLennan, D. A., 254, *285*
MacNeilage, P. F., 69, *77*
Macphail, E. M., 253, 282, *287*
MacWhinney, B., 350, *358*
Maki, W. W., 317, *333*
Makim, S., 297, *313*
Malloy, P., 35, 36, *52*
Mandler, J. M., 166, *197*
Marler, P., 84, *94*, 326, *330*, *333*, *334*
Marr, D., 167, *197*
Martin, R. D., 136, *142*, 259, 283, *287*
Marzke, M. W., 65, *77*
Mason, W. A., 87, *94*
Matama, H., 85, *93*
Mateer, C., 111, *115*
Matelli, M., 69, *77*
Mathur, A. K., 308, *314*
Matsudaira, P., 233, *249*
Maturana, H. R., 270, 275, *287*
Matyniak, K. A., 318, *333*, 335
Mauthner, N., 34, 46, *53*
May, D. L., 327, *333*
Maynard Smith, J., 21, *24*
McCulloch, W. S., 270, 275, *287*
McDonald, K., 44, *53*
McDonald, M., 152, *197*
McDonough, L., 166, *197*
McGinn, C., 365, *367*
McGowan, K. J., 326, *333*
McGregor, P. K., 318, 319, 321, *335*
McGrew, W. C., 85, *94*, 219, *222*
McGuire, M., 14, *25*, 213, 215, *222*
McKinley-Pace, M. J., 33, *52*
McLachlan, D. R., 36, *53*
McNeill, D., 136, *141*
McShea, D., 233, *249*
Mead, M., 353, *358*
Mech, L. D., 277, *287*
Meehl, P. E., 16, 17, *25*
Mehlman, M. J., 137, *144*
Menzel, C. R., 243, *249*
Menzel, E. W., 44, *52*
Mercier, T., 346, 347, *357*
Mesterton-Gibbons, M., 213, *222*
Mesulam, M. M., 59, 67, *77*

Mika, S., 297, *313*
Miles, H. L., 131, *142*
Miller, G. F., 238, 246, *249*
Mills, C., 73, *77*
Mineka, S., 168, *197*
Mishkin, M., 130, *144*
Mitchell, R. W., 72, *77*
Mitchell, S., 309, *313*, 324, *334*
Mithen, S., 22, *25*, 28, 32, *52*, 139, *142*, 181, *197*
Moadel-Shahid, M., 297, *313*
Moane, G., 297, *313*
Monaco, A. P., 68, *76*
Montero, M., 297, *313*
Moore, B. S., 322, *336*
Moore, C., 121, *142*
Moran, N., 237, *249*
Mori, M., 57, 58, *78*
Morton, J., 166, *196*
Moscovitch, M., 36, *53*
Mowdray, K., 65, *78*
Mowrer, O. H., 318, *333*
Moxon, E. R., 17, *24*
Mpongo, E., 85, *93*
Müller, R., 67, 68, *77*
Mundy-Castle, A. C., 297, *313*
Murdock, G. P., 353, *358*
Murphy, J., 47, *53*, 89, *94*, 276, *288*
Murphy-Cowan, T., 307, *314*
Murray, C., 14, 19, *24*
Murray, K., 42, *52*

N

Nadasdy, Z., 166, *196*
Naguib, M., 321, *333*
Nallan, G. B., 319, *337*
Neisser, U., 125, *142*
Nelson, D. A., 321, *333*
Nelson, K., 132, *142*
Nelson, K. E., 87, *94*, 131, 132, *143*
Neuchterlein, K. H., 3, *6*
Nevin, J. A., 317, 322, *329*, *336*
Nidditch, P. H., 348, *358*
Niit, T., 297, *313*
Nims, P. J., 316, 317, *333*
Nishida, T., 85, *94*
Nissen, C. H., 320, *331*
Noakes, J., 301, *314*
Noble, W., 129, 139, *142*
Noonan, K. M., 40, *50*
Northcutt, R. G., 262, *287*

Subject Index